GAMELAN

D1563388

GAMELAN

Cultural Interaction and
Musical Development
in Central Java

SUMARSAM

The University of Chicago Press / Chicago & London

Sumarsam is an adjunct professor of music at Wesleyan University and an internationally known gamelan musician who conducts workshops and concerts throughout the world.

The University of Chicago Press, Chicago 60637
The University of Chicago Press, Ltd., London
© 1992, 1995 by The University of Chicago
All rights reserved. Published 1995
Printed in the United States of America
04 03 02 01 00 99 98 97 96 95   5 4 3 2 1

ISBN (cloth): 0-226-78010-4
ISBN (paper): 0-226-78011-2

Earlier versions of parts of chapter 3 appeared in the journal *Seni Pertunjukkan Indonesia* (1992): 72–91, and in Margaret J. Kartomi and Stephen Blum, eds., *Music Cultures in Contact: Convergences and Collisions* (Sydney: Currency Press, 1994).

Library of Congress Cataloging-in-Publication Data

Sumarsam.
     Gamelan : cultural interaction and musical development in central Java / Sumarsam.
          p.   cm. — (Chicago studies in ethnomusicology)
     Revision of the author's thesis (Ph.D.) — Cornell University, 1992, originally presented under title: Historical contexts and theories of Javanese music.
     Includes bibliographical references and index.
     ISBN 0-226-78010-4. — ISBN 0-226-78011-2 (pbk.)
     1. Music — Indonesia — Java — History and criticism.   2. Gamelan.
     I. Title.   II. Series.
ML345.I5S86   1995
780′.9598′2 — dc20
                                                                94-43013
                                                                CIP
                                                                MN

In memory of my parents

Contents

Illustrations

Preface

The all-night shadow puppet play wayang purwa had reached the midnight "flower battle." A few musicians were tired and sleepy. They may already have accompanied wayang performances for several days and nights consecutively. The saron player was so sleepy that he had to lay his head on the saron's keys. I was a seven-year-old boy then. Noticing that I was among the onlookers, the drummer called me and asked me to play the saron, telling the sleepy saron player to rest. (The drummer knew that some of my friends and I often got together to play gamelan at our neighbor's house). That was the beginning of my gamelan training. When I was about eight years old, the musicians let me join their group to perform in Dander (a small village in East Java, the place where I was born in 1944) and its vicinity.

This does not mean, however, that I spent my teens doing nothing but playing gamelan. I had to balance school work and playing music. In fact, during junior high school I quit playing gamelan. I remember vividly my experiences after graduating from junior high. After learning that I had passed my final exam, I spent the next two months playing gamelan almost every night in the traveling kethoprak company that performed in my village.

Musically, this was a pleasant ending to my teens in a small village. After that, I began my formal gamelan education at the Konservatori Karawitan Indonesia (KOKAR) in Surakarta (now Sekolah Menengah Karawitan Indonesia) in 1961. This is a high school of Javanese performing arts. Indeed, it was quite a move for me, from a small village to a court city commonly thought of as the center of Javanese culture, from informal gamelan training to formal training.

Soon after I began studying at KOKAR, the school community began to notice my musicianship. I was often asked to participate in out-of-school gamelan performances. I was involved in the activities of a group of close friends; the group was active in performing gamelan (for money or not) in Surakarta and its vicinity.

In 1964, I graduated from KOKAR. In the same year, I began my career as a part-time gamelan teacher at the Kasatriyan Junior High School, which was founded by the Kasunanan court of Surakarta. A year later I was appointed gamelan teacher at KOKAR, teaching classes on gamelan performance and a course called Teori Menabuh (theory of gamelan playing) for the first-year students.

In the year that I started to teach at KOKAR, the Akademi Seni Karawitan

Indonesia (ASKI; now Sekolah Tinggi Seni Indonesia, STSI) was founded. Besides teaching at KOKAR (in the morning), I enrolled as a full-time student at ASKI (in the afternoon). In 1969, ASKI appointed me a part-time assistant lecturer, helping R. L. Martopangrawit to teach classes in gamelan performance and a course called Pengetahuan Karawitan (knowledge of gamelan) for first-year students. I graduated from ASKI in 1968.

Besides local activities, KOKAR and ASKI are often asked to select faculty members or students to participate in the government's cultural missions abroad. I participated in a cultural mission to the seven-month World Exposition in Osaka, Japan, in 1970. After returning from Japan, I spent only one year in Surakarta. In 1971, I taught gamelan at the Indonesian Embassy in Canberra, Australia. From Australia I went directly to the United States, to become a visiting artist at Wesleyan University, teaching classes on gamelan performance.

Two years of exposure to the intellectual life at Wesleyan inspired me to pursue graduate study. In 1974, while teaching gamelan, I enrolled in the Master of Arts Program in World Music at Wesleyan. In 1976, I graduated. My thesis was entitled "Inner Melody in Javanese Gamelan." Subsequently, I continued teaching and performing gamelan at Wesleyan and in other cities and colleges in the United States. Occasionally I wrote and published essays on gamelan practice and wayang. In 1976, Wesleyan made me artist-in-residence.

During my subsequent years of teaching at Wesleyan University, I became interested in the history of gamelan. In 1983, on sabbatical leave from Wesleyan, I began working for a Ph.D. at Cornell University. My course work at Cornell was in Ethnomusicology and Southeast Asian studies. It was at Cornell that my interest in the historical approach to the study of gamelan developed. In 1992, I graduated from Cornell. My dissertation was entitled "Historical Contexts and Theories of Javanese Music." The present book is a revised version of this dissertation.

After I returned from Cornell to Wesleyan, in 1990 Wesleyan made me adjunct associate professor. After completing my dissertation in 1992, I was named adjunct professor.

In retrospect, the perspectives and content of my book embody almost my whole life experience, from being a young musician in a small village in East Java, through my formal education and experience in gamelan playing in the court city of Surakarta, to being a gamelan teacher, performer and *homo academicus* in an American university.

I am greatly indebted to my mentors at Cornell University for their guidance, support, encouragement, patience, and example. From the start of my writing to the completion of this book, Professor Martin Fellows Hatch patiently guided me in developing my ideas and strengthening my argument, and he checked and rechecked my English. Professor Benedict R. O'G. Anderson, whose knowledge of Javanese culture is unsurpassed, has given me invaluable direction through his sometimes sharp questioning and criticism. Professor William Austin always made certain that I progressed in my work. Through his gentle advice, he directed me to the awareness of a broader view of music.

I would like to thank Wesleyan University, which has given me unfailing support for my research for this book. As I mentioned earlier, it was at Wesleyan that I began my training in ethnomusicology and the development of my intellectual life. I would like to thank my mentors, my colleagues, and my students there, in particular Jon Barlow, Fredrik DeBoer, Barry Drummond, I. M. Harjito, David McAllester, Maria Mendonça, Kay Shelemay, Mark Slobin, Marc Perlman (to whom I am also grateful for the use of figure 3.2, from his personal collection), and Jennifer Thom, for their continuing support, useful comments, and criticism.

I would like to extend my thanks to my teachers, friends, colleagues and students at Cornell and elsewhere, in particular to Judith Becker, Kathy Bergeron, Suzanne Brenner, Lenore Coral, Anthony Day, Sal Murgiyanto, John Pemberton, Harold Powers, Amrih Widodo, Philip Yampolsky, and many others, who have given support, useful comments, and criticism.

I am grateful to the musicians in Dander, many now gone, who trusted an eight-year-old boy to join their group. To the kethoprak musicians, wherever they are now, I give my thanks for allowing me to play with them.

I thank my teachers and colleagues at KOKAR (1961–1964) and at ASKI (1965–1971) for their guidance and support. I am especially grateful to Pak Martopangrawit (d. 1985), Pak Mloyowidodo, and Pak Ngaliman for their continuing advice. I also thank many faculty members and students of ASKI–STSI for their responses to my lectures during my occasional visits to the institution.

Special thanks are due to Philip Yampolsky, who helped me so much in putting the final touches on the book; and to Jennifer Thom for her help in proofreading the manuscript. To two anonymous readers, I offer my gratitude for their invaluable comments and constructive criticism.

Lastly, I express my gratitude to my wife Maeny and my children Tistha and Dwi for their moral support. They know that the research for this book and my writing it demanded much of my time. I am grateful for their patience and understanding.

I would like to close this preface with a song , sekar tengahan Girisa pélog.

5 5   5 5 5̲6̲   5̲3̲ 3̲5̲6̲ 6̲5̲
Sarwi èstuning hyang e- sa   With God's blessing

5 6 i̇ i̇2̣   6 5 5̲6̲5̲ 3̲ 2̲
ulun sung karya si- nas- tra   I offer you my work,

6 5 i̇6 2 2 2̲3̲ 1 2̲1̲6̣
mugi kersa anampi- a   hoping you're willing to accept it,

2 3̲5̲   5 5   5̲6̲ 5̲3̲ 3̲5̲6̲ 6̲ 5̲
akan-thi dhanganing na- la   with delight in your heart.

  5 6   i̇   i̇2̇ 6 5 5̲6̲5̲ 3 2
ruhur ing pangangkahi- ra   The intention [of the study] is noble.

6 5 i̇ 6 2 2   2̲3̲ 1 2̲1̲6̣̲
sada-ya ki- laping ba- sa   For all inapt words

2 1 2 3̲5̲6̲ 2 2 2̲3̲ 1 2̲1̲6̣̲
awit ceguk bali- lu' mba   because of my shortcomings,

  3 3 3̲5̲ 3̲ 2̲ 2 3 5̲ 6̲ 5 6̲5̲3̲
minta ak-sa- ma pa-du- ka   I ask of you an apology.

Note on Orthography

With the exception of personal names, the spelling of Javanese and Indonesian words cited in this study follows the orthographic conventions officially adopted by the Indonesian government in 1972, but citations from materials written in Indonesian are written in their original spelling. The difference between the old (Dutch-based) and modern transliteration lies mainly in the following spellings: *dj* became *j, tj* became *c,* and *oe* became *u.*

In Javanese, *e* can take certain diacritical marks. The following is a list of vowels and consonants in Javanese that require particular notice.

	English equivalent	Javanese example
a	1. In a closed syllable (ending with a consonant), as in father	lekas
	2. In an open syllable (ending with a vowel), like <u>aw</u> in l<u>aw</u>	buk<u>a</u>
c	<u>ch</u>urch	<u>c</u>elempung
d	pronounced with tongue-tip touching inside upper teeth (i.e., dental; no English equivalent)	<u>d</u>emung
dh	pronounced with tongue-tip touching palate (i.e., palatal), e.g., <u>d</u>ay	<u>dh</u>alang
e	<u>a</u>bout	<u>e</u>mbat
è	l<u>e</u>t	gend<u>è</u>r
é	<u>a</u>te	p<u>é</u>log
i	1. In a closed syllable, as in b<u>i</u>t	al<u>i</u>t
	2. In an open syllable, as in pol<u>i</u>ce	kinanth<u>i</u>
ny	ca<u>ny</u>on	<u>ny</u>ela
o	1. In a closed syllable, as in b<u>o</u>re	pél<u>o</u>g
	2. In an open syllable, as in zer<u>o</u>	b<u>o</u>nang
r	rolled <u>r</u>	salisi<u>r</u>
t	pronounced with tongue-tip touching inside upper teeth (i.e., dental)	ke<u>t</u>ipung

th	pronounced with tongue-tip touching palate (i.e., palatal), e.g., la<u>t</u>er	pa<u>th</u>et
u	1. In a closed syllable, as in p<u>u</u>t	w<u>u</u>s
	2. In an open syllable, as in tr<u>ue</u>	mlak<u>u</u>

Unless indicated otherwise, all translations are my own. Only the first occurrence of a Javanese word is italicized.

Introduction

At twenty-one past seven,
the king emerged from his inner chamber,
[and was] honored by the sound of
Gendhing Sri Katon, exquisite,
moving, and pleasant-sounding.
The *irama* (tempo) was steady and even;
its pace was appropriate.
Intertwined with ornaments,
[the playing] was harmonious, firm, assiduous, and soft.
The whole sound was heartily felt.

The *laras* (tuning system) was sweet, pleasing to the heart—
[gamelan] Kyai Kaduk Manis [and] Manis Rengga.
The gamelan Cara Balèn,
Kyai Sepet Madu
Madu Pinasthika was its name,
[and] the [European] string orchestra
[playing] Wihèlmis were sounded loudly.
The courtiers stood in a humble attitude.
The king sat on a chair carved with
gilded *lung-lungan* (curling tendril) ornaments.

The king sat facing the east,
in the middle of Parasdya Hall.
Beautiful was [the king's] attire.
He was dressed in the Dutch style.
. . . .[1]

(Purbadipura 1913, 1:5)

As students of musical culture we learn a great deal about the important functions of music in society. Merriam (1964:224–25) identifies three of these functions: enforcing conformity to social norms, validating social institutions and religious rituals, and contributing to the continuity and stability of culture. He goes on to say that "every society has occasions signalled by music which draw its members together and reminds [*sic*] them of their unity" (227).

1

I do not question the validity of this idea of functionalism in music. We are confronted with different kind of issues, however, when we encounter a musical event like the one described in the above quotation. The playing together of two Javanese gamelans and a European string orchestra rendering the Dutch national anthem would undoubtedly produce musical chaos, especially because the three ensembles would be playing different compositions in entirely different tuning systems. This would be true regardless of when or in what context such a musical event occurred. Here it is a question not so much of music as a symbol of social unity (how could such a combination of musical sounds represent a unity?) as it is an allegory of the dynamics of Java's social and cultural history. That the musical sound combination described above emerged in the nineteenth- and early twentieth-century court of central Java needs to be explained in connection with other aspects of culture in this period. This approach is crucial, since in order to fully understand a musical event, we need to examine the context of its performance, the sociopolitical and technological characters of the period in which the event takes place, and its historical background. Like most cultures in the world, Javanese culture should be viewed as the "product of a history of appropriation, resistances, and accommodations" (Marcus and Fisher 1986:78).

In this sense, the key for understanding musical culture lies in its historical perspective. One of the characteristic features of Javanese history is the continuous exposure of the Javanese people to foreign cultures and ideas. In essence, contact with foreign cultures stimulates the development of Javanese culture. Viewed this way, in the Java of the fourteenth century to the present, one cannot properly speak of a single culture; one can properly speak only of cultural pluralism. Moreover, even within any of Java's historical periods, we always have to be aware of its plural character because of the existence of different ethnic groups (Javanese, Europeans, Eurasians, Chinese, Arab, Malay), class systems, rural–urban differences, and gender.

The musical combination described above raises a larger question about how traditions survive when foreign elements and ideas are imposed on them. Traditions are man-made and are therefore invented, developed, and changed according to the perspectives of their carriers. Cultural changes affect the worldviews of those who sustain a tradition and produce continuity, development, or change in traditions. When there is contact with foreign cultures, cultural change and development is likely. In order to fully understand the development of Javanese culture, we must discuss Java's long contact with foreign cultures.

Cultural events of the nineteenth- and early twentieth-century Javanese court, such as the ceremony described above, represent a mixture of Javanese (indigenous) and European (foreign) ideas. The hybrid event which brought about such a peculiar musical phenomenon was a result of the reaction of the Javanese to particular political circumstances during Java's long contact with Europeans and European colonialism.

The presence of European culture and European music in Java can be traced back to the seventeenth century. By the late eighteenth century, as a result of the increasing intervention of Europeans in the life of the Javanese aristocracy, European culture had already become a part of court life. Already in the second decade of the nineteenth century, Thomas Stamford Raffles, the British governor general of Java (1810–1816), saw many changes in court customs: "The ceremonies and state of the native courts have lost much of their genuine character, from the admission of European customs, introduced by the Dutch after the last Javan war" (Raffles 1817, 1:311). Among others, contact between the women of the court and Europeans (men and women), the customs of European drinking (toasting) and ballroom dancing, and Western music were all established parts of court life (see Taylor 1983:108–9).

The period after the last Javan war Raffles refers to was after the long power struggle among the princes that led to the division of the court of Mataram in 1755. This was a period when Dutch administrators, planters, and managers of trading companies, and later scholar-officials, became more and more deeply involved in the political and social life of the aristocrats. Consequently this group of Dutch were Javanized; they lived in a mixture of cultures, part European and part Indonesian, called mestizo culture (a culture made up of different influences); they built up close relationships with Javanese aristocrats. Conversely, Javanese aristocrats were Europeanized to the extent that they felt compelled to use some European elements in court rituals, producing many hybrid court cultural expressions.

Another important aspect of the presence of Europeans in Java was the contact between Indonesian women and European men. The contact resulted in Eurasian offspring who were known among the Javanese as Indos. Raised in European settlements in Indonesia, these mixed-blood children grew up and lived in a mixture of European and Indonesian cultures. In fact, it was among Indos that the mestizo culture I mentioned above developed.

Before the coming of the "liberal policy" of the Dutch government, the mestizo culture of Indo and Javanized Dutch men and women influenced Javanese society. This changed after the coming of the new policy in the third decade of the nineteenth century. The new policy allowed for many more *totok* (pure-blood Dutch) to enter the East Indies. This resulted in a *totok*ization of the Dutch already there and of the Javanese elite and a marginalization of Indos. This did not mean the end of mestizo culture, however. Mestizo culture lived on with the addition of totok elements.

As mentioned above, in Central Java, Indos (especially wealthy Indos and a handful of Indo intellectuals) and Javanized totok had an intimate relationship with aristocrats. Knowing both Javanese and European customs, these upper-class Dutchmen and Indos took on important roles as intermediaries between Dutch authorities and Javanese courtiers. Their mestizoness influenced the performance of certain court rituals, especially those that included European elements. This resulted in the hybrid character of much court culture. An example was the peculiar mixture of musical sounds mentioned above. Indeed, we cannot underestimate the heterogeneity of the Central Javanese court cultures. Many European elements, including military marching bands, popular dance music such as waltzes and polkas, cannon and salvo salutes, and the display of fireworks, were integral parts of important Javanese court rituals.

The political culture of the Central Javanese monarchy in this period had made possible the development of hybrid court cultures. The relationships between the Dutch political leaders and Javanese rulers determined the hybrid character of court cultural expressions. Similar relationships existed in British India. Cohn (1983:173) explains:

> Indian "kings" who were allowed internal autonomy over their domains were reduced to the status of "chiefs and princes." They were controlled through treaties which were contractual in nature, as they guaranteed the boundaries of the states, pledged the support of the Company to a royal family and its descendants, in return for giving up the capacity for making war, and effective as long as they "practised good government" and accepted the supervision of an English official.

This kind of political relationship made the Javanese aristocrats feel compelled to establish ritual courtesy out of respect to the European elite. Such courtesies included the incorporation of European customs (including European music) in court rituals.

The fact that Javanese rulers were willing to display ritual respect to the Europeans, and in European ways, can be explained in terms of the familiar phenomenon whereby the oppressed identifies himself with the oppressor (Ranger 1975; Nandy 1983). On the other hand, the Javanese ruler also considered it important to maintain traditional court rituals essential to him and his Javanese subjects. Consequently, the incorporation of European ideas and elements into traditional Javanese rituals was a natural development of Javanese court cultural practices. We shall return to the atmosphere, the tension, the process, and the contradictory richness of Java's encounters with the West.

Besides the interaction of Java with the West that produced hybrid cultural expressions, were there also cultural expressions representing traditional, pre-Westernized, Javanese value systems? The answer is yes. But it would be naive to attempt to give a simple answer to the question, since even before the intrusion of European culture into Java, Javanese traditions had already experienced a long development in which many foreign elements had been incorporated. These foreign elements—Hindu, Buddhist, and Islamic elements—were all syncretized and absorbed into the complex indigenous matrix of Javanese court culture.

It should be emphasized here that religion provided the foundation for traditional Javanese court culture. The borrowed European culture was profoundly different because it was basically secular (European religions did not have a strong impact on Java). In essence, religion was the common ground for the Javanese perception of society.

The role of religion in the spread of foreign cultures in Java makes the term "Hinduization," instead of "Indianization," an accurate description of the impact of Indian culture. It was not simply a matter of Hinduism replacing Javanese belief systems, however. It was a long process of adaptation in which

> Indian materials tended to be fractured and restated and therefore drained of their original significance by a process which I shall refer to as "localization." The materials, be they words, sounds of words, books, or artifacts, had to be localized in different ways before they could fit into various local complexes or religious, social, and political systems and belong to [a] new cultural "whole." Only when this had happened would the fragments make sense in their new ambiences. (Wolters 1982:52)

In his study of Hindu-Javanese musical instruments, Kunst (1968:10) concludes that the performance of Indian music was confined to the ruling castes. Was there Indian influence on Javanese music? Lack of evidence prevents us from knowing the extent of Indian influence on Javanese music during the Hindu-Javanese period. There is evidence, however, that Indian literature and *kawya* sung-poetry had a significant impact on the development of genres of Javanese literature and vocal music. The Javanization of Indian sung-poetry followed the process described by Wolters. The Indian kawya was gradually localized. At the end, only the rules of poetic meter remained Indian. The kawya became Javanese *kakawin* poetry. In the later period of Javanese history, the kakawin were given new melodies and were called *sekar ageng* ("great song").

It is commonly held that the long and gradual syncretization of Hindu-Buddhist elements into Javanese belief systems formed the traditional Javanese value system and indigenous customs of Javanese life; they became a long-lasting Javanese weltanschauung. (I shall say more later about this view of the traditional Javanese value system and its relevance to my discussion of contemporary Javanese performing arts.) The traditional Javanese value system was so well grounded that the coming of Islam did not cause major changes in it. This was because "a large element of congruence and compatibility [existed] between the types of Islam that entered Java in the fifteenth and sixteenth century and the cultural tradition that they encountered" (Anderson 1972:68). Anderson treats the expansion of Islam in Java as more an assimilative than a revolutionary process, which

> can be attributed to the fact that Islam came to Java "on the heels not of conquest but of trade." It was first brought by traders and has never

lost the marks of its provenance, developing its strongest hold in the intermediate, commercial, rather than the upper, official or lower, peasant strata. After an initial period of zealotry, the devout Islamic groups were more or less absorbed into the patrimonial state. On the one hand, an Islam which had passed to Java through Persia and India was already patrimonialized and thus generally congruent with the traditional Javanese world-view (particularly with regard to the role and significance of the ruler). On the other hand, after the fifteenth century, the rulers assumed Islamic titles, kept Islamic officials in their entourage, and added Islam to the panoply of their attributes. Yet this overt Islamization of the rulers does not seem to have caused major alterations in their way of life or outlook. (68f.)

It is important to mention here that Sufi Islam dominated the early Islamization of Java. This helped older Javanese traditional performing arts to endure and develop, since Sufism believes in the power of music as a conduit for the union of man with God. This positive stance of Sufism toward music encouraged the development of Javanese and Islamic music. There is even evidence that these two musics interacted, contributing to the development of Javanese gamelan and the Javanization of Islamic *terbang* (frame drum) music.

As mentioned earlier, Hindu, Buddhist, and Islamic elements were syncretized and localized, forming the indigenous matrix of Javanese court culture. In his *State and Statecraft in Old Java,* Moertono (1968) explains an important component of the broader value systems of traditional Javanese culture. According to him, the traditional Javanese weltanschauung is governed by the *kawula-gusti* ("servant and master") relationship, a kind of relationship that is manifest in all aspects of Javanese life, religious and secular. One of the important aspects of the relationship between servant and master is a personal and close bond of mutual respect and responsibility. Another aspect of the kawula-gusti relationship is a belief in fate, a belief that events are preordained. In other words, fate determines the place of a man in society. Consequently a man must do his duty according to his fate. The personal relationship and the belief in preordination results in a sense of obligation of the master to care for and protect his servant.

Stories of the shadow puppet play (*wayang*) are often the best sources in which to find the ideal kawula-gusti relationship. The position of the four *panakawan* in the wayang story is a good example. Represented as physically deformed and outcaste figures, panakawan are not only servants "but also inseparable companions and at times the mentors of their respective masters" (Moertono 1968:23). Moreover, Semar, the oldest panakawan and the father of the other three, is a manifestation of the most powerful god Sang Hyang Ismaya. At times the deity Bathara Guru (the younger brother of Sang Hyang Ismaya) must submit to Semar. It is true that in the wayang performance the panakawan seem to be little more than clowns or jokers. But they are also thought to personify time: Semar is identified "with the formlessness of eternity, while his sons Garèng, Bagong and Pétruk are thought to personify the past, present and future" (p. 24). This all implies that "the people as a whole are regarded by Javanese as sacred and therefore to be taken seriously into account" (ibid.).

Javanese court performing arts developed and were cultivated in the milieu of the kawula-gusti relationship. This kind of relationship permitted the artists (who were considered servants of the court, *abdi dalem*) to have close relationships with their masters (the princes and rulers). Not only were the masters required to receive art education as a part of their upbringing, but the artists and their masters also had a close relationship and were able to exchange ideas. Anderson (1984:210) summed up the intimacy of the court milieu within which Javanese performing arts existed:

> In a context where poetry and song were inseparable, and both were tied to music in a wider sense (as well as dance), it is not surprising that artists in these fields mingled easily, exchanged ideas, and often had equivalent ranks and emoluments calibrated within the palace ranking system—for example, Nyai Lurah Bedhaya (dancer), Nyai Bèi Ma[r]dusari (singer), Radèn Tumenggung Warsodiningrat (musician).

In his important study of Javanese power, Benedict Anderson (1972:28) argues that the core concept of traditional Javanese power lies in one's ability to gain power in the following ways: "To focus his own inner Power, to absorb Power from the outside, and to concentrate within himself apparently antagonistic opposites." It is relevant to see Javanese gamelan and theatrical performances during the centuries of the Mataram aristocratic rule in the context of the view of traditional Javanese Power as outlined by Anderson. The most notable connection is the belief that in acquiring power "the ruler should concentrate around him any objects or persons held to have or contain unusual Power" (p. 27).[2] Most of the palace gamelan instruments and wayang paraphernalia were considered to be magically charged items. Thus, the ruler could enhance his power by concentrating these items around him. The *bedhaya* dance and dancers were considered to be the ruler's emblems of Power. The duty of bedhaya dancers was not only to perform the most refined and sacred dances of the court but also to accompany the king when he went off to battle (29 n. 30).

The most obvious example of the importance of performing arts as a sign of the ruler's power was the holding of ceremonies or exciting court occasions in which gamelan and theatrical performances were included. It is true that the holding of court ceremonies was intended partly to perpetuate the loyalty of the ruler's entourage. But it was also "intended to concentrate and display Power absorbed from various sources" (Anderson 1972:26).

In the middle of the nineteenth century the syncretic worldview of the Javanese began to change. The spread of the "pure doctrine" of Islam brought by

Javanese pilgrims returning from the Near East resulted in the so-called Islamic Reformation. This period was concurrent with the deepening impact of European colonialism and the Europeanization of the Javanese elite.

The Islamic reformation and the deepening penetration of European colonialism into Java led Javanese court culture to another phase of development: the old, syncretic Islamic tradition declined, eventually disappearing from the court, and the intimate social milieu in the court within which the Javanese arts had developed also disappeared. The intrusion of Europeans into the lives of Javanese aristocrats intensified the Javanese class system, resulting in the breakup of the close relationship between Javanese artists and their masters. Anderson points out that the expansion of print technology in Java is one of the underlying causes of this breakup. Print technology makes mass distribution of an author's work possible. Thus,

> Javanese writers were confronted with an invisible, atomized public. Silent prose rather than sung poetry quickly became the norm. But the central problem for anyone writing now in Javanese was what one might call the "problem of pronouns." For it became more and more difficult to sustain the old pronominal forms in the world of the market.[3] One can see this on both sides of the I–you divide. The old ingsun-I might be the singer, the composer, the sovereign praised, or a particular character in a poem's narrative, but the identity of this "I" was clear to everyone listening. (Anderson 1984:210)

Anderson explains further that the print market created a situation in which the readers would never encounter face to face the "I" (the author or the singer), except on the printed page. It also created a multiplicity of "yous"—readers with many different social statuses.

> The print-market thus created speakers and interlocutors wholly outside the existing convention of the language. What was the right "you" for all these collections of putative social superiors, equals, and inferiors? With the market came also the breakup of other old connections. Gifted authors [court poets known only within the court] became famous as authors; good singers fell steadily in status until the coming of the cassette; good Javanese musicians rapidly lost caste. (210f.)[4]

The expansion of capitalism in late nineteenth-century Java resulted in the deepening penetration of European value systems into Java. Furnivall (1939:225) summed up the economic conditions of this new colonial era as follows:

> In this new world the balance of economic power in Java no longer lay with Government but with private capital. In 1870 the few wealthy planters were isolated individuals, but in 1900 the far larger and far wealthier non-official community was directed by a few powerful cor-

porations which could easily take common action to protect their interest; the economic structure was no longer individualist but capitalist.

On the one hand, capitalism might have resulted in the expansion of the economy. On the other hand, it had an impact on the increasing distance between social classes. Furthermore, each segment of the population—the Europeans (whose numbers increased), the Indos, the Chinese, and the Javanese elite—competed with each other to make political alliances and to gain status. Consequently, the mestizo culture in which these groups existed began to dissolve. The Indos themselves were pushed to the margin. The Chinese continued to strive for greater status. Hybrid court rituals gradually disappeared, although they could still be found at the beginning of the twentieth century.

In the hybrid Javanese court culture of the nineteenth century, two kinds of Javanese–European social relationships can be seen. First, the close social intercourse between Dutch and Indo officials, planters, and managers of companies and Javanese aristocrats inspired mixed Javanese-European court rituals. Second, by the mid nineteenth century, another group of Europeans and Indos, namely, scholar-officials and art connoisseurs, had close intellectual relationships with Javanese aristocrats and court poets. They interacted on equal terms. The relationship between these Javanese, European, and Indo intellectuals characterized the intellectual atmosphere of the time. These intellectuals often produced work that sheds light on the cultural practice and perspective of nineteenth-century Java.

The late nineteenth century witnessed the expansion of European-style education for Javanese, Chinese, and Indos. This was especially true at the beginning of the twentieth century when the Dutch colonial regime adopted the Ethical policy, based on a humanitarian concern for the economic condition of the natives (Ricklefs 1993:151). One means of carrying out this policy was the expansion of European-style education. This meant the intensification of the exposure of these groups to European modes of thinking. An important consequence of the European style of education was the rise of Indonesian nationalism among Dutch-educated Javanese and some prominent Indos and Chinese.

With a background of nationalism, gamelan music, along with other Javanese performing arts, lived on. Music also became the subject of controversy among Indonesian nationalists. In their attempt to define Indonesian national culture, they had difficulty finding a single cultural expression that all Indonesians could appreciate together. A prominent nationalist, Ki Hadjar Dewantara, suggested that the national culture should be *puncak-puncak kesenian daerah* (the peaks of regional culture). As a member of the Javanese aristocracy, Dewantara had in mind Javanese gamelan, dance, and theater as one, indeed the most prominent, of these peaks of regional culture. He and other aristocrats advocated the gamelan as being comparable to European art music. But some nationalists, especially non-Javanese nationalists, could not accept Dewantara's notion of Indonesian national culture. Consequently the question of whether gamelan should be encouraged as a national music lingered on.

After Indonesian independence, state-sponsored gamelan schools were opened in the 1950s and 1960s. As in the early period of nationalism, the schools had to justify the relevance of gamelan in modern Indonesia. A prominent leader of one gamelan academy, Sediyono Humardani (1972), also promoted the idea of gamelan as classical music, music that, he said, had to have a sense of universalism. As part of contemporizing gamelan, the academy also encouraged its faculty and students to create new gamelan compositions.

Actually the ideas about gamelan proposed by some prominent nationalists and the founding of the gamelan schools were the result of the expansion of European-style education, which began in the late nineteenth century. Western-style education also brought about the development of gamelan scholarship. In particular, the intellectual atmosphere in the late nineteenth and early twentieth centuries led to a European way in which the Javanese elite and Europeans elucidated Javanese performing arts. With the expansion of print technology and the presence of Dutch scholars and connoisseurs of the arts, this period witnessed a proliferation of writings on gamelan. The work of a Dutch scholar, Jaap Kunst (1973), was widely known to both Western and Javanese scholars. It was through Kunst and his works that gamelan became an important subject of study in Western ethnomusicology, a discipline Kunst had an important role in developing. Subsequently, gamelan study, its theory and practice, flourished in Western countries. Gamelan theories developed by Western ethnomusicologists became important references in the circle of ethnomusicology.

In Java, from the 1970s onward, as a consequence of the expansion of research in gamelan schools, gamelan scholarship expanded. The theorizing of Javanese musicians about gamelan caused European-inspired gamelan theory to mix with the perspectives of Javanese musicians. This also resulted from increased cooperation between Javanese and Western gamelan theorists. In this period gamelan theorists called attention to the importance of Javanese musicians' perspectives as a part of the impulse to indigenize gamelan theory. The intellectual atmosphere in the 1970s reminds us of the nineteenth-century intellectual climate, when Javanese, Indo, and European intellectuals had close relationships.

To summarize: In discussing group identities around the world, Appadurai (1991:191) points out that "groups are no longer tightly territorialized, spatially bounded, historically unselfconscious, or culturally homogenous. We have fewer cultures in the world and more 'internal cultural debates' (Parkin 1978)."

Group identity in contemporary Javanese society conforms well to Appadurai's line of thought. It also applies to group identity in the early history of Java. The "internal cultural debates" in Java were already going on in the period of

Java's contacts with the Hindu-Buddhist and Islamic traditions. These contacts brought about the localization of foreign elements and the formation of a syncretic traditional Javanese culture. The Europeanization of Java in the eighteenth and nineteenth centuries profoundly altered the life of Central Javanese aristocrats and their cultural productions. The religiously based Javanese tradition had to encounter, interact, and interplay with the secular, technologically oriented Western world of capitalism. This development provided the Javanese with wider possibilities to adapt or imagine many aspects of modern social life, resulting in a culture that was a heterogeneous, hybrid, and sometimes contradictory complex of Javanese and Western elements. The presence of Europeans and Indos, the influence of European colonial cultural power on Javanese society, the Islamic Reformation, and the active role of the Chinese in Javanese society all created complex cultural dynamics. Such dynamics evoked profound interactions among social-ethnic and intellectual groups that operated in ways that "transcend specific territorial boundaries and identities" (Appadurai 1991 : 192). The hybridity of Javanese cultural reproduction and intellectual life resulted in rich variants in the contexts and contents of Central Javanese gamelan and the development of gamelan scholarship.

ONE

*From Hindu to Islam: The Early
History of Javanese Music*

Hinduized Javanese Culture

It is commonly held that the influence of Hindu culture in Indonesia at the
beginning of the Christian era stimulated the development of Javanese culture.
Perhaps the rise of the early empires in Indonesia after the fifth century (e.g.,
Sriwijaya, Mataram, Majapahit, and others) could not have happened without
the kind of intellectual and technological revolution introduced by Hindu culture. These Hindu or Hindu-Buddhist kingships became the centers of power,
promoting the development of not only social, political, and religious life but
especially literary and artistic endeavors. The Indian writing system, poetry, and
Hindu epics were adapted and localized by the Javanese. Various kinds of performing arts (e.g., dance drama, various kinds of puppet theater, dance, masked
dance drama) existed in this period. In particular, the Indian epics *Mahabharata*
and *Ramayana* caused the arts to flourish. These Javanized Indian epics became
the source material for many forms of the performing arts that developed in Java
later on.

The history of Javanese music can be traced from the early period of the
Hinduized court of Central Java (8th to 11th centuries). Unfortunately, musical
evidence from this period is scarce. A number of depictions of musical instruments and musical scenes on the walls of temples and monuments, such as the
ninth-century Buddhist monument of Borobudur, while affording tantalizing
glimpses, do not give us enough data to make an accurate description of the
musical activities of that time.[1] Entering the period of the Hindu-Buddhist court
of East Java (12th to 15th centuries), we begin to see more evidence of music. It
can be found in literature and on temple reliefs. For an invaluable study of musical instruments in this period, see Jaap Kunst's *Hindu-Javanese Musical Instruments* (1968). Examining the available data, he compiles names and suggests the
backgrounds of hundreds of musical instruments that existed in the period from
the eighth century to the fifteenth century. Here I merely wish to describe certain features that convey the atmosphere of musical life in the later period of
Hinduized Java. In addition to Kunst, I draw my discussion primarily from Zoet-

mulder's *Kalangwan* (1974), a study of Javanese literature from the ninth century to the sixteenth century, and the *Wangbang Wideya* (edited and translated by Robson, 1971), a sixteenth-century poem written in Bali.

One feature of musical life in the later period of Hinduized Java (11th to 14th centuries) was the importance of music and other performing arts (including writing and reading kakawin poetry) as parts of the general education of courtiers and the royal family. Almost all levels of courtiers—priests, princes, princesses, ladies-in-waiting—had to learn to play music, sing, dance, or recite poetry. The ideal prince was judged not only by his good looks and intelligence but also by his accomplishments in the fine arts and music (Zoetmulder 1974: 152, 154). It was also common for the court poets (*kawi*) to perform "mask dances and comical intermezzos, as story tellers and bards" (p. 156), perhaps to try out their works. As for the court ladies-in-waiting, they too were encouraged to practice these branches of the arts. Awards were given to mark their proficiency in such arts as playing musical instruments, singing, and reciting poetry (p. 160). These examples suggest that music had an important role in creating an intimate social atmosphere among all levels of courtiers and the royal servants.

As is mentioned in the fourteenth-century kakawin poem *Negarakertagama,* the court of Majapahit had a special division whose responsibility was, among other things, to supervise programs in the performing arts.

> What is the *rakryan děmung*'s office? To take care of the Seven Musics, singing, dancing, things of beauty, and especially excursions, and the organization of the delights, entertainments, to make designs for luxury and clothing, to make various arrangements for voluptuous displays of art, the charm of amorous poetry, the making of *kāwyas* (high poetry), [the making] of all kinds of musical instruments, especially *salukats* (instrument with brass keys, *saron*), *samahepas* (*samepa,* not identified), *měrdanggas* (ceremonial drums), . . . the loveliness of the *ringgitan* (dances or female dancers). . . . (Pigeaud 1960, 3:122)

Although the poem does not offer a detailed explanation of this passage, it does suggest that music and the other arts played important roles in the lives of aristocrats. We also cannot find any information on the nature and significance of the "Seven Musics" mentioned in the passage. We can only be sure that various musical ensembles existed, and special care was given to them. Probably each ensemble was played for a particular purpose, either for its own sake or as accompaniment to theatrical performances.

Old Javanese literature frequently mentions wayang ensembles. In many cases the literature does not give direct descriptions of the performances but, as Zoetmulder (1974:209) puts it, "illustrative simile[s]" by which an author seeks to attract the attention of his readers. For example, this is a passage from the long twelfth-century poem entitled *Bharatayuda:*

In the river the [bamboo] clatterers arranged in rows were like the [instrument] *salunding* of the *wayang*. The hollow bamboos through which the wind played were like flutes, following its lead. The small gongs (gendhing strinya)[2] were provided by an orchestra of *kungkangs* (a big frog producing booming sound) in the ravines.[3] The shrill sound of the grasshoppers constituted the incessant accompaniment of the cymbals (*kamanak*).[4] (Ibid. 211)

It is not clear from this passage whether wayang was accompanied by an ensemble consisting of flutes, small gongs, and kemanak, as well as salunding. But the possibility of such an ensemble should not be ruled out. The first sentence of the passage suggests, however, that salunding, a metallophone or perhaps an instrument that had bamboo keys, was an important instrument for accompanying wayang at that time.

Another source, the thirteenth-century kakawin entitled *Wretasancaya*, also mentions salunding and flutes, as well as singing. A very vivid description of a wayang ensemble is given in the sixteenth-century *kidung* poem *Wangbang Wideya*. Here we find reference to the singing of kakawin poetry in a wayang performance to the accompaniment of an ensemble consisting of *gendèr* (perhaps a later name for salunding), *redep* (a frame drum), and a gong or gongs (Robson 1971:35). Another poem, the sixteenth-century kidung named *Malat*, mentions a wayang performance in which the kidung melody Wukir Polaman was sung to the accompaniment of *guntang* (Zoetmulder 1974:154). This instrument is still in use in Bali. It is a bamboo-zither instrument that is used in the gamelan Arja and gamelan Gambuh, ensembles used to accompany singer-dancers in the dramatic performances of those names.

The examples suggest that the singing of the puppeteer (*widu*) or another performer was important to the wayang (Zoetmulder 1974:210–11; Robson 1971:35–36) and other productions. Perhaps the singing was the localized version of the Indian poetry, the kakawin. Whether accompanied or not, the kakawin became an important genre of the singing tradition in this period. Another important genre was the indigenous sung poetry, kidung.

We also learn from the examples that there were different kinds of ensembles for wayang, perhaps depending on the kind of wayang being performed or the changes in the nature of the ensemble throughout its history. Different genres of Balinese wayang have different accompanying ensembles even today.

I now list some of the ensembles existing in the Hindu-Javanese period. The *Wangbang Wideya* mentions the chief musician (*luwarak*), who was an accomplished player of the samepa (a string instrument?) and *cantung*, as well as a skillful *dhalang* (Robson 1971:72–73). The poem also mentions the sound of the *gendhing gong* (unidentified ensemble) that heralded armed men who were ready to march (p. 117); the sound of a percussion ensemble, accompanied by the conch, trumpet, and bells; and the sounding of gendhing Rara Buyut, accompanied by *kangsi* (small cymbals) (p. 196).

A discussion of music in the Hindu-Buddhist period in East Java would not be complete without mention of its connection with Balinese music. As early as the tenth century, the Balinese had come into contact with the Javanese (Vlekke 1959:39). The contact continued during the reign of Erlangga of Kediri in the twelfth century. Zoetmulder (1974:19) even speculates that Erlangga was the son of a Balinese prince. Subsequently, the contact between Balinese and Javanese courts intensified during the period of the Majapahit kingdom (fourteenth century), during which Majapahit sent expeditions to Bali and established Javanese courts there (ibid.). By the middle of the fourteenth century, as Zoetmulder puts it: "Bali entered the orbit of Hindu Javanism . . . and that in consequence Bali must be considered, from this time on, as belonging to Hindu-Javanese cultural world" (p. 21). Wolters (1982:26) reminds us, however, that this does not mean that the Balinese became Javanese; instead, the Old Javanese traditions were made to fit into a different cultural tradition (p. 54).

The early mode of contact between these two islands ended when Islam came to Java.[5] But in his study of Balinese literature, Vickers (1987) perceptively identifies various sorts of ongoing contact (trade is one of them) between Java and Bali after the Islamization of Java. The contacts resulted in the introduction of Islamic literature to Bali and its subsequent adaptation into the stories of Balinese dance dramas such as *gambuh*.

This historical background suggests that certain musical ideas and musical instruments that developed in Bali originated in fourteenth-century Java. Some of the evidence I have used as the basis for my discussion of music in the Hindu-Javanese period is drawn from Balinese literature. Despite the evident weaknesses of this approach, scholars usually agree that, to a certain extent, Balinese literature can be relevant to Hindu-Javanese musical practices. In fact, one aspect of Hindu-Javanese culture that is still used in Bali today is the Old Javanese language. This language is used in contemporary Bali in Balinese theatrical performances, in narrative as well as musical form (Wallis 1980:130–34). Furthermore, a form of Kawi poetry known in Bali as *wirama* and another old genre of sung poetry, *kidung,* are closely related to Javanese poetic genres (pp. 211–12).[6]

Unfortunately, there is not enough evidence to draw any firm conclusion about the transfer of musical practice from Java to Bali. Hood (1984:94–95) suggests that gamelan Gambuh and four types of sacred ensembles (Selonding, Caruk, Gambang, and Luang) originated in Hindu Java. Hood thinks that gamelan Gambuh is a living continuation of an east Javanese ensemble because it has seven tones; this fits in with his theory that ensembles employing a seven-tone system originated in east Java in the twelfth century or earlier.

Two reasons are given by Hood (1984:93) and McPhee (1966:256–57) for supposing the Javanese origin of Salunding (also spelled Selonding): the word occurs in twelfth-century Javanese literature, and in the oral accounts of Balinese musicians. For gamelan Luang, the shape of *saron* and *bonang* is similar to Javanese instruments of the same names, and a playing technique, *sekatian,* is related to Sekatèn, the name of a Javanese gamelan set which is considered to be archaic (Hood 1984:94–95).

It should be mentioned that the Balinese *gambang,* a bamboo xylophone with fourteen keys that is played with a pair of Y-shaped sticks, is identical to pictorial representations of instruments of the same shape depicted on the walls of the fourteenth-century temple Panataran in East Java (McPhee 1966:25, 272–73).[7] The *réyong,* an instrument consisting of two small gongs attached to the two ends of a pole, is also identical to the instruments of the same form that are found depicted in the temple (p. 25).[8] These instruments do not exist in contemporary Java. We also do not have evidence to show that the Balinese gambang and ré-yong originated in East Java or vice versa. We can only say that the relations between the two islands must have been quite intensive.

In conclusion, it is almost impossible to know precisely what other instruments or ensembles were brought to Bali during the period of Hindu-Javanese contact. In any event, I am inclined to think that instruments or ensembles that were brought from Java to Bali did not remain the same; they developed according to local tastes.

In general, our curiosity about the history of Javanese music focuses on the larger gamelan ensemble we know today. The evidence, however, does not give a clear idea about the development of a large ensemble. Rather, we learn of the existence of a number of smaller ensembles and the importance of singing in them. In contemporary Java we still find several small gamelan ensembles, such as the ensemble for *wayang bèbèr, wayang klithik, réyog* (a folk dance drama), and an ensemble for certain bedhaya dances.[9]

We have no firm evidence of their direct links with Hindu-Javanese ensembles, however, since for the early period of Islamized Java, cultural history is poorly documented. We can only assume that after the decline of Majapahit, Hindu-Javanese art and literature underwent a period of chaos. Some of the arts seem to have disappeared, only to reappear again (perhaps in a different form) much later on.[10]

Thus it appears that the transmission of Indian culture was first concentrated at the level of the court, especially through language and literary expression that was closely associated with court rituals.[11] Gradually the Javanese localized and popularized many aspects of Indian culture. For example, the kakawin, a localized form of a genre of Indian poetry, became the possession of not only elite literary circles, but also all levels of courtiers, perhaps even commoners. (It appears that the Indian caste system did not develop in Java.) The kakawin was sung by all levels of courtiers, from Brahman priests to ladies-in-waiting, and was an important genre in wayang and other popular dramatic plays. This suggests that the localization and popularization of Indian sung-poetry created an atmosphere of intimacy among all levels of courtiers and commoners. The ability of the Javanese to domesticate foreign materials shows they were tolerant and flexible toward Indian cultures.

Examples drawn from Balinese and Javanese literature indicate that smaller ensembles, whether or not they accompanied singing, characterized Hindu-Javanese ensembles. We may assume that the diverse smaller musical ensembles we find in Java and Bali today are based on certain remnants of Hindu-Javanese music. The present form of grander *sléndro-pélog* gamelan, which is commonly found in Central Javanese courts, was absent from the musical scene in the Hindu-Javanese period. I discuss the development of this grander gamelan in the next chapter.

The Early Period of Islamized Java and Early Contacts with Europeans

In spite of their strength, in the beginning of the fifteenth century the power of Hinduized Javanese monarchs began to decline because of the expansion of Islam. The gradual rise to power of Muslim traders and their consequent conflict with Hindu-Javanese royalty were largely responsible for the decline of Hinduized Javanese court centers such as Majapahit.

The conversion of many Javanese to Islam did not bring about the total collapse of the Hinduized Javanese cultural traditions, however. Although a new cultural heritage was introduced, much of the Hindu-Javanese cultural tradition continued to exist, either in independent pockets of the population or in combination with or as a complement to Islamic traditions.

We know almost nothing about cultural life in the early period of Islamized Java (15th to 17th centuries), the early period of cultural transition. This period of cultural crisis involved not only class warfare between Muslim traders and Hindu-Javanese royalty (Pigeaud and de Graaf 1976:6), but also power conflict among the Muslim rulers themselves (p. 9). The crisis continued with the shifting of power from the north coast, namely Demak, to the interior of Central Java, first to Pajang and then to Mataram.

It is significant that despite continuous political and religious instability, much of Hindu-Javanese culture continued to exist, largely because Muslim traders, having themselves been under the suzerainty of Hindu-Javanese rulers for many years, were well acquainted with Hindu-Javanese culture (ibid.). In other words, Hindu-Javanese and Islamic cultures met and interacted over many years.

In any event, the period of adjustment and exploration continued after the center of power shifted and individuals in those power centers changed. The process of cultural adjustment was very complex and delicate[12]—delicate indeed, since it involved not only a changing religion, but also socio-political and economic conflict. In the first place, from the time of the shift of power from the north coast to the inland Mataram, the rulers of Mataram were engaged in an effort to subjugate the Islamic coastal suzerainties. Second, the spread of Islam was uneven; thus, antagonism to the rulers was not uncommon (Ricklefs 1974: 16). Consequently, the rulers of Mataram were always on their guard for any suspicious development of rebellion. Perhaps because of this, Amangkurat I ordered the massacre of a group of Islamic leaders and scholars who allegedly supported a rebellion led by his brother, Pangeran Alit.

This period of crisis and adjustment coincided with the first contacts between the Javanese and another new element—European traders. The Portuguese were the first to arrive in the Indonesian islands. Possessing a good knowledge of navigation, in the middle of the fifteenth century Portuguese seamen and adventurers began to widen their trade by circumventing the Muslim traders who had held a monopoly of the spice trade with Europe.[13] In the second half of the sixteenth century, after conquering Malaka, the Portuguese entered the Indonesian archipelago, where, through force and political maneuvering, they began to engage in the spice trade in the islands (Ricklefs 1993:22).

Throughout the sixteenth century, the Portuguese held a dominant position in maritime trade in the Indian Ocean and thus had a strong impact on commerce. The Portuguese language became the lingua franca for trade in most of the coastal regions at that time and remained so until the end of the eighteenth century. Portuguese cultural influences were introduced that had an impact on Indonesian society: the borrowing of Portuguese words into Indonesian, such as *pesta* (party), *meja* (table), *bendera* (flag), *sabun* (soap), and *sepatu* (shoes); the use of Portuguese units of weight; and the use of Portuguese money for currency. The Portuguese also brought missionaries, who achieved the earliest Catholic conversions in the eastern archipelago, especially in Maluku.

The Portuguese also, by having intercourse with Asian women, some of them slaves, conceived children of mixed blood, the Eurasians or Indo-Portuguese. In fact, in order to promote trade colonization, the Portuguese encouraged their men to marry Asian and later Eurasian women, a policy that was also followed by the Dutch in the early period of their trade, in the middle of the seventeenth century (Boxer 1965:220).

Perhaps the most memorable and long-lasting remnant of Portuguese culture in Indonesian society was an Indonesian musical genre now known as *kroncong*.[14] The origin of this music can be traced back to the Portuguese music of sixteenth-century Java. This was a type of music played by the Christianized slaves of the Portuguese—Africans, Indians, and Malays—who lived in a settlement of the village of Tugu, near Batavia (now Jakarta) (Heins 1975:21–22; Kornhauser 1978:109–10). From Tugu the music spread throughout Java, and after more than three centuries, it formed into several musical sub-genres which are known collectively as kroncong (ibid. 127–37).

In the late sixteenth century, a major competitor to the Portuguese, the

Dutch, arrived in the archipelago. Well prepared materially (i.e., having better ships and better guns), as well as organizationally and financially, the Dutch surpassed the Portuguese (Ricklefs 1993:26–27). After trading under the banner of the Vereenigde Oost-Indische Compagnie (the Dutch East India Company, abbreviated V.O.C., founded in 1602), the Dutch company gradually increased their intervention in the political life of Indonesian states. Sultan Agung (r. 1613–1645), who had been successful in consolidating the Javanese states into the Mataram kingship, took a strong stand against the presence of the Dutch in Java. In 1628 and again in 1629, he went to war against the Dutch in Batavia, but both times he was defeated (ibid. 42–43; Pigeaud and de Graaf 1976:42–43).[15]

After his death, the Javanese regional rulers became politically and economically more dependent on Dutch advice. Power struggles between the royal family and religious factions created a series of crises throughout the seventeenth century and up to the middle of the eighteenth.

For lack of evidence, we are left with almost no knowledge of music and the other performing arts in the early period of Islamized Java. Our eagerness to learn about artistic life at this time grows out of Javanese cultural memory itself, which insists on the high artistic achievement of this period. The Sekatèn ensemble, a special gamelan which is played once a year to honor the birth and death of the Islamic Prophet Nabi Muhamad, was believed to be the creation of the Islamic saints (*wali*). The development of the sacred dance called bedhaya and significant developments in the practice of wayang and gamelan are attributed to the court of Sultan Agung. Moertono calls this view of tradition "the cult of glory in the legitimation of kingship" (1968:52–82). In this case it was not the status of the king that was legitimized, but the court performing arts. Eventually the royal glory was enhanced as well, since the court performing arts sought to maintain or increase the extent to which the king was held in esteem by his people. The more august the person, real or legendary, to which the art was attributed, and the further back it went, the greater the prestige of that art.

In any event, there is almost no historical evidence to substantiate the claims of high artistic development during Sultan Agung's reign. The only written evidence about the music and dance of this period comes from a handful of Dutch accounts; that of Rijklof van Goens (1856 [1656]), the V.O.C. ambassador to the kingdom of Mataram during the reign of Amangkurat I (r. 1646–1677), provides the only substantial information about music and dance in Mataram.

Van Goens saw several ensembles, each consisting of from twenty to thirty or fifty small and large gongs,[16] which were played to honor the appearance of the king at Monday and Saturday tournaments (1856:322–23). An ensemble consisting of predominantly gong-type instruments known to have accompanied Saturday and Monday tournaments in nineteenth-century Central Javanese courts was gamelan Monggang. But in this gamelan there is also a pair of drums (kendhang) and cymbals (*rojèh*). According to present-day court musicians, gamelan Monggang is an archaic ensemble.

Did Van Goens see a drumless gamelan Monggang? A firm answer cannot be given because Van Goen's descriptions lack detail. We can only observe that an ensemble consisting of different sizes of gongs, a gamelan Monggang type of ensemble, is first mentioned in the early period of Islamized Java.

Van Goens (1856:327) also saw five to nineteen maidens, whose torsos were barely covered, dance before the king. About the fabric the dancers wore, Van Goens wrote:

> This fabric is variously adorned, often black mixed with gold stars, blue with gold or silver flowers, red, green, white, etc.; all adorned with gold or silver; on which they know how to paint with water-color in a very unusual technique.[17]

This fabric appears to be similar to that worn by the nine female dancers in the most sacred dance, called Bedhaya Ketawang, in the Surakarta court. We also learn from Van Goens that this "bedhaya Mataram style" was presented in an atmosphere of drinking parties among the noblemen.

> Now, the King, being in a good mood, even claps his hands, encouraging these young maidens in a loud voice to do their best, promising them some gold rings and jewelry. Then, when they are tired, the other great noblemen must get their maiden dancers from their lodges in order to compete against his [the King's dancers] for the prizes, which frequently takes the whole night. In order to enjoy themselves during the performance, they drink among themselves of a certain drink called *brem,* made from a particular sticky rice (called *plut*). The drink tastes almost like our Spanish wine, and, if drunk moderately, is healthy for thin bodies. However, if you drink too much, it strongly warms you up, and one becomes very quickly drunk from it (as with Spanish wine).(1856:328)[18]

The accompaniment to this dance consisted of "many small gongs and a soft melody provided by a few flutes and viols" (p. 327).[19] We have no idea if the "viols" here were rebab, the bowed-stringed instrument which is commonly used in today's gamelan ensemble. At any rate, this instrumental combination has no equivalent in today's Javanese ensemble. But an ensemble consisting of small gongs, flutes, and samepa was mentioned in Old Javanese literature (Robson 1971:73). And if samepa refers to a bowed-string instrument, as Kunst (1968:86) suggested, this ensemble might well be a survival of Hindu-Javanese ensembles.

An ensemble whose main instruments are four flutes and a rebab is known in Bali as gamelan Gambuh. The ensemble also includes several percussion instruments of gong and other types, and a pair of drums. As I mentioned earlier, the gamelan Gambuh is thought to be one of the remnants of Hindu-Javanese ensembles. In any event, an ensemble that has more than one rebab, like the one Van Goens saw, cannot be found in Balinese or Javanese gamelan practice today. It is possible, as Kunst (1973, 1:116) suggested, that Van Goens described the instrumental composition of this ensemble incorrectly.

Van Goens (1856:328) mentions a dance contest between two men, one carrying a pike and the other a shield and sword, accompanied by great gongs. He also mentions "many kinds of fools and clowns, covered with masks of many kind of animals, who also play a few comedies of older times, in which they know how to sing amusingly" (ibid.).

Such accounts do not substantiate traditional claims that the present-day gamelan and dances, with their deep social significance and religious meaning, originated in the early period of Islamized Java, especially in seventeenth-century Mataram. However, Van Goens's accounts were limited to a single occasion. Were there performances inside the court? What about wayang performances? For these questions I can provide no firm answers.[20]

I have already mentioned the time of crisis and adjustment in the early period of Islamized Java. This period of contention is well described in some poetic works written in the eighteenth century, among them the *Serat Cabolèk*. Composed by the court poet Yasadipura I, from the late eighteenth century to the early nineteenth century (Soebardi 1975:18), the *Serat Cabolèk* reflects

> the tensions in Javanese religious life resulting from [increased] contact with Islam. The principal of these tensions was that between the *'ulamā'* (Islamic scholars), the defenders of the *sharī'a* (Islamic law) and those who rejected legalistic forms of religion and professed Javanese mysticism. (Ibid. 52–53)

Thus, the tension was now not between Islamic and Hindu-Buddhist views, but between two varieties of Islam: a legalistic form of Javanese Islam, and a syncretic, mystical Javanese Islam. The passage below illustrates such a tension in music. It is a conversation between the king Paku Buwana II of Kartasura and Radèn Demang Urawan, who was summoned by the king to investigate a religious and social movement led by Haji Amad Mutamakin.[21] The king recalls Adipati Jayaningrat telling him about Ketib Anom of Kudus, who, besides being a *santri*, was also a dhalang and wayang actor whose performances were accompanied by the terbang ensemble.[22]

> At that time I have [*sic*] invited/Jayaningrat's *wayang-wong*
> [company] to come/together with the carver of *wayang*-
> puppets./Indeed I invited [him] on that occasion/together
> with Cakraningrat,/when there were still no *gambuh*-dancers.

It was Jayaningrat who said/jokingly in my presence:/ "My Lord,/every time you wish to have/a *gambuh*-dancer and *ringgit-tiyang*,/there is [always] one thing missing,

and that is a tambourine,[23] my Lord."/I laughed heartily [and said]:/ "Now *Adipati*, is there ever/a tambourine played to accompany a puppet-show?/I think it is unusual."/The *Adipati* said:

"As a matter of fact the *bupati* of Kudus/has a son-in-law, who is a *santri*,/his name is Kĕtib Anom;/he was the first to give performances with a tambourine my Lord."/Then I burst into laughter,/I thought he was joking.

Yet *Adipati* Jayaningrat/said to me/that he [*Kĕtib* Anom] was a *ḍalang* as well as a *wayang* actor,/and that Kĕtib Anom himself had played/the role of *wong agung Menak* [= Amir Hamzah]/who was a warrior and powerful on the earth.

So, I wanted to invite him,/[but] Cakraningrat restrained me /saying: "Please, do not/hold a performance, my Lord,/in which the relatives of the Prophet of God take part/for this [means] rejecting their example.

Indeed formerly my father,/your servant, was forbidden/to give a tambourine performance with the *menak* repertoire,/ this is not permitted in Madura./Stories about *Muhamad* and *Mursada*,/*Sapingi* and *Asmarasupi*,

[may not be included] in the repertory./[As for] the Madurese tambourine performance, my Lord,/[the story] is only read from a book,/this is not forbidden;/indeed my father, your servant,/inherited [the book] from Mataram."

(Soebardi's translation, 1975:88–89)

This passage reflects a conflict between doctrinaire Islamic practice and the Javanese performing arts. On the one hand the king sees nothing wrong when he hears that wayang and a musical instrument associated with Islamic music (terbang) could coexist. He even gives an example of Ketib Anom, both a religious leader and an actor, who performs wayang with the terbang accompaniment. On the other hand, Cakraningrat takes the stance of rejecting such combination.

These lines represent a specific example of the process of cultural adjustment after the introduction of a new musical genre associated with Islam, namely, Islamic terbang music. The passage captures the conflict between the old and new traditions and also shows the necessity for Islamic leaders to embrace old traditions in order to spread Islam. Such conflict and resolution is well illustrated in the general content of the *Serat Cabolèk*.

It is commonly held that the Javanese have great tolerance for foreign cultures. Such a view cannot be taken for granted. This is because sociopolitical conditions take precedence in determining the kind of tolerance the Javanese needed in order to adopt foreign elements. The fact that after two centuries of Islam the Javanese still had some reservations about the experiment that combined two musical cultures indicates the delicacy and intricacy of the process of Islamization of Java. On the other hand, the mention of such an argument in the literature indicates the openness of the process of adaptation.

Early Views of Javanese Islam: Sufism and the Javanese Court

As was mentioned in the *Serat Cabolèk,* a wayang performance to the accompaniment of Islamic terbangan music was the subject of a debate and a reflection of cultural adjustment after the arrival of Islam. However, the *Serat Centhini,*[24] a poetic work compiled and written in the late eighteenth to the early nineteenth centuries, offers several different views of the effect of Islam on Javanese music. Let us consider this passage:

10. About the marriage [of gamelan] with *èlmu* (sacred knowledge),
    the sound of gamelan
    is the same as the sound of the lips.
    Gendhing is the true *niat* (striving after the sublime).
11. The sound of the *dhikir* prayer is analogous with
    the clanging of gamelan instruments,
    yet without gendhing.
    Praying dhikir without niat,
12. the prayer is the same as the sound of kethuk
    as it is played alone.
    Its sound does not become gendhing.
    Praying dhikir incessantly is as a broken *kecèr* (cymbals):
13. noisy and disturbing to the ears, heard
    as if breaking [the eardrum].
    Even [if one prays] until one's jaw is broken,
    and praying dhikir is only measured by the mouth,
14. thus expecting to receive what is asked for
    at once,
    even if [one prays] until one's throat is sore,
    in the end what is wanted will never arrive,
15. because [the prayer] is without gendhing in the heart.
    The sound of [the piece] Okrak-Okrak,
    if it contains gendhing,
    will inevitably be very enjoyable as a piece in *pathet sanga.*[25]
    (Serat Tjentini 1912–15, 7–8:204–5)

In this passage we notice a sense of readiness (or eagerness) on the part of the author(s) to present an analogy between gamelan and Islamic prayer. The fact that gamelan music is compared with dhikir ("recollection"), prayer for achieving mystical insight, demonstrates the authors' views on the significance of playing or listening to music—namely, that through such musical-religious activity one may have deep spiritual experiences. In light of the frequent condemnation of music by many Javanese Muslims in today's Java, such great tolerance of music at the time of the *Serat Centhini* is indeed worthy of closer inspection.

As I said above, before Islam arrived in Java in the fifteenth century, Javanese culture was based on pre-Hindu culture infused with Hindu-Buddhist philosophies. I also indicated that the introduction of Islam brought about a period of cultural crisis and adjustment—a period of encounter between the older traditions and Islam. To a certain extent, however, some compatibilities between the two traditions eased the process of Islamization in Java.

One of the reasons for the successful spread of Islam in Java was the dominance of Sufism, which was brought to Indonesia by Islamic traders. Developed in the middle of the ninth century, Sufism is an ascetic movement that "embraces those tendencies in Islam which aim at direct communion between God and man" (Trimingham 1971:1). Thus Sufi, as it is commonly known, emphasizes the practice of mysticism, which Trimingham defines as "a particular method of approach to Reality (*Ḥaqīqa,* another special Sufi term), making use of intuitive and emotional spiritual faculties which are generally dormant and latent unless called into play through training under guidance" (ibid).

The fact that this Muslim mysticism was introduced earlier and was regarded highly and became dominant in the early period of Islamization in Java helps us to understand the relatively peaceful acceptance of Islam by the Javanese later on. During the pre-Islamic period, the Javanese had a dynamic, syncretic Hindu-Javanese mystical tradition.[26]

It is worth noting that music has an important role in the ritual of the Sufi brotherhoods. Trimingham (1971:195) observes that, in Sufism,

> music, with its vagueness and lack of precise images, not only has mystical power to draw out the deepest emotions, but also, when coordinated with symbolic words and rhythmical movements, has power over man's will.

Thus, music is an essential means for religious devotion and communion with God. It may help a Sufi to achieve a state of ecstasy. In other words, unlike other streams of Islam which emphasize legalistic Islamic law, Sufi brotherhoods are more concerned with an emotional approach to achieving religious enlightenment. This is why music has an important role in the life of the Islamic community.

Sufi brought an inherently positive attitude to music to Java. Consequently, not only was Islamic music, such as the terbang ensemble and various Islamic prayers, introduced and promoted in Java and other parts of Indonesia; but Sufi leaders also regarded indigenous Javanese music and related arts as important. As a result of the encounter of the Sufi worldview with Javanese musical culture, a unique Javanese perspective on the performing arts came into being. It is this particular worldview that I wish to discuss.

There is some evidence that Islamic music was an essential part of cultural life both inside and outside the courts in the eighteenth and early nineteenth centuries. A long poem written by a lady scribe and soldier of the court of Mangkunegaran, the *Serat Babad Nitik Mangkunegaran* (abbreviated *Serat Babad Nitik*) (1780–1791), testifies to the dynamism of Islamic religious life in the court of the Mangkunegaran in Surakarta. In this treatise we find descriptions of various musical and other performances with characteristics of Islamic as well as pre-Islamic customs, which were performed in conjunction with royal rituals, such as the observance of the weekly Friday prayer (*Jumungahan*) and the birthday of the prince Mangkunegara. Dhikir and terbangan music were two exogenous Islamic musical forms that were performed every Thursday evening as part of the Jumungahan observance.

> 130b-6.   Again on the evening of Thursday
> the prince's retainers stayed awake.
> *Kaum* sang dhikir and played terbang.
> *Demang* played archery.
> *Ngabèhi* were in the front hall.
> The prince's children and *tumenggung*
> were served food,
> rice, side dishes, and from time to time drink.
> At midnight all were served food [again].[27]
> (*Serat Babad Nitik* 1929, 2:248)

Sometimes the religious observance was on a grand scale, as when hundreds of *santri* (Islamic devotees) performed prayers during the celebration to commemorate the prince's birthday (1:24). We learn from these passages that Islamic life had a lively atmosphere and there were various rituals in the Mangkunegaran palace at that time. Various Islamic rituals were performed in conjunction with or alternating with non-Islamic entertainment. In essence, the court rituals promoted a close relationship between Islamic and other Javanese customs in Islamic religious as well as secular contexts. Ann Kumar (1980) stresses this point in her article on the subject. She points out that as part of the Friday ritual, "Mangkunĕgara and his followers frequently kept watch the preceding night, listening to santri reciting the Kuran or performing the dhikir in unison, as well as enjoying more secular amusements" (p. 13).[28] To illustrate this point, I translate a passage from the *Serat Babad Nitik* that describes a ritual which was held for the *tingalan ageng* ("big" or annual birthday) of Mangkunegara I.[29]

13a–13. . . . .
    Then the month changed
    to the month of Arwah.
    On Monday-Wagé
    the fourth day,
    the honorable Prince
    held his annual birthday [celebration].
    His age was
13a–14. already fifty
    and eight years.
    The year was Ehé with the chronogram
    "elephant sees the sound of human."
    In the afternoon santri were praying,
    [their numbers] consisting of seven hundred and
    seventy-four.
    Reverberating was the sound of the santris' prayer.
    Santri meri crowded in the courtyard.[30]
13a–15. At midnight there was a *kondangan* (ritual meal).
    Food [was then served] after midnight.
    Santri meri overflowed everywhere,
    and money was distributed to them.
    In the morning gamelan Monggang was sounded.
    Cannons were booming,
    followed by the continuous shooting of
    rifles, all were sounded,
    reverberating as if the mountain was exploding.
13b–16. Then male *srageni* (marching army)
    followed by female srageni
    fired their rifles in the *paringgitan* hall.
    The prince gave them commands.
    In uniform was the female srageni,
    more impressive than the male srageni.
    Most astonished were the spectators.
    The drummers and flutist were all female.
    After kondangan [santri] were praying,
13b–17. and money was distributed
    evenly to them all.
    Then *ringgit tiyang* [was staged],
    taking turns with *serimpi* dance,
    and dancers danced before the screen,
    all were petite and beautiful maidens.
    Open-mouthed with wonder was everyone who was
        watching,
    the spectators were astounded.
    Then the beautiful female bedhaya dance intervened.

13b-18. The soldiers were all drinking.
Cannons were sounded repeatedly.
People applauded frequently.
The number of spectators increased.
Lurah, soldiers, and *mantri* were
all drunk with liquor,
extremely intoxicated.
Pangéran dipati [Mangkunegara],
the prince Jayèngasta and his entourage were also drunk.

13b-19. They held entertainment all day along.
In the late afternoon there was a ringgit performance
as well as continuous *talèdhèkan* dancing party.
Showers fell all night.
In the morning they staged ringgit once again—
the leather puppet show. And also
blankets were distributed to soldiers.
At night *wayang wong* dance drama was performed again.
Then in the morning there were talèdhèkan.[31]

(*Serat Babad Nitik* 1929, 1:24–25)

These descriptions indicate the unique and lively Islamic practice of the Javanese courtier. Islamic rituals were held side by side or in turn with worldly entertainment (including drinking and gambling), two activities that would now be considered mutually contradictory. The descriptions also show that in religious activities and secular entertainment Islamic and Javanese customs existed side by side with no conflict.[32]

It is not clear what stream of Islam existed in the courts of Central Java at that time. It is known that Sufism was popular in the rural areas. It was also taught in the *pesantrèn* (the Islamic religious schools), which were usually in the countryside. While the meaning of Islam in Central Javanese courts cannot yet be ascertained, it seems clear, as Day (1983:153) points out in the context of the development of the court literature, that the court was well aware of the "rural pattern of religious activity which served as cultural matrix for the reception of Sufi Islam in Java." Thus, rural cultural activity contributed to the shaping of the courtier's worldview.[33]

As is shown in some of the court literature, apparently the court world of Surakarta tried to keep a balance between legalistic and mystical Islam. From the eighteenth century to the mid nineteenth century, Javanese aristocrats seem to have been more receptive to Islamic practice. In this period, support from Islamic leaders was still essential for Javanese rulers to enhance their political power. From the mid nineteenth century onward, conditions changed as the Dutch consolidated their control of Java. As a consequence of the dependence of the Javanese rulers on the Dutch, Islam gradually became only a formal religion in the courts. Eventually, old Islamic practice disappeared in the Central

Javanese courts. Consequently, cultural life in the Central Javanese courts shifted away from Islam (see chapter 2).

How much the positive attitude of Islamic Sufism to music actually influenced the perspective of aristocrats cannot yet be determined. However, oral accounts and traditional literature indicate that the Sufi worldview existed in the court.

It is known that Sufism assigns important roles to spiritual leaders. These Islamic leaders are known as wali, the saints who were credited with introducing Islam to Java. Legend has it that the wali were directly involved in the development and refinement of wayang and gamelan. Such a view existed in the minds of both the court elite and the masses.

Kusumadilaga, in his *Serat Sastramiruda* (1930), provides a list of wali and Islamic leaders and their contributions to the development of wayang. According to him, the wali helped to alter the shape of wayang, giving the puppets a very stylized form so that images of human beings were not directly represented (p. 10). Any representation of a human being in the form of an animated object is forbidden by Islamic law.[34] More specific examples of their contributions appear in Kusumadilaga's work. Sunan Giri is said to have created additional monkey characters in the shadow puppet play *wayang purwa* and to have revised the order of the story (*gancaring lalakon*); Sunan Bonang created left and right arrangement of wayang puppets (*simpingan wayang*). Sultan Ngalam Akbar added elephants, horses, and army figures; Sunan Kalijaga created the screen, added the banana trunk for staging the puppets, created the *baléncong* (an oil lamp for creating shadows in the wayang performance), the wayang chest and the *kayon* (tree or mountain) figure (and also created *wayang topèng,* mask dance drama); and Sunan Bonang created the story of Damarwulan, which is used in the wayang klithik or *kerucil* (a wayang performance with flat wooden puppets).

Warsadiningrat also attributes to some wali the creation and refinement of gamelan. For example, he (1987:59) states that Sunan Tunggul of Giri created a gamelan with an additional saron and an additional pitch for certain instruments: the bonang, the gendèr, and the saron family. Like many other Javanese, Warsadiningrat (pp. 55–59) also believes that Sunan Kalijaga was responsible for creating gamelan Sekatèn, an extremely large and loud sounding gamelan that was (and is now) played in the courtyard of the court mosque.[35] In addition to being played to commemorate the birth and death of Nabi Muhamad, it is commonly believed that the gamelan Sekatèn was also played to persuade people to convert to Islam. In addition, Sunan Kalijaga was responsible for composing a number of gendhing.

There is no evidence to support Kusumadilaga's and Warsadiningrat's claim about the important role of the wali in the development of Javanese arts. The point here is that they think of the artistic development in Javanese court in terms of its linkage with Sufism.

The Javanese themselves also encouraged the expansion of Islam. The work of the *pujangga* (court poet) Yasadipura is a case in point. Besides his works that illustrate the process of Islamization of Java (such as the *Serat Cabolèk*), he also translated a number of works of Islamic literature. For example, he translated *Tajusalatin* (an Islamic book about religion and statecraft), *Serat Ménak* (a story about the heroism of an uncle of the Prophet Muhammad, Amir Hamzah), and *Serat Ambiya* (stories about Islamic prophets) (Soebardi 1975:23).[36] In Central Javanese courts, the *Serat Ménak* formed the basis for the story of a dance drama and wayang kulit Ménak; in the outlying regions of the kingdoms it was the basis for the story of wayang Thengul or *wayang golèk* Ménak. Nowadays these Ménak theatrical forms are vanishing.

In his *Serat Sastramiruda,* Kusumadilaga sees a strong link between Javanese and Islamic customs. In particular, he sees a close relationship between Javanese tayuban and Islam. Explaining the history of tayuban, he says:

> Concerning travelling *talèdhèk* dancing group during the time of De-mak, its musical accompaniment consisted of terbang and kendhang. Gendhing began with vocal introductions. This [practice of tayuban] originated in the time of Buddhism; it was the dancing of celestial nymphs to the accompaniment of the sound of *katawang*.[37] At the time of the court of Janggala, it is said that when Prabu Suryawisésa entered the inner palace, he was met by the queens in the middle of the paring-gitan quarter. There the queens danced to the accompaniment of gamelan sléndro. Thus, tayuban dancing originated in the reign of Prabu Suryawisésa. At the time of Demak, tayuban was performed by santri [of an Islamic sect called] Dulguyering Birahi. The introduction [of the piece] was dhikir prayer. The song was accompanied by angklung, kendhang and terbang. There were also male or female santri who were summoned to dance. The melody was similar to gendhing sléndro or pélog. Later, tayuban became the entertainment of Javanese people both in the village and in the city. The commoners or the elite, if they held wedding celebrations, circumcisions and the like, held tayuban entertainment.[38] (Kusumadilaga 1930:48–49)

In this passage we note that Kusumadilaga, a leading court artist, perpetuates the view of the courtiers about Islam, particularly Sufism. He sees tayuban, the court, and Islamic customs as having something in common. In fact, as is mentioned in the *Serat Babad Nitik,* tayuban was often a part of Islamic ritual, as when Mangkunegara I (r. 1757–1796) observed the Jumungahan ritual. More important for courtiers, tayuban and drinking liquor became standard customs and entertainment for men. Thus, the courtiers must have known of these two related entertainments.

An incident that occurred during the visit of the Yogyanese crown prince to the court of Surakarta at the time of the reign of Paku Buwana III (r. 1749–

1788) illustrates the importance of tayuban and drinking for courtiers.[39] The reason for the visit was that the Yogyakarta sultan wished to ally himself with Paku Buwana by ordering his son to seek in marriage a Surakarta princess. In honor of the visit of the crown prince, Paku Buwana held a lavish tayuban.

> . . . .
> In the tayuban dancing party,
> the gamelan sound could be heard from afar,
> The cheer "hurrah" [was heard] repeatedly.
> They ate and drank.
> Many were very drunk.
> At the time the crown prince
> did not want to drink *arak* (an alcoholic drink),
>
> only eating rice belatedly.
> After eating, talèdhèk entered in [the hall].
> [They], four of them, were special.
> They were very pretty,
> wearing batik colored with green *kenanga* flower
> gilded with dark red,
> [as if these talèdhèk] could fly.
> The king [Paku Buwana] was first to dance,
> heralded by the thundering sound of cannons,
> together with the immense sound of cheering.
>
> . . . .
> After the king finished dancing,
> then danced the *Huprup* (Dutch chief official), after which
> Mangkunegara danced.
>
> After Mangkunegara finished dancing,
> then the crown prince
> was asked [to dance] by Paku Buwana:
> "Please, my younger brother, you
> will satisfy my heart,
> All your subjects
> are filled with expectation?"
> The crown prince of Jogjakarta [replied]:
> "Thank you, [but] I have never done
> this kind of business.
>
> I surrender my death and life to you my older brother king."
> Paku Buwana approached where he sat,
> stood up in front of his chair.
> His brother got down [from his seat],
> squatting before the king
> . . . .[40]

(Yasadipura 1854 [late 18th century]: 160–61)

Then Paku Buwana again begged the crown prince to dance. But he again refused, giving as his reason that from his childhood he had been brought up as a santri and was prohibited from dancing and drinking.[41] The point here is that the noblemen in Central Java at the time were expected to know how to dance and drink in tayuban, a skill that was important for a courtier.

It is possible to treat this incident as an example of the conflict of religious values among the courtiers: the Yogyanese courtiers seem to follow the path of Islamic orthodoxy, in opposition to their Solonese rivals. Actually, the story is based on a particular political affair at the time: an ongoing feud between Central Javanese rulers seeking to inherit the Mataram kingdom legitimately through marriage.[42] The announcement of the marriage of Mangkunegara's son and the oldest daughter of Paku Buwana III was the beginning of the animosity between Mangkunegara and the Sultan of Yogyakarta (the latter had failed to do the same for his daughter). With the involvement of the Dutch in a series of negotiations and the threat of renewed warfare between Mangkunegara and the Sultan with the help of the Dutch, the dispute between these two rulers resulted in the divorce of Mangkunegara and his wife, Ratu Bandara (the Sultan's oldest daughter).

A similar incident occurred during the second visit of the crown prince to Surakarta in his second attempt to see his prospective wife. *Babad Mangkubumi* describes a tense incident, as summarized by Ricklefs (1974:116):

> On the occasion of a *wayang-topeng* (masked dance) performance, at which the Susuhunan danced the role of Pandji, the young Crown Prince was too embarrassed to dance, professing that he had not yet learned. The Susuhunan said he, too, was no expert and the Crown Prince then accepted the invitation to join him. But the performance provoked Mangkunĕgara's anger when the Susuhunan and the Crown Prince became too tired to continue. The situation became so tense, says the *babad,* that the Crown Prince's entourage prepared against possible hostilities on their trip to Jogjakarta, for it seemed that Susuhunan would be unable to curb Mangkunĕgara.

It is possible to assume that the portrayal of the dance performances during the Crown Prince's visit was a way for the poet to present a historical event dramatically. It is also possible to connect the incident involving tayuban to the Dutch government's awareness of the potential power of Islam against the presence of Europeans in Java. It was thus essential for the Dutch government to begin to prevent the aristocrats from embracing Islam. The *Huprup*'s anger at the crown prince because he consistently refused to dance in tayuban (because of his devotion to Islam) indicates the Dutch hostility to Islam. The hostility continued when Paku Buwana IV, starting when he was still a crown prince, demonstrated publicly his wish to practice Islam strictly. He even allied himself with a group of "religious zealots" linked to a rebellious religious family (for further discussion, see Ricklefs 1974:285–341). In any case, tayuban dancing and the-atrical performances were essential in the cultural life of the court at the time.

Tayuban continued to be an essential part of the court celebrations into the nineteenth century. In the *Wiwahan Dalem* (mid 19th century), a poetic work recounting the wedding celebrations of K. P. A. A. Prangwedana, the son of Mangkunegara IV (r. 1853–1881), the poet mentions tayuban several times. Significantly, the groom also had to dance in the tayuban, a tradition which is still followed in most wedding celebrations.

6. After the end of the dinner party,
   the Dutch guests and their wives wished to leave.
   Their departure is not told here.
   In the meantime, in the *pandhapa* (front hall),
   the preparations for the tayuban dance party were carried out.
   Juru alok, juru senggak (interjectory singers), and
   juru keplok (clappers) were made ready.
7. The prince [Mangkunegara] gave a cue to his son,
   the groom, asking him to dance first.
   The one who was given a cue responded,
   then faced left,
   instructing his soldiers to order
   [the musicians] to play gendhing Boyong *pathet barang*.
   It was loudly cheered, together with the sound of gong.
8. The clapping was immense,
   issuing from south, east, north, west, in groups,
   impressive,
   coming from all directions.
   The loud cheering was comparable to the loud sound of gamelan.
   With the singing of *ronggèng* dancers, the gendhing could
      be heard from afar,
   like the sounds of battle.
11. Well timed were the neck movements,
    The intertwining dance movements attracted the hearts.
    The *larih* session was performed three times.
    The prince's son
    opened his *sampur* (scarf for dancing), cueing the music to stop.
    Then the dancers danced in succession.
    The noble families also took turn,
12. alternating with the guests from outlying regions,
    continually until the morning came.
    . . . .[43]

("Wiwahan Dalem" 1927:28:250–53)

Tayuban was also held in the court *pakajangan*. Pakajangan refers to an occasion when the king's high-ranking subjects (*bupati*) from the outlying regions of the kingdom stayed in a temporary camp which was built at the open square (*alun-alun*) of the palace. Here each bupati provided all sorts of entertainment for his subjects. Often this entertainment was tayuban. Such tayuban might last for many days, in accordance with the wish of the king. An early report on tayuban by Soewandi (1938) describes at length a pakajangan tayuban which was held during the royal marriage of Paku Buwana X (r. 1893–1939). I translate and summarize below:

> In such tayuban, the bupati must be responsible for the cost of the event. This includes the cost of food, drink, liquor, and hiring talèdhèk. Coinciding with a dance introduction by the talèdhèk [he mentions ten talèdhèk for this particular pakajangan tayuban], a glass of gin was served to all who were present. Then all the talèdhèk danced *gambyong*. After the gambyong ended, junior bupati was the first to dance. This was because the senior bupati himself did not want to dance. After receiving a sampur from the talèdhèk, the junior bupati asked for a blessing from the senior bupati. He then asked the musicians to play gendhing Boyong. When the gendhing entered the *minggah* section, the junior bupati offered a salute of honor to the senior bupati and then proceeded to dance. He summoned four of his subordinates to be *larih* (people who are in charge of offering a drink to the male dancer). At each gong stroke, the larih offered the junior bupati a glass of gin. Subsequently, the bupati's entourage took turns dancing and drinking. The dancing style of each nobleman was determined by his rank. When night fell, foolish behavior began, such as pulling the talèdhèk's ears, to which the talèdhèk responded by pinching the nobleman's thigh. When many were drunk, tayuban became disorderly. They kissed and touched the talèdhèk's breasts. At dawn, the tayuban ended. Many were drunk and could not walk by themselves. (Soewandi 1938:116–21)

This description of tayuban indicates that the court tayuban did not differ much from the tayuban outside the court, such as the many described in the *Serat Centhini*. In particular, liquor and "foolishness" were part of the tayuban. The description of pakajangan tayuban also reminds us of Van Goen's account of the dance party in the time of Amangkurat I (r. 1645–1677), (see above).

Early Islamic Perspectives toward Music: Outside the Court

We can conclude that in the early stages of its introduction to Java, Islam encouraged both Islamic music and the indigenous Javanese performing arts. As is described in the *Serat Babad Nitik*, gamelan and wayang were presented side by side or alternately with Islamic music.

Away from the court, some evidence suggests that the interaction between

Islamic and indigenous musical performances brought about all sorts of musical syncretism. There seem to have been experiments with ensembles with different instrumentation and various repertoires of terbang and gamelan music.

Clear descriptions of syncretic musical phenomena can be found in the *Serat Centhini* (early 19th century). A particularly striking example is the use of the terbang ensemble to accompany a tayuban or talèdhèkan. This differs from the accompaniment of the tayuban mentioned in the *Babad Nitik* and "Wiwahan Dalem" (see above) and from tayuban accompaniment as we know it today. These tayuban were and are accompanied by gamelan music. But the presentation of the two kinds of tayuban may have been similar.

The following passages from the *Serat Centhini* indicate that a syncretic ensemble consisting of three terbang, angklung, kendhang, *calung,* and *calapita* was also used to accompany tayuban.[44] The story is about a terbangan performance held in the house of a bupati (a regent) to fulfill his *kaul* (vow) for the safe birth of his child. After the presentation of the music, the regent asks the talèdhèkan dancing party to begin.

20. Mas Cebolang accepted the command,
     starting to sing a *bawa* (vocal introduction) to Gambir Sawit.
     The essence of his voice was exquisite and sweet,
     flexible was its *wilet* (ornament), attracting our hearts.
     Santri replied,
     reverberating together with the terbang sounding "brung."
     Uniform was its ornamentation (*ukel*),
     repeated without any strange [treatment].
     Mas Cebolang played terbang skillfully.
21. Then the *tandhak* dancers danced.
     Excited were the spectators.
     The regent was very happy.
     He asked his servants to enter [to dance],
     taking turns, and was ordered
     to pay *tombok* (a fee for requesting a gendhing) *nyuku* (fifty cents).
     They were happy taking turns dancing.
     Dipati's servants
     asked for gendhing according to their pleasure.
22. Some of them danced together
     to the accompaniment of gendhing Gonjang-Ganjing
     . . . .[45]

(*Serat Tjentini* 1912–15, 1–2:5)

What is striking in this description is not only that the tayuban was a common activity in the Islamic community (an activity carried out and participated in by Muslims), but also that the syncretic ensemble combining Islamic terbang with Javanese musical instruments and playing gamelan gendhing was used to accompany the dancing party. I have yet to find a remnant of this curious tayuban practice in Java now.[46]

There must have been a certain musical dynamism when two musical genres, Javanese gamelan and Islamic terbangan, were mixed together. Their interaction must have resulted in new musical ideas and the exchange of repertoire. In fact, we learn that there were musical practices with other kinds of instrumental combinations. For example, the jathilan group was accompanied by an ensemble consisting of kendhang, salomprèt, angklung, *kekemong, kempul,* and terbang (*Serat Centhini Latin* 1988, 4:183).

Other clues to this dynamism are the interchangeable use of musical terminology and the sharing of musical repertoire in gamelan and terbangan music. Terms such as bawa and wilet, as in the above passage, were used in both musical genres. Gonjang-Ganjing, Petung Wulung, Lompong Kèli, Onang-Onang, Gambir Sawit, and many more pieces were given as the repertoires of both terbangan and gamelan music.[47]

The aristocrats also supported the Sufi view in their positive attitude toward music. As mentioned above, Kusumadilaga sees terbangan and tayuban as derived from a custom of the court of Jenggala—the dance of the queen in honor of the king's entrance to the inner palace. Pertinent to our discussion of Sufism is his explanation of tayuban's association with an Islamic practice of Dulguyer ("Whirling Dul").

The *Serat Centhini* also has a section on the practice of this Islamic sect. It is possible that Kusumadilaga used information from the *Serat Centhini* as a reference for creating his historical account of tayuban. But the point here is that Sufism had become part of the aristocrat's worldview.

In any event, the practice of Islamic Dulguyer continued to exist in the nineteenth century. An early-nineteenth century Dutch report of an Islamic ritual in Madiun clearly indicates the existence of Islamic Dulguyer (quoted by Onghokham 1975:70–71):

> Only here and there in a few villages are followers of a Moslem sect, the teaching of Abu Bakr (?) a disciple of Mohamad which differs from ordinary Islam . . . they call themselves the religion of *Dul* and have their own clergy. They had their own rites which were celebrated if the pryayi did not know about them and when they did not have to be afraid of persecution. Their ritual consisted of beating on the drum and singing continuously "Ha-Illa-Lah, Ha-Illah-Lah" while moving their bodies back and forth or side ways, until they got into a trance and became unconscious. Men, women and old invalid people who could not even walk ordinarily then began to dance (tandakken). The unconscious followers were believed to be in the happiest of states since they were in communion with God. Yellow water (*boreh?*) would be smeared on them and they then become conscious again while every-

body was offered yellow water to drink. Their leader (the guru) would burn incense and everybody made the *sembah* (salutation) to him before dancing.

It is clear that in this particular practice of Javanese Islam, prayer and dancing or whirling are inseparable religious events. The *tandakken* section—when entranced followers begin to dance (perhaps still accompanied by the beating of drums)—seems to be an essential part of the ceremony, an indication that the highest religious ecstasy had been reached.

These descriptions seem to refer to a kind of Sufi spiritual recital in which music and dancing are important means of achieving religious ecstasy. In fact, some evidence shows that in the nineteenth century, leaders of a Sufi order often traveled around Java as dervishes (Drewes and Purbatjaraka 1938 and Kraemer 1924, quoted in Kartodirdjo 1966:145). Moreover, the spiritual recital of a Sufi order is described clearly in the *Serat Centhini*.

> 44. Having eaten, all were full.
> Then they began a mass dhikir,
> forming a full circle,
> fastening their eye-covers
> of batik cloths and papers.
> That is the opening of Sufi dhikir.
> 45. The dhikir was whirling.
> There were many kinds of behavior,
> holding breath intermittently,
> and their sounds varied.
> The whole day
> the dhikir expert twirled.
> 46. Those who had long ago lost consciousness,
> woke up to cry and sing dhikir again.
> Standing up were the conscious ones.
> Some were shaking their heads.
> Of many kinds was the behavior
> of all male and female santri.[48]
> (*Serat Tjenṭini* 1912–15, 5–6:66–67)

It is clear that the authors are describing Sufi spiritual dances and songs. They refer to them as the practice of Sufi dhikir. Singing the litany, controlling the breath, whirling, and entering into trances—these common modes of behavior in the dhikir ritual are all found in the above poem.[49]

As indicated in the poem, the participants in the dhikir were both male and female santri. Qureshi points out that in Sufi practice in South Asia, the participants are commonly men, and only rarely women (Qureshi 1986:1). Qureshi does not say whether women participate differently from men. But the description of Sufi practice in the *Serat Centhini* suggests a unique picture of dhikir ritual. As the following passage shows, it included erotic behavior.

> 50. . . . .
> Early in the morning all of
> their heads began to turn,
> they fell, making a resounding sound,
> causing them to catch their breath.
> They were everywhere, one on the top of the other,
> like banana trees that had been cut down.
> 51. Men and women mixed together.
> Those who were on the top of the other did not mind.
> The ones who were naked were not concerned;
> there was no punishment.
> That was the way of the people of Dul Birahi,
> whoever achieved superiority, no questions were asked
> about their behavior.
> Those santri whose èlmu was inferior
> surrendered their wives' bodies and souls,
> presenting them [to the superior ones] for whatever purposes.[50]
> (*Serat Tjentini* 1912–15, 5–6:92)

This passage shows that the terms Dul Birahi and Santri Birahi allude to passionate Islamic practice. The word *birahi,* which means "passion," emphasizes passionate or erotic behavior. The passage also tells of the power of religious practice, when the inferior santri must surrender their wives to the more accomplished ones.[51]

Although the description in the *Serat Centhini* of eroticism in the practices of the nineteenth-century Sufi in Java is clear, we are not sure whether it is fact or fiction. Is the eroticism intended to make the story more interesting? On the other hand, it is important to note, as Trimingham (1971:199) observes in his study of Sufi orders in the Arabic and Persian world, that by the twelfth century,

> the dervishes had acquired a complete technique. They employed all sorts of methods to condition the person, open up his consciousness to the attractions of the supra-sensible world: sacred numbers and symbols; colours and smells, perfumes and incense; ritual actions and purifications; words of power, charm-like prayers and incantations, with music and chant; invocations of angels and other spirit beings; even the use of alcohol and drugs.

The discussion above suggests that, in Sufism, music can help to channel the listener's emotions toward the divine and "can also stir [the listeners'] emotions of love toward profane purposes" (i.e., erotic behavior) (Qureshi 1986:107).[52]

For further discussion of the erotic character of Sufi practice, and to provide a wider context for my discussion of Sufi practice, I now turn to Sufi practice in Aceh as reported by Hurgronje (1906).[53] This is especially important, since Hurgronje's report represents the earliest scientific account of Islamic practice in Indonesia. In addition, northern Sumatra was where Islam was first introduced into Indonesia (Ricklefs 1993:4). The assumption here is that Islamic practice in Aceh represents the early kind of Islamic customs that were similar to the practice in Java before orthodox Islam began to dominate both islands.

In Aceh there was an Islamic dhikir practice known as *ratib* (or *rateb*).[54] There were different kinds of ratib. Ratib Samman and Sadati (now commonly spelled Seudati) are discussed at length by Hurgronje. Hurgronje also states that these two ratib had a tendency to contain "unnatural" elements. He says that the orthodox, indigenous teachings of ratib "require of all who perform rātib or dikr, that they pronounce clearly and distinctly the words of the confession of faith and the names and designations of God" (1906:217). He goes on to say:

> But in the East Indian Archipelago the performers of the rātib Sammān have strayed far from the right path. In place of the words of shahādah, of the names or pronouns (such as *Hu,* i.e., He) used to designate Allah, senseless sounds are introduced which bear scarcely any resemblance to their originals. The votaries first sit in a half-kneeling posture, which they subsequently change for a standing one; they twist their bodies into all kinds of contortions, shaking their heads too [*sic*] and fro till they become giddy, and shouting a medley of such sounds as *Allahu éhé lahu sihihihihi* etc. This goes on till their bodies become bathed with perspiration, and they often attain to a state of unnatural excitement, which is by no means diminished by the custom observed in some places of extinguishing the lights. (1906:217–18)

This passage reminds us of the dhikir practice in Java discussed above. Hurgronje also notes that the practices of ratib Samman in Aceh "have strayed far from the right path." This refers to the process in which Sufism had to mix with local customs. Apparently such a mixture also took place in the transmission of Sufism in Java.

In Aceh, women had their own ratib (Hurgronje 1906:219). This suggests that the dhikir with mixed participants existed only in Java. It is probable that pre-Islamic Javanese customs, in which women were active participants in dance rituals, contributed to the creation of Javanese dhikir. As reported by Dutch writers (Domis 1832 and van Lerwerden 1844, quoted in Hefner 1987:88), ordinary women were still involved in village dance rituals (in wedding celebrations, the ritual purification of the dead, village festivals) among the Tenggerese in the middle of the nineteenth century.[55]

Hurgronje states that ratib Seudati was the favorite ratib in Aceh. Unlike ratib Samman, in which boy spectators might join in, the ratib Seudati was a public theatrical performance. The ratib company consisted of fifteen to twenty men, called *dalems, aduens,* or *abangs* (elder brother), and young boys in female dress were called *sadati*. In addition, the Seudati company had a *chèh* (from Arabic *shaikh*, leader) and one or two *radat* (singers).

The performance of ratib Seudati was always in the form of a contest between two groups. Lasting all night and half a day (from 8:00 P.M. to noon of the following day), the performance consisted of antiphonal singing and a story and choreographed movements led by the radat or the chèh, consisting of different sections.

It is not my intention here to go into detail about the practice of ratib Seudati, except to say that the performance consisted of elaborate poetic singing and complex, choreographed movements. (The former had a substantial erotic content.) What is important here is a link between the performance and "immorality." The center of attraction in this performance was the charm of the transvestite sadati dancers. About the link between the dancers and immorality, Hurgronje (1906:246) states:

> The manner of dress and appearance on the stage of the sadatis must be admitted to have some connection with the general prevalence in Acheh of immorality of the worst kind; but . . . it cannot be said that such immorality is directly ministered to by these performances.

Whether or not religious performance directly or indirectly caused immorality, the fact remains that there was an intimate linkage between religious activity and secular emotion, which was, in the case of the Acehnese seudati, possibly homosexuality.

Returning to Java, the *Serat Centhini* describes at length and in unambiguous terms the intimate linkage of music, religion, and eroticism. The story of Cebolang in the poem illustrates this. Cebolang is the son of a *kyai* (Islamic priest). Because of numerous offenses, including adultery with married and unmarried women, he has been evicted from his home by his father. With his four santri companions, he forms a troup of itinerant musicians, playing the Islamic-influenced terbang music.

14. Traveling along the coastal regions,
    frequently he got syphilis,
    caused by [his intercourse with] many ronggèng.
    In Sedayu, he was surrounded [by people there],
    because he had illicit love with santri wives.
    He departed to Daha.
    He boarded in the house of
    ki Jamal, the *pengulu* (religious official) of Daha.
    Ki Jamal had many santri, indeed.
    Ki Jamal was very happy
15. [to receive] his guests in his house.
    All Ki Jamal's santri

cherished dearly the newcomers.
When [Cebolang] was asked to perform [the terbangan],
for *pakaulan* (vow)—
e.g., the bride and groom do not get along,
a vow [was declared] to ask Cebolang to perform [his music]—
he was escorted by many santri.
His own santri companions were only four,

16. who accompanied him when he was sent away [by his father].
 They alone were assigned as tandhak.
 All four were skillful in dancing.
 Although people knew
 that they were truly professional male dancers,
 when people fought [because of the rivalry to entice the dancers],
 many stabbed each other.
 . . . .[56]

(Serat Tjenṭini 1912–15, 1–2:2–3)

The fact that Cebolang and the members of his terbangan dancing troupe were happily received as the family of the pengulu indicates the intimate relationship between music and religion, a theme that appears very frequently in the poem. Moreover, Ki Jamal's santri also became participants in the troupe.

Another theme mentioned is the practice of transvestism—four santri were assigned to become tandhak dancers, wearing women's dresses. Later in this section of the *Serat Centhini,* the linkage between music and transvestism is described at length. But first the poems introduce the topic of music and erotic behavior.

The regent of Daha was to fulfil a vow by calling on Cebolang's troupe to perform terbangan. After offerings were provided and hundreds of guests and onlookers had arrived, the regent asked Cebolang to start the performance. He picked up his terbang and began to sing an introductory song, a poem Sekar Lémpang:

13. His voice rose, clear and bright,
 rang out loud, fragrant and sweet.
 Appealing his wilet, carried heart away.
 His terbang playing resonated.
 His friends answered at once.
 Three terbang were rumbling,
 together with angklung and kendhang,
 calung, ivory calapita,
 vibrant, resonant, resounding, shaking and thundering.
14. Mixed in with the loud singing of the Lempang melody,
 in tumult were the onlookers.
 It was jam-packed, crowded,
 pressing and pushing against each other.

Many kinds were their manners.
The pickpockets were glad,
busily stealing.
Many people were losing their possessions,
shouting, in chaos; in a short time, turmoil.

15. After a while people were not aware
of losing anything, [because] they needed to watch [the performance].
Men and women were mixing and jostling one another.
People with disgraceful behavior wanted
women to feel a tickling sensation.
Their hands rubbed the women's breasts,
groping and searching unsurely.
Women were firmly held at their "padlocks" (genitals).
There were many who let themselves be fondled that way.[57]

(Ibid. 4)

Did the sound of music provoke the behavior that the passage suggests? Or did the social circumstances at the time permit such behavior to occur in any kind of gathering? The precise answer to these questions is difficult to find. I assume that both factors contributed. In any event, the point here is that the linkage between music and eroticism is one of the themes of the *Serat Centhini*. In fact, in the context of same performance, the poems describe frenzied sexual acts committed in the middle of the crowd while the sound of the terbang music went on (ibid. 5–6).

In the same story of Cebolang's adventures, the poem also describes the intimate linkage between erotic transvestite behavior and music. The story of the transvestite erotic behavior begins with the regent's desire for one of the male tandhak dancers, Nurwitri. After the performance, the regent asked Cebolang to allow Nurwitri to stay in the regent's house.

21. . . . .
Meanwhile, the regent's
heart was carried away
by the male ronggèng, Nurwitri.
The regent was a bit intoxicated
by *brem tape* liquor.

22. He was drunk and charmed
by his new lover, Nurwitri;
his desire was just satisfied [?].
Then he brought Nurwitri
to the rear room.
The regent said:
"Nurwitri, come forward,
I will sleep in your arms,
while you sing softly Lompong Kèli,
Montro, Petung Wulung,

23. Gambir Sawit and Gandrung Manis."
     Nurwitri answered "yes" with a flirtatious look,
     while biting his lips.
     The regent hurriedly
     embraced Nurwitri's neck.
     Eager with desire, he pinched
     Nurwitri's lips and cheeks,
     sucking and kissing them.
     Nurwitri said: "Oh, wait a moment master,
     I thought you ask me to sing."
24. The regent answered: "Yes, that would be nice."
     Then Nurwitri sang softly; his voice was enjoyable.
     Lompong Kèli was well rendered,
     thinly bright and sweet.
     After only two *gongan,*
     the regent spoke:
     "Stop, I have accepted [your songs].
     Come forward, don't be afraid."

· ·[58]

(Ibid. 12)

After this, the poem describes at length and step by step the homosexual intercourse between the regent and Nurwitri. As the passages show, music was
used as a prelude to erotic acts. It is possible that such descriptions of erotic
scenes were merely poetic. However, the frequency of references to transvestite
practice in the poem and the continued existence of such practices in contemporary Java suggest that the existence of the phenomenon cannot be ruled out in
nineteenth-century Java.[59]

The *Serat Centhini* describes a variety of performance contexts for music, either religious or secular or combinations of both. One of these contexts is the
magic spectacle, which is described in the following:

256. Jamal and Jamil performed *gabus* (magic spectacle) immediately,
      hitting each other with iron crowbars.
      Jamal was hit in his face,
      so hard that a cracking sound was produced.
      His forehead was split open, and, falling to the ground,
      the blood poured out.
      [His body] writhed in agonizing pain.
      Subsequently, [his body] was crushed with a rock.
      His head was broken into pieces, his bones were crushed, and
          his body
      collapsed in fatigue with blood streaming everywhere.
257. The spectators grieved intensely,
      profoundly shocked, their hearts were troubled.

The faces of all onlookers were pale.
Jayèngwesthi nodded.
Jayèngragi shook his head.
Suarja, Wiradhusta
and Kulawirya,
all were incredulous.
[They wondered] what Jamil would do next.
[These were] unbelievable events.

258. Ki Jamil asked [the musicians] to change gendhing,
to the long drawn-out and slowly played Sekar Gadhung.
The song in reply was as follows:
"Eagle strikes eagle.
Yes master, the eagle is death,
pale, yes master,
rokepida yakun."[?]
Jayèngraga said quickly
to Surat and Senu: "Let us stand up to sing *singir,*[60]
following behind Jamil."

259. Those who were asked obeyed the command.
Then they stood up and were taught by Jamil [to dance].
The motionless [dead] body was covered.
Jamil stood behind it,
bringing with him two angklung,
and moving around the lifeless body.
Sindhèn sang Ulung-ulung:
"Striking hawk yes master.
The hawk is death, pale master *rokin.*[?]
That is *pida yakun.*"[?]

260. [The melody] rose very high,
loud as if pressing the heart,
as if they appealed
to the inert, dead body.
Many onlookers cried.
[The sound of] a single terbang was soft,
with three angklung,
and a kendhang.
Quietly played was the interlocking technique,
the sound of [terbang] *kempyang* was exposed and very
enjoyable.

261. *Ting* and *tik pang ping pek pak pik pik*
thung plek thung plek tong ting bung pang peng byang
nguk nguk dhung dhung thong thung thur thèr.[61]
The incense was wafting.
The dead body moved and came to life.
The cover was removed.

Ki Jamal sat down.
His breath was coming in snorts.
He faced two ronggèng dancers and Ki Jamil.
Jamil watched, as if he were full of pity.[62]

> (*Serat Tjenṭini* 1912–15, 1–2:146–47)

It is possible that the descriptions of magic spectacles in the *Serat Centhini* are exaggerated—to heighten the excitement of reading the poems. In any event, such spectacles fall into the category of mixed religious and secular activities.[63] In particular, they can be related to the knowledge of invulnerability (*èlmu kadigdayan*), which was part of the esoteric knowledge of the Islamic Sufi brotherhoods. Kartodirdjo (1972:78–83) points out that the knowledge of invulnerability is common among the peasant community. Such knowledge can be gained from holy men in the community. Oftentimes these holy men are also Islamic leaders.[64]

It is worth noting that the magic spectacle as described in the *Serat Centhini* existed in late nineteenth-century Aceh. Hurgronje was an eyewitness of such a spectacle, which he reported at length (1906:249–53). Classified as a ratib performance, this magic spectacle was called a *rapa'i* or *ripa'i* performance (named after the great saint of the Islamic mystics, Ahmad Rifa'i). Like the *gabus* performance described in the *Serat Centhini,* the ripa'i might be performed to fulfill a vow. For example, should one escape some danger or should a member of one's family recover from an illness, he would vow to hold the rapa'i performance. According to Hurgronje's description (p. 253) of such a dervish miracle:

> The brethren divide into two equal sides, which take up their position opposite one another in several parallel rows. At the top, between the two parties, sits the guru, who is respectfully saluted by all present. He begins by reciting *fātiḥah,* the Mohammedan Lord's Prayer, and other passages from the holy writ; then he leads off the ratéb, which is intoned to the Achehnese and Malabar tune, as they are called, alternatively slow (*jareuëng*) and quick (*bagaïh*). It consists of Achehnese verses, two at a time being sung to each tune, mixed with corrupt Arabic expressions the meaning of which is unknown to the hearers.
>
> The leader sings alone three successive times the words: *ya hō alah, ya mèëlòë;* then all intone in chorus after him, "*o sòydilah,* oh my lord Amat! (i.e. Ahmad Rifa'i)." Thereupon commence the verses, the recitation of which is accompanied by an orchestra of great *rapa'i's,* while the actual performers occasionally strike smaller tambourines or wave them in the air with graceful motion.

Hurgronje provides a translation of some of the verses sung in the performance. He then describes (pp. 256–59) the center of attention, the most intense part of the performance:

The recital grows louder and quicker, and between this and the clashing of the tambourines and the constant motion of the head and limbs, the desired state of transport is at last reached. Then those possessed with the *efflatus* rise from the ranks of their fellows and after a respectful salutation to their teacher, receive at his hands the weapon or instrument which he selects. In Acheh the *dabōïh* is used, the weapon specially appertaining to this performance, but most of the common weapons of the country (*rinchōng, sikin* and *gliwang*) are also employed. The performer begins by making various half dancing movements in unison with the time of the recitation, which continues without a pause; meanwhile he draws his weapon, which he regards from time to time with tender looks and even kisses, in sundry different directions along the hands and arms.

Presently he begins to stab and smite these extremities with (to all appearance) a certain amount of force, and finally attacks other portions of his body, maintaining all the time the same rhythmic movements. The skilful tricksters among the brethren draw a little blood perhaps but generally confine themselves to causing deep depressions in their skin with point or blade, apparently using great force, and so giving the impression that their skin is impenetrable. But actual believers not unfrequently go so far as to inflict deep wounds on their arms, hands or stomachs, to knock holes in their heads or to cut pieces off their tongue.

A rapa'i representation which included the *sawa' ranté* i.e. "throwing (red-hot) chains round the shoulders" is regarded as particularly complete. The performers seldom escape without burns, but even in this case there appears to be no lack of artificial devices which increase the efficacy of the incantations. Such for instance is the preliminary moistening of the body with lime-juice.

In spite of Hurgronje's skepticism about the self-inflicted injury, his descriptions point to an intimate linkage between religion, music, dance, and invulnerability. The Acehnese evidence also shows that the nineteenth-century practices of syncretic, mystic Islam, a local form of Sufism, were not uniquely Javanese.[65]

To recapitulate: In early periods of Javanese history, the indigenous pre-Hindu culture, Hindu-Buddhist culture, and Islamic culture all encountered one another, interacted, hybridized, and complemented one another, resulting in the dynamic growth of Javanese culture and the formation of the traditional Javanese worldview. Religion is the foundation of Javanese culture. Besides their political and technological impact, Hindu-Buddhist traditions led to the development of Javanese literature and the performing arts. The localization and popularization of the Hindu literature and sung poetry brought about the atmosphere of intimacy in which the court artists and their masters lived and exchanged ideas.

The Islamization of Java did not change this intimate atmosphere. This is because Sufism, the dominant force behind the early expansion of Islam in Java, had a positive attitude toward the performing arts. There was a period of exchange of musical ideas and repertoire between Islamic and Javanese music. As I have emphasized, Javanese culture did not recognize any separation between religious and secular activity.

I briefly discussed Java's early contact with European culture. Later the expansion of trade and political domination by the Europeans, together with the decline of the early worldview of Javanese Islam, led to the more complex and heterogenous character of contemporary Javanese cultures.

TWO

Javanese Interaction with European Colonialism, Islam, and the Peranakan *Chinese: A Period of Intensive Cultural Development*

Background and Theory of the Development of the Javanese Performing Arts

In the preceding chapter I pointed out that the early period of Islam in Java was a period of not only cultural adjustment, but also of political crisis. The Javanese princes struggled for power, and a new foreign element, the Dutch East India Company (V.O.C.), was present. Historians summarize the activities of the Dutch in Java (Steinberg 1987:151):

> In the seventeenth century, the Dutch on Java had been diligent servants of a great merchant company, and in the nineteenth century they gradually became civil servants of a colonial state. In the eighteenth century, however, they were essentially an alien war band, extracting what they could from conquered territories by the most expedient means.

In the eighteenth century, a series of court intrigues in Central Java began with the sacking of Paku Buwana II's court of Kartasura by Chinese and Javanese rebels in 1742.[1] Subsequently, the Dutch defeated the rebels and reinstalled Paku Buwana on the throne. (At this point, because of the destruction of his court in Kartasura, Paku Buwana moved his palace to Surakarta.) But a number of princes, especially the nephew of the king (Mas Said) and the king's half brother (Pangeran Singasari), who had opposed the king and helped the Chinese insurrection, continued their insurgency. The intrigues worsened when the king's own brother Mangkubumi defected to the rebels. Thus, two sides were established in the eighteenth-century Javanese war of succession. The rebels, led by Mas Said and Mangkubumi, contended with the men led by Paku Buwana II, who was assisted by the Dutch. After the death of Paku Buwana II in 1749, the war continued into the reign of Paku Buwana III (r. 1749–1788). The young king governed the court so poorly that many of his officials, including the crown prince, defected to the rebels.

Having experienced almost continuous war since the Chinese rebellion in 1743, in 1752 all parties began to take another course of action: the way of negotiations. First, Mas Said began to negotiate with the Dutch. Then Mangkubumi and Mas Said broke their alliance, and Mangkubumi began separate negotiations with the Dutch. These negotiations resulted in a division of territorial control between Paku Buwana and Mangkubumi, and in Mangkubumi's agreement to help the Dutch defeat Mas Said. In 1755, a treaty was signed at Giyanti. The Mataram kingship was then permanently divided between two major courts, the Susuhunan (Kasunanan) of Surakarta and the Kasultanan of Yogyakarta. Mangkubumi became the first sultan of Yogyakarta, taking the name Hamengku Buwana I.

The division of Mataram was only a part of the solution to the court intrigues. The two rulers, with the support of the Dutch, confronted Mas Said. Mas Said held his territory for a while; and sometimes he even won a battle. But because his forces were insufficient to achieve his goal, the conquest of all Mataram, he eventually had to negotiate with the Dutch. In 1757, under the supervision of the Dutch, Paku Buwana II and Mas Said reached an agreement for the establishment of Mas Said's territory and his Mangkunegaran court, although Hamengku Buwana I did not agree to this settlement.

With the permanent division of the Mataram kingship and the establishment of the Mangkunegaran court, the long battle for power among the princes apparently ended. Actually the search for the "true" sovereign of Mataram continued in other ways. Marital diplomacy was one of the means, although it never succeeded in producing a legitimate heir to all the areas or in unifying the court. Suspicion continued among the rulers. The Dutch government was in the middle. The Dutch provided support to all three rulers, preventing the victory of any one over the others.

At the beginning of the nineteenth century, war in Europe interrupted the Dutch control of Java. After the Dutch surrendered to the British in the first Napoleonic war, they turned over Java to the British. The British interregnum (1811–1816) brought about a division of the Yogyakarta court, as the result of a conflict between Hamengku Buwana II and the British government. The British were assisted by Natakusuma (an uncle of the sultan). In 1813, after the British besieged the Kasultanan and exiled Hamengku Buwana II to Penang, the British government rewarded Natakusuma by allowing him to establish the Paku Alaman court in Yogyakarta, with its own territory taken from that of the Kasultanan. Then the British installed the Hamengku Buwana's son as the new sultan.

The permanent division of the Mataram kingdom into two major and two minor courts led each of these courts to search for a special identity in court customs, rituals, and artistic expression. These courts were intense rivals, especially the Kasunanan of Surakarta and the Kasultanan of Yogyakarta, so that each found it necessary to distinguish many aspects of its life from that of the other, ranging from attire to the style of the performing arts.

There were notable distinctions in style between the Yogyakarta and Surakarta courts in gamelan, dance, dance drama, and puppet theater. Because of lack of evidence, it is difficult to document the process of development of these styles. The question of which of the two major court styles of gamelan represents the older practice has become a subject of discussion among today's musicians. Musicians generally believe that the Yogyanese gamelan represents a continuation of the style from before the division of the kingdom, while the Solonese gamelan style was developed after the division of Mataram (Sutton 1984a:225).

On the other hand, Sutton suggests that Mangkubumi, the first sultan of the Yogyakarta court, "may have become concerned to develop not just an impressive [and new] court culture, but one which would represent both continuity with the past and an identity distinct from that of Surakarta" (p. 224). His reason is that

> because Surakarta had been an established court center before the partition, and possibly also because Paku Buwana III is characterized as somewhat weaker and, at least after 1774, less able to exercise authority, there may have been less concern over rigorously redefining Surakarta court tradition in contradistinction to Yogyakarta's.

Although it is difficult to describe the process of development of these two gamelan styles, it can be emphasized that the political circumstances of the period were a major factor in the emergence of the rich variety of Javanese arts.

It is beyond the scope of this chapter to discuss the stylistic differences between the Yogyanese and Solonese gamelan. Many of the differences are very subtle. It can generally be said that the Yogyanese gamelan is noted for its robust or strong playing style, and the Solonese for its softness and florid style of playing. At times even now, as an extension of the rivalry between the Yogyakarta and Surakarta courts, musicians and gamelan connoisseurs of the two cities joke about their stylistic differences.

Some evidence suggests that musical interchange between the two traditions has taken place in the past. There were two common causes: political alliances as a reaction to the rivalry between the courts which included exchanging artists or music and dance practice or repertoire, and the defection of musicians and dancers from one court to the other.[2]

It is true that because the Mangkunegaran court is near the Kasunanan court, the difference between Mangkunegaran and Kasunanan gamelan practice is not very great. However, by close inspection of musical and dance practices and repertoire in the courts, one can establish the general characteristics of the political alliances of the courts.

Lindsay (1980) observes that in the early nineteenth century the Paku Alaman allied itself with the Mangkunegaran.[3] This alliance reflected the attempt of these minor courts to stand apart from the major courts. In other words, the Mangkunegaran distinguished itself from Kasunanan; Paku Alaman, from Kasultanan.[4] Thus each minor court created distinctive art forms. The minor courts also exchanged musicians and music and dance practices. For example, the Paku Alaman artists created a dance opera called *banjaran sari*,[5] which was an imitation of *langendriyan*, a dance opera that originated in the Mangkunegaran.[6]

The relationships between these two minor courts diminished, however, over the nineteenth century. The court alliances changed especially at the beginning of the twentieth century when Paku Alam VII (r. 1906–1937) married the daughter of Paku Buwana X (r. 1893–1939); and Mangkunegara VII (r. 1916–1944) married the daughter of Hamengku Buwana VIII (r. 1921–1939) of Yogyakarta. These marriage alliances led to the incorporation of the Kasultanan's musical and dance practices into those of the Mangkunegaran,[7] and the incorporation of the musical and dance practices of the Kasunanan into those of the Paku Alaman. The Paku Alaman often sent its leading musicians to the Kasunanan of Surakarta to be trained by the leading musicians there, and the leading musicians and dancers of the Kasunanan taught their arts in the Paku Alaman. Thus, although the Paku Alaman is located in the same city as the Kasultanan, its gamelan practices are closer to those of the Kasunanan of Surakarta.

After the permanent division of Mataram, there was a remarkable development of cultural and artistic life, especially in literature. About this development Soebardi (1969:83) writes that after the signing of the Treaty of Giyanti in 1755,

> Surakarta appeared to come to life. It entered a period of gradually increasing order and tranquillity; the kingdom was consolidated; the damage left in the wake of the struggle of several years before was repaired.[8] At the same time, there was a marked revival in Javanese cultural life. Great efforts were made to produce new works on Javanese literature and to replace books which had been destroyed or had disappeared during the Chinese rebellion and the Mangkubumi war.

Scholars call this period the renaissance of classical literature (Pigeaud 1967, 1:235). The subjects of this renewed literature were now drawn not only from Hindu-Javanese culture but also from Islamic culture, or from a culture that showed a combination of both (pp. 235–45).

The flourishing of literature had an impact on the development of the various genres of Javanese performing arts. In gamelan, this development manifested itself in the fitting of poetic texts to gendhing and the composing of new gendhing that were based on the melodies of macapat sung poetry. (I discuss this in chapter 4). In this period, court pujangga also revived pre-Islamic literature. For example, Yasadipura I rewrote the *Mahabharata* and *Ramayana* Hindu-Javanese epics in modern Javanese language and metrical form. Ronggawarsita wrote the monumental work *Serat Pustaka Raja,* which was based on the *Mahabharata.* Subsequently, Yasadipura's and Ronggawarsita's works became important sources of inspiration for the court dhalang, who created and performed wayang stories based on them.

Another manifestation of the flourishing of Javanese literature was the writing of *pakem*—concise prose outlines of wayang stories (*lakon*). In the nineteenth century, hundreds of these pakem were written. Some pakem give very detailed contents of wayang lakon. I will give as an example a pakem from the *Serat Sastramiruda.*

Serat Sastramiruda is a manual for dhalang written by Kusumadilaga in the mid nineteenth century. Written in the form of a dialogue between Kusumadilaga (the author) and his pupil Sastramiruda, the first part of the book contains a historical account of various wayang performances, gamelan ensembles, and Javanese dances, a description of gamelan accompaniments for wayang, a description of *sulukan* (songs of the dhalang), and a discussion of the iconography of wayang puppets. The rest of the book contains a complete pakem, including dialogue, narration, and indication of actions, and directions for sulukan and gendhing accompaniment.

From this pakem we learn that in the middle of the nineteenth century, the dramatic structure of a wayang story did not greatly differ from today's wayang lakon. The gendhing accompaniment was also similar to today's.

It is difficult to say how much *Serat Sastramiruda* was used and known by dhalang in Surakarta at the time of its composition. Considering the eminent status of Kusumadilaga as a court musician and dhalang (Warsadiningrat 1987: 148), however, he was in a better position to set a standard for wayang performances in the court of Surakarta. Nyai Nyatacarita, a lady dhalang of Kartasura, who was a court dhalang during the reign of Paku Buwana X (1893–1939),[9] mentions Kusumadilaga, especially his role in disseminating the knowledge of wayang to other dhalang (Sears 1987:97). Discussing the way court dhalang prepared wayang stories, she says:

> If something was not refined enough, not good enough, it was built up. Certain parts were decreased and others were supplemented. We were told to create stories . . . the type of stories from Paku Buwana IX's. The inferior stories were discarded and the good stories were increased . . . In the old days, originally it was Panjenengan Dalem Gusti Kanjeng Kusumadilaga who gathered the dhalangs. On the first day of the month of Sura, dhalangs were called from near and far, from far and near. They were summoned and invited to a discussion, to analyze a set of stories one by one. This is what Sakri is like, Arjuna is like this, Salya

is like that . . . once a year. Then afterwards we would walk home to eat and then come back to listen again, to listen to them again, then we would break again. There was the expression "kembul nadhah" when Kusumadilaga would eat with the simple folk (*wong cilik*), with the dhalangs. Then when the celebration of the first of Sura was over, those who lived far away would be given some money for their trip home, those who lived close would only get a little money.

This passage indicates not only the eminent role of Kusumadilaga as a court dhalang but also the process of dissemination of the Surakarta court style of wayang performance in the vicinity of the court.

The flourishing of literature also had an impact on the creation of a new wayang, namely, *wayang madya*. It is commonly held that this wayang was created by Mangkunegara IV (r. 1853–1881). Mangkunegara IV's interest in *Serat Pustaka Raja Madya* inspired the creation of this new wayang; that is, the stories in the *Serat Pustaka Raja Madya* inspired Mangkunegara IV to create wayang madya (Soetrisno n.d.: 4).[10]

Mangkunegara IV also composed new gendhing sléndro for accompanying wayang madya (Soetrisno n.d.: 11). However, these gendhing existed for only a short time. When the wayang madya was presented to Paku Buwana X (r. 1893–1939), he ordered his musicians to accompany the wayang madya with pélog gamelan. For this purpose, musicians did not use new or existing pélog gendhing. Instead, they accompanied the wayang madya with the sléndro gendhing and sulukan for accompanying wayang purwa, but played them in pélog. Soetrisno (p. 12) suggests that the use of the wayang purwa sléndro pieces in pélog gamelan of wayang madya was parallel to the chronological position of this wayang in relation to the other two forms of wayang: wayang madya was invented as a bridge between the time of the stories of wayang purwa and that of wayang gedhog. That is, sléndro pieces played on sléndro gamelan accompany wayang purwa; pélog pieces played on pélog gamelan accompany wayang gedhog. Thus, accompanying wayang madya with sléndro pieces played on pélog gamelan represents the musical counterpart of the bridge between wayang purwa and wayang gedhog.

The writing of wayang pakem followed the trend of the flourishing Javanese literature at the time. Tsuchiya (1990:93–94, based on Ricklefs 1974) suggests that the impetus for these writings came from the relative peace after the division of the Mataram, but also from the ongoing rivalry between the four Central Javanese courts. He explains:

Competition among the royal houses now took the form not of disputes leading to invasion or political subjugation but of rivalry that spurred each royal house to try to outdo the others in establishing, in the eyes of its own vassals and subjects, the superiority of its claim to legitimacy as inheritor of the great tradition of Java. This became still more crucial at the time of the emergence of a new royal line. Anxiety over the advent of a new century in 1774 (the year 1700 in the Javanese calendar), an occurrence that in Javanese tradition coincided with the rise and fall of kingdoms, spurred the royal houses to embark on great new undertakings. All these factors stimulated the mystical act of recording events, in other words, the creation of *serat* and *babad* [and wayang, and the writing of wayang stories]. A new kingdom and a new age were to be created through language.

I should also mention that the importation of Chinese and Arabian paper and writing tools from the Netherlands facilitated the increased production of literary works in this period (Pigeaud 1967, 1:35–37). Finally, relationships between Javanese pujangga, European and Indo Javanologists, and the Chinese characterized the intellectual climate in this period. In Surakarta, a new literary community was formed, consisting of some Indos, Europeans, Chinese, and Javanese. This literary community disseminated and subscribed to the writings of pujangga in print (Day 1981:257). In other words, the court pujangga did not write for the court circle alone, but for a Javanese, European, Indo, and Chinese literary circle (Shiraishi 1990:7). In short, it was the politics, the increased accessibility of writing tools, and the intellectual climate of this period that influenced Javanese authors to write *serat, babad,* new wayang stories, wayang pakem, and treatises on Javanese music.

The interest in and flourishing of Javanese literature in this period was also responsible for the cultivation and development of court dances and dance dramas. Court poets composed hundreds of stanzas of verse for the bedhaya and *serimpi* dances. Though the Javanese may now insist that these dances are of ancient origin, especially the present-form bedhaya (see, for example, Hadiwidjojo 1981), there is no evidence to support this claim. Clear evidence of these dances began to appear only in Javanese literature of the late eighteenth century. Nineteenth-century manuscripts of bedhaya show that throughout that century the repertoire of this dance genre increased. The *Serat Pesindhèn Badhaya* (SMP KS 156/10) written in 1832–33, lists seven titles of bedhaya dances. By the end of the century, as indicated in a manuscript with the same title (SMP KS 156/14), written during the reign of Paku Buwana X (1893–1939), twenty-six titles of bedhaya were listed.

The nineteenth century also witnessed the development of dance dramas. Wayang wong and langendriyan are the two best-known dance dramas created in this period. Wayang wong is a dance drama which presents the stories of wayang purwa shadow theater. In fact, the stories presented in this dance drama now follow the content and dramatic structure of the stories in wayang purwa.[11] In wayang wong, the dialogue and actions are done by the human actors, and the narration is delivered by the dhalang, who sits with the musicians. Langendriyan is a dance-opera (i.e., the dialogue, in the form of poetry, is sung by the dancers and accompanied by gamelan). The stories of langendriyan are based on the *Damarwulan* epic of East Javanese origin.[12]

Scholars have long debated the place of origin of wayang wong. Some scholars believe that it was created in Surakarta by Mangkunegara I (r. 1757–1790). Other scholars suggest the first Sultan of Yogyakarta, Hamengku Buwana I (r. 1755–1792). Scholars also suggest a link between wayang wong and the Hindu-Javanese dance drama *wayang wwang*.

It is not my intention here to discuss the origin of wayang wong. For a discussion of its origin, see Lindsay (1985:82–87).[13] My point here is that the development of wayang wong and langendriyan in the nineteenth century was part of the intensive development of Javanese arts in the courts of Central Java.

How could the development and refinement of cultural traditions occur simultaneously with political crisis and decline? Moertono (1968:50) suggests that this happened because "the relative peace of that period or the lack of opportunity in the political field might have caused the Javanese, or at least the Javanese courts, to turn their activity inward towards culture and art."

Moertono's explanation is typical of the opinions of many scholars (e.g., Sutherland 1979; Soebardi 1969:81; Ricklefs 1993:126–27). In the words of Sutherland (1979:vii):

> No innovation, no creative political response to social and economic change could be tolerated by colonial dogma. The effects of this enforced stagnation were later to feed new images of exotic Java, in which a *priyayi* elite was seen to be, by nature, more concerned with mysticism and the reenactment of ritual than with the hard exercise of power.

I believe that this assertion needs to be qualified. The question of whether cultural development was the expression of the "political impotence" of the courts should be reexamined. We need to further consider the influence of political and cultural conditions in the Javanese courts on the flourishing of the Javanese arts there. Three factors come to mind: the relative peace, the economic growth, and the dynamic interaction between Javanese and various population groups on the island: Europeans, Indos, Chinese, and other ethnic groups such as Arabs, Indians, and Malays.

As Moertono observes, after the permanent division of the Mataram kingdom, the Javanese enjoyed a period of relative peace. Not only had longstanding warfare ended, but it was also a time when some Dutch administrators became advisors to and companions of Javanese princes.[14] The aristocrats had to rely on Dutch help not only in matters of finance but also in settling family conflicts and in mediating court domestic affairs, such as the marriages of princes and princesses. This relative peace was accompanied by population growth and increased prosperity (Ricklefs 1993:109), which contributed to the remarkable development of cultural and artistic life in Central Javanese courts.

Dutch and Indo researchers, of whom a handful resided in Central Java in the nineteenth century, called the eighteenth and nineteenth centuries in Central Java a period of renaissance in classical literature. But they did not find a true return to the notable literature of Old Javanese, which they considered the literary golden age. A conversation between a Dutchman and his Javanese informant (presented in an 1848 language textbook written by an Indo scholar, C. F. Winter) shows how difficult it was for a Dutchman to find a Javanese who understood the Old Javanese language, Kawi.

Mr. What's-His-Name: How can the Javanese people understand Kawi, since there is no instruction?

Raden Ngabehi Gunawan: With the exception of pujongga [court poets], it can be said that in the realm of Surakarta no one understands Kawi. Those who understand Kawi are the descendants of pujongga; ability in Kawi only descends to their own children. For the Javanese who are not descendants of pujongga, only a very few are willing to learn Kawi, because it cannot be used for talking. It is only used for reciting [singing] poetry. Besides, there is almost no benefit in learning it. Thus, the Javanese are compelled more to earn a living. Unlike you, the Dutchmen, you care to expand your skill, knowledge, and ability, because these will lead to profit in fame and respect.

MW: If many Javanese do not understand Kawi, why do many of them like to recite [sing] poetry—what for?

RG: As for the *priyayi* (aristocrats/gentlemen), their purpose is to understand the story, without thinking about the meanings of the words. But for the commoner, most of them only do it to stay awake, so that the thief will not come. While those who read [sing] usually understand only the outline of the story; they do not understand the words. People seldom understand ordinary Javanese texts, let alone Kawi poetry. Thus people sing loudly every evening only behaving like watchmen; some sing in order to show off their voice to the neighborhood, so that they will be praised for knowing how to recite [sing] and for their good voice.

MW: I get the impression from what you have said that many Javanese do not understand their own words.

RG: Actually, that's true—I myself have had occasion to question men who were fond of reciting [singing] poetry. Everything I have asked them, they have been unable to answer. If there are people who are willing to give the meanings [of the Kawi poetry], their explanations were not accurate; they even make many mistakes.[15] (Winter 1882:35)

As they searched for a literary golden age, Dutch scholars found (what many of them thought were involuted and overrefined) literary forms of the eighteenth and nineteenth century. Besides Javanese, however, Indos and Chinese became important patrons of these "decadent" arts. It is even probable that Mr. What's-His-Name was C. F. Winter himself. In any event, there is no question that in the eighteenth and nineteenth centuries Javanese poets produced a wealth of literary works.

Our knowledge of Javanese culture in and before the seventeenth century is very meager. It is only in the eighteenth century that we begin to know a little more about artistic life in Java. From the wealth of literature produced at this time, we learn that the "artistic renaissance" in this and the following centuries included not only literature, but also gamelan, as well as other genres of the performing arts.

It seems appropriate to locate the roots of this artistic development in the beginning of the eighteenth century. In literature, Ricklefs (1993:54) notes the author Carik Bajra, who was active at the court of Kartasura in the first half of the century. Soebardi (1975:19) considers numerous works of the well-known Yasadipura I (1729–1803), who by the late period of the court of Kartasura (1680–1745) had earned the title of "Young Court Poet."

With regard to the gamelan, a manuscript written in the middle of the eighteenth century, *Serat Pakem Ringgit Purwa* (SMP KS 145/6), mentions gendhing for wayang performance, a number of which contained what we now know as developed and sophisticated melodies (e.g., gendhing Rondhon, *sléndro sanga;* gendhing Dhalang Karahinan, *sléndro manyura;* gendhing Tunjung Karoban, *sléndro nem*).[16]

Most of the works of literature from this period were written in macapat poetic meters. Defined by certain poetic conventions,[17] these poems were meant to be sung. Evidence from the early nineteenth century shows that singing sung-poetry (*tembang*) was a lively activity. Besides macapat, the singing of *sekar kawi* was also common. Originally, sekar kawi (also called sekar ageng, great songs) were Indian-influenced, Sanskrit poetic forms.[18] By the early nineteenth century the language of sekar ageng had been updated to the modern Javanese language, and the melody and poetic rules were changed. Day (1981:40–42) notes that the updating of Old Javanese poems to Modern Javanese "involved a singing rewriting" that signified "the mutually reinforcing aims of literary comprehensibility and embellished melodiousness, as defined by current [i.e., 19-century] practices and tastes."[19]

Nowadays, the singing of sekar ageng is practiced only as a vocal introduction (bawa) to gendhing. However, descriptions of Javanese song in the *Serat Centhini* give evidence of a rich tradition of singing poetry in the early nineteenth century and before. In one section of the *Serat Centhini* on tembang, the poems begin by listing the names of songs according to their song genres; and the poems also explain the poetic rules for each meter. Forty-nine sekar ageng, twenty-nine *sekar tengahan,* and seven sekar macapat are given (*Serat Tjentini* 1912–15, 3–4: 12–40). Then a man named Lawatan, an expert in the singing of sekar ageng, is asked to sing.

> 228. . . . .
> "Please uncle Lawatan,
> you sing [*sekar ageng*] Sulanjari."
> Lawatan accepted the order.
> Shifting his sitting position
> 229. [and] clearing his throat by rapid coughing,
> he prepared his voice.
> He smiled and composed himself in a *sila* posture.
> His hands lay on his thighs.
> The position of his hat (*dhestar*) was fixed.
> Then he sang Sulanjari.
> 230. The singing of the vowels was long and bright,
> even, intricate and sweet.
> He moved his neck from side to side.
> His hips moved back and forth.
> His fingers counted [the meter],
> taking the 8 plus 6 syllabic counts twice.[20] (p. 18).

Lawatan sang two stanzas of Sulanjari. After a brief pause, in which a listener praised his singing, Lawatan sang Sasadara. After the completion of two stanzas of Sasadara, a conversation ensued. It was about the appropriateness of dhalang learning sekar kawi. Then Lawatan sang a song that was appropriate for accompanying the scene of the entrance of a king in wayang gedhog.

Raffles (1982) also provides evidence of the lively tradition of singing poetry in eighteenth- and nineteenth-century Java. He classifies Javanese poetry into three categories: sekar kawi, *sekar sepoh,* and *sekar gangsal* (vol. 1, p. 398). In particular, Raffles's descriptions of the singing of sekar gangsal (five modern measures) suggest the richness of the tradition of singing tembang then. Raffles points out that each of the five sekar could be sung in several ways.[21]

In short, the discussion points to the richness of the tradition of singing poetry in the early nineteenth century and before. The extent to which the melodies of these poems relate to the melodies of gamelan gendhing is not known, but it is safe to suggest that there were affinities between these two kinds of music; and in chapter 4 I show the connection.

Late eighteenth-century and early nineteenth-century literature also gives us information about many extravagant artistic displays which were presented at royal celebrations. In chapter 1 I describe several of these splendid artistic activities at the court of Mangkunegaran as they were reported in the *Serat Babad*

Nitik, especially in the context of the Islamic influences in this court. Various performances were staged to celebrate every birthday of Mangkunegara I (r. 1757–1796). Such extravagant royal occasions were also common in the Kasunanan court of Surakarta. Describing the wedding of Paku Buwana III to the daughter of Mangkunegara I, in his *Babad Prayud,* Yasadipura (1854) recounts a splendid celebration. For seven days the celebration was heralded by the simultaneous sounding of a large number of musical ensembles. A week before the ceremony, during the pakajangan (camp waiting), all dipati (the king's outlying regents)

> brought gamelan with them.
> The sound reverberated.
> And in the inner palace [of the Kasunanan],
> the gamelan Sekatèn was played for seven days.
> Pélog and sléndro gamelan
> were placed in the outer hall.
> In the mean time, in the Mangkunegaran
> the gamelan Sekatèn was sounded for seven days,
> in the east of the main hall.
>
> Pélog and sléndro gamelan [were played] in the outer hall.
> People were jam-packed in the court yard,
> dancing [to the accompaniment of] gamelan Cara Balèn.
> . . . .[22]
>
> (Yasadipura 1854:265)

The poet goes on to describe all sorts of entertainment, including nightly tayuban. As can be seen in the above passages, the Javanese enjoyed festive occasions in which a large number of gamelan ensembles were played simultaneously. Even what we now know as a sacred gamelan Sekatèn, which is played only once a year to commemorate the birth and death of the Prophet Muhamad, was at the time played together with other gamelan to celebrate secular occasions.[23] Javanese enjoyed a *ramé* (boisterous/complex/busy) atmosphere. We have seen the love of the Javanese for this ramé atmosphere in the seventeenth-century court of Mataram (see chapter 1). The ramé atmosphere continued to be a feature of many court occasions. The inclusion of foreign elements, such as cannon salutes, European music, and Chinese firecrackers added to these tumultuous events. (I discuss below the many peculiar combinations of indigenous and foreign elements in court rituals.) Perhaps these lavish, festive rituals and ceremonies prompted court artisans to enlarge the ritual apparatus, such as musical ensembles and the music and dance repertoire.

On royal occasions different kinds of ensembles played simultaneously in different locations. On another aspect of gamelan practice, the *Serat Babad Nitik* describes the placing together of pélog and sléndro sets. At times the poet specifies that the double sets were played by two groups of musicians, male and female players: "The *niyaga* (gamelan musicians) consisted of two groups. There were two gamelan sets. The sléndro set was played by a group of male niyaga, the pélog set by female niyaga" (*Serat Babad Nitik* 1929, 2:211).[24]

It is not clear exactly when the practice of combining sléndro and pélog gamelan sets began. In the late eighteenth century, this practice became very common, especially in the Central Javanese courts.[25] This was a consequence of the desire of aristocrats to make court rituals more festive and lavish.

Court manuscripts also do not tell us the instrumentation of these mixed sléndro and pélog gamelan. However, the poet of the *Serat Babad Nitik* mentions the names of three gamelan: Kanyut ("Swept Away"), Mèsem ("Smile"), and Udan Riris ("Misty Rain") (p. 448). The first two names are those of a sléndro and a pélog set. Nowadays these two sets are usually known as a single set in an ensemble called Kanyut Mèsem. This ensemble is considered to be a full (*lengkap*) ensemble by today's standard.[26]

Kunst (1924:26) notes that the year of A.J. 1700 (A.D. 1778 [*recte* 1770]) was carved in the wooden frame of a *demung* of Kanyut Mèsem.[27] According to an oral account (Brown and N. Pemberton 1977), originally Kanyut Mèsem was owned by Paku Buwana II (r. 1726–1749). The set was given to the king's son-in-law, the regent of Panaraga. During the warfare between Mas Said (the would-be Mangkunegara I) and Paku Buwana III, the set was captured by Mas Said, around 1753. According to legend, it was the dispute over Kanyut Mèsem that caused a division of the forces of Mas Said and the forces of his uncle, that is, Mangkubumi, the Paku Buwana's younger brother.

Babad Mangkunegara I (as quoted in Suparno 1990) confirms the mid eighteenth century as the date of the origin of Kanyut Mèsem and two other gamelan sets.[28] The poem mentions the period when Mas Said was allied with Mangkubumi in their war against Paku Buwana II and III (1746–1755) as the time of the origin of Kanyut Mèsem and several other gamelan. The poem says that during this warfare, Mas Said and Mangkubumi ordered craftsmen

> to make a gamelan Monggang
> and a *saléndro* [gamelan] in Yogyakarta in Mataram.
> The saléndro set was named Kanyut.
> The gamelan maker, who
> resided in Mataram, also made pélog gamelan.
> The first one was named Lipur,
> [the second] Mèsem, and [the third] gamelan *carabali*.
> (Suparno 1990: 39–40)

Two instruments in Kanyut Mèsem (slentho and gambang gangsa) are rarely found in present-day gamelan. Slentho is a single-octave keyed metallophone; each key has a knob (or raised boss) on its center. The instrument is functionally a member of the saron family. Gambang gangsa is a keyed metallophone, like a xylophone in shape but with bronze keys. It is commonly held that these instruments are very old (Kunst 1973, 1:371; Vetter 1986:119; Warsadiningrat 1987: 54 n.). The inclusion of these two archaic instruments suggests that Kanyut Mèsem is a relatively old gamelan. From the evidence presented, early to mid eighteenth century may have been the period when Kanyut Mèsem was made.

This does not mean, however, that the instrumentation of Kanyut Mèsem has never been altered. The alteration of a gamelan's instrumentation seems to have been common in the past. Researching gamelan in the Kasultanan court of Yogyakarta, Vetter (1986:119) found that some older ensembles (which can be identified by the inclusion of a few archaic instruments) have undergone changes in their instrumentation to bring them up to their present size. These changes in instrumentation consist of the addition of instruments "that are now considered standard (e.g., *gender panembung* [metallophone], *gender panerus* [metallophone], *celempung* [plucked zither], *suling* [end-blown flute] and *kendhang batangan* [membranophone]" (ibid., 119–20). The changes also include the addition of several kenong kettles and kempul gongs, so that each set increased from two or three to five or more tones.

There is no evidence to prove that the gamelan Kanyut Mèsem developed in the way that Vetter suggests. However, the development of dance drama in the Mangkunegaran court in the mid nineteenth century could be one of the reasons for the increase in the number of kenong tones.[29] I suggest that the addition of kenong tones was associated with the birth of the langendriyan "opera," a specialty of the Mangkunegaran court. In this dance drama, the kenong is a crucial part of the accompaniment of songs that are sung by the dancers. Sung in the form of palaran, these songs employ a wide melodic range; hence, a full gamut of kenong tones is necessary.[30]

Some evidence about the instrumentation of gamelan ensembles from this period can be found in Raffles's *History of Java* (1817). Besides being the British governor of Java during the period of the British interregnum (1810–1816), Raffles was also a scholar. His well-known *History of Java* is an important pioneering work on the history and ethnography of the island. In 1816, Raffles returned to England. The collection of thirty tons of Eastern treasures and novelties that he brought with him to England included a gamelan ensemble. He left no information about the origin of his gamelan. Raffles's gamelan was peculiar because of the animal shapes of the wooden frame and resonators on almost all the instruments.[31] Such instruments cannot be found in Central Javanese courts.[32]

This does not mean, however, that Raffles was not familiar with court gamelan ensembles. His description of gamelan in his book indicates that he knew of different types of court gamelan. Besides the usual sléndro and pélog gamelan, he mentions gamelan Miring, Monggang, Kodhok Ngorèk, Chara bali, Sekatèn, and Srunèn (Raffles 1982:469).[33] Except for gamelan Miring, all these ensembles still exist in the courts.

In the *History of Java,* Raffles also provides an illustration of the instrumentation of a gamelan ensemble. The gamelan instruments drawn in this illustration are not as zoomorphic as Raffles's own gamelan instruments. On the basis of this illustration, Raffles's description of gamelan instruments, and the gamelan ensemble he owned, we may conclude that the instrumentation of a gamelan ensemble in early nineteenth-century Java was similar to today's.[34] In other words, by the late eighteenth and early nineteenth century, a gamelan ensemble of a size not very different from today existed.

Besides the reasons stated, another reason for the increasing number of instruments into the gamelan ensemble may have to do with the need to add strength to the festive, noisy ramé mentioned earlier. Typically, a ritual was celebrated with a combination of the sounds of various gamelan ensembles, including gamelan Sekatèn, gamelan Cara Balèn, gamelan Monggang, and gamelan Kodhok Ngorèk. Pemberton (1987:23) summarizes the significance of the loudest sound and the ramé atmosphere of nineteenth-century court musical events:

> Gamelan had long performed as an emblematic sign of the king's authority, but by the nineteenth century the royal noise transmitted from the palace was far more formidable. Its volume seems to have grown in inverse proportion to the king's power—power that was, of course, rapidly decreasing under Dutch colonial rule. Numerous gamelan from the king's storehouse, drum and fife corps, chanting, Islamic officials, brass bands, mantra-ing palace divinators, waltz orchestras, and twenty-one cannon salutes all served as signals of royal occasions; the greater the occasion, the more of these were sounded, often simultaneously.

I suggest that the competition between Javanese and European sound in the court ritual, musical or non-musical (e.g., between the sound of gamelan and cannon salutes), provided a basis for developing a musical style that emphasized the production of the loudest sound; hence, the increasing size and number of instruments in the gamelan ensemble. The making of a gamelan Sekatèn larger and heavier than the original one was a case in point. It was made under the auspices of Paku Buwana IV (r. 1788–1820) (Warsadiningrat 1987:108).[35]

For another example, in an imitation of the gamelan Sekatèn, a complete pélog-sléndro, a rather large, low-pitched gamelan was built during the reign of Paku Buwana IV (Warsadiningrat 1987:114). Named Kyai Kutha Windu–Windu Sana, this gamelan is especially suitable for playing gendhing bonang, a genre of instrumental pieces in which the last section of the piece (the *inggah* or *sesegan*) is always played loud and fast.[36] In fact, according to Warsadiningrat (1987:109), Paku Buwana IV composed many gendhing bonang.

The distinctive feature of gendhing bonang is loud playing of a sesegan section in a fast tempo, the climax of the piece. Hence, it is very appropriate to play the sesegan section with a great number of loud gamelan instruments.

Another good example of this development was the gamelan Monggang named Kyai Surak. The gong of this particular ensemble was made extraordinarily large. Several players must take turns playing this gong. With a large gong mallet, each of them must stand up and strike the gong as hard as he can, trying to produce a loud, powerful sound. Perhaps this is an attempt to compete with the sound of the cannon.

Strong, powerful musical sound was also a musical trend in the court of Mangkunegaran. As in the Kasunanan court, Mangkunegara II (r. 1796–1835) ordered a larger, heavier, and lower-pitched gamelan to be built in the Mangkunegaran court. It was named Kyai Udan Asih–Udan Arum (*Serat Babad Panambangan* 2, 32).[37]

The splendid display of the arts in the courts of Central Java did not always reflect musical events in an "orderly" manner. Instead, sometimes the combination of the sounds of different ensembles that heralded various royal events produced chaotic or ramé sounds. For this reason I suggest that musical presentations should be thought of as reflections of the sociopolitical circumstances of their time. The mixture of sounds of various kinds of ensembles and other such grandiose artistic displays demonstrated to the populace the power of the court in the face of the Dutch colonial government in Java.[38] In fact, in order to display the glory of the court, the courtiers even incorporated "non-traditional" sounds into the court rituals, that is, the sounds of cannon, rifles, and European music.

Crucial to understanding this cultural co-optation is the political and psychological relationship between the colonial rulers and their subjects, the Javanese rulers. The inclusion of European sounds and customs in court rituals can be explained in terms of the oppressed identifying themselves with the oppressor, a phenomenon commonly found in colonial cultures (Nandy 1983; Ranger 1975). Javanese rulers saw the Dutch as their overlords, or even their parents (Javanese rulers often addressed the Dutch as their grandfathers). This process is what Nandy (1983:7) calls "an ontogenetic legitimacy for an ego defence" for "a normal child in an environment of childhood dependency to confront inescapable dominance by physically more powerful adults enjoying total legitimacy." Javanese rulers were caught between acknowledging the Dutch as their parents, on the one hand, and as the aggressor, on the other. For the Dutch to maintain their rule, from beginning to end they had to make alliances with Javanese rulers. Consequently, rituals of appropriation were exchanged between the rulers and their subjects. It is these rituals of appropriation, their backgrounds, and the process of their creation that I would like to discuss now.

Mestizo Culture: Relationships between Europeans and Javanese Courtiers

It can be seen that the Dutch colonial government on Java increasingly interfered in the political life of the Javanese. On the one hand, intrigues within the Javanese royal family were used by the Dutch to manipulate Javanese political life. On the other hand, for political and social reasons a common society between Dutchmen and Javanese courtiers formed. The Javanization of the Dutch and Indo administrators, planters, and managers was an important factor in the creation of this common society. Many of the upper-class Dutch and Indos lived most of their lives in Java; they became familiar with Javanese people and culture. This facilitated the close friendships between the Dutch and Javanese aristocrats and the feeling among Europeans that they were very comfortable living among the Javanese in the Javanese environment. Boredom on the part of Dutch and Indos (having nothing to do in their leisure time) may have been another factor that encouraged them to establish relations with Javanese aristocrats.[39]

In essence, the Dutch and Indos who settled in the East Indies lived in a culture made up of different influences, especially European and Indonesian cultures. This culture is appropriately termed mestizo culture. Mestizo is a Portuguese word which refers to people of mixed blood. (It was the Portuguese who first engendered children of mixed blood in Asia.)[40] Here I use the term to characterize a mixture of European and Asian cultures.

Actually, it was among the Indos that the mestizo culture developed. As children born of unions between Europeans and Asians and raised in European settlements in Asia, the Indos grew up and lived in a mixed culture. From an early age, they were raised by Asian mothers, always with the help of Asian slaves or an Indonesian *babu* (maidservant). They were sent to the Dutch school. They received only secondhand knowledge of European culture, from the schools and their parents. Only a few of them actually visited Europe. Thus Indos had a unique sociopolitical and cultural background.

In the two Javanese court cities of Surakarta and Yogyakarta, a somewhat closer relationship existed between some Indos and the indigenous population (Van der Veur 1955:92). Van der Veur (pp. 92–93) suggests that

> the existing agrarian legislation as laid down in the Javanese code, the
> *Angger Sepoeloeh* of 1818, helped such relations to a limited extent. The
> Angger Sepoeloeh permitted the renting of land in Solo to "Dutch-
> men, Chinese and other such nations [*sic*], white of skin" [*sic*] and Java-
> nese "for a period of three or six years" by officials of the Sultan. The
> Eurasian family of Dezentjé, well-known to many inhabitants of the
> Indies, is one example of a Eurasian family which took advantage of
> this opportunity from the very beginning.

Evidently many Indo children were born in Central Java from the unions of European fathers and Javanese wives or concubines (Marle 1951–52:317, 507). It is true that mixed marriages were most common between European men and Javanese women of the lower class. But occasionally marriages also occurred between a European man and a Javanese woman of the elite. For example, in the early nineteenth century, there was a marriage between Johannes Augustinus Dezentjé and the Solonese "princess" Raden Ajoe Tjondro Koesomo; the latter was given the baptismal name Sara Helena (ibid. 317). The daughters of the regent of Karanganyar and Demak also married Europeans (ibid.). It was only well-to-do Indos, such as planters and managers of the companies, who had close contact with the aristocrats.

Apparently the mestizo culture in the East Indies made the upper-class Europeans enjoy living there. The lives of Dutch Residents and the European community in these court cities illustrate this point.

> Life at the *kraton* Residencies must have been a strange affair for the small European communities in the centre of the exotic *kraton* towns. In particular the Residents, who often served for many years at the *kratons,* must occasionally have come to lose something of their sense of identity. The cases of Palm and Hartsinck in Surakarta will be recalled. Of the latter the Company was even prepared to believe that he was conspiring with the Susuhunan to slaughter all Europeans. The Jogjakarta Resident J. M. van Rhijn, who had been Second Resident at Surakarta for four years before being made First Resident at Jogjakarta, retired after thirteen years at the Sultan's court in 1786. By that time Europe was apparently more foreign to him than Java. He asked to be repatriated to the Netherlands with his Dutch wife, but wished to be allowed to return to Java if either of them should prove unable to adapt to a European climate. . . . The Surakarta Resident van Straalendorff (1767–84) took an Indonesian mistress, by whom he had eight children. He applied to Batavia to have these children declared legitimate, which was granted. (Ricklefs 1974:366)

This quotation shows not only close relationships between Dutch Residents and Javanese aristocrats, but also the Javanization of the Residents and, by extension, other Dutch men and women in the court cities. To illustrate the extent to which the upper-class Dutch and Javanese aristocrats had close social relationships, consider the following stanzas, taken from *Serat Babad Nitik* 1:1.

1a-2. From the room, four [individuals] had exited.
       Then the king sat down
       on a chair; everyone else sat down.
       They all sat down in an orderly manner.
       [The sound] of gamelan was very pleasant;
       the king's [gamelan]

1a-3. was sounded together with trumpet and violin,
       mixed with the drum.
       Then eating together with the king's subjects were
       the wives of the Dutch Officers,
       and the princesses.
       All were eating at the table.

1a-4. The *wadana* (regional officials) and *pasisir* (coastal officials)
ate [while sitting] on the floor.
The bedhaya dancing alternated
between those of the wadana and *patih.*
They drank continuously.
They ate for a long time,

1a-5. [and] were saluted by the frequent sounding of the cannon,
and mixing with [the sound of] gamelan.
For a long time they all ate,
sitting down, and drank [liquor] continuously.
All the wadana
and pasisir were intoxicated.[41]

Such occasions, with Javanese gamelan and Javanese dance presentations, were
often held in the palace of the Paku Buwana or the Mangkunegara. This one,
however, was held in the headquarters, the *loji,* of the Dutch Resident. The
occasion was called Tedhak Loji, the "royal progress" to visit the Resident there.
As the poet goes on to say:

1a-6. Then the Sri Bupati (Paku Buwana) took a walk
with the Dutch governor close by,
walking around to the west and to the east.
The [governor's] wife, the [Javanese] queen, and the
wives of the Dutchmen walked behind them,
so did the officers.
Then the king returned, and

1a-7. sat down in the loji again.
They all sat down
on chairs, continuing to drink.
Then pangéran dipati [Mangkunegara]
presented his bedhaya dancers.
Then Paku Buwana's bedhaya danced

1a-8. bedhaya Kuwung-kuwung; it was very beautiful.
The *senggak* (vocal interjection) was noisy.
At dawn the bedhaya ended.
At that time the fireworks [began].
They all watched it.
Paku Buwana sat down on the platform.[42]

We get a sense of the informal atmosphere of the events. The bedhaya
dances—the refined female dances that evoked feelings of serenity—were performed while people were eating and drinking or in turn with it. From another
section of *Serat Babad Nitik* we learn that each round of the bedhaya dancing
took its turn with eating and the playing of Dutch card games.

9b-4. The king ate in the loji
        with the Officers and the king's subjects.
        Cannons were sounded repeatedly.
        For a long time they ate and drank,
        while [the staging] of the Patih bedhaya
        took turns with the Wadana's
        bedhaya.
        After they finished eating,
        the [Javanese] Queen and the [Dutch] Ladies played
            a Dutch card game.
        For a long time they entertained themselves.
9b-5. They played the Dutch card game until late at night.
        Then the bedhaya of the king's son,
        the crown prince,
        emerged two times.
        Then the king's bedhaya
        appeared two times.
        After midnight,
        the king departed.
        ·[43]

(*Serat Babad Nitik* 1:17–18)

We see that the Dutch appreciated the Javanese performing arts. That is, when
the Solonese king Paku Buwana made a journey to meet the Dutch Resident
and his entourage in the loji, Javanese music and dance were important parts of
the reception held by the Dutch.

Many social and ritual events in the court also indicate close social intercourse
between the upper-class Dutch and Javanese aristocrats. European dancing was
often a feature of the court events. The poet of the *Babad Krama Dalem* (1865–
66)[44] describes the dancing enthusiastically. Having seen the behaya and *serimpi,*

the guests were happy. Then
all the Dutch ladies
danced with their husbands.
It was bustling, the song kept changing.
If tired, they stopped,
and were served drinks.

The spectators were happy.
The [dance] movements of the Ladies,
[carried out] in groups, were like the *lèyèk* dancing style,
like a chain they were holding each others' hands.
[When they] released their hands, they changed
their partners, [the Gentlemen] held

> the hips of the Ladies tightly,
> very tight and intense.
> [They acted] as if to amuse their children,
> moving their necks, to entice for love.
> The Ladies smiled
> at the intense embracing.[45]
>
> (*Atmadikara* 1865–66:59)

Evidently European social dances were commonly held in the palaces of the Susuhunan and Mangkunegaran and in the house of the Resident. Waltzes, polkas, quadrilles, and other such popular dance songs were familiar. It was this type of popular music and dance that the Dutch Residents, their entourage, and the Dutch Company's employees knew well. The Dutch were often men of commoner origin (Ricklefs 1974:366). Their exposure to European art music may have been limited. This is especially true with the Indos, who had only second-hand knowledge of European culture.

Indeed, mestizo culture facilitated fluent social interactions between Javanese aristocrats and Europeans. The atmosphere of the visit of the British Governor-General of Java, T. S. Raffles, and his party to the court of Surakarta in 1813 illustrates clearly the working of the mestizo culture in the ceremonial meeting between European and Javanese elites. On the basis of the accounts in the *Java Government Gazette,* a weekly British government newspaper published in Batavia, Taylor (1983:107–8) summarizes some of the events:

> The evening of December 6 included staging of a "Javanese comedy" at the [Dutch] residency and the reception of the susuhunan and his consort. All the local Europeans attended the evening's festivities, at which there were a fireworks display, a conjuring demonstration, and an exhibition of dancing by palace women who had been transported to the residency in enclosed palanquins. Supper ended with toasts to "Mrs. Raffles" proposed by the susuhunan and "Her Highness the Empress," "Souracarta and prosperity to it," and "the Ladies of Java" proposed by the guests. "These and some other toasts having been drunk," the report continues, "the party adjourned to the Ballroom, where his Highness the Emperor led off a country dance with the Lady Governess. *The Hon. the Lt. Governor danced a few couple with the Empress.* Reels concluded the festivities of the evening." [Emphasis added]
> The seventh opened with tiger fights staged by the Javanese and attended by Raffles, Olivia, and the susuhunan. From there, all moved into the kraton. "The Emperor and Empress then conducted the Lt. Governor, with his Lady and their Suite, to an interior chamber of the Palace, where the Daughters and other female relatives of their Highnesses were presented in form."

The physical contact between Javanese ladies and strange men, the admission of European men to the princesses' chamber, the drinking of wine—all forbidden by Javanese religion and custom—were tolerated and adopted by Javanese courtiers for their ritual courtesy to the Europeans. Such tolerance was possible because of the effect of the mestizo culture.

Apparently the relationship between the upper-class Europeans and the Javanese courtiers was very intimate. The important role of the Dutch government in finding peaceful solutions to longstanding court intrigues—thus permanently dividing the Mataram kingdom—strengthened this association. In essence, Javanese rulers saw the Dutch bureaucrats, Dutch planters, and managers of the Company as their social equals in many respects.

European music had an important role in marking the intimate social intercourse between European elite and Javanese aristocrats. European popular music was heard on many court occasions. Sometimes European music was played in turn with gamelan, and sometimes they were played together.

It is likely that the Portuguese were responsible for the earliest instances of European music in Java, in the sixteenth century (Kornhauser 1978:111). Portuguese themselves never settled in Java, however. (Their headquarters were in the Maluku and Malacca.) Their music was brought and performed in Java by their Indian, African, or Southeast Asian slaves. By the late seventeenth century, slave music was still a very common sound in the residences of Dutch merchants. An account by a Dutch bride in Batavia (now Jakarta) in 1689 indicates that she had a slave orchestra (consisting of harp, viol, and bassoon) that played at mealtimes (Boxer 1965:240).[46]

Subsequently, military music was introduced into Java by the Dutch East Indies Company (the V.O.C.) and other European trading companies. The merchant Jean-Baptiste Tavernier states in 1648 that when he "was invited by Governor-General van der Lijn to dine with him and his party and then to join them in an outing '[t]wo trumpets began blazing'" (Taylor 1983:36). In 1673, the Sultan of Banten received the Danish trading delegation, whose guard of honor included a European tenor drum (Dam-Mikkelsen and Lundbæk 1980:134).[47] Thus it is safe to say that some types of European military music already existed by the middle of the seventeenth century.

It seems that by the period of Kartasura (1680–1749) European military music had been fully adopted in the Javanese court. Yasadipura in his *Serat Babad Giyanti* (late 18th century) mentions a European military band that played together with gamelan Cara Balèn. Describing the royal procession of the move of the palace from Kartasura to Surakarta, Yasadipura wrote:

> Upon the appearance of the King,
> the Dutch Company and the Javanese troops
> saluted with a loud salvo,
> and were answered by the great cannon's
> shattering thunder.

> The music troop played trumpets, the drums,
> flutes, *bendhé,* together with
> the loud sounding of Munggang and Kodhok
>   Ngorèk,
> Cara Balèn gamelan, beautifully sounded.
> Tumult was the people of the capital.[48]

This passage mentions marching music that consisted of trumpets, drums, flutes (or fifes), and a *bendhé* (a small gong). The first three instruments were European and the last was Javanese. In other passages, the *Babad Giyanti* mentions *musikan kumpeni* (the Dutch Company's music troop) playing trumpets, drums, flutes, bendhé, and kendhang, three European and two Javanese instruments.[49]

In another passage, the *Babad Giyanti* mentions that the Company's music troop played drums, trumpets, and flutes. Perhaps by this time there were already two kinds of Javanese marching band: one of mixed European and Javanese instruments and one of entirely European instruments. Groneman's account (1895:80–86) shows that in the late nineteenth century, prajuritan music in the court of Yogyakarta also consisted of these types of ensemble. For example, some prajuritan musical groups consisted of two European drums and a fife, while others consisted of European trumpets, drums, and fifes, together with the Javanese instruments bendhé and kecèr.

Unfortunately, there is no substantive information concerning the origins of the use of the European military marching music in the courts of Central Java. We do not know when hybrid prajuritan music was invented. Most likely, European soldiers first played this kind of military marching music. Subsequently, under the tutelage of European soldier-musicians, the court founded its own corps of soldier-musicians (abdi dalem musikan). We know from Groneman's account that in the late nineteenth century, all prajuritan music in the Yogyakarta court was played by Javanese soldier-musicians. Musicians in almost all the prajuritan groups wore uniforms modeled after nineteenth-century European military dress.

The *Serat Babad Nitik* of the Mangkunegaran court also mentions a military marching band consisting of drums, flutes, trumpets, and violins. The poem clearly states that the musicians were Javanese women soldier-musicians (1:2–3). Thus, as early as the late eighteenth century, there were already Javanese musicians playing prajuritan music. In another passage the poem mentions an ensemble of drums, flutes, and violins accompanying European social dances in the Javanese court (2:202).

We can assume that European music in the courts of Central Java served two functions: as military marching music and as musical accompaniment for European social dances. Subsequently, sometime in the late nineteenth century, European string ensembles were instituted in the courts. Dhesibel (1915, quoted in Perlman 1991:64) suggests that in 1894 the first string ensemble in Surakarta was instituted in the Mangkunegaran; that is, at the end of the reign of Mangkunegara V (1885–1896). As mentioned in the *Serat Sri Karongron* (1913), during the reign of Paku Buwana X (1893–1939) a European string ensemble is known to have had important functions in the court (see below).[50] I will show that the different kinds of incorporation (or the lack of it) of European music into Javanese court events was a reflection of a general pattern of the colonial cultural experience.

Evasion and Expression of Colonialism in the Javanese Court Culture

We have seen the development of hybrid cultural expression in the Central Javanese courts in the period roughly from the mid eighteenth century to the second decade of the nineteenth century. Court ritual events now incorporated European elements as a result of European mestizo culture.

In the nineteenth century and up to the beginning of the twentieth, hybrid court cultural reproductions developed vigorously. In this period, European elements became more prominent in court culture.

The third decade of the nineteenth century marked the beginning of a new era of colonialism in the East Indies. After the Java war—a great revolt against European colonial rule in 1825–30—true colonialism was established. This meant that "for the first time, the Dutch were in position to exploit and control the whole island, and there was not to be any serious challenge to their dominance until the twentieth century" (Ricklefs 1993:119).

One consequence of the consolidation of Dutch control of Java was the gradual application of pure-blooded colonial policy, the totokization of the Dutch in East Indies. This totokization was the result of the growing number of educated Dutch officials and immigrants from the Netherlands, which meant that the composition and the intellectual atmosphere of the European settlements changed. The totok educated Dutch became influential in the European settlements. They tried to maintain their connections with Europe and their bourgeois intellectual status: by importing newspapers and periodicals from Europe, by increased networking with other educated totok in the island, and by increasing the number of clubs whose activities included sports and music.

The longstanding colonial mestizo culture continued, however, and the upper-class European way of life became another layer of the culture. Taylor's elucidation of the totoks' adaptations and Javanese responses to them is instructive. Using the concept of "intermediate society" of Indonesian-Chinese culture proposed by G. W. Skinner, Taylor (1983:132–34) explains:

> Newcomers did not adjust to an Indonesian style of life, whether variants of Sundanese, Javanese, Ambonese, or whatever. Their adaptations were conditioned, molded and guided, by all the years of earlier responses that had resulted in a Mestizo culture which had taken on a life

of its own. All Europeans participated in it to some extent, from ardent devotees of the opera to the great-grandchildren of immigrants and Asian women. Similarly, Indonesians who had any contact with Europeans participated in it too. This was as true for the upper class whose members could afford pianofortes as it was for the women entering the white man's household as mistresses and domestic servants.

Central Javanese aristocrats responded to the new colonial era by establishing a more clearly defined, well-ordered court cultural landscape (Pemberton 1989: 115). The strong control of the colonial government over the Central Javanese *Vorstenlanden* (Principalities) is manifested in the well-ordered court ritual, which involved the inclusion of European elements and the presence of Dutch authorities. Consider a passage from the *Wiwahan Dalem Kangjeng Pangeran Adipati Ariya Prangwadana* (mid 19th century). In the wedding celebration of the son of Mangkunegara IV, it was the Dutch Resident himself who gave the order to begin the *paningkah* and *panggih* ceremonies:

11. After the completion of the recitation of *musikum,*
    the pangulu recited a prayer.
    All answered "amen."
    Having finished offering prayer,
12. [the pangulu] was allowed to exit, followed by a line of ulama.
    Soon the Resident
    held up a glass, wanting to toast.
    All the guests stood up.
13. The Resident's words were calm, loud, and sweet:
    "Hallo, all dignitaries
    and guests present.
    Please witness my desire
14. to offer my best wishes to the honorable crown prince
    and his wife.
    My prayer is
    for a long and happy marriage."
15. At the end [of his speech], the guests cheered.
    [European] music and [gamelan] Monggang
    were heard loudly; three
    officers offered a salute with nine salvos,
16. supported by cannons sounding nine times continuously.
    After the salute was completed,
    the honorable pangéran dipati [Mangkunegara]
    stood up to offer a toast for the safety
17. of the guests who were present there.
    Afterward, they cheered.
    [European] music and [gamelan] Monggang sounded to honor.
    The soldiers prepared to march.[51]

(*Wiwahan Dalem* 1927:184–85)

It is true that the Mangkunegaran was the only court in Java that adjusted very well to colonialism (Ricklefs 1993:127). The military, agricultural estate, and salary systems were Europeanized (ibid.). Under Mangkunegara IV, the Mangkunegaran was a microcosm of the Dutch East Indies state. But the reason for featuring a Dutch official in the court ritual was a Javanese aristocrat's response to the new political and cultural circumstances. The metaphor used by the poet of *Wiwahan Dalem* demonstrates this point well.

19. After both [of the newlyweds] asked blessing [from their elders],
    then his highness (Mangkunegara IV) exited
    to accompany the Resident and his wife,
    who bestowed their best wishes [on the newlyweds].
    Following behind was
    the crowd of the ladies (*nyonyah*)
20. with the gentlemen (*tuwan*) who offered their blessings.
    They stepped forward one after another.
    Upon reflection, it seemed as if
    the gods and goddesses
    descended bringing a prayer of safety
    to the newlyweds.[52]
                                        (*Wiwahan Dalem* 1927:205–6)

The metaphor "the ladies and gentlemen" (referring to the Dutch men and women) "seemed like gods and goddesses," who descended from heaven, signifies the deeper involvement of the Dutch in the life of the Mangkunegaran and vice versa. Topics, language, and references of the poem reflect Mangkunegara IV's court in colonial times. This means that European customs had Javanese meanings as well as European ones. In other words, European customs had an appropriate and proper place in a nineteenth-century court. In fact, the final event of the panggih ceremony was celebrated with a European dance party.

The ceremony began with the arrival of the groom, who was greeted by Dutch ladies and gentlemen as well as the royal family and was heralded by the sound of European and gamelan music. Subsequently there was a sequence of formal events in the panggih ceremony in the paringgitan (an area between the outer and inner hall) and the inner hall of the court.[53] As the main events of the ceremony were completed, Mangkunegara asked the Resident and his wife to bless the newlyweds. Then the other Dutch ladies and gentlemen followed suit.

21. Upon the completion of the offering of best wishes,
    the Resident exited,
    together with all other guests.
    At about 8:00 P.M.,
    the feast began.
    The great hall was full.

22. The gamelan on the platform was not allowed to be played.
    It was moved into the gamelan storage.
    Only [European] music was heard throughout,
    giving pleasure to the hearts:
    [groups were located] on the left and right sides,
    sounding alternately.
25. After the feast ended
    to their satisfaction,
    many guests dispersed.
    The Gentlemen and Ladies
    walked, holding each other's hands,
    circling in line.
26. They danced to a waltz encircling the hall,
    changing their dancing styles continuously:
    Galop and Quadrille were varied in their presentation.
    Only the old Dutchmen
    remained seated playing [cards]
    in groups.
27. In the inner palace, the feast ended.
    The newlyweds
    entertained themselves in the middle of the hall.
    Ladies were in groups,
    entertaining themselves in different manners
    to suit their pleasure.[54]

(*Wiwahan Dalem* 1927:206–9)

We see that the court ceremony consisted of the "coinciding" or "competing" of two traditions, Javanese and European. Sometimes the ceremony was exclusively Javanese, as with the series of formal panggih ceremonies according to Javanese custom, and other activities of the newlyweds and Javanese ladies after the panggih. At other times, European elements dominated, as with the speech by the Dutch Resident and the European social dancing. From time to time the two traditions coincided. For example, in the beginning of the ceremony in the paringgitan, both Javanese aristocrats and European authorities and guests were present together. This event was heralded by the playing together of gamelan and European music. Another example of "coinciding" occurred when the Dutch ladies and gentlemen gave their blessings to the newlyweds in the inner palace.

"Competing" and "coinciding" of the two traditions in a court ceremony occurred not only socially but also in sound production. For example, the passage mentions the sounding together of gamelan Monggang, European music, and cannon. Thus, the atmosphere of boisterousness created by the "peculiar mixture" (or "odd" sequence) of different elements became a feature of the court ceremonies.

Plate 1 Fifth page of *Serat Sri Karongron* (Purbadipura 1913): on the playing together of the Dutch national anthem Wihèlmis, gamelan Cara Balèn, and gendhing Sri Katon. (Reprinted with permission from Kraton Surakarta).

Plate 2 A type of Islamic-Javanese ensemble called Majemukan or Perjanjèn, consisting of three terbang, kendhang, and three singers. Surakarta, circa 1930s. (Photo courtesy of Agus Sutopo).

Plate 4 The refined bedhaya dance, evoking the feelings of serenity, was performed while the audience (Javanese courtiers and Dutchmen and women) was chatting, eating, drinking, or playing a Dutch card game. Bedhaya at the court in Yogyakarta, circa 1870. (Photo courtesy of Koninklijk Instituut voor Taal-, Land-, en Volkenkunde).

Plate 3 (left) Four beautiful dancers dance serimpi Sangupati. The dance includes the use and shooting of nineteenth-century revolvers (Photo courtesy of Sardono W. Kusuma).

Plate 5 The court tower Songga Buwana (Buttress of the World) is a designated place for the ruler of Surakarta to have spiritual and sexual union with the Goddess of the South Ocean. (Photo courtesy of Agus Sutopo).

Plate 6 Radèn Mas Harya Tondhakusuma, a dancer–musician, the creator of *langendriyan,* and the author of *Serat Gulang Yarya.* (Photo courtesy of Ethnomusicology Center 'Jaap Kunst', University of Amsterdam).

Plate 7 Soewardi Soeryaningrat (*right*) and Noto Soeroto (*left*) perform the Bandayuda dance in "De Indisch Kunstavond" in Haagschen Schouwburg (Borel 1916–17:124).

Plate 8 A canthang balung. Extraordinary behaviors were regarded as ways to enhance the power of the ruler. (Photo courtesy of Nancy Florida).

Plate 9 Martopangrawit (1912–1986) delivered a public lecture on pathet at the first ASKI commencement in 1968. His assistant played musical examples on gendèr.

Plate 10 Jaap Kunst (1891–1960) created a large body of literature on gamelan and music from other Indonesian islands. He was also known as one of the founders of ethnomusicology. (Photo courtesy of Ethnomusicology Center 'Jaap Kunst', University of Amsterdam).

Plate 11 Mantle Hood playing rebab. A student of Jaap Kunst, Mantle Hood is an influential ethnomusicologist, founder of the first gamelan program in the U.S. at UCLA, who has written numerous works on gamelan. (Photo courtesy of Mantle Hood).

Plate 12 Judith Becker and her students (1970s). Judith Becker is an influential ethnomusicologist, who focuses on Javanese gamelan. (Photo courtesy of Judith Becker).

Plate 13 Warsadiningrat (1882–1975), a gamelan expert and musician from the palace of Surakarta, one of the founders of the KOKAR, and lecturer at ASKI. His important work includes a six-volume *Serat Wédha Pradongga*. (Reprinted with permission from SMKI).

The poet of the *Babad Krama Dalem* (1865–66) often described the boisterous atmosphere. For example, at the elaborate toasting ritual (*kundhisi*) in the celebration of the marriage of Paku Buwana IX (r. 1861–1893) and the daughter of the Sultan of Yogyakarta, drunkenness and blaring of European music and gamelan were parts of the kundhisi event. The poet wrote:

> . . . .
> After a while,
> the Dutch Resident offered a toast.
> All the glasses were filled.
> [The Resident] asked for the safety
> of the marriage of the king.
> Then they all replied "hurrah."
> It was very boisterous repeatedly.
>
> They all drank at the same time,
> the sound of *tanjidhur*[55] honored [the toasting] at once.
> Tanjidhur ended, and was followed by
> the soft sound of gamelan.
> . . . .[56]
>
> (Atmadikrama 1865–66:61)

As the poem continues, tanjidhur and gamelan, which were first played consecutively, after seven rounds of toasts, are played together. On the last round of toasts, the Resident offers

> . . . .
> words of safety for the land of Java.
> "Hurrah" [they all replied] then stood up to disperse for eating.
>
> Gamelan and tanjidhur were played.
> Pélog, sléndro, and Senggani [ensembles were played]
> simultaneously [with tanjidhur] without pause [?]
> The sound of calapita indicated
> the king's departure toward
> the northern pendhapa, and also [the departure of] the guests.
> ; . . . .[57]
>
> (Ibid. 62)

Except in a limited way, such as *gendhing mares* (see below), syncretism between European music and Javanese gamelan did not really occur. The incompatibility of the musical elements of the two musical systems (the tuning system, modal classification, and formal rhythmic structure) may be the reason for their continuing independence from each other.

The independence of gamelan and European music can also be seen as a reflection of the general colonial experience. This general pattern concerns the nature of the relationship between the colonizer and the colonized: the ruled must recognize the ruler as both ally and enemy. Instead of syncretizing, the two musics competed with each other, indicating their animosity. They were often played together, but each kept its own identity and repertoire. In short, the relationship between gamelan and European music falls in the category of "competing" and "coinciding" but not "complementing" or "syncretizing."[58]

As mentioned earlier, the division of Mataram and the establishment of minor courts caused competition among the Central Javanese principalities in claiming legitimacy as inheritor of the Mataram kingdom. This was another kind of "competing" in colonial Java that contributed to the creation of a rich variety in hybrid cultural expression in the Central Javanese courts. One of the consequences of this rivalry was the different ways each royal house integrated European elements.

In spite of the fascination of Surakarta aristocrats with European music, apparently there were no attempts by Surakarta court musicians to compose for mixed Javanese gamelan and European musical ensemble.[59] Musicians of the Yogyakarta court showed interest in incorporating European musical instruments into the gamelan ensemble in a genre of gamelan compositions called gendhing mares ("march," from the Dutch *mars*). The invention and the use of gendhing mares exemplified the character of the hybrid court culture.

The invention of the gendhing mares was inspired by the European military marching band; thus, in the performance of gendhing mares, European field drums and wind and string instruments were played together with gamelan in order to reinforce the feeling of a military march.[60] Significantly, these marches were played to accompany the entrance of the most refined court female dances, the bedhaya and serimpi.

A lack of evidence prevents us from knowing the process and the intention behind composing gendhing mares. Clearly the creation of gendhing mares was the result of the interest of Javanese court musicians in incorporating European elements into their music. But the use of gendhing mares to accompany a refined bedhaya or serimpi dance is a unique phenomenon. This indicates that the incorporation of European music into gamelan symbolizes both the invasion by foreign elements and the expression of Javanese court culture in the context of European colonialism.

Another adaptation of European music in the Yogyanese court was in the prajuritan (military) music.[61] Played in court parades (especially in the *garebeg* procession), this music was a combination of European instruments (fifes, trumpets, and tenor drums), and Javanese instruments (gong, bendhé, kecèr, kendhang, and ketipung). In addition, the uniforms of these musical groups were modeled after nineteenth-century European military uniforms. Kunst (1973, 1: 294) identifies some of the names of the pieces as having corrupted Dutch names ("Pandhebruk" = "Van Den Broek," "Setok" = "Stroke").

Earlier, I mentioned the *Wiwahan Dalem*'s description of the important role of European officials and customs in the wedding celebration of the son of Mangkunegara IV, signifying the prominent role of Europeans in the court ritual events. The following shows not only that European elements became conspicuous in court ritual but also the way the Surakarta court incorporated European elements.

> The bedhaya dancers entered the court chamber.
> They were very beautiful.
> Their costumes resembled wedding dresses.
> Then the gamelan played *sendhon.*
> [The dancers] entered the hall,
> according to prescribed manner.
>
> They began to dance before the king.
> The king enjoyed watching the dance.
> The spectators watched with astonishment.
> In the middle of the dancing, the dancers held and shot off pistols;
> [their sounds] was pleasant to hear.
> After a while, the dance ended.
>
> Then a serimpi dance was presented,
> consisting of four very beautiful dancers.
> They wore the same dance costumes.
> They danced before the king
> gracefully and skillfully.
> When they shot their pistols,
>
> the sound was startling but pleasant to hear.
> The spectators were startled.
> [The serimpi danced] only once; then they stopped and rested.
> After the serimpi ended,
> all [the guests] drank
> whatever they wanted.
> None of them was disappointed.[62]
>
> (Atmadikrama 1865–66:59)

Bedhaya and serimpi are two genres of court female dances that epitomized the *alus* (refined) character of the court culture. We may wonder about the significance of pistols in the most refined court dances. Significantly, in the court of Yogyakarta, pistols were used by dancers in the most sacred bedhaya dance, the now defunct bedhaya Semang. (Parallel to bedhaya Ketawang Ageng of Surakarta, bedhaya Semang was one of the ruler's emblems of Power.)

Did the use of pistols in a bedhaya or serimpi dance symbolically signify the adjustment of the Javanese to European colonial power? In a broader context of cultural life in the Javanese court in colonial time, the question is: What did the inclusion of European customs in the life of the Javanese court mean to the Javanese? Conversely, what did Javanese customs mean to the Dutch? In his *Netherlands India,* Furnivall (1939:457–58) suggests that in a plural society,

> each [group] lives within a closed compartment and life within each section becomes narrower; . . . to most Europeans oriental music is unmeaning, and to Orientals a band of fife and drum is just a noise. As with music, so with the other arts and graces of humanity; the social heritage of each community takes a bias and is incomplete.[63]

Indeed, Furnivall conveys a strong image of the nature of a plural society. It is possible, however, that Burmese colonialism (his earlier study) was still in his mind when he wrote his *Netherlands India;* the occupation of Burma by the British was much shorter than the Dutch occupation of Java. But evidence of life in nineteenth-century Javanese courts suggests a different picture—a Javanese version of the plural society whose different ethnic groups had known each other for two centuries. The inclusion of aspects of European culture in the life of the Javanese courtiers was both a form of evasion and an expression of the extent to which European power had imbued the fabric of Javanese cultural and political life. Thus, the frequent sounding together of European and Javanese music, gamelan Monggang and cannons, pistols and gamelan, each contributed to a unitary political and cultural statement, a "noise" that definitely had a meaning.

In any event, that pistols were used in the most refined and (at least in the case of Yogyakarta) the most sacred dance suggests, on the one hand, a form of symbolic cultural expression of Java's adjustment to colonial power (i.e., the invasion of foreign elements into Javanese court culture). On the other hand, it could be thought of as a way for an aristocrat to adopt foreign elements in order to enhance royal power (i.e., the expression of Javanese court culture in the context of colonialism).

The bedhaya and serimpi dances epitomized the alus character, that is, a sign of Power of Javanese court culture. Contemporary views testify to the high aesthetic and spiritual quality of this dance. In the nineteenth century, however, when European guests were present at the performance, the atmosphere of the performance of bedhaya was very informal. Drinking, eating, and even the playing of European card games were parts of the dance presentation.

The secularization of court ritual reached its high point at the beginning of the twentieth century. European popular culture penetrated the spiritual realm of a Central Javanese court.

. . . .
Every Thursday night
the players of European music entered
the court tower Songga Buwana,

playing [several] compositions in turn:
Quadrille, Schottische, Polka,
March, Pasodoble dance,

Fantasia, Galop, Kris Polka,
and the Canter Mazurka.
The Officer Parade March was heard loudly.
The Waltz could be heard from afar.

When the hour of 12:00 midnight strikes,
the music stops and [the musicians] disperse.
. . . .[64]

(Purbadipura 1913, 2:268)

Two sacred aspects are involved here. First, the tower Songga Buwana is a meditation tower. It is believed that the tower is a designated place for the Goddess of the South Ocean (the spirit guardian of the kingdom) to visit the kingdom or to have spiritual and sexual union with the king. Second, at the time when the account was written, and even today, Javanese courtiers believed that Thursday night was a religiously auspicious time, an evening that is most effective for acquiring ancestors' and gods' blessings, for example, by staying awake until late at night. It is an appropriate evening for providing offerings to the guardian spirits, to the spirit of death, and to magically charged objects such as *keris* (daggers), lances, and gamelan. In fact, in the time of Paku Buwana X (r. 1893–1939), every Thursday night the king performed a ceremonial offering of flowers to his *pusaka* (heirlooms or magically charged items).

It has long been the custom that
every Thursday night,
after putting on his attire, the king
enters the pusaka room.
He offers flowers to
his revered [objects]:
the pusaka called Kyai Ageng.

The first to be given the offering
was his pusaka [weapons]
named Kyai Gondhil;
then that called Kyai Prajuritan,
Sangupati;
subsequently,
flowers were offered to

the king's attire
called Kyai Ageng Wangkingan.
The smoke of incense was always billowing.
The next item was [the horse whip] called Kyai
Camethi Sapujagad.
Then the pusaka the venerated hat
called Kyai Basunanda.[65]

(Ibid.)

So far the discussion has described the mixing of secular elements of European culture and religious aspects of Javanese court culture. I will discuss further the reasons for such an odd mixture.

The European mestizo culture in Java had made it possible for the Dutch and wealthy Indos to become close friends of Javanese aristocrats. Social interaction between Surakarta aristocrats and Europeans was encouraged by the close proximity of the centers of activities where the two groups of people met. The ruler (*Susuhunan*) lived with his wives and family in the inner compound of the palace. Other courtiers, officials, and workers lived around the palace, inside the palace wall. To the south and north of the palace lay large squares (alun-alun). Further north of the northern square lay the sections of the town where the Europeans lived and participated in social activities. There were the residency house, the church, offices, clubs, theaters, and schools. To the north of the European section lay the *Kepatihan* (grand vizier's compound). In other words, the European quarters were in close proximity to the Susuhunan's palace, the courtiers' residences, and the Kepatihan. There was also a club (*societeit*) located near the Mangkunegaran court.

This setting facilitated social interaction between Javanese aristocrats and Europeans. An account from the early part of the twentieth century captures well the social interaction between Yogyakarta aristocrats and the Europeans who resided there. The report is based on the experience of Walter Spies, the director of the European musical ensemble in the court of Yogyakarta in 1920s.[66] Spies was also a pianist who regularly played the piano in the club near the Yogyakarta palace.

> In Jogyakarta two worlds [Javanese and European] existed in close proximity. On one side of the *alun-alun,* a great grassed area set with ancient banyans, was the Kraton of the Sultan of Jogyakarta, looking like some fairytale palace. The many millions of Islamic Javanese looked upon the Sultan as an overlord endowed with magical powers. On the other side stood the imposing building of the Dutch Resident, and next to it the club, 'De Vereeniging'. Every afternoon the prominent members of the ruling hierarchy met here for drinks, while the band played light classics with Walter Spies at the piano. Talk on the wide cool verandah among the government officials, planters and managers of trading companies was of the current prices of sugar, tobacco and other commodities; dividends, percentages and promotions, while the silent, barefoot Javanese boys served Dutch gin and anything else the masters might call for. It was the colonial world at the apogee of its power. (Rhodius and Darling 1980:21)

It should be noted that the Surakarta and Yogyakarta courts had similar layouts. I believe that the kind of social interaction seen by Spies happened in both major courts in the nineteenth century as well; at the very least, the kinds of events where Europeans, Indos, and Javanese aristocrats socialized started when European clubs (De Vereeniging and societeit) were founded in the two principalities during the third decade of the nineteenth century.[67] This kind of social interaction was one of the means by which Javanese aristocrats were culturally Dutchified—by going to the club; intermingling with the Dutch bureaucrats, planters, and managers (Dutch totok and Indos); listening to light music; and engaging in other European social customs. It was partly in the European club culture that the penetration of European influences into the life of Javanese aristocrats occurred. My assertion here is that the social life in the club influenced the appropriation of court rituals—by juxtaposing European elements in them. Besides instances of European social dancing in the palace, it was in the European clubs that the aristocrats became familiar with polkas, waltzes, and other genres of European popular music. This musical repertoire was then adopted as part of the repertoire played by court music ensembles; for example, waltzes and polkas were played in the court meditation tower and in other places in the court (see above). In essence, genres of European popular culture were appropriated into Java's high court culture.

Some oral and written evidence from the late nineteenth and early twentieth centuries shows the role of Europeans as patrons of Javanese art. There is evidence of direct involvement of Europeans in the development of Javanese music and dance. In his *Serat Sastramiruda,* which was written in the mid nineteenth century, Kusumadilaga (1930:27) mentions a European woman (*sawijining nyonyah bongsa Eropah*) who in the early nineteenth century created a masked dance drama presenting stories of the wayang purwa. I cannot determine the identity of this European woman, but it is most likely that she was an Indo or a Javanized Dutch woman.

For another example, according to tradition, the rise of langendriyan (a Javanese "opera," a specialty of the Mangkunegaran court) was the result of the direct involvement of Tuwan Godlieb (Soetrisno pers. comm., 1979; Murgiyanto pers. comm., 1987) or Godlieb Kiliaan (Partohudoyo 1924–44:4), either in artistic conception, through financial support, or both.[68] An early written source also indicates that Tuwan Godlieb was known for his interest and expertise in Javanese dance (Djakoeb & Wignjaroemeksa 1913:106). Another source suggests that he was a Chinese who was raised by the Kiliaan family (Supriyanto 1980:90). He then became a financial expert and director of the treasury for the Mangkunegaran court (*Majalah Pusaka Jawi* 11–12 [1924]:193–94).

There is some evidence to show that Indos were generally interested in music and theater (Van der Veur 1968:48–49), particularly *kroncong* and *komedie stambul.*[69] Many performers and owners of these musical and theatrical genres were Indos and Chinese; an Indo named Mahieu was one of them (ibid. 52). In the 1930s, as reported by Pigeaud (1938:36), the professional Indo, Javanese, and Chinese *peranakan* komedie stambul troupes were among the most popular forms of drama during sekatèn celebrations and the pasar malam fairs. During the reign of Paku Buwana X (1893–1939), kroncong was one of the musical activities of the Surakarta court. As reported in *Serat Sri Karongron,* kroncong was played during the rest time in the king's hunt.

> . . . .
> the king short a deer
> from the water,
> as he rode a small boat.
>
> Then he sat down again,
> [and] the servants served
> food and drink.
> The queen and court ladies
> had been served.
> They took [food] they liked.
>
> And children and servants
> who were present
> were all served food and drink,
> none was forgotten.
> [They ate] while listening to
> the enjoyable sound of violin,
>
> guitar, flute, terbang, and mandolin.
> [The music] was played softly
> by blind and handicapped musicians.
> They began to play Kembang Kacang,
> preceded by a solo vocal introduction,
> the song Megatruh.
>
> Next the song Pinggir Kali [was played],
> then the sound of a kroncong
> song Bintang Surabaya. They rested
> briefly; then they played again.
> Stambul began,
> [Song number] one, two, and three.
>
> The players [while playing their instruments] also sang.
> Two of them moved to the front.
> Their hands and mouths were working together.
> In this way, they had a good time.
> . . . .[70]
>
> (Purbadipura 1913, 3:30–31)

From the foregoing we see the complexity of the political and cultural conditions of nineteenth-century colonial Java. As can be seen in Javanese literary works, court pujangga were very perplexed about the complexity of their world. Day has perceptively analyzed Javanese literature from this period. He concludes that nineteenth-century literary works feature the world of *kaélokan,* portraying a world of the mysterious, wondrous, marvelous, strange, and obscure (Day 1985:259–65).[71] Such a mixed quality is characteristic of the Javanese cultural hybrids discussed above, resulting from the Javanese-Western encounter in the court centers of Java. The interactions between Javanese aristocrats and upper-class Dutch and Indos formed a culture "somewhere between the primitive spirit world of Java and the 'modernity' of nineteenth-century Europe" (ibid. 264) in which the world of kaélokan was expressed.

Chinese Patronage of Javanese Arts

We have seen the political and cultural interaction between Javanese aristocrats, their subjects, Europeans, and Indos, and how these interactions gave impetus to the remarkable development of Javanese art. Besides Javanese and Europeans, there were also Chinese, Arabs, Malays, and Bugis. Among these non-Javanese ethnic groups, aside from the Europeans and the Indos, the Chinese had the most prominent role in the society. Raffles (1982:75) describes them as "the life and soul of the commerce of the country." The Chinese also became important patrons of Javanese arts.

Like the Europeans, the Chinese in Java consisted of two groups: totok or *singkèk,* the pure-blood Chinese, and peranakan, mixed blood, usually from a Javanese mother and a Chinese father.[72] Having been raised by Javanese mothers, the peranakan were particularly well integrated into the Javanese way of life. They also appreciated and were often practitioners of Javanese arts. Gamelan, wayang, and Javanese literature (including writing and reading of the Javanese script) became important parts of their lives.

Hybrid Javanese-Chinese entertainment was already known as early as the middle of the eighteenth century: tandhak dancing and wayang wong (Seltmann 1976:54). Gambling and prostitution added to the popularity of these forms of entertainment, so that the Dutch East Indies Company wrote a decree to set the conditions and fix the payment when these entertainments were held.

Liem Thian Joe (1931–33:130) describes well-known tandhak dancers from Sangklahan and Ambarawa at a Chinese wedding in Semarang. These tandhak could sing *pantoenan* (poem), which was accompanied by gambang (xylophone), *djie-hian* (Chinese rebab), *soeling* (flute), and *keprak* (wood block).[73] Liem Thian Joe also mentions that Ambarawa was also the place of well-known *pat-im* (a Chinese ensemble), which were often invited to perform, taking turns with tandhak dancing. Liem Thian Joe also states that tandhak dancers from Solo (Surakarta) and Yogyakarta were often invited to dance in turn with the Ambarawa tandhak.

It is not clear from Liem Thian Joe's account whether Chinese men danced in Chinese or Javanese style. Another early account of tayuban (Soewandi 1938:

23–26, 63–78) [74] explains, however, that some Chinese in Surakarta were good dancers; they were taught by court dancers, indicating they danced Javanese style. In a Javanese style of tayuban for the Chinese, Chinese men could choose whether to dance or not.

Another unique aspect of the Javanese tayuban for the Chinese was the tandhak dancer's obligation to dance and sing to *moesikan* (a European music ensemble). According to this early account of tayuban, a dancer who could sing both gamelan songs and European music was very rare.

Several reports cited by Seltmann indicate that in the nineteenth century the Chinese were fond of all kinds of wayang: wayang kulit, wayang topèng, wayang golèk, and wayang wong. There were also two kinds of Chinese wayang: *wayang cina* and *wayang potèhi*. There were also forms of wayang wong singkèk and wayang golèk that were performed in Chinese style and the Chinese language. Seltmann speculates that there was a Javanese-inspired Chinese wayang kulit. In 1976 he found evidence in Yogyakarta of such wayang, called *wayang thithi* (see Seltmann 1976:54–76).

Other accounts indicate that the Chinese love for Javanese performing arts included support of these arts for personal entertainment, used as a sign of wealth and personal status. Liem Thian Joe (1931–33:144) noted the life of a prominent, well-to-do Chinese Kapitein,[75] Tan Tiang Tjhing, in the early nineteenth century, who built his own park for entertaining himself and his family. There was a section of the park called *paséban* (a gathering place of Tan Tiang Tjhing and his family).[76] Liem Thian Joe (1931–33:85) wrote:

> During the full moon, Mr. Tan Tiang Tjhing and his family often entertained themselves at the paséban, while listening to sindhèn singing or *klonengan* (gamelan playing). For that reason, the Kapitein had his own gamelan players and an exquisite sléndro/pélog gamelan. Or sometimes, he and his friends entertained themselves, playing Chinese music, while drinking arak and composing Chinese poems (Sie).
>
> He was considered to be a Chinese who paid attention to the indigenous art of gamelan. At that time gamelan was not yet popular among Chinese. Only during the time of Tan Tiang Tjhing did gamelan begin to take part in various celebrations held by Chinese.[77]

The Chinese love for Javanese arts was also shown in Chinese literary work. Concerning the content of the newspaper *Slompret Melajoe* in the late nineteenth century, Liem Thian Joe (1931–33:144) said:

> The newspaper was published three times a week, and added [a section written in] Javanese script, containing various tembang. This was because at that time many Chinese knew well the Javanese script and Javanese language. This was the result of their consideration that the

Chinese language was a more difficult language to learn. Therefore, the newspaper published the serialized story of Sam Kok in Javanese script and in tembang form. This attracted many Chinese subscribers. The author of the story was R. Goenawan of Maospati, Madiun. He received much praise because of his excellent writing. He even cleverly adopted the Chinese rank/status for the rank/status in wayang. Also in another section of Central Java, the progress of Chinese in the study of Javanese script and literature was quite great, so that at that time many books of translations from Chinese characters to the Javanese language were produced, using tembang: among these were the stories Siek Djien Koei, Yo Tjong Poo, Tek Thjing, Nyonyah Koewi, and others.[78]

In spite of the interest of the Chinese in Javanese arts and letters, commerce was still the basis of life for most Chinese. It was primarily in economic terms that the Chinese had a special relationship with Javanese courts. Besides their function as tax collectors for the courts, Chinese were also moneylenders and rice brokers for the aristocrats.[79]

The relationship between the Chinese and the courts strengthened Chinese appreciation of Javanese court arts. Discussing a particular Chinese affair in the court of Yogyakarta, Carey (1984) demonstrates this. The Chinese had important positions in the courts—as tax collectors, moneylenders, and businessmen. Carey identifies one Chinese peranakan in Yogyakarta during the reign of Hamengku Buwana III (1810–1814), Tan Jin Sing, who also had an important role as a political middleman between the court and the British colonial government. So essential was the position of Tan Jin Sing in the court that the Sultan promoted him to Bupati (the rank for a high court administrative official) with the title and name Raden Tumenggung Secadiningrat (ibid. 28). Certainly it was a great privilege for Tan Jin Sing to receive this high court rank. Moreover, his promotion thereto was a confirmation of his appreciation of the Javanese arts. This is because the Sultan also gave him the privilege of having his own bedhaya dancers in his residence, a prerogative of Javanese princes. We do not know how his Chinese background influenced the development of Javanese dance, but it is clear that the Secadiningrat matter exemplifies the role of the Chinese peranakan as patron of Javanese art, and shows the close relationship between the Chinese and Javanese aristocrats.[80]

In essence, contacts between the Chinese and the court circles encompassed both business or financial matters and cultural or political affairs. Such contacts obliged the court to show courtesy to the Chinese. For example, Chinese theatrical shows were often parts of the performances held at court celebrations. As described in the *Wiwahan* poem, a Chinese puppet show from Singapore participated in the wedding celebration of the son of Mangkunegara IV (r. 1853–1881).

13. . . . .
   For the celebration,
   a Chinese puppet show
   from Singapore [will be staged].
   When the show begins
   will be decided today.
14. There will be ten days of performances.
   It was planned that the performance
   during the daytime will begin
   at 3:00 [in the afternoon], and will end
   at sunset.
   The evening performance
   will begin at 8:00,
15. and will end at midnight.
   . . . .[81]

       (*Wiwahan Dalem* 1927 : 143 – 44)

The *Wiwahan* also describes *jenggi* (a Chinese theatrical procession) as a part of the wedding celebration. It was held on the night after the panggih ceremony. The guests sat in the middle of the hall, and the newlyweds and Mangkunegara exited from the front of the hall.

15. . . . .
   At that moment,
   at the eastern door one saw
   dazzling, red torches.
16. The music of gongs was in the front:
   the bronze slit-gong (*thong-thong grit*) and
   the trumpet, drum (*puksur*), and flutes.
   The spectators were in tumult,
17. blustering and noisy, searching for
   the best place
   and the closest,
   so that they can view
18. the jenggi procession which had just arrived.
   Then, they marched in,
   and leading the procession,
   many types of crazy buffoons,
19. appearing as snakes, tiger[?], buffalo[?],
   bird, pig,
   deer, orangutans, and lady ogres.
   They shouted excitedly.
20. The procession marched along the side of the hall,
   to the paringgitan.
   Slowly they marched to the west.
   After the procession of crazy buffoons ended,

21. the lead jenggi marched in,
    in the form of a big eagle.
    Riding [the lead jenggi dancer] was a beautiful lady
    with light skin.[82]

    (*Wiwahan Dalem* 1927:212–14)

The *Wiwahan* continues to describe the jenggi, focusing on the elaborate costume of the beautiful lady riding on the lead jenggi dancer. Then the lead jenggi dancer encountered the newlyweds.

26. When the [lead jenggi dancer] arrived in front of the newlyweds,
    it stopped moving.
    The jenggi watched
    the sitting newlyweds closely.
27. For a long time the [lead jenggi stood there] not greeted
        [by the newlyweds];
    it marched again,
    moving slowly, as if it was disappointed,
    having paid its respects without result.
28. When the jenggi arrived outside, at the west side of the hall,
    it marched south.
    It seemed
    as if it was disappointed, unhappy.[83]

    (*Wiwahan Dalem* 1927:214–15)

The fact that Chinese theatrical performances were included in such important court occasions indicates how important relations were between the court and the Chinese. As I mentioned earlier, in this period of the *Wiwahan Dalem* a new literary and artistic community was established, consisting of the Javanese elite, Europeans, Indos, and Chinese, which was an important patron of Javanese art and literature.

Present-day oral and written accounts show the extent to which the Chinese admired Javanese culture and arts. Older musicians still remember performing wayang kulit for several days in the *klenthèng* (the Chinese temple) as a part of the religious services. Kunst (1973, 1:166, 244) states that the best gamelans were in the possession of wealthy Chinese music lovers—like the kind of exquisite gamelans (often having four demung and eight saron) that were commonly owned by the ruling princes of the principalities and by other members of the nobility. According to oral sources (cited in Warsadiningrat 1987:147), one of the best gamelans of the Surakarta court, named Kyai Kaduk Manis and Manis Rengga, came from Pacinan (the Chinese section of town) and was once owned by a Chinese named Babah Ting, also known as Bah Mayor (meaning he was head of the local Chinese community). Paku Buwana IX found out about this gamelan while touring the city and asked for the gamelan to be delivered to the palace.

In the late nineteenth century, some Chinese combined their expertise as businessmen with their love of Javanese music and dance. The birth of the commercial troupes of wayang wong actors and musicians is a case in point. It is commonly held that wayang wong was a dance drama that was developed in the nineteenth century in the minor court of Mangkunegaran, and also in the Yogyakarta court. Perhaps for economic reasons, wayang wong in the Mangkunegaran declined after the death of Mangkunegara V (r. 1881–1896), a prince who was known to have been a great supporter of the dance drama. According to Raden Mas Said, the Mangkunegaran wayang wong was discontinued during the reign of Mangkunegara VI (1896–1916).

> Many wayang wong servant-actors were discharged. Since then, performances [in the Mangkunegaran] were simple, not as grand as before the year 1896. Then the discharged wayang wong actors founded wayang wong groups in villages. Not long thereafter, there appeared a handful of Chinese, Dutch, and Indonesians who organized these actors to perform wayang wong, traveling in many places; hence the beginning of the expansion of wayang wong in Indonesia.[84] (Sayid 1981:58)

Sayid gives the names of the sponsors of commercial wayang wong from Surakarta: Babah Lie Wah Gien, Babah Lie Wat Djien, Babah Lie Yam Ping, Tuan Rieneeker, R. M. Sonder Suryoputra, R. M. Sastratanaya, Bapak Paira Sandi, Bapak Kartadiwirya, and Bapak Sastra Sabda (1981:59).

A Dutchman named J. L. Rineker[85] was a sponsor of a commercial wayang wong in Pasar Pon, Surakarta, at the beginning of the twentieth century (Soewandi 1938:156). A dancer named Murgiyanto (pers. comm. 1987) was told by his grandfather, who was the first artistic director of the Sri Wedari wayang wong of Surakarta, that Rademaker (a Dutchman) and Bah Wang Hin (a Chinese) were co-founder with him of the troupe. Thus, the founders of the Sri Wedari wayang wong[86] were a Javanese, a Dutchman (perhaps Indo), and a Chinese.[87]

Chinese publishing houses were important in publishing writings on Javanese arts and literature, especially in the early twentieth century. For example, the publishing house of Tan Khoen Swie of Kediri published many books on Javanese literature, most of them written in the form of tembang. Sie Dhian Ho, a Chinese publishing house in Surakarta, published *Serat Lagu Jawi,* a three-volume book by Wirawiyaga containing the notation of gamelan gendhing and Javanese vocal repertory. And Chinese became the middlemen in the early production of gamelan recordings in Java in the 1920s (P. Yampolsky, pers. comm., 1990).

Commercial gain was not the only motivation for Chinese involvement in the Javanese performing arts. Evidently Chinese also had a growing interest in becoming performers in wayang wong. As early as the 1920s, a Chinese wayang wong company was founded in Surakarta.

To recapitulate, beginning almost a century ago Chinese peranakan became prominent in Javanese arts and letters. The role of the Chinese is particularly evident in the dissemination of Javanese arts and literature through Chinese publishing houses, but Chinese were also important patrons of gamelan and wayang, sponsoring many performances of these arts. Chinese also had an important role in the development of commercial wayang wong troupes, and thus made it possible for the Javanese court arts to become accessible to a wider public.

The Decline of Islamic Ritual in the Courts of Central Java

Music was important in eighteenth- and early nineteenth-century Java, both inside and outside the courts (see chapter 1). This does not mean, however, that there was no argument in the Islamic community about the place of music during this period. In fact, the *Serat Centhini* has a section about this argument. Kunst (1973, 1:267–69) suggests that it represents a conflict between religious orthodoxy and a more modern, tolerant point of view. But the debate was not this simple.

In the *Serat Centhini,* Wiracapa leads a discussion of the relationship between music and religion. After a gendhing and pathetan are played, Wiracapa says:

> 40. Oh, what a pity, the handsome one [the rebab player]
> truly is very keen for gendhing,
> aware of the intricacy of its soul,
> overcoming [even] a gendhing expert.
> He is in no way the son of ulama.
> He is skillful in the practice of the art.
> 41. But my brother,
> a person who practices music,
> becomes an opponent of religion.
> Ultimately [music] leads to poverty
> in this world and the world hereafter.
> The musician has no faith in religion.
> 42. This is because the musician, in
> his heart, worships gendhing.
> Nothing else is in his mind
> except the feeling of a gendhing,
> which he strives for in his heart
> when playing a gendhing.[88]
>
> (*Serat Tjenṭini* 1912–15, 7–8:203)

Wiracapa makes other points about music and religion.[89] After mocking the musician, he suggests a way to make music a valuable experience, an experience which may be considered analogous to a religious experience.

1. Therefore, my "Brother" Kulawirya,
   concerning the playing of a gendhing,
   in order to fully understand its meaning,
   the *ilmu* (sacred knowledge) of its *rasa* (inner meaning)
      should be explained.
2. The sound of a set of gamelan
   is merely the sound of metallic instruments.
   It alone will not reveal the true meaning of the ilmu.
   Only the gendhing, my brother, can become rasa.[90]
                  (*Serat Tjenṭini* 1912–15, 7–8:204–5)

Wiracapa discusses at length the compatibility between playing gendhing and practicing religion. I translated part of this discussion in chapter 1, relating it to a possible positive stance of Islam toward gamelan. Although Wiracapa at times mocks the musician's lack of faith in religion, he finally makes a point of the importance of knowing the ilmu (sacred knowledge) of a gendhing. Religion will fail those who like gamelan but do not know the ilmu. He concludes:

3. [To those] who have known the rasa of the gendhing
   and the essence of its meaning,
   gendhing becomes the intermediary
   of true meaning,
   until the end of life,
   . . . .[91]
                                 (Ibid. 206)

The benefits and dangers of certain genres of music within Islam have been debated by Muslim scholars for centuries (al-Faruqi 1985:9). al-Faruqi discusses the debate in terms of the hierarchization of different genres of sound-art expression (*handasah al-sawt*), "separating the more appreciated and encouraged genres in a class apart, and . . . categorizing certain forms and occasions for sound art or *sawti* performance as controversial or disapproved" (p. 7).

The debate in the *Serat Centhini* reflects these Islamic debates. In fact, it is reflected in the doctrine of the Sunni school of Islamic law. As al-Faruqi (1985: 22–23) points out:

> The jurists of all four Sunnī schools of Islamic law have maintained that the testimony of the public mourner or singer, for example, is not admissible evidence in any legal case tried in a court. It should be noted, however, that the authorities of the various madhahib have drawn a clear disinction between those persons who are involved in musiqa under the permitted circumstances that have been outlined earlier and those who participate under religiously and socially disapproved circumstances. For the former, no denial of testimonial right is prescribed, while the professional, the person addicted to this occupation, the one who takes money for it or who is involved commercially in this activity

is considered untrustworthy. The musician therefore becomes suspect not because he performs mūsīqā but because he takes on a profession that has negative social and moral associations in the culture. Such a choice reveals in him a lack of concern for his position in the community and a disregard for safeguarding his integrity and reputation. These are characteristics that could cause him to involve himself in other activities rejected by the society and the religion.

A parallel between this passage and the debate in the *Serat Centhini* is that what is condemned is not musical experience but the behavior that is associated with music. When the *Serat Centhini* attributes a positive value to music, it judges music to be not only legitimate but an experience that is synonymous with the highest form of religious ecstasy.[92] This can all be achieved when one is equipped with proper knowledge of the music.

The point here is that the *Serat Centhini* recognizes the problem of the relationship between music and religion. The poem places its argument appropriately within the framework of both orthodox and traditional syncretic-mystical Islam; hence, the debate is not about a conflict between those two streams of Islam. Geertz describes Javanese religious life at the time of the production of the *Serat Centhini:*

> At the heart, geographically as well as socially, the civil service version of (to coin a small neologism) Madjapahit exemplarism; along the margins and in the interstices, Indonesianized renditions of medieval Islam, now occult and emotional, now crabbed and scholastic, now dogmatic and puritan; and under, or behind, or around them both, the syncretistic folk religion of the mass of the peasantry . . . which at once drew upon them, naturalized them, and resisted their intrusion. Never really reconciled to one another, these various strands were anyway reasonably well contained in a system which was less a synthesis than a sort of spiritual balance of power. (1968:42–43)

These are the religious conditions of Javanese society that produced the *Serat Centhini.* They were also an important part of the intense cultural development in the eighteenth- and early nineteenth-century Javanese courts. For example, there is evidence from late eighteenth-century Mangkunegaran of the rigorous activity of syncretistic Islam in the court (see above). Javanese and Islamic traditions existed side by side harmoniously. Islamic prayers were delivered and terbangan music performed regularly in the courts, together or in turn with Javanese gamelan or other related performances. Pujangga such as Yasadipura I extended their work to include Javanizing Islamic literature. It seems clear that in its early years Islam had a role in the life of the Javanese courtiers, and contributed to the intense cultural development in the court.

However, the religious climate described by Geertz did not continue. In the middle of the nineteenth century, the pace of "crystallization" of Javanese Islam into more orthodox, legalistic Islam accelerated. Geertz explains:

> The immediate agents of this crystallization were the pilgrimage to Mecca, the boarding school, and the internal market system. They were not new either, but each grew enormously in importance after 1850, when steamships, trains, and the Suez Canal suddenly shrank the world to domestic dimensions. The pilgrimage, on which some two thousand Indonesians were departing by 1860, ten thousand by 1880, and fifty thousand by 1926, created a new class of spiritual adepts: men who had been to the Holy Land and (so they thought) seen Islam through an undarkened glass. Upon their return the more earnest of them founded religious boarding schools, many of them quite large, to instruct young men in what they took to be the true and neglected teaching of the Prophet. Called either *ulama,* from the Arabic term for religious scholars, or *kijaji,* from the Javanese for sage, these men became the leaders of the santri community, a community which soon expanded to include anyone who had been in a religious school at any time in his life or who even sympathized with the sentiments fostered by such schools whether he had in fact been in one or not. (Geertz 1968:67)

Geertz describes a period of reform for Javanese Islam, which brought a different kind of dynamism to the cultural life of Java. In the Javanese courts, the Islamic reformation in the middle of the nineteenth century caused the assiduous practice of the Sufi Islam to wither away. The practice of dhikir, the Islamic terbangan music, Islamic prayers at the court celebrations, and wayang with Islamic story themes declined or disappeared entirely. In the middle of the nineteenth century, these Islamic activities receive only brief mention in court literature. They became marginal activities, or formalities of religious requirements, in the life of the courts. For example, during the annual ceremonial celebration of the birthday of Mangkunegara IV (r. 1850–1881), as reported in the *Babad Mangkunegara IV,* the Islamic prayer was said only briefly by the pengulu and two *ketib:*

> Then Jeng Gusti [Mangkunegara] summoned his brother Jeng Pangéran Suryadiningrat. He responded and passed on the order to the pengulu, who was asked to offer a prayer for the celebration of prince Mangkunegara's birthday on Sunday Legi. The pengulu accepted the order and offered a prayer at once. His voice was loud, sweet, clear, precise. He recited *kiratilapal* three times. He offered a prayer, taking turns with two ketib.[93] (*Babad Mangkunegara IV* 1853–63:67)

The Islamic prayer at the annual birthday party of Mangkunegara IV was not as grand as at the birthday party of Mangkunegara I. At that party, hundreds of santri prayed together in the courtyard. In spite of the frequent mention of presentations of gamelan and Western music in various royal celebrations in the late nineteenth century, Islamic terbangan music was absent from these events. And although *Babad Mangkunegara IV* reports a *selawatan* (=terbangan) performance, it was held outside the court (ibid. 36).

So far our discussion of terbangan music in the court has been limited to the Mangkunegaran. I have not yet found evidence in eighteenth- or nineteenth-century Javanese manuscripts of the performance of terbangan ensembles in the Kasunanan court. The *Serat Babad Nitik* often suggests, however, that the courtiers in the Kasunanan court did practice Islamic rituals assiduously. In fact, Paku Buwana IV showed himself to be a devoted Muslim, "attending the mosque and reading the *kutbah* [sermon] . . . instructing his men to perform their prayers properly, sending a party to inspect the Dĕmak mosque with a view of building a replica, forbidding alcohol and opium, replacing European clothes with Javanese or Middle Eastern styles. . . ." (Kumar 1980b:84).

Nevertheless, there is no clear evidence of the playing of terbangan music in the Susuhunan court. It is only in present-day writings that such a suggestion is made. Warsadiningrat (1987:126–28) comments on terbangan music in the Kasunanan. He even suggests that Paku Buwana V (r. 1820–1823) was a composer of gendhing terbang. He acknowledges that this ensemble had almost disappeared in the 1880s. But during the reign of Paku Buwana X (1893–1939), under the auspices of the prime minister, Bandara Kangjeng Raden Adipati Sasradiningrat IV, the terbangan ensemble was revived in his residence. The prime minister summoned a number of musicians, including Warsadiningrat himself, to learn terbangan music from Paku Buwana IV's grandson, Bandara Raden Mas Harya Sumaningrat, who knew how to practice it (ibid.). Two court musicians, Raden Mas Kodrat and Raden Mas Wiradat, assisted in the attempt to revive terbangan music.[94] At the time of the terbangan revival, in 1907, kemanak was added to the ensemble, and the ensemble was then given a new name, santiswaran (ibid.).

Pigeaud (1938:295) also mentions santiswaran as a musical ensemble which was commonly performed in Surakarta. He was told that not too long ago this santiswaran singing was part of performances in the court of Surakarta, which were held regularly on various occasions and holy days.[95] Pigeaud (p. 296) also quotes passages from Ki Padmasoesastra's *Sekar Oerapsari* (1895:237) which contain information about the performance of Islamic rituals in wedding ceremonies at the Susuhunan court during the reign of Paku Buwana VII (1830–1858). According to Padmasoesastra, during the wedding ritual,

> every Thursday evening the court religious scholars came to fulfill their duty to stay awake in the Panepen (a building in the middle part of the *kraton*) and recited the Koer'an (or singing, in a chorus, of something

other than Koer'an) until midnight (bedhug). At that time santiswaran singing did not yet exist, at least not in its present form.[96]

This passage suggests that in the middle of the nineteenth century a type of terbangan ensemble and other Islamic rituals were performed inside the court of Surakarta.

Earlier, I mentioned the revival of terbangan music as reported by Warsadiningrat in his *Wédha Pradangga*. It is not clear what the motivation was for reviving Islamic terbangan music. In this period an intellectual atmosphere was developing that resulted from interaction between European and Javanese elite intellectuals in Central Javanese courts (see chapter 3). For the Javanese elite this meant that incorporation of European ways of thinking was a sign of progress.[97] Sasradiningrat, in his work as a patron of the arts, is a product of this intellectual climate. As reported by Warsadiningrat (1987 : 166), he was known as an expert on Javanese culture and a great patron of the arts whose interests included the cultivation of Javanese music and dance of the past. Concurrently, he experimented with playing the celempung Eropah (European guitar?) and gamelan together. He also adapted Western musical techniques into gamelan playing, by providing program notes for gamelan concerts and, for example, by adapting articulation techniques of the fortepiano (*porto piyano* or *seru-lirih*) in gamelan playing.

The revival of terbangan music represented an interest of a circle of court intellectuals in which European modes of thought were part of the intellectual outlook. In other words, the revival of terbangan music did not represent a general trend in the cultural expression of the court in this period.[98] In fact, an account from the Mangkunegaran court gives a different picture of the attitude of one Javanese court toward terbangan music. As reported in the *Serat Babad Mangkunegara VII,* at the wedding celebration of Mangkunegara VII, terbangan music had no legitimate place. The passage below is about commoners who were so excited about the wedding that they could not resist celebrating; but they did so in a "ridiculous manner" (*ngédan*): they played terbangan music.

> Because they were so happy,
> the commoners fully anticipated [the opportunity]
> to offer their services.
> This was because their king had married
> the daughter of the king [of Yogyakarta].
> Thus [the commoners] gathered around foolishly.
> They insisted on paying respects to the king.
>
> As they entered the courtyard,
> they danced happily, accompanied by "*mung mung jir.*"[99]
> Some just walked
> together in rows of four.

They shouted and yelled, accompanied by the terbang sound
  "brang brung,"
moving their heads back and forth
[while reciting] "Lailah, Muhamad Rasullulahi."

They went straight north, [and] entered the hall;
they exited to the east, turning north to enter the
paringgitan hall, still [playing the terbang] *"brang brung
lat dholit pak pak dhung blang."* [100]
They arrived at the northern end, turned to the south, then left.
Then they walked around the streets;
many children following behind them. [101]

(Citrasantana 1920s:457)

The ever-increasing Dutch control of Indonesia also contributed to the decline of Islamic practice in the courts. As a result of the expansion of Western
culture and Dutch political power on Java, "the nobility, i.e., the traditional
aristocracy, was degraded and disposed, and consequently deprived of political
power, although they still retained social prestige"; concomitantly, the religious
elite was deprived and frustrated (Kartodirdjo 1966:22). This resulted in the
religious elite secretly seeking a political alliance with the nobility and the development of many religious rebellions throughout Java.

In Surakarta, the turmoil in the late eighteenth century created by the crown
prince, later Paku Buwana IV (r. 1788–1820), is the best case in point. The
crown prince became involved with a group of "religious zealots" linked to a
religious rebellion. Then, after coming to the throne, Paku Buwana began replacing court officials with his own devoutly mystical Islamic advisors. Disturbed
by Paku Buwana's actions, the Dutch colonial government forced the Susuhunan
to replace his advisors. From then on, the Dutch colonial rulers were very strict
in their prohibition of the strict practice of Islam in the courts.

Thus Islamic reform accelerated the decline of unreformed Islamic practice
in the court. More important, the pacification of the court by the Dutch resulted in the marginalization of Islam there. This resulted in two currents of
influences in the performing arts. On the one hand, Islam became only a superficial religion in the court, which diminished the development of syncretistic art
forms that had existed before, such as terbangan music and wayang with Islamic
stories. On the other hand, the decline of Islamic practice in the court encouraged the unsyncretized Javanese arts to flourish in their own right, using pre-
Islamic cultural characteristics as a source for their development. [102]

The Flourishing of Literature Influenced
the Development of Gamelan Gendhing

We have considered the rich contents and contexts of Javanese performing arts
in the courts of Central Java during the colonial era. European control and

the suppression of syncretic Islam encouraged Javanese courtiers to search for a "sense of Javaneseness" in the development of their culture. One way in which Javanese arts developed during this period was by using Hindu-Javanese cultures as a source. This is clear in the field of literature. In the middle of the literary renaissance period (the mid 18th to the 19th century), many Hindu-Javanese literary works were rewritten and reinterpreted in the contemporary Javanese language, using the macapat metrical and melodic forms. New versions in macapat of the two well-known Indian epics *Mahabharata* and *Ramayana* became standard references in the stories for wayang performances.

Such a vigorous growth in written and oral literature had an impact on the development of Javanese music. The influence of literature on the development of gamelan music can be seen in various forms of gendhing.[103] Perhaps the earliest consequence of this development was the creation of a genre of gendhing used to accompany bedhaya and serimpi dances.

There are two sub-genres of these types of gendhing: gendhing kemanak (or kethuk-kenong) and gendhing bedhaya-serimpi. In both cases, unison mixed choral singing called *pesindhèn bedhaya* is employed. In gendhing kemanak the mixed choral part is accompanied by a small ensemble consisting of kemanak, kethuk, kenong, gong, and a pair of drums (*kendhang ageng* and *penunthung*). In this genre, the gendhing are identified by their choral parts. In the other genre of gendhing bedhaya-serimpi, sung-poetry was fitted into gamelan gendhing in the form of a chorus of mixed singers. That is, the new choral part was composed to fit with the already existing gendhing melody. Originally these gendhing had no choral part. When they were not played to accompany bedhaya and serimpi, a single pesindhèn might sing to them.

Poetic texts consisting of hundreds of stanzas were composed for the choral parts in the gendhing bedhaya-serimpi. For each of the dances, a dozen or more stanzas were necessary. (Some gendhing have as many as two dozen stanzas.) Written mostly in the form of *wangsalan* (poetic riddle), the texts contain many different subjects: stories, praise for the nobility, moral advice, expressions of love, heroism, and war, among others.

It is difficult to establish the exact date of the creation of gendhing kemanak and bedhaya-serimpi. We know, however, that bedhaya and serimpi dances already existed at the time of Mangkunegara I and Paku Buwana III, as they are often described in the *Serat Babad Nitik* (1781–91). In 1832–33 a manuscript entitled *Serat Pasindhèn Bedhaya* (SMP KS 156/10) was written in the Surakarta court, containing the singing texts of bedhaya Ketawang Ageng (fragment), bedhaya Ela-Ela (incomplete), bedhaya Sumreg, bedhaya Kuwung-Kuwung, bedhaya Gandrung Mangun-Kung, bedhaya Dora Dasih, and bedhaya Bujong-ganom. With the times of the first mention of bedhaya and serimpi in literature and the writing of their lyrics established, it is reasonable to place the beginning of the creation of gendhing bedhaya, or the conversion of regular gendhing into gendhing bedhaya-serimpi, around the beginning of the eighteenth century.

Another type of gendhing which developed as a result of the influence of the literary renaissance of this period was gendhing that employed *gérongan:* unison choral singing of three or more male singers. Present-day musicians think that this type of gendhing is relatively recent. Using information received from Jayamlaya, Martopangrawit (1984) states that gérongan and bawa (the singing of poetry as an introduction to a gendhing) were invented at the time of Paku Buwana IX (r. 1861–1893). Jayamlaya said that:

> 2. The creator of bawa and gérong was K[anjeng] P[angéran] Kusu-mabrata, and the first singer of bawa was R[aden] M[as] Hesmubrata, at the royal estate, Langen Harja. The bawa he sang was [sekar ageng] *candra kusuma* as an introduction to the gendhing *Pangkur Paripurna,* performed in honor of the visit of Kangjeng Gusti [Pangeran Adipati Arya] Mangkunegara IV. The singer wore the *Langen Harjan* style costume. (Translated by Martin Hatch, in Becker and Feinstein 1984:209)

It is difficult to establish the precise date of the invention of gérongan pieces.[104] The authors of the *Serat Centhini* did not describe gérongan or imply that they existed, and the term is absent from the poem. However, the poem does clearly describe the performance of terbangan music that employs both bawa and unison choral singing.

> 12. . . . .
> Then [Cebolang] picked up the terbang.
> His manner was enthralling,
> as he was excited.
> The terbang was on his lap,
> prominently facing up on his knee.
> Proud as [the character of] Gunungsari,
> He introduced the piece [with the Javanese] poem of
> Sekar Lémpang.
> 13. His voice was strong and crisp;
> it rang out, fragrant and sweet;
> appealing, the wilet so moving.
> Unceasing was his terbang playing.
> His friends answered at once.
> Three terbang rumbled,
> together with angklung, kendhang,
> calung and ivory calapita:
> resounding, vibrant, festive, and thundering.
> 17. Those who replied competed in volume.
> Their voices strongly echoed together

in joy, surpassing, and being surpassed.
[That was the way] santri answered together
When moving toward the ending-phrase,
the answer was resounding.
When they came together at the gong,
then Mas Cebolang took over [the song];
[his voice was] sounding out, rising, expanding and echoing.[105]

(*Serat Tjenṭini* 1912–15, 1–2:4)

These passages describe the singing of Sekar Lémpang as the introduction of a piece. The author referred to this introduction as *adan* (which literally means "call to prayer"). But in other passages the *Serat Centhini* also uses the word bawa (a more common word for vocal introduction), as in the sentence "lekas bawa Gambir Sawit" (sing the bawa for Gambir Sawit at once) (ibid. 5). The poem also describes unison choral singing (*sauran*) in the terbangan ensemble. It seems that the singing was done antiphonally.

With no evidence of bawa and choral singing before the middle of the nineteenth century (see below), it seems reasonable to assume that bawa and the choral singing style in the terbangan ensemble predate bawa and gérongan in the gamelan. We do not know for certain if the practice of bawa and unison choral singing of the terbangan inspired the creation of gendhing gérongan.[106] In view of the intimate relationship between terbangan and gamelan music, as often described in the *Serat Centhini* and *Serat Babad Nitik,* such transmission cannot be ruled out. In fact, evidence from the mid nineteenth century seems to support this.

A manuscript entitled *Sendhon Langen Swara* (1853–81) is pertinent to a discussion of gendhing gérongan. The manuscript describes the background and performance of nine pieces: Langen Gita, Wala Gita, Raja Swala, Sita Mardawa, Puspa Warna, Puspanjala, Taru Pala, Puspa Giwang, and Lebda Sari. Tradition attributes the composition of these pieces to Mangkunegara IV (r. 1853–1881).[107] The following is the preface of the manuscript:

> This is *Sendhon Langen Swara,* composed by Kangjeng Gusti Pangeran Adipati Harya Mangkunegara IV. [The pieces were] performed at the time when the Mangkunegara was eating with his children, subjects, and soldiers. *Each of the pieces is introduced with bawa, followed by the gamelan [playing]. The melodies of the gendhing are based on sekar* (sung poetry).[108] (Ibid. 1; emphasis added)

As the quotation indicates, each of the Sendhon Langen Swara pieces had bawa.[109] Each piece is composed in the structure of ketawang (16 beats per gongan). Each gendhing consist of two parts: *ompak* and *ngelik*. The ompak, consisting of one gongan, contains a simple melody in a narrow range—a kind of refrain but without a gérongan. The ngelik part, the section which has the gérongan, is the melody proper of the piece. In essence, the compositional presentation of the *Sendhon Langen Swara* pieces resembles the performance of a terbangan piece: Bawa – ‖: Ompak – Choral Singing :‖. The fact that the author states clearly that the melodic basis of the gendhing derives from sung-poetry seems to indicate that the gérongan was composed first.

This genre of gendhing is distinctive also because each gendhing has its own gérongan text, thus differing from today's common practice in which many gendhing have "generic" gérongan with texts that are poems in the Kinanthi or Salisir meters. Indeed, usually the same text is sung in many different gendhing.

There are two other kinds of gendhing gérongan that were created as a consequence of the interest in turning the tembang into gamelan gendhing. The first type is gendhing gérongan that are based on the melodies of tembang macapat. The second type is gendhing with new gérongan melodies composed for sections of the gendhing. Today there are many gendhing gérongan of these two types. But a treatise written in the late nineteenth century, *Serat Kikidunganing Gendhing Ingkang Sampun Kalebet Langen Swara* (SMP MN 193/6) specified the gendhing that were in these categories at that time. They were: Gambir Sawit, Sembung Gilang, Sekar Tanjung, Kinanthi Langendriya, Kapi Dhondhong, Genjong Goling, Sekar Gayam, Kinanthi Sinom, Boyong, Ketawang Raras Madya, Tunggul, Lobong, Brakutut Manggung, Ginonjing, Kinanthi Saléndro, Kinanthi Pélog Nem, and Kinanthi Pélog Barang—seventeen in number. These gendhing use for gérongan texts in the macapat form of Kinanthi meter. Gendhing in which texts in the *salisir* form (type of wangsalan) are used as follows: Calunthang, ladrang Manis, and Longgor—three in number. The list of twenty gendhing gérongan in this manuscript may indicate that the other gendhing with gérongan which we know today were composed after the late nineteenth century.

Gendhing gérongan were born as a result of the Javanese literary circle's practice of bringing Javanese literature into the gamelan. The religious and political circumstances (i.e., the ever-growing influence of the Dutch in court life and the decline of syncretistic Islamic practice in the court) were responsible for the rapid development of art in the court. They provided an impetus for the creation of a rich variety of newly invented contexts and contents for Javanese arts. Gendhing *panembrama* is one of the results of the sociopolitical influences of the court in the late nineteenth and early twentieth centuries. Panembrama means "greeting song." These are songs which were composed to embellish special events and honor special visitors. In most cases only the texts were newly composed, and then sung in the gérongan singing style to existing gendhing.[110] But in some cases both the text and the gendhing were newly composed.

As the Dutch control over Java increased, so did the Dutch influence on the lives of the courtiers. Thus, almost all aspects of court life were under the influence of Dutch authority. Consequently, a unique relationship was created between the Dutch and the native rulers. The native rulers were bound to offer the Dutch ritual public display of respect, and the Dutch gave the rulers special treatment, the kind of treatment the rulers expected.

One of the Paku Buwana's ritual appropriations of respect facilitated by the Dutch colonial ruler was that of the king accepting numerous honorary titles and medals from foreign dignitaries. These honorary awards began at the time of Paku Buwana IX (r. 1861–1893). But during the reign of Paku Buwana X (r. 1893–1939), literary circles began to glorify these events by composing and performing panembrama texts and gendhing. Warsadiningrat (1987:154–61), who was a court musician in the reign of Paku Buwana X, lists panembrama pieces, indicating the events for which they were composed. They commemorated other royal occasions besides the king's acceptance of titles and medals, such as the birthdays and circumcision of the prince.[111]

In short, the social and political circumstances that caused a unique relationship between the colonizer and the colonized inspired the creation of gendhing panembrama. The interest in literature at the time encouraged the creation of these pieces. Indeed, the literary aspect was very important in panembrama, since eight or more stanzas were composed for a panembrama piece, and some panembrama have as many as forty-nine stanzas.

Were all the stanzas sung in the panembrama presentation? A definitive answer to this question is hard to find. From the perspective of music, it would be boring to repeat a piece forty-nine times (as many repetitions as the number of stanzas requires). It is possible, therefore, that the panembrama verses were written for the sake of documentation and publication. If this was the case, the production of these texts might have been sponsored and enjoyed by the Indos, Chinese, and Javanese elite who were important patrons of Javanese arts at that time.

To summarize: It is commonly assumed that cultural developments in nineteenth-century colonial Java, especially in the courts, reflected the political impotence of the courts. Consequently, the arts have been characterized as involuted, over-refined, or byzantine. I have suggested that such an assumption fails to account for the complex background of political and cultural life of nineteenth-century colonial Java. Nineteenth-century Javanese court culture should be viewed not only as the consequence of an "inward focus" of court activity, but also as an "outward expression" of court attempts to accommodate the diversity of society. More importantly, the development of Javanese culture should be understood as the result of complex interactions in the multi-class and multi-ethnic population of Java: Javanese (aristocrats and common folk), Dutch, Indos, and Chinese. Such interactions involved competing and conflicting models of culture, religion, and ideology. The heterogeneous court culture was the result of a cultural consensus between the colonizers and their Javanese subjects.

In the subsequent colonial years, the accessibility of Western education to the Javanese elite, Chinese, and Indos strengthened the close relationship between these groups and Europeans. Consequently, by the twentieth century, European modes of thought were important in the intellectual outlook of these groups in Java, and, for that matter, throughout Indonesia. In the next chapter, I discuss the impact of these changes on the intellectual life of Java, especially their impact on the Indonesian national movement, how gamelan became a subject of controversy among the Indonesian nationalists, and how the changes influenced the character of writings on gamelan and gendhing theory.

THREE

*The Impact of Western Thought
on Javanese Views of Music*

The Early Impact of European Intellectualism on Gamelan

The preceding chapter discusses how the interactions between different groups of people (Europeans, Indos, Chinese, and Javanese elite), each with their own value systems and ideologies, created an unusually rich variety in the contents and context of Javanese arts. Relationships between the Javanese elite, the Dutch (both totok and Indos), and the Chinese had a significant impact on the development of court cultures. The Dutch and Indos, consisting of mostly upper- and middle-class bureaucrats, planters, and managers of trading companies, had social and cultural relations with Javanese aristocrats. Most of the Dutch and Indos were practical people with minimal education. Beside any political motivation, their relationships with Javanese aristocrats were merely casual social intercourse. But these relationships had a significant impact on court rituals.

The social relationship between Javanese aristocrats and this group of Dutch and Indos was generally one of equality. Dutch and Indo officials and planters often spent time with Javanese aristocrats in the courts, loji, and European clubs. Together they participated in ballroom dancing, listening to gamelan or waltzes, watching bedhaya or serimpi dances, playing cards, drinking, boating, and other social activities.

In the second decade of the nineteenth century, another group of Dutch and Indos emerged, the group of scholar-officials, who had an important role in the development of Javanese studies. The reason for this emergence of intellectuals was the colonial government's need for more officials who could communicate better with native officials and who had expertise in Javanese culture. For this reason, the colonial government trained its young officials in indigenous languages. In Central Java, such training was begun in Yogyakarta in 1819 (Tsuchiya 1990:79).

Subsequently, because the need for well-informed Dutch officials expanded, in 1832 the Institute for Javanese Language in Surakarta (Het Instituut voor de Javaansch Taal te Soerakarta) was established. Here Dutch students (prospective officials of the Dutch government) not only learned the Javanese language but also learned about Javanese arts and culture, through weekly attendance at the wayang performances and occasional field trips to historical sites such as the Borobudur, Prambanan, and Dieng temples (Kraemer 1932:273).

From the language training in Yogyakarta and the Institute for Javanese Language in Surakarta, eminent Dutch scholar-officials emerged. They were missionaries, such as J. F. C. Gericke (a German); academicians, such as T. Roorda; and serious students of Javanese culture, such as A. D. Cornets de Groot, Jr., P. P. Roorda van Eysingga, F. W. Winter, and J. A. Wilkens (the last two scholars were Indos). These Dutch and Indo scholar-officials engaged in intellectual discourse with learned aristocrats, court poets, and leading artists on more or less equal terms. Their relations with Javanese aristocrats were academically motivated. They initiated modern European scholarly methods in the study of Javanese culture.[1]

As a dominant force of intellectual thought in Surakarta, the Dutch Javanologists led the way toward the legitimation of Javanese culture. The Dutch Javanologists identified the pre-Islamic, Hindu-Javanese period as a golden age in Javanese culture (Florida 1987:1). After studying the literature of eighteenth- and nineteenth-century Java, Dutch Javanologists viewed Javanese culture at that time as decadent and involuted (ibid. 2). According to them, the literature "corrupted" the works of the "golden age" of literature. In spite of these Dutch views,

> there arose in Surakarta an Indo-Javanese-Chinese community that, being essentially amateur, loved and patronized "modern, decadent" Javanese literature and all the other cultural activities ignored and disregarded by the Dutch Javanologists. (Shiraishi 1990:7)

In connection with the Institute for Javanese Language in Surakarta, I should mention C. F. Winter, who was born in Yogyakarta and died in Surakarta. As an Indo growing up in Java, he had an intimate knowledge of Javanese culture and language. In 1825, he succeeded his father, F. W. Winter, as an interpreter in the court of Surakarta (Uhlenbeck 1964:45). In 1834, he became the director of the Institute, succeeding J. F. C. Gericke, its founder and its director for two years. Winter was a serious Javanologist. He published several books and articles on Javanese language and culture, including Javanese music. He was the first scholar to attempt to standardize Javanese singing by transcribing songs in Western staff notation.

The establishment of the Institute for Javanese Language in Surakarta characterized the intellectual atmosphere at the time: the Dutch researchers focused their work in the Surakarta courts, and they built a close relationship with Javanese courtiers and pujangga (court poets). As Tsuchiya (1990:81) suggests, by the nineteenth century, the Dutch were able to approach the heart of Javanese *kraton* culture. A situation was thus created in which the bearers of that culture, the *pujangga,* discussed Javanese language and culture with Javanologists and "nutrient sources" like Winter and Wilkens. The nineteenth-century Surakarta *pujangga,* one might say, inhabited two worlds, two cultures. On the one hand, they were at the cutting edge of the tradition of esoteric knowledge that flourished in court culture during the literary renaissance; on the other hand, they were in direct contact with the agents of the Dutch academic world.

In this period of colonialism, the most prominent court poet, Ronggawarsita, did not view himself as the legitimizer of his ruler Paku Buwana IX (r. 1861–1893). Instead, his work was aimed at Dutch Javanologists and the growing community of non-courtier patrons, Indos, Chinese, and educated Javanese. This is because he knew he did not need to legitimize his ruler, since cultural legitimacy had been preempted by the Dutch.[2]

The mid nineteenth century to the beginning of the twentieth century was a period of rapid expansion of European colonial cultural power and the introduction of modern aspects of European life, such as European-style education, modern scientific scholarship, research in the natural sciences, printing technology, the phonograph, radio, steamships, railways, and telegraph. At this time the scientific study of Javanese culture was gradually expanded, first by European intellectuals and then by the Dutch-educated Javanese elite.

For the Dutch scholar-officials who resided in Java, it was not enough only to listen to gamelan or to watch Javanese dance and wayang. Instead they felt compelled to study them using European scientific methods, showing to the world of European academia and to the Javanese elite the complexity and intricacy of the history, theory, and practice of Javanese gamelan and vocal music. In doing so, they transplanted to Java the notion of "high culture" from eighteenth- and nineteenth-century Europe; hence, Javanese court arts were defined as high culture.

The initial contact of Javanese intellectuals with written traditions and European intellectualism influenced certain modes of perception expressed in nineteenth-century Javanese literature. Day (1986:18) describes these modes of perception as "partly oral, partly chirographic traditional form." The writing tradition often represents "a personal collection or compendium of one person's knowledge and interests" (Zurbuchen 1987:86).[3] These modes of perception are quite different from the Western, typographic tradition, whose aim is to present an abstracted, unified topic of study.

The introduction of a typographic tradition in Java inspired the writing of treatises exclusively about Javanese performing arts. *Serat Gulang Yarya* (Joy of learning) falls in this mode of presentation. It is the earliest text devoted mostly to gamelan and Javanese vocal music,[4] written in 1870 by Radèn Harya Tondhakusuma of the Mangkunegaran, a son-in-law of Mangkunegara IV (r. 1853–1881) and the creator of the langendriyan dance opera. Written in macapat poetic meters, the treatise is in the form of a dialogue between a servant, Setu, and his master, Kyai Gulang Yarya. To promote understanding of the treatise, I will discuss a fragment of the poem that concerns gamelan theory.

The master says: "Setu, I would like to ask: How many keys/slabs (*wilahan*) are there in sléndro? And what are their names."

> 9. Setu replies: "Master, in sléndro
> there are only five principal slabs.
> First, *enam*,
> means *pangumpul* (that which brings together)
> and *panata* (arranger).
> This means that enam arranges the *laras* (tuning system),
> [and] brings the *embat* (temperament) together.
> Second, *geng Asal.*
> Geng means *ageng* (low/large), Asal means *wiwinih*
>   (that which inseminates).
> Thus, it means
> 10. that if one is going to create a seed,
> the *sorog ageng* (low key) should be the key *gengsal.*
> That is the fact.
> The third [slab] is
> *tengah* (middle) because of its middle position.
> The fourth key is *jongga* (neck),
> located at the 'neck.'
> The key *barung* is the fifth,
> meaning in accord or replicating—
> balancing the key *gengsal.*[5]
>
>   (Tondhakusuma 1870:2)

What is of particular interest in this passage is the way Tondhakusuma gives meaning to the names of the pitches, by *jarwa dhosok* (etymologizing or, more accurately, imposing an interpretation). He alters the names of three pitches to fit his interpretation: *enem* becomes enam, *gangsal* becomes gengsal, and barang becomes barung. Jarwa dhosok is an indigenous explanatory strategy which attempts to reveal the intrinsic meanings of words (Becker 1979:236).[6]

It is difficult to determine Tondhakusuma's reasons for this explication. Possibly his desire to give meaning to the names of the keys[7] grew from his discussions with his Dutch and Indo colleagues, who by this time had become important patrons of the Javanese arts and literature. It is probable that Tondhakusuma had discussions with the prominent Indo scholar C. F. Winter. In fact, in the same treatise he refers to the work of this Indo-Javanist Karel Pedrik (Carel Fredrik) Winter on tembang (sung-poetry).

6. About the names of tembang and sekar kawin (*kawi*),
   ageng and *madya,*
   macapat and *talisir,*
   their specifications
7. are found in a book published (*pèngetan piningit*)
   at the time when
   the Dutch government sponsored
   a school in Java.
8. An interpreter, Mr. Karel Pedrik Winter,
   was assigned to gather
   numbers and names
   of all types of tembang.[8]

(Tondhakusuma 1870:20)

Certainly Tondhakusuma was familiar with the work of C. F. Winter, namely his well-known *Javaansche Zamenspraken* (Javanese conversations). Written entirely in the form of a conversation between the Dutchman Tuwan Anu (Mr. What's-His-Name) and his Javanese informant, the book was written for Dutch students of Javanese in the Dutch Java Instituut voor de Javaansch Taal te Soerakarta. Perhaps this is the school for learning the Javanese language that Tondhakusuma mentions. Tondhakusuma mentions that Winter was assigned by the Dutch government to gather numbers and names of tembang. These appeared in Winter's *Javaansche Zamenspraken.* Tondhakusuma (1870:19) also mentions Yasadipura II[9] and Ronggawarsito (1802–1873), the tembang experts who helped to put together Winter's section on tembang.

Thus it is clear that by the middle of the nineteenth century, Java's leading artists were good friends of the Dutch and Indo scholars in Java.[10] Searching for the logic of gamelan composition, which was emphasized in the European mode of thought, Tondhakusuma based his writing on gamelan theory on etymological interpretations of gamelan terms. This kind of explanation was the Javanese scholarly tool he had at the time.

In the period of *Serat Gulang Yarya,* an important impact of European typographic tradition was being felt in gamelan practice and discourse: the introduction of notation for gamelan. As will be discussed later on, the introduction of notation for gamelan caused gendhing theories to develop in certain ways, particularly regarding the formulation of a melodic theme of gendhing. Subsequently, from the beginning of the twentieth century onward, the Javanese elite used the gamelan notation to legitimize the status of gamelan as a "high art," in accord with the status of European music.

The earliest source for Javanese gamelan notation indicates that its introduction began with the use of the Western staff to notate Javanese vocal music; this was the notation of forty-nine sekar ageng in a book entitled *Sekar Kawi* (1870) (see figure 3.1).[11] Already in use in the 1850s and 1860s, this notation of tembang

2.

Figure 3.1 Notation of *sekar ageng* Patra Lalita (an excerpt, *Sekar Kawi,* 1870)

was intended to aid the teaching of Javanese song in the elementary schools (Perlman 1991:47). There is no indication of the author of the book.

Subsequently, the same approach to notating Javanese song was used in Winter's *Tembang Jawa Nganggo Musik Kanggo ing Pamulangan Jawa* (Javanese song written in [Western staff] music to be used in Javanese educational institutions) (1874). It is in this context that we begin to see the emergence of one important European attitude toward Javanese music: the necessity to standardize the melodies of Javanese songs. The preface of *Layang Wuwulang Nut* (1874) says this explicitly:

> But Javanese teachers cannot use notation, since they were not taught it. Thus Javanese teachers teach their students without the standardization of sound. That is why [songs are] always incorrectly sung, since they teach aurally. And [each teacher] has his own melody. If this teaching method continues, the publication *Sekar Kawi* will be useless, and there will be many different melodies for each sekar kawi; the correct melody will not be known.[12]

Subsequent gamelan notations were inspired by Western staff notation. *Nut ranté* (chain notation) was developed in Surakarta and *nut andha* (ladder notation) in Yogyakarta. The ranté notation consists of six horizontal lines with dots above or below the lines, representing pitches (see figure 3.2). The dots are connected with lines, giving a chain-like appearance; hence the name of the notation.[13] The andha notation consists of a combination of vertical and horizontal lines (see figure 3.3). The vertical lines indicate the pitches, the horizontal lines (garis wirama) mark a steady flow of beats.[14]

According to Warsadiningrat (1987:164–65), nut ranté was invented during the reign of Mangkunegara IV (r. 1853–1881) by Kyai Demang Karini, a member of the European music staff of the Mangkunegara court.[15] The assumption here is that the Western staff notation, with which Karini was familiar, influenced the shape of nut ranté.[16] Subsequently, Karini passed on the notation to his first cousin, Mas Nèwu Sudiradraka, a court musician with the rank panèwu of the panakawan group. Later he was promoted to the rank panèwu of the kasepuhan group with the new name Kyai Demang Gunasentika. As an expression of gratitude for his promotion, he announced the notation to the government and presented it to the prime minister Sasradiningrat IV (1889–1916).

Regarding the invention of the nut ranté, Perlman (1991:46) asks a relevant question: why did members of the European music staff of the Mangkunegara court (perhaps Karini and his colleagues)[17] need to invent new notation for gamelan? Why did they not use the Western staff to notate gendhing? Perlman (pp. 52–53) suggests that the ranté notation was well suited to the notation of gendhing melody because of its ability to notate the multi-octave balungan melodies—notes above the line indicate pitches in the medium or upper octave, notes below the line show pitches in the low octave.

Perhaps another reason for the newly invented notation is that Karini felt that the Western staff was a difficult system for learning gamelan. Thus he adopted only the horizontal staves and notes, disregarding the stems, flags, and other signs.

It is not clear, however, how much the early notations were used for teaching gamelan. According to Warsadiningrat, Gunasentika used the ranté notation to teach his students and the children of the king. Djoko Walujo (pers. comm., 1994), is of the opinion that nut andha was used to teach gamelan. For this purpose, the notation was written on a large, door-shaped blackboard. Djoko Walujo saw this notation in the residence of Purwadiningrat (the son of Wiraguna, one of the inventors of the andha notation). My guess is that the early notation was used for teaching gamelan only in the circle of the Javanese royal family, especially for children of the princes.

Evidently, the main purpose of the early gamelan notations was to save gendhing from loss. This is stated explicitly in the preface of Serat Pakem Wirama, a treatise containing the andha notation: "By command of His Highness Sultan Hamengku Buwana VIII . . . to write Serat Pakem Wirama Wileting Gendhing Pradongga . . . , whose purpose was to save from extinction the trace of the melodic basis of the old Mataram gendhing" (1934:2).

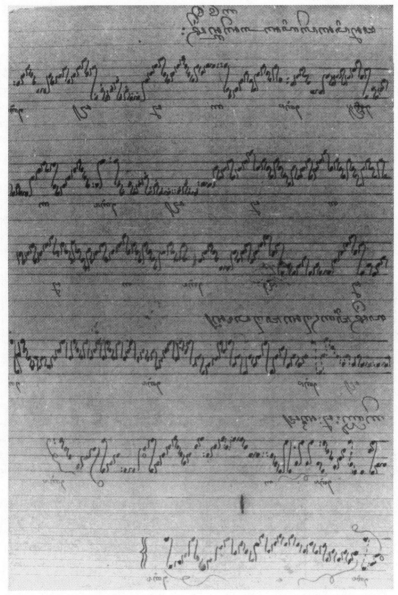

Figure 3.2 Nut ranté (chain notation), an excerpt (Gunasentika early 20th century)

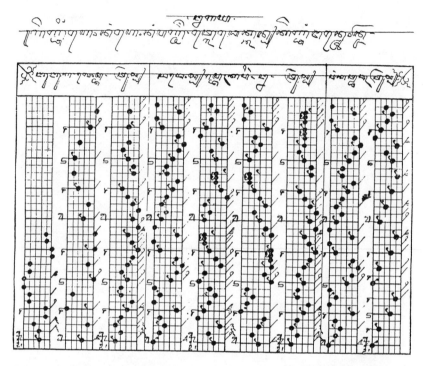

Figure 3.3 Nut andha (ladder notation) *gendhing* Onang-Onang Pantheng Tlèdhèkan (an excerpt, *Serat Pakem Wirama* 1934)

In the late nineteenth and early twentieth centuries, the notion of preservation was common among European Javanologists in Java, whose interest included archaeology and antiquity.[18] The project of notating gendhing was a reflection of this general interest in preserving old objects. In this sense, the impetus for notating gendhing came from European modes of thought.

Lindsay (1985:210–11) offers a different interpretation, however. She suggests that the impulse to preserve gendhing was a reflection of a larger Javanese cultural reaction to the stronger colonial control in Java.[19] Reaching a sense of alarm at losing their political and cultural identity, the Javanese people felt compelled to preserve their past. Lindsay's reasoning is valid. However, one can not underestimate the influence of the Dutch Javanologists on the attitude of the Javanese elite toward their arts. These Dutch Javanologists led the way for the legitimation of Javanese culture of the past.

Subsequently, notation for gamelan was used by the Javanese elite to justify the status of gamelan as a "high art." In this legitimization, "conservative *priyayi* worked together with sympathetic Dutch Javanologists towards a spiritualized codification of elite culture" (Florida 1987:3). The inception and the execution of nut andha in the *Serat Pakem Wirama* reflect a European intellectual atmosphere in Java in the late nineteenth and early twentieth centuries.

The inception of the treatise was in 1889, with the instruction of Hamengku Buwana VII (r. 1877–1921) to his brother, Mangkubumi. Mangkubumi's son, Kertanagara, supervised the project. It is not clear when the actual writing of the treatise began. But the writing was carried on into the turn of the century by Kertanagara's younger brother Wiraguna and his assistants (Mas Lurah Brangtamarta, Radèn Lurah Puspakanthi, Mas Panèwu Demang Angon-gendhing, and Radèn Lurah Babarlayar) during the reign of Hamengku Buwana VIII (1921–1939). The treatise was completed in the 1930s.[20]

The completion of the andha notation coincided with the movement of the Javanese priyayi, with the support of their sympathetic Dutch colleagues, to define Javanese gamelan as a classic work, in accord with the status of European music. In other words, initially the purpose of writing *Serat Pakem Wirama* was to save gendhing from extinction; subsequently, it was used by the Javanese elite to justify the classicity of the gamelan. In doing so, it was felt necessary to include reference materials on various gamelan topics in the treatise,[21] including the list of the gendhing being notated and a detailed explanation of the apparatus of the notation. The authors present their topic in a unified way, a sign of a European mode of presentation.

It is important to mention here that a middle density level of the multi-layer gamelan texture, the saron part, was chosen for notation. Perhaps this is because the saron part is the most easily identified part of the gamelan melodic texture. Another important reason for the choice was that the Javanese musicians already sensed that the saron played a melodic abstraction of gendhing. As shown in the ranté notation, Javanese musicians were even aware of the existence of a multi-octave melodic framework of gendhing (later known as balungan).

In the beginning of the twentieth century, a theory developed, identifying the saron melodies as the principal melody of gendhing from which other parts are derived. This assumption had a strong influence on the future development of gendhing theories. Further analysis will show, however, that the melodic structure of a gendhing is far more complex than that. Moreover, by establishing the saron part as the melodic theme of a gendhing, gamelan theorists neglected the vocal element in gendhing; it never entered the theoretical consideration of the gendhing structure. (Chapter 4 deals with this issue.)

In short, the early notation for gamelan was used initially for the purpose of preserving gendhing and, in a limited way, as a learning aid. Subsequently, these notations and other notations thereafter were used by the Javanese elite to justify the classicity of gamelan. The introduction of notation for gamelan also channeled the development of gendhing theories in a certain direction.

In the late nineteenth century another system arose, called nut angka or ci-

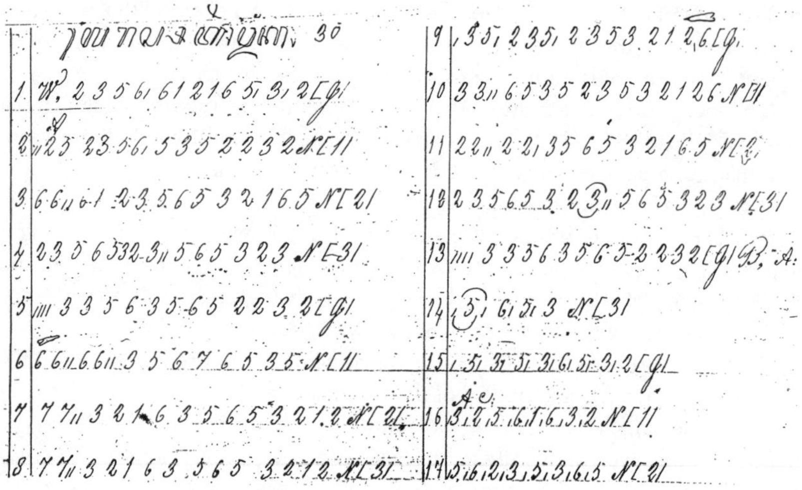

Figure 3.4 Cipher notation of *gendhing* Larasati (Gondapangrawit, late 19th century) (Reprinted with permission from Istana Mangkunegaran)

pher notation. There is no clear indication of the reasons for its invention. The only explanation is provided by Warsadiningrat (1987). He suggests that when the nut ranté was used by Gunasentika to teach his students, including the children of the king, the notation was difficult to understand. So Wreksadiningrat, a younger brother of the Surakarta prime minister, found a way to simplify the notation. He assigned numbers, from 1 to 7, to the keys of the pélog and sléndro saron. For sléndro, number 4 was omitted; thus, the arrangement was 1 2 3 5 6 7, 7 being the upper octave of 1. This made learning gamelan easier, and Wreksadiningrat's notation system (also known as Kepatihan notation) gradually replaced nut ranté.

The precise date of the invention of nut angka is not known. Sindusawarno (1960:61) suggests the years around 1890 as the time when Wreksadiningrat was turning nut ranté into nut angka. The earliest extant source is a manuscript entitled "Buk Gendhing Sléndro," written by Ki Gondapangrawit (SMP MN 85/3; see figure 3.4). There is no information about when Ki Gondapangrawit wrote this book of gendhing notation. The manuscript describes him, or perhaps the copyist, as a rebab specialist (*miji pangrebab kiwa*); and according to Martopangrawit (cited in Florida 1981:2), he held that position under Paku Buwana IX (1861–1893).

In addition to 151 sléndro gendhing, the manuscript contains twenty-five pélog gendhing; and on page ii, there is drumming notation for gendhing Kabor, Jungkang, Kawit, Semedhang, and Lala. The drumming notation uses the onomatopoeic designation of "dhang" [𝕒] in the lower position and "dhung" [𝕒] in the upper position on the page, with dots in between to indicate the duration.

One of the characteristics of early nut angka is the absence of the division of metric phrases into units of four basic beats, which nowadays is commonly known as *gatra*. The main markers of musical phrases in nut angka notation are kenong and gong, abbreviated N or Kn, and G. When the Western solfège system[22] was introduced at the beginning of the twentieth century, nut angka adopted a designation of metric units. At first, bar lines were employed. As in the solfège system, these bar lines were placed before the accented note in a measure (see Komisi 1924 and Dewantara 1936). In the middle of the century, bar lines were omitted and metrical units were separated by placing spaces between the groups of four pulses. The spaces are located between the accented note and the note which follows it. This second method of separating metrical units became more common than the first, and it is still used.

Nut angka also adopted other features of the solfège system: a dot above or below the number indicates an upper or lower octave; a dot in place of a number indicates rhythm and a sustaining of the sound of the previous note; occasionally, a small zero is employed, indicating a rest or a place to breathe; and horizontal lines above ciphers or a cipher and a dot indicate the degree to which the beat is subdivided.[23]

In summary, the expansion of Western education in the late nineteenth century stimulated the development of writings on gamelan. Interaction between Dutch and Indo scholars and Javanese court and non-court intellectuals characterized the intellectual climate of the time. The interest of European scholar-officials in preserving old objects inspired the introduction of notation for gamelan. Subsequently, the Javanese elite used notation to legitimize the status of gamelan as a "high art."

The use of notation in gamelan had a long and strong impact on the development of gendhing theories. In particular, the notation led to the positioning of the saron or balungan part as the melodic theme of the gendhing. The vocal element in gendhing did not enter into consideration in the formulation of gendhing theories. In spite of early evidence of the importance of the vocal element in gendhing, it is only recently that some theorists have taken this matter into account in their work (see chapter 4).

The impact of European culture on the intellectual outlook of the Javanese elite can be strongly felt in twentieth-century Java. Before I discuss further the development of notation and gendhing theories, it will be instructive to describe the political dimension of this impact.

The Art of *Adi luhung* and Indonesian Nationalism

One important result of the expansion of colonial cultural power in Java was that in 1908 Dutch-educated Javanese courtiers and non-courtiers and a handful of prominent Indos founded a political-cultural association called Boedi Oetomo. Copying Western learned societies, Boedi Oetomo held congresses, opened branch offices, and published a newsletter.

It was through Boedi Oetomo that the Indonesian national movement arose. The association became an important arena for Dutch-educated Javanese to discuss the present and future of Javanese society and culture. It was also through Boedi Oetomo that Javanese learned about the heterogeneous character of the Javanese elite, whose perspectives were not always in harmony (Scherer 1975). The discordant views were often manifested in the debates between members of the association, the debate between Soetatmo Soeryokoesomo and Tjipto Mangoenkoesoemo being a case in point. The debate appeared in a special issue of the Dutch-language journal *Wederopbouw* (Reconstruction) (1918): "Javaansch of Indisch Nationalisme" (Javanese or Indies Nationalism). The following is a summary of the debate.[24] Soetatmo advocated a national movement aiming at the founding of a nation on the basis of common culture, language, and history. He argued that "Javanese nationalism was the means of self-expression for the Javanese." On the other hand, the "Indies nationalism" of national organizations such as the Indische Party or Sarikat Islam could at best be described as a reaction to Dutch colonial domination of the Indies. Therefore, "only Javanese nationalism had the sound cultural basis on which the Javanese could establish their future political community."

Tjipto disagreed with Soetatmo's campaign to Javanize Indies nationalism. He defended Indies nationalism as an ideology which could serve the national spirit of the diverse people of Indonesia. He said that

> Europe was clearly more advanced than Asia, and therefore the Javanese could learn from European historical experience the direction in which the national formation in the Indies would go. [Since] Java had lost its sovereignty and was only a part of the Dutch-dominated Indies, the Fatherland of the Javanese was no longer Java but the Indies, and the task of the national leaders was to work for Indies.

Tjipto argued that traditional Javanese Hinduism had

> suffocated the creativity and initiative of the people and brought about their moral death. The people's liberation from moral death could only be realized, in his view, with the destruction of Javanese culture and the reincarnation of the Javanese into "Indiers."

Seeing himself as representing the common people (he was an educated non-courtier),[25] Tjipto started an anti-aristocrats' campaign, especially aimed at the Surakarta court (but extended by implication to the Mangkunegaran, Kasultanan, and Paku Alaman as well) for its "feudal," "outdated" Javanese traditional ruling system during the time of *pergerakan* (the Indonesian national movement) in the second decade of the twentieth century.[26] Tjipto was very aggressive in exposing and condemning the ruler of Surakarta for his pomp and ceremony, which Tjipto said he used to conceal from the people his political impotence. Using the language of wayang, Tjipto gave speeches, rallied public support, and wrote in the *Panggoegah,* the Javanese-language publication of Insulinde (a nationalist organization of which he was a member), of which he was the editor. In one of his speeches, Tjipto compared the Dutch Indies government to Pandhita Durna (a cunning priest in the kingdom of Ngastina), the Susuhunan to the greedy king of Ngastina (the antagonist of the Pandhawa), and the Sarekat Hindia (a nationalist organization) to the Pandhawa (five brothers who had to fight for their right to rule the kingdom of Ngastina). Thus the Sarekat Hindia had to fight against the Dutch Indies government and the Javanese ruling aristocrats.

Thus it is clear that some nationalists held the Javanese aristocracy in disdain. Javanese aristocrats desperately tried to defend themselves, asking the Dutch government to help them. In essence, because of the rise of the Indonesian nationalist movements, the ideal conception of the Javanese court as the center of the world faded. The argument about the role of the court arts was set into motion for a long time to come.

As noted earlier, Tjipto often used the language and ideology of the wayang. Javanese gendhing, wayang, and dance had a strong influence on the thinking and actions of several important nationalists. This is especially true for Soewardi Soerjaningrat and Soetomo.[27] However, the rise of Indonesian nationalism provoked questions about the relevance of Javanese traditional arts to a modern, ultimately plural Indonesian society. These questions generated anxiety among Indonesian intellectuals when they discussed the future of Javanese traditional arts, an anxiety that is felt by many even today.[28]

Soewardi was an important figure as a promoter and cultivator of Javanese performing arts. Soewardi (1898–1952) was educated in Dutch schools in Java and the Netherlands. Because of his radical opinion against the Dutch and his activity in the Indonesian political organizations which were critical of the Dutch rule, he was exiled to Holland in 1913. During his exile, Soewardi refrained from making political criticism of the Dutch. Instead he turned his interest to education and culture. For these activities, he often worked with three Javanese students from the family of the Paku Alam: Noto Soeroto, Soeryo Poetro, and Jodjana.[29]

After his return from Holland in 1919, Soewardi resumed his involvement in political activity. He was appointed chairman of the central committee of the National Indische Partij-Sarekat Hindia (National Indies Party Association of the Indies) and made his first public appearance in a Sarekat Hindia rally together with a commissioner of Sarekat Islam, Tjokroaminoto (Shiraishi 1990:185). Although the rally was meant to show the united front of Sarekat Hindia and Sarekat Islam in their anti-aristocrats campaign, Soewardi, a member of the nobility himself, did not feel his royal blood presented a problem in leading the campaign.

Subsequently, he did not continue in politics. Instead he devoted his time to creating an educational system, Taman Siswa (founded in 1922), that combined the Western system of education (fashioned on educational models promoted by Montessori, Frobel, and Dalton) with traditional Javanese cultural forms. Thus, Soewardi (by 1928 he had changed his name to Ki Hadjar Dewantara) was known as both a nationalist and an educator.[30]

Dewantara vehemently defended the important role of Javanese gamelan and dance in modern Javanese society. For him it was crucial that Javanese performing arts should be mandatory in the Taman Siswa curriculum:

> Instruction in gendhing not only has importance *for searching out the knowledge of and the ability to play gendhing,* but is also essential for *the growth of inner life.* This is because gendhing always guide *rhythmic feelings . . .* enliven *aesthetic feelings . . .* purify *ethical feelings . . .* as stated in the instruction of *Sultan Agungan* and *Western scholars.* (Dewantara 1936:41; emphasis in original)[31]

To strengthen his argument about the value of teaching gamelan, Dewantara also pointed out the compatibility of gamelan and Western church music in imparting spiritual power:

> In Java it is said that the Javanese *priests and saints* have paid attention to the art of gendhing. Moreover, many of them took part in composing gendhing and sung-poetry (e.g., Sunan Kali Jaga, Sunan Giri, Sri Sultan Agung, and others). This is also the case in the West, where *the religious and church leaders* (priests and ministers) have applied the power of music to *impart religious feeling* and *strength of character,* both of which are based on the sharpness of creative force (*cipta*), refinement of feeling (rasa) and strength of mind (*karsa*). (Ibid. 41–42)[32]

In spite of his anti-Dutch stance at the beginning of his political activity and his anti-European lifestyle, in the end Dewantara "used the respect of Europeans for Javanese art as his strongest argument for the cultural equality of the Javanese" (Lindsay 1985:23). It is difficult to explain Dewantara's reasons for this. As McVey (1967:130) points out, it is "difficult to discuss the ideological concepts put forth by the national movement [such as Dewantara's ideology] according to whether they were traditional or modern in origin and thrust." For one thing, in a transitional period the most creative ideas tend to come from the confluence of traditional and modern thought and it is impossible to credit the one or the other exclusively."[33] However, in his discussion of gamelan, Dewantara used Western culture merely to justify Javanese arts as high art. In fact, he directly adopted the rudiments of Western music theory in his theory of gamelan composition. In other words, in discussing gamelan, Dewantara sided with Western culture almost without reservation. This created a conflict between Dewantara and other gamelan intellectuals, especially Purbacaraka and Najawirangka. These two intellectuals charged Dewantara with lacking knowledge of gamelan.

At any rate, in his stance as both an educator and a nationalist Dewantara defended the importance of gamelan. He was convinced that gamelan would help the nation to feel superior. He says:

> At this period it is very important that cultural experts pay attention to *the instruction in gamelan for youth* . . . because *the form of Javanese gendhing* is indeed *beautiful* and dignified, appropriate to be the apparel of a superior nation. Besides this, the feeling of having an art which is adi luhur may create *sturdy and pure national feelings.* (Dewantara 1936:42)[34]

In this period, the Javanese elite increased the fervor with which they defined their music (also wayang and dance) as high art, the art of *adi luhung* (beautiful and glorious).[35] This is parallel to the twentieth-century Javanese view of the court literature of the nineteenth century, elucidated in Florida (1987:3).[36]

> The cult of the adiluhung idealizes a refined Javanese culture through the lenses of the "traditional" elite—that is the priyayi or neo-priyayi— who are remarkable for their insistent preoccupation with the deep symbology they want to see underlying Javanese life. This preoccupation tends to linger on the alleged "high" arts, "traditional" rituals, linguistic etiquette, and the like.[37]

In the period of Indonesian national awakening, the presence of Western thought in Java began to have a particular impact on the Javanese elite view of Javanese arts. Subsequently, gamelan and its relationship with national ideologies continued to be important issues among Indonesian nationalists.

In the meantime, the question of the identity of Indonesian culture became very complex, an identity that had to involve the role of regional cultures throughout the archipelago. Responding to this complexity, Dewantara proposed to define Indonesian national culture as "the peaks or high points and the essences of all invaluable cultures in the archipelago, either the old ones or the new creations—those that have national spirit" (Dewantara 1967:96).[38] This expression of national culture was even included in the *Undang-Undang Dasar 1945* (the 1945 Constitution).[39] Article 32 of the U.U.D. 1945 says:

> National culture is the culture that came about as the fruit of the effort of all of the Indonesian people working together. Old and original [aspects of] culture that are found to be *the peaks of culture of regions throughout Indonesia* are counted as national culture. (*Undang-Undang Dasar* 1945, emphasis added)[40]

It is clear that what Dewantara meant by national culture was the best of cultural expression in each of the regions of Indonesia. But neither Dewantara nor article 32 of the U.U.D. 1945 specified "the best cultural expression." There is no question, however, that for Dewantara, Javanese gamelan was an excellent example of a peak in a regional culture: it was a music that should have been elevated to become part of the national music of Indonesia.[41]

The desire of Dewantara and other members of the Javanese elite to legitimize the status of gamelan had to face two basic questions often asked by other Indonesian nationalists. What was the relevance of Javanese gamelan to Indonesia's future? And might elevating Javanese gamelan to become the national music of Indonesia be an example of Javanese cultural imperialism?

The Javanese-Indonesian nationalist Tjipto disdained the elevation of Javanese court culture. Moreover, non-Javanese nationalists were also strong opponents of this idea. The views of the Minangkabau-born nationalist Tan Malaka are a case in point.[42] Tan Malaka had experienced *rantau,* a Minangkabau tradition which motivates a man to leave his ancestral home to gain experience in the wide world and thereby to learn his place in the Minangkabau world (Mrázek, 1972 : 4). Tan Malaka's rantau took him first to a teacher-training school at Fort de Kock (Bukittinggi), to more teacher-training in Holland, then to Semarang, and then to Moscow and to other Asian countries. The rantau experience led him to become a prominent Indonesian nationalist and a leader of the Indonesian Communist Party. His rantau also led him to an antagonism toward colonialism and toward the Javanese way of life. He charged that the Javanese had been too much influenced by Dutch and Indian cultures. Mrázek (p. 26) summarizes Tan Malaka's attacks on Javanese culture, including wayang and gamelan:

> He was virtually systematic in his attacks on everything of any popularity, influence and value in Hindu-Javanese culture, as representing the bad qualities of the dark period. He described the *wayang*— shadow-play—as having devastating effects, especially on Javanese pemuda [youth]. He saw the wayang as "childish stories, nonsense, unbelievable chatter." Wayang tales "do not stimulate intelligent thinking"; on the contrary, "none of their answers make sense." It may be that the musician in Tan Malaka made his criticism of *gamelan* (traditional Javanese music), another of the more important Hindu-Javanese cultural values, more ambivalent:

>> For the author [i.e. Tan Malaka], the gamelan and the atmosphere around it have no equal in this world. The movements of the body in the *serimpi* [dance] make us feel we are lifted high above this vain world. The five tones of the Javanese scale often arouse feelings of sadness, serenity, depth and mysteriousness.

> The Minangkabau in Tan Malaka, however, had the last word: "The objection to gamelan is perhaps that it is too soft [*halus*] for struggle [*perdjuangan*].

Javanese dance and gamelan were capable of transporting Tan Malaka to another world: to serenity, depth, and mysteriousness. It appears that Tan Malaka did not search for the individual, spiritual effect of gamelan; rather, he looked for music that could awaken the spiritual need of the masses for a struggle for independence. For this he felt that gamelan was insufficient. He condemned not only the forms and practices of the gamelan and the serimpi dance, but, more importantly, the environment in which these arts were cultivated—that is, the court environment.

For another example of the debate on the issue of national music, I turn to a polemic which appeared in *Poedjangga Baroe* (1941). What sparked the polemic was a radio program called *Indonesisch volksconcert* which aired on January 11, 1941, sponsored by Perserikatan Perkumpulan Radio Ketimuran (The Association of Oriental Radio Broadcasting).[43] PPRK devoted its first broadcast to kroncong music.[44] A Java-born Indonesian nationalist, Boediardjo (1941), condemned the association's kroncong program. He claimed that by broadcasting kroncong, the association promoted this music as a collective Indonesian music (*kesenian moesik Indonesia oemoem*), while gamelan, which was enjoyed by the majority of Indonesians, was categorized as a very exclusive or exceptional music (*moesik ketjoealian jang loear biasa*) (p. 253). According to Boediardjo, when they listened to kroncong, people were dazzled by the glory of the West, as manifested in the shallow romanticism of this music (p. 254). This shallow feeling paralleled the shallow lifestyle of many modern Indonesian people who were much happier, in a frivolous way (*lebih gembira*) and more mobile (*lebih soeka bergerak*) than they had been before. But these people

> could not feel any longer the difference between refined (*haloes-haloes*) [and coarse] music; they could not experience any longer the smoothness (*kelemasan*) of Puspa Warna, [and] the pent-up passion (*hawa nafsoe yang tertahan-tahan*) in Asmaradana; they could not feel any longer the dignified (*keagoengan*) mérong (the first section) of Gambirsawit, [and] the happiness (*kegembiraan*) of the *dhawah* (the second section). (Ibid.)

Defending the association's kroncong program, the Batak-Indonesian nationalist Armijn Pane reminded *Poedjangga Baroe*'s readers that by promoting gamelan music for Indonesians, Boediardjo neglected the Sumatran, Menadonese, and Ambonese who could not find agreement (*tidak dapat tjotjog*) with the gamelan (Pane 1941 : 257). Pane described kroncong as having an international character because its elements were not only Western, but were also drawn from Chinese, Arab, Rumanian, Javanese, Sundanese, Batak, Menadonese, and Ambonese sources (p. 259).[45] "This is proof that *kerontjong* contains a fresh force (*tenaga jang segar*). Kerontjong widens a person in all directions, outward and inward" (ibid.).[46] Pane suggested that even though kroncong reflected aspects of regional music, it should be recognized as a collectively Indonesian music (p. 260).

Several Dutch and Indonesian writers other than Pane also commented on Boediardjo's essays: G. J. Resink, A. Brandts Buys–van Zijp (1941), and M. R. Dajoh (1948). Resink (1941) supported Boediardjo's views. He said that gamelan

(Javanese, Sundanese, or Balinese) was the most highly respected music in the islands. It was listened to and enjoyed by the majority of Indonesians (pp. 74–75).[47] Furthermore, the quality of gamelan music was as high as that of Western classical music. Therefore, it was appropriate to call gamelan a collective Indonesian music.

Note that Dutch participants in this debate defended Boediardjo's view of gamelan. In fact, as I have discussed earlier, the interaction between the Dutch and Dutch-educated Javanese priyayi had first evoked the notion of gamelan as a high art, the art of adi luhung.

Not by coincidence, Javanese arts were legitimized during the period when Western modes of thinking became a platform for communication between the Dutch-educated Javanese elite and sympathetic Dutch Javanologists. This happened not only because the Javanese elite had received European educations, but also because their intellectual activities followed the model of European academic activities. For example, the court intellectuals and Dutch-Indo Javanologists belonged to learned societies such as the Java Instituut, the theosophical circle, and Cultuur-Wijsgeerigen Studiekring (Cultural-Philosophical Study Circle). These societies held congresses and study groups and sponsored publications, lectures, and music and dance performances. Thus the Javanese court elite and the Dutch and Indo intellectuals had a special relationship. In 1939, Furnivall (1939:119–20) noted this special relationship:

> The freedom of social relations between the native aristocracy and Europeans [in Indonesia], which Money in 1860 noted as so refreshing a contrast with conditions in British India, was an inestimable privilege, and has grown still more valuable during the present century in proportion as European society has developed wider cultural interests.

This special relationship encouraged the cultural activities necessary for intellectual stimulus for both Europeans and the educated Javanese elite. Moreover, the atmosphere brought about a characteristic intellectual outlook among the Javanese elite, resulting from viewing Javanese arts in Western terms—Javanese arts as the product of high culture, of the Classic tradition.

It was against this background that court gamelan, wayang, and dance were performed. Besides performances in regular court ceremonies, such as for sekatèn week or for honoring distinguished guests, there were also performances meant to demonstrate (especially to the Europeans) the deeper meanings of Javanese arts, those meanings that advanced the arts as the product of Javanese high civilization. Such performances were presented in congresses, study groups, and lecture series.[48] Often, program notes were printed and distributed to the participants. Sometimes, even in the context of a court occasion such as a court wedding ceremony, the prince and his entourage provided program notes for the Dutch guests.[49]

For another example, some older Javanese musicians still remember playing gamelan for the annual meetings of societies, especially one remarkable event— a gamelan performance during a kunstkring (art circle) program, which was held in a princely residence, the Kusumoyudan of Surakarta. During the playing of the gendhing, the lights in the hall were turned off, and the music was performed in the dark. It was the understanding of all who attended that music was for the purpose of meditation.

I have discussed the importance of tayuban in nineteenth-century court rituals in Surakarta. By the early part of the twentieth century, this male dance party began to decline, and it eventually disappeared from the court cities of Central Java. The movement of the Javanese elite to elevate the status of Javanese arts may have been the reason for the disappearance of tayuban. This is because the status of talèdhèk dancers and the practice of tayuban were not compatible with the notion of Javanese arts as the product of a high culture. It will be instructive here to examine the background of the talèdhèk's life in the court city of Surakarta.

There is evidence of a close connection between talèdhèk and prostitution (Soewandi 1938, Stutterheim 1956). In the court of Surakarta, the court jokesters, *lurah badhut* or *canthang balung,* had an important role in the patronage of ringgit or talèdhèk dancers in the whole realm of the principalities.[50] The lurah badhut called Gunaléwa sponsored all talèdhèk in the western realm of the court and one called Sukaléwa in the eastern part.

The tasks of the canthang balung included guard duty, performing senggak or *alok* (short vocal interjections) and *keplok* (clapping) with the gamelan to accompany serimpi dances, and to dance at the garebeg festival when the king departs to the inner court (Stutterheim 1956:95).[51]

But the once-a-year special duty of the canthang balung was to play the clown in a procession of the *garebeg mulud* festival to celebrate the birth of the Prophet Muhammad. In this procession, when the canthang balung arrived at the outer hall of the court (*pagelaran*), they clown in as funny a way as they could, including imitating dogs mating. This was because if the prime minister laughed at the clowning of the canthang balung, he had to pay them. This was no longer done at the time of the writing of Soewandi's report in the late nineteenth- or early twentieth-century (1938). According to Stutterheim (1956:96), "this custom was abolished probably for the sake of decency because many Europeans of the Resident's (later the Governor's) retinue were present at the grebeg ceremony."

In any event, the old practice of canthang balung was part of an old Javanese tradition: various types of extraordinary human beings and behaviors were regarded as ways to enhance the power of the ruler. In essence, the practices of canthang balung, including their duty to administer the talèdhèk in their role as prostitutes, were connected to this old tradition.[52]

The duties of the lurah badhut included issuing identification cards (*serat pikekah*) to be purchased by the talèdhèk, to show the dancers' legal status as dancer and prostitute.[53] To get this identification card, the dancer had to pay to Guna-léwa an annual fee of ten *wang* (equal to 8½ cents in Javanese currency at the time). If the dancer did not have this identification card, she could be reported to the government (*nagari*) and be arrested.

It was also the duty of the lurah badhut to always be ready whenever the court officials demanded that the dancers perform in a court celebration. For this reason, the lurah badhut had their own talèdhèk living in their houses, which were also brothels. Besides Gunaléwa and Sukaléwa[54] of the Kasunanan court, the Kepatihan and the Mangkunegaran also had their own lurah badhut.

The practice of prostitution presented the courtiers and the Dutch colonial government with moral problems, including the exploitation of the talèdhèk by lurah badhut, fighting between the clients of the lurah badhut in their brothels, and the breakup of marriages caused by the prostitution.[55] Therefore, sometime around the beginning of the twentieth century the courtiers and the Dutch government abolished the authority of the lurah badhut to control talèdhèk, and the court administered the talèdhèk directly. They were given the same status as lurah badhut, as abdi dalem (persons in the service of the king). Perhaps at this time two low-ranking canthang balung, Sukaastama and Gunaastama, were added.

As a consequence of the loss of the authority of the lurah badhut over talè-dhèk and prostitution, and the elevation of the status of the talèdhèk, tayuban disappeared gradually from the court and court towns. I assume that the Dutch government encouraged the abolishment of tayuban because of the moral problem mentioned above. That is, tayuban were connected with talèdhèk, and talèdhèk were connected with prostitution. (Tayuban continued to exist on the peripheries of the cities.)

Thus, from the early to the mid twentieth century, Javanese gamelan and other performing arts became the subject of arguments among Indonesian nationalists. Influenced by Western modes of thinking, one segment of the Western-educated Javanese elite considered Javanese gamelan to be a classical art, an art of adi luhung. (The disappearance of tayuban in the court and court cities was also caused by this attempt to redefine the status of Javanese arts.) But another segment of Western-educated Javanese (and non-Javanese) questioned the relevance of Javanese court culture to modern Indonesia. In the debate over ideologies at the beginning of the twentieth century, the debate about gamelan arose: a debate concerned with the contrast between the Javanese past and its future. The proponents of Javanese nationalist ideologies, as Quinn states in his discussion of contemporary Javanese literature,

> found themselves caught between the desire to capitalize on images of glory in the Javanese past, and the fear of Javanese chauvinism in the present. Consequently, Majapahit and Dipanegara [and gamelan] have

become prize exhibits in the gallery of the national ideology, but at the same time the Javanese past is depicted as feudal and static, and this image, picked up and used to characterize present-day Javanese society, has become an instrument to quell resistance, perceived or real, to propagation of nationalist ideology of the multiethnic unitary state with its political order and national language. (Quinn 1978:36)

Against the backdrop of this dilemma, gamelan lived on and developed, even until today. An important development in Javanese performing arts was the founding of state-sponsored gamelan and dance schools in the 1950s and 1960s.[56] Scholars have written about these schools (J. Becker 1980, Hatch 1979, Lindsay 1985). These schools were founded against the background of the nationalist ideologies mentioned above. Therefore, the schools were also caught between the desire to capitalize on the glory of the Javanese past and the fear of Javanese chauvinism in the present. This can be seen in the schools' attempts to justify their existence in relation to Indonesian national culture. For example, in "Konservatori Karawitan and Kebudayaan Nasional," Soekanto (1953) said he hoped for the creation of an Indonesian national music by artists trained at KOKAR:

> Thus, later will come to pass results from all the Indonesian artists of the new generation, because there (at the conservatory) all the above-mentioned artists have the opportunity to organize a thousand and one varieties, experiments, until finally, with contented hearts, they will meet that which they are always seeking, that is Indonesian music that is truly based upon the foundation of national culture. (Cited in and translated by J. Becker 1980:34)

Two years after Soekanto made this statement, another spokesman of the school, Soerjaatmadja (1957:211), still expected the same formulation of Indonesian national music. He said he hoped that in the future, after the school's graduates worked in the offices of cultural affairs in many provinces in Indonesia, "They will promptly carry out research on the diverse arts in their regions. Indirectly, I believe the indigenous regional arts could thus become the material for the development of a collective Indonesian music."[57]

The fact is that from its beginning to the present, the focus of the curriculum of the KOKAR has been Javanese gamelan. Except for a few courses in Sundanese and Balinese gamelan, and rudimentary theory of Western music, no music from other parts of Indonesia has been included. Most of the KOKAR graduates found employment in Java, and only a few took jobs outside Java. In other words, the education had insufficient scope for the kind of experiment Soekanto and Soerjaatmadja envisioned.

It is possible to suppose that Soekanto's and Soerjaatmadja's statements were merely rhetorical and were meant to justify the relevance of gamelan education in the modern, independent Indonesian nation. While I was a student and teacher at KOKAR (1961–1971), I never heard any discussion of a curriculum that would include music from other parts of Indonesia. Besides, most of the teachers employed at KOKAR were court musicians and dancers and the graduates of the same school. Significantly, the first two directors of KOKAR were aristocrats, the prince Soerjohamidjojo and his brother Djojokoesoemo, who were Dutch-educated princes. Djojokoesoemo even received some education in Holland, studying Javanese culture. Thus, the atmosphere of the school did not provide any impetus to search for an Indonesianized curriculum. The backgrounds of and relationship between the faculty and students at KOKAR form the character of the school. J. Becker (1980:35) describes this character:

> They [the faculty and students at KOKAR] are for the most part intellectually committed to modernizing gamelan traditions while at the same time emotionally attached to the old traditions. This curious ambivalence leads to conservative, traditional gamelan style that is taught in a radical nontraditional way. Old court gamelan compositions are taught with notation. A thin, delicate old man in traditional dress may be found presiding over a class of rebab players, all playing in unison. Because of the background of its teachers, the Surakarta conservatory, far from becoming the fountainhead of experimentation and synthesis as was originally hoped, is now one of the few viable institutions sustaining court traditions.[58]

New schools of performing arts also inherited the perspective of *seni adi luhung*—gamelan as classical art. In the context of the adi luhung-ness of gamelan music, the students and teachers at KOKAR attempted to suppress traditional terms and to promote new terms for the players and singers of gamelan. The traditional words niyaga, *pesindhèn,* and *penggérong* were thought to convey an image of inferior status for gamelan musicians. Consequently, the term *pangrawit* (maker of the beautiful) was advanced in lieu of niyaga (gamelan player);[59] the term *swara wati* (the voice of female beauty) in lieu of pesindhèn (a female singer-dancer); and the term *wira swara* (hero in voice) in lieu of penggérong (male singer).[60]

The word niyaga was particularly disparaged. The word was said to derive from an abbreviation of the sentence *niyeg-niyeg nggawa sega* (too heavy bringing rice). The image implied is of a village musician who, after finishing his performance, brings home the food the sponsor of the performance gives him, including the leftovers of food served to him during the performance. Yet in spite of the inferior image implied by the word niyaga, in the past the term was commonly used to refer to court musicians.

The word pesindhèn was often associated with talèdhèk, the dancer at the tayuban dancing party. (Sometime in the 1930s the tayuban had vanished from the courts and court cities, and existed only in the rural areas.) Often the talèdhèk was also a prostitute (see above).[61] Yet the compound word pesindhèn-talèdhèk (female gamelan singers and dancers) is often found in nineteenth-century court literature.

Finally, the word karawitan was preferred to the word gamelan; hence, the names Konservatori Karawitan Indonesia and Akademi Seni Karawitan Indonesia. It is true that the term karawitan was already used in print in the late nineteenth century by Tondhakusuma in his *Serat Gulang Yarya* (1870). Then Sumanagara used it in the title of his book *Serat Karawitan* (1935),[62] and Wirawiyaga used it in his *Serat Lagu Jawi* (1935). But the term was never widely known until the founding of KOKAR and ASKI.

I have noted that even gamelan practice itself is not a homogeneous phenomenon. Some Javanese aristocrats, nationalists, and the musicians and administration at KOKAR promoted the Yogyakarta and Surakarta court gamelan practices. But there were other gamelan practices in Central Javanese villages and in other regions of Java.[63] In defending court gamelan as an art music according to the Western European music category, the Javanese elite applied Western classical-folk musical paradigms to distinguish court gamelan from the village gamelan.

Generally speaking, the classicalness of Western music can be determined by two components: the sound (such as harmonies, instruments, and timbres) and the context in which the music is transmitted (such as with or without notation, on or off a concert stage, by professional or nonprofessional performers, in cities or rural areas, and so on; Hatch 1980:39). This means that European classical music is differentiated from folk music because of the high level of complexity of its sound, its use of notation, its presentation on the stage by professional musicians, and its urban environment. In addition, the term "classic" is also commonly associated with a standard of excellence.[64]

It was on the basis of the Western European paradigm of classical/folk that Humardani, the director of ASKI from 1976 until his death in 1983, proposed a distinction between court and non-court Javanese arts.[65] Using the term *seni tradisi* (traditional art) for court arts, and *seni rakyat* (folk art) for village arts, he says:

> Seni tradisi lives in the city. This art represents a continuation of the art which lived and developed around the kraton [palaces] or places of power and patronage . . . seni rakyat appears in the village, in the midst of common [lit. small] people. And in every way the difference between them is evident.
>
> A characteristic of seni tradisi, because it developed constantly over the past hundreds of years, is [its] intricate detailed form. Its content is in harmony with the wishes/interests of people in areas of authority/power. There is reflection on (a) view of life and so forth. But seni rakyat grows directly from the people (rakyat). As the common people know each other intimately, so is the form of this art like that. It is intimate and communicative. In seni rakyat every villager enjoys the

artistic product. This is not the case with city people; a work of art has those who like it and those who do not like it.

One element which can arise in seni rakyat is a spontaneous and open/direct quality. (Translated by Lindsay, in Lindsay 1985:41–52)

Humardani applied the Western European concept of the distinction between folk and classical music. Consequently, he made far too great an opposition between Javanese court art and village art. It is only in the degree of refinement of musical practice and the size of the repertory that the two gamelan practices differ; basically they are the same. But Humardani felt that like his predecessors, the early Javanese nationalists and the administrators of KOKAR and ASKI, he had to justify the continuation of court arts in modern Javanese society. And the distinction between court and village arts has led ASKI to develop court gamelan performance in a Western setting. Lindsay (1985:76) describes ASKI's activities as follows:

> Over the 1970s, under Humardani's directorship, ASKI Solo took the lead in analyzing, documenting and codifying aspects of musical technique and nuances of performance style. Humardani enforced rigid standards, and the students had to face tough practical examinations (called *resital*). To all appearances, the direction chosen for ASKI in the 1970s appeared to be that of Western music conservatories, conserving high standards and rules of classical art.

Humardani also justified the classical status of Javanese seni tradisi by pointing out the universal quality of the Javanese arts; this is no different from the common opinion of the proponents of Western classical music. He argued that "the true character of traditional arts" was "nonrepresentational" or "*tan wadag* [non-corporeal]"—that is, art was the performance or the treatment of a medium (*medium dalam garapan*), which was to be experienced directly (Humardani 1972:56).

> This is the foundation of truly traditional karawitan: it never tries to imitate the plain sounds of everyday life, such as rain, thunder, people weeping, [people] lamenting [other people], galloping horses, and so forth. Truly traditional karawitan creates its tones in association with definite musical intervals; and its arrangement [is presented] with tempo and rhythm that directly reach us.
>
> > "Gamelan cannot be heard as *nang, nong, gung* and *thathé théthé.*
> > All of these discrete sounds cannot be heard;
> > only the full feeling of gendhing, that carries away hearts." [66]

It was his conviction that gamelan had classical and universal status by which he justified the existence of this music as an integral part of the cultural life of modern Indonesian society. For this, Humardani called for "*peng-Indonesiaan kehidupan seni tradisi*" (the Indonesianization of the life of the traditional arts).

How did Humardani think seni tradisi ought to exist and develop in the modern world of Indonesia? First, he suggested (1972:61) that the content and quality of art rests on the connoisseur (*penghayat*) of the art and the artists. Artists, after observing (*menyelami*) the spiritual issues of their epoch (*masalah-masalah rohani jamannya*), should, according to their technical abilities (*kemahiran teknik*), materialize their inner struggle with these issues. It was today's world and perspectives (*dunia/kiblat kini*) that Humardani emphasized.

> Today's perspectives, although the continuation of [the perspectives of] yesterday, are also our own current creation. The values [of our world today] are not necessary identical with the values of yesterday's tradition, but they are the ones that we experience and believe in, whether [these values] originated in our tradition or not. (1972:62)[67]

Humardani also suggested that the Indonesianization of seni tradisi had to be carried out with the participation of the whole society, especially the support of the government. This statement is very general, indeed. But Humardani's vision had a lot to do with the policies of institutions that have promoted Javanese seni tradisi in recent times. He says:

> There can be different kinds of form and direction to this development, starting from developing traditional practices and creativity by using traditional vocabulary as it is experienced by the individual [composer], to the forms that only contain the breath of tradition. (Ibid. 63)[68]

Humardani's attempt to contemporarize seni tradisi was responded to positively by the faculty and students of ASKI. Initially most of their work focused on condensations (*pemadatan*) of the dance and wayang repertory. This can be thought of as falling in the category of "the creative use of traditional vocabulary." Subsequently, ASKI's experiments included the composition of new gamelan pieces.[69] The earliest of the new compositions were a mixture of characteristic elements of Javanese gamelan and vocal music with non-traditional elements of gamelan. For example, Sri Hastanto's composition "Dhandhang Gula" (1979) consisted of the singing of the traditional macapat Dhandhang Gula by a soloist or chorus. Passages from traditional instrumental melodies, sometimes mixed with the sound of the gong ageng hit in an unusual way,[70] are played in between the lines of the song.

It is interesting to note the language these young composers used to explain the basis on which they composed their new pieces. Often their statements about their works reflected contradictory feelings. On the one hand, they felt obliged to respect the principles of composition in older gamelan pieces. On the other hand, they felt they had to justify any changes or additions they made in these principles as needed to create new pieces in the context of the new status of gamelan. The statement by one of the first young composers of new compositions for gamelan, Supanggah (1986:39), reflects this feeling.

> My composition is a new work that originates from the material of traditional karawitan. The basic idea rests on the fact that, in karawitan, tradition has a strong potential for musical [development]. The facts indicate, however, that there are weak elements: among others, a lacking in the treatment of volume, timbre, tempo, dynamics, and so forth. Besides [using] the positive aspects, such as the freedom of each musician [to interpret] within the structure of gendhing and the sound qualities of each gamelan instrument, my work develops these other qualities.[71]

What Supanggah and other new composers attempted to do was to compose pieces that had new qualities of sound and many changes in volume, tempo, and dynamics.[72] They hoped that the pieces would become more interesting to listen to. Subsequent experiments involved compositions that mixed Javanese gamelan practice with some aspects of other Indonesian gamelan traditions, notably those from Bali.

It is beyond the scope of this work to discuss further new gamelan compositions by the faculty and students of ASKI. My point is that the creation and performance of new compositions by ASKI composers invoked the new role of gamelan as "concert music," especially in the circles of gamelan schools and academies. It is true that the practice of *resital* in ASKI, as I noted earlier, was the foundation on which this new role of gamelan was built. But the creation and practice of new compositions certainly strengthened it.

We should remember, however, that the performance contexts of gamelan music differ from those of concert music in the West. Performances of Western classical music are usually important formal and public events, whereas almost all gamelan performances are parts of ceremonies and celebrations (e.g., wedding receptions, circumcisions, before or after the birth of children). And many gamelan events are held in informal and private settings. In fact, written evidence from the past and from the twentieth century suggests that the worthiness and the religious or spiritual quality of gamelan is only achieved when the performance is held in such informal and intimate milieus.

In chapter 1 I mentioned the informal contexts for and the spiritual quality of listening to and playing gamelan music as recounted in the early nineteenth-century *Serat Centhini*. The poem describes the compatibility between playing gamelan and praying dhikir, an Islamic prayer for the remembrance of God. Specifically, the poem explains that one should feel the sound of gamelan most deeply when one is *kapanjingan* (integrated) into the *kaklimahé* (essence) of the gendhing.[73] The essence of the gendhing is contained in the sacred knowledge (èlmu) of its rasa. It is through the *ngèlmu* and rasa that Javanese explain the deep meaning of gamelan, ideas that appear again in later writings on gamelan, such as the Serat *Titi Asri* (1925:25).

> The essence of the knowledge of gendhing
> and the knowledge of pathet

if [they] cannot be felt,
indeed we are at a loss
as to the essence of gamelan.
But this is the instruction of reality,
and can truly be felt in the mind.

One who wishes to be enlightened
should, when listening to the harmonious sound of
gamelan, find happiness in his rasa,
followed by rapture in his heart and mind.
Listening to gamelan causes a sudden awakening,
as if knowing the ultimate,
as when knowing the sacred knowledge of god.[74]

The issue of the spiritual qualities of gamelan is rarely talked about among contemporary gamelan players. To many of these niyaga, the worthiness of playing gamelan can only be felt, and cannot be discussed. But Martopangrawit ends his major work on the theory of gendhing with a beautiful poem containing the deeper experience one searches for in learning gamelan.

Strive to understand the wisdom contained in gendhing,
be diligent in feeling its irama,
its development and treatment;
feel the essence of the *lagu,*
know where lies the origin of pathet,
seek there
the meaning of lagu,
feel it until your soul
is made clear, bright, and your view unclouded—
a clarity that penetrates the universe[75]
(Translated by Hatch, in Becker and Feinstein 1984:242).

The last three lines of the poem say: *Rarasen nganti kajiwa, Karya padhang narawang nora mblerengi, Tatas nembus bawana.* There is no question but that for the reader who is familiar with Javanese, these three lines strongly suggest that a spiritual experience can be achieved through playing gamelan.

In the *Serat Centhini,* klenèngan performances as private events are described at length. The klenèngan are portrayed as informal gatherings of musicians and listeners.[76] According to the poem, it is the private klenèngan performances that can make one experience enlightenment. Gamelan performances in the court were held in an intimate atmosphere. There were close relationships between the musicians and their patrons (i.e., Javanese rulers and princes). This implies not only that court musicians carried out their duties in the context of the traditional power politics of the court (one of the functions of music was to enhance the power of the ruler), but also that their activities had religious meaning. Thus, according to this nineteenth-century Javanese perspective, the practice of gamelan has deep, spiritual significance only when it is held as an intimate, informal, and private affair. In essence, the legitimization of the status of gamelan according to the dominant Western European concept of classical music, in which public performance is essential, does not conform to the point of view of Javanese musicians about the worthiness of gamelan.

However, this does not mean that gamelan music is intended only as "musical yoga." Gamelan gendhing may express a wide range of meanings, from meditative gendhing Tali Wangsa to playful *jineman* Uler Kambang, from peaceful gendhing Bandhilori to lighthearted Witing Klapa, and from tense Sampak to melancholy pathetan Tlutur. These various meanings of gendhing suggest that gamelan can express the whole of human behavior; it can convey the wide range of human feelings and experiences, including the religious, the profane, the intellectual, and the emotional.

The Development of Theories of *Gendhing* in the Twentieth Century

I have pointed out earlier that as a result of the increase in European colonial cultural power at the beginning of the twentieth century, there was an increase in the influence of Western thought on Java. Dutch intellectuals used European scientific methods to explain Javanese cultures. This was the period when European researchers believed that a high art could be proved scientifically; one criterion Kunst proposed to prove the "high culture" of Javanese music was the existence of gamelan tuning systems.

> It was not until man learned how to make musical instruments on which a sequence of tones could be produced that real tonal scales came into being, i.e., sequences of fixed intervals, and often, in such cases, vocal music would follow suit at least for the greater part. *Only in the higher forms of culture was this stage of development reached.* . . .
>
> In Java and Bali . . . we have to deal with a "Hochkultur" (= high type of culture), or the remnants of it; in these regions, therefore, we find the above-mentioned fixed, or, to use another expression, "objectivated" tonal scales. (Kunst 1973, 1 : 11–12; emphasis added)

Kunst's and other Dutch Javanologists' view on the classicity of Javanese performing arts influenced the perspectives of the Javanese elite. Moreover, the accessibility of European-style education to the Javanese elite caused Javanese intellectuals to adopt European tools for the study of Javanese culture. Imbued with the notion of gamelan as a high art, the Javanese elite used the methods of Europeans to explain their own music.

This way of approaching Javanese music poses a special problem: the imposition of one system of musical analysis on another kind of musical system. Since cross-cultural study of music theory is still in its infancy, the application of one system of musical analysis to another should be closely inspected for its advantages. In addition, special care is needed in the study of music. This is because, when we theorize about music, essentially we are transferring one system of communication to another—that of music to speech. In his study of Western musicology, Charles Seeger (1977:66) warns us of the hazards of this transfer:

> If we use the term *logic* to designate the musical device that results in or characterizes the inner order of music as known to its makers, this must be in a sense consistent with its use in designating the speech device that results in or characterizes the inner order of speech as known to its makers. We must distinguish what, if any, procedures of a music logic show homology, analogy, and heterology to them. And we must always bear in mind that the presentation of the results of our observations and reflections will be in terms of speech, not of music.

In other words, it is often the case that "music is reported upon by speech, but speech is not reported upon by music. In this one-sided relationship, there is, thus, no direct check upon the former" (ibid.). The hazards and complexity of the transfer from speech logic to music logic are bound to be greater in a culture (such as Javanese) in which the study of the relationship between traditions of speech and of music is still in its infancy. Therefore, it is crucial that we examine critically the development of gamelan theory.

With regard to gamelan scholarship, certain developments emerged: the increased use of notation for gamelan, the increased interest of European and Javanese intellectuals in scientifically explaining Javanese arts, and the availability of print technology to disseminate gamelan writings. In other words, the atmosphere of European intellectual life and printing technology in Java provided an impetus for Dutch researchers and connoisseurs of Javanese arts, Javanese priyayi, and Javanese musicians to write about Javanese arts.

The presence of Dutch and American musicologists in Java in the twentieth century has kept Euro-American perspectives in view during the formulations of contemporary gamelan theory by Javanese musicologists. Moreover, since the middle of the century, opportunities have arisen for Javanese gamelan students to study ethnomusicology in Western countries. From the 1960s, gamelan theory has entered a new phase: the direct involvement of some Javanese musicians in formulating it. And in the 1970s, Javanese theorists often had the opportunity to exchange ideas and to work with their Western counterparts. This is reminiscent of the intellectual atmosphere in the nineteenth century when Javanese aristocrats, poets, and leading artists had close intellectual relationships with Dutch and Indo scholars.

When theories of gendhing are formulated, insufficient attention is often paid to perspectives on gamelan that can be found in early writing about gamelan, such as in the *Serat Centhini* (early 19th century) and the *Serat Gulang Yarya* (1870), and to other oral–chirographic perspectives, such as those projected in the works of Warsadiningrat and Martopangrawit. I will take these oral-chirographic theoretical perspectives into consideration in my reexamination of contemporary gamelan theories.

The Western education and *ethische politiek* for the Javanese adopted by the colonial government increased the exposure of court intellectuals to European modes of thought. Besides education, there were other elements that enhanced the intellectual atmosphere I described earlier. One of these elements was the accessibility of published monographs and articles about the performing arts. The increased availability of paper at the turn of the twentieth century, when the Dutch began to manufacture paper in Java, and the advent of printing technology boosted publication. More writings on gamelan began to appear. Publishers such as Widya-Poestaka and the Dutch learned society Java Instituut often provided opportunities for special publications on gamelan or Javanese dance.

The Java Instituut, in particular, had an important role in institutionalizing relations between Dutch, Indo, and Javanese scholars and intellectuals. Founded in 1919, the Java Instituut held annual congresses, sponsored special events, and published a bimonthly journal, *Djawa*.

In short, the increased possibility of publication and the activities of the Instituut provided even more opportunities for Javanese and Dutch scholars to interact and exchange ideas, informally and formally, in person as well as in writing. Javanese and Dutch authors collaborated on some of the writings about vocal music and gamelan. For example, *Serat Rarya Saraya* (Child's companion book), giving the meanings and notation for children's songs, was written by K. P. A. Kusumadiningrat and D. van Hinloopen Labberton (1913).[77] Djakoeb and Wignjaroemeksa[78] wrote two volumes of gamelan instruction, one on the playing and making of instruments (1913) and the other on the notation of gendhing (1919). In the chapter "Maskerspelen in de Vorstenlanden," (Masked plays in the principalities) of his famous *Javaanse Volksvertoningen* (Javanese performing arts), Pigeaud relied heavily on the written works of Javanese court intellectuals and artists (1938:39–90). These collaborations indicate close relationships between Dutch and Indo Javanologists and Javanese intellectuals.

The gamelan writings produced at the turn of the twentieth century differ from earlier writings. First, these writings use gamelan notation. Second, they contain elementary descriptions of gamelan performance practice. In addition, many were intended as manuals on how to play gamelan. These features are found in the books of Djakoeb and Wignjaroemeksa mentioned above and in Soelardi (1918).

Written at an introductory level, these books attempt to explain some basic aspects of gamelan, including its history (as in Soelardi), methods of making and tuning the instruments (as in Djakoeb and Wignjaroemeksa), and the relationship between gamelan and wayang or dance. In their function as teaching manuals, they also include guides to the use of notation, as well as the notation for many gendhing.

117

ꦭꦏ 68

[Javanese script:]

|| ꦲꦶꦔꦶꦔꦺꦴꦛꦭꦥꦵꦪꦔꦏꦴꦩꦃꦄꦏꦴꦏꦗꦚꦛꦏꦴꦤꦚꦛꦏꦴꦤ꧀ꦄꦔꦏꦴꦤꦭ
ꦩꦴꦪꦭꦩ꧀ꦲꦺꦴꦏꦴꦂꦲꦶꦤꦩꦵꦙꦔꦚꦛꦏꦗ꧀ꦤꦭ
ꦲꦶꦔꦴꦃꦂꦲꦶꦏꦴꦤꦱꦭꦏꦴꦤꦭꦤꦱꦴꦂ꧉ \\

```
W,  5 , 5 , 6 5 3 2 3 5 5 , , 5 6 1 2 , 3 2 1 6

    5 3 5 G,
      . . .

A , 5 5 5 2 2 3 5 1 2 1 6 5 3 1 2 6 7 6 5 ,
            ●                   ●

    3 1 2 1 3 1 2 , 1 6 5 N₁,
            ●           . .

  , 5 5 5 2 2 3 5 1 2 1 6 5 3 1 2 6 7 6 5 , 3 1
          . .     ●               ●

    2 1 3 1 2 , , 1 6 5 N₂,
            ●

  , 5 5 5 2 2 3 5 1 2 1 6 5 3 1 2 6 7 6 5 , 3 1
            ●     ●           ●

    2 1 3 1 2 , 1 6 5 N₃,
          ●         ⌣

  2 3 5 6 5 3 2 3 , , 5 6 5 3 2 3 5 5 , , 5 6 1
  . . . . .     ●         . . .     ●     . .

    2 , 3 2 1 6 5 3 5 G, B, A,
          ●

  , 1 , 6 , 5 , 3 , 5 , 6 , 5 , 3 , 6 , 5 , 3 , 2 , 3 , 2
    ⌢       .     ●           ●               ●

    , 6 , 5 G,
      .

A C , 6 , 5 , 6 , 5 , 1 , 6 , 3 , 2 , 6 , 5 , 3 , 2 ,
      ●     .     ●           ●

    3 , 2 , 6 , 5 N₁,
    ●         .
```

Figure 3.5 Cipher notation of *gendhing* Madu Kocak (Djakoeb and Wignjaroemeksa 1913)

The books use cipher notation (see figure 3.5). These authors did not employ spaces to separate basic metrical units (gatra). In fact, the authors do not use the term gatra. Kenong and gong strokes were the only important markers of the musical phrases (see figure 3.1). This practice is characteristic of early notation systems, such as that employed by Ki Gondapangrawit in the late nineteenth century (see figure 3.4).

The way these authors assigned numbers to the gamelan tones differs somewhat from that in use today. Djakoeb and Wignjaroemeksa used the same order of numbers as in today's Kepatihan notation system, except that in sléndro they assigned the number 7 to the upper octave of pitch 1. Thus, their order of sléndro was 1 2 3 5 6 7 instead of 1 2 3 5 6 i̇. Soelardi, however, used a quite different set of numbers. He assigned the number 1̲ for pitch *nem,* 5 = barang, 4 = *gulu,* 3 = tengah, 2 = *lima,* 1 = *nem alit,* and 5̅ = barang alit. This is similar to the Sundanese *Daminatila* notation system.[79]

	Nem	Barang	Gulu	Tengah	Lima	Nem	Barang
Kepatihan	6̣	1	2	3	5	6	i̇
Djakoeb/Wignja		1	2	3	5	6	7
Soelardi	1̲	5	4	3	2	1	5̅
Daminatila	1̲	5	4	3	2	1	5̣

Soelardi's (1918) and Djakoeb and Wignjaroemeksa's (1913) books also contain basic drumming notation. Explaining the drumming technique called *kendhang satunggal* (one drum [style]), both books list and discuss most of its patterns.[80] Djakoeb and Wignjaroemeksa go into greater detail than Soelardi. He provides only examples of the notation of various drumming patterns.[81]

It is interesting that both books exclude the other two drumming techniques (i.e., kendhang kalih and ciblon). Perhaps they were not equipped with a notation system that could adequately present the complex rhythms of those two techniques. In any event, the various kendhangan styles discussed in the two works are still known in today's kendhangan practice.

The Java Instituut, whose members were both Dutch and Javanese intellectuals, maintained and fostered the intellectual climate. Its activities included conferences whose discussions might include topics on Javanese performing arts, and music and dance performances. Program notes for the performances were printed and distributed.

A competition was sponsored by the Java Instituut in which Javanese were invited to write essays on Javanese music. As reported by Brandts Buys (1924),[82] the announcement of the competition was published in *Djawa* (1921:303–4). The jury received the monographs in September 1923. Seven essays were submitted, written in Javanese. Some of them included Western staff notation of gamelan pieces. The jury consisted of both Dutch and Javanese: J. S. Brandts Buys, R. Ad. Ar. Danoesugonda, J. Kats, J. Kunst, and R. M. Ng. Soedjanapoera. The first prize, 300 gulden, was given to M. Ng. Lebdapradongga (mantri niyaga [the head of musicians] of the Kepatihan of Surakarta), who wrote the essay in collaboration with M. P. Djatiswara (the Second Lieutenant music director of the European string ensemble of the Surakarta court). The two second prizes of 175 gulden each were given to R. T. Djajadipoera, who wrote the essay in collaboration with Mevrouw Hofland, whose pseudonym was Linda Bandara,[83] and R. Ng. Soetasoekarya, *mantri-tjarik kaboepatèn* (the head copyist of the regency), who wrote the essay with the help of M. Ng. Mlajadimedja, mantri niyaga (the head of musicians in the court of Surakarta). In addition, there were four honorable mentions: R. Soelardi Hardjasoedjana of Surakarta, R. Loerah Dajengoetara of Jogjakarta, R. M. Ad. Ar. Tjakrahadikoesoema of Temanggung, and R. Tirtanata of Temanggung.

The competition had an influence on subsequent writing about gamelan. For one thing, it stimulated attempts to draw closer analogies between gamelan and Western musical practice, as can be seen in the work of the Committee on Gamelan Instruction (Komisi Pasinaon Nabuh Gamelan) of the museum of Radyapoestaka of Surakarta. It was not merely coincidence, perhaps, that two of the committee members received the first prize in the competition: M. Ng. Lebdapradongga and M. P. Djatiswara. The other members were Mas Ngabehi Sutasukarya, Mantri Garap Bumi Gedhé (the head of the territorial division of a core region of the court), Mas Ngabehi Atmamardawa, Mantri Ordenas Kamisepuhing Niyaga Panakawan (the head of *ordenas* and of musicians of the panakawan group). This committee was assigned the job of writing a book for teaching gamelan. The book, *Buku Piwulang Nabuh Gamelan* (Book of instructions for playing gamelan; Komisi Pasinaon Nabuh Gamelan 1924), contains an introductory explanation of gamelan and notation of gendhing in the Western solfège system.

Despite the inclusion of gamelan musicians on the committee and the committee's statement that they used an earlier notation system invented by Wreksadiningrat,[84] the book follows a Western approach to notating and teaching gamelan, including the use of Western music terminology in Dutch and the use of bar lines (see figure 3.6).[85] Certainly this is a departure from the earlier notation system employed by Ki Gondapangrawit in the late nineteenth century and Djakoeb and Wignjaroemeksa. These authors employed neither bar lines nor spaces to separate basic metrical units (gatra). Kenong and gong strokes are their only important markers of musical phrases.

I mentioned earlier that Dutch-educated aristocrats had increasingly emphasized that gamelan had the same value as Western music. At this time the Javanese elite equated the high value (the adi luhung-ness) of the gamelan with the high status of Western art music, but this equation was superficial. The myth of Javanese arts as adi luhung was propagated only in a limited circle of Javanese society.

Dewantara felt deeply that Javanese arts and European arts were compatible, so he also discussed gamelan theory in Western musical terms. In his *Sari Swara* (1930:10) he explained gamelan modal practice (pathet) by using the analogy of the Western concept of the changing of keys (or the concept of movable *do*). He assigns the cipher 1 as the tonic or *dhasar* of each of the three pathet. In pathet nem, pitch 2 functions as the dhasar; in pathet sanga, 5 functions as dhasar; and in *pathet manyura,* 6 functions as dhasar.

Pathet nem	Pathet sanga	Pathet manyura
1, ji = gulu	1, ji = lima	1, ji = nem
2, ro = dhadha	2, ro = nem	2, ro = barang
3, lu = lima	3, lu = barang	3, lu = gulu
4, pat = nem	4, pat = gulu	4, pat = dhadha
5, ma = barang	5, ma = dhadha	5, ma = lima

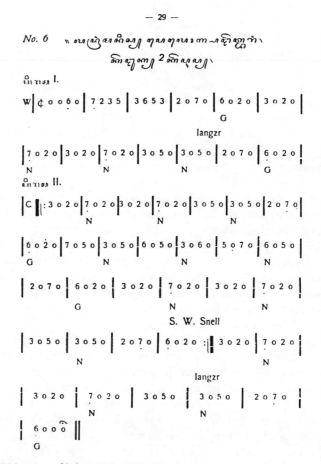

Figure 3.6 Notation of *ladrang* Manis (*Komisi Pasinaon Nabuh Gamelan ing Paheman Radyapustaka* 1924)

Furthermore, Dewantara thought of wirama as the equivalent of meter in Western music. He employed the meter 4/4 and illustrated his explanation with the hand gestures of a Western conductor and fractional durations appropriate to this meter (pp. 12–18). Using the time signature 4/4 and the Western concept of the changing of keys, he notated thirty-one songs of different genres of vocal music (pp. 23–124).

In a later publication, Dewantara (1941–48:2–8) confirmed that the Sari Swara system was adopted from a notation system created by Chevé. He said that his reason for adopting a Western notation system for gamelan was that the Javanese did not have an adequate notation system, and by borrowing a Western system of notation he could quickly establish one; that is, he would not have to go through many years of experimentation.

In the Sari Swara system, the cipher arrangement for the sléndro tuning system is 12345 (see figure 3.7). This differs from the already existing Kepatihan system in which the sléndro arrangement is 12356.

Furthermore, Dewantara suggested that the arrangement 1234567 used in the Kepatihan notation system for pélog was incorrect,[86] because pitch 4 was actually a half step higher than pitch 3 (1941–48:3), and pitch 7 was a half step lower than pitch 1. Thus, Dewantara was convinced that both the sléndro and pélog tuning systems had only five basic tones (*lima soeara yang pokok*).

Dewantara's proposal for Sari Swara notation drew heavy criticism from Poerbatjaraka (1941), a Surakarta intellectual, a lower-rank courtier, and a Dutch-educated scholar of Javanese literature. He objected to Dewantara's claim that the reason for adopting a European notation system was that gamelan did not have an adequate notation system. Poerbatjaraka felt that in Surakarta and Yogyakarta there were already notation systems that were adequate for learning gamelan (p. 289).

Poerbatjaraka's criticism centered on Dewantara's assigning of numbers to the gamelan tuning systems. I provide a translation of Poerbatjaraka's response to Dewantara, especially his elucidation of the relationship between sléndro and pélog ciphers.

> Ki Hadjar says that the big mistake of the Kepatihan system is that pitch 4 is skipped, but actually there is no sound that is skipped over. If we had only sléndro, there would perhaps be some truth to this statement; but we also have pélog, and pélog is older than sléndro. Therefore a discussion of Javanese gamelan must be based on pélog. In pélog, one octave consists of eight pitches [*sic*]. Pitch 1 (bem) and pitch 7 (barang) should be made parallel (not equal) to pitch 1 and 1̇ in sléndro. Thus, the comparison is as follows:

pélog	1	2	3	4	5	6	7
sléndro	1	2	3		5	6	1

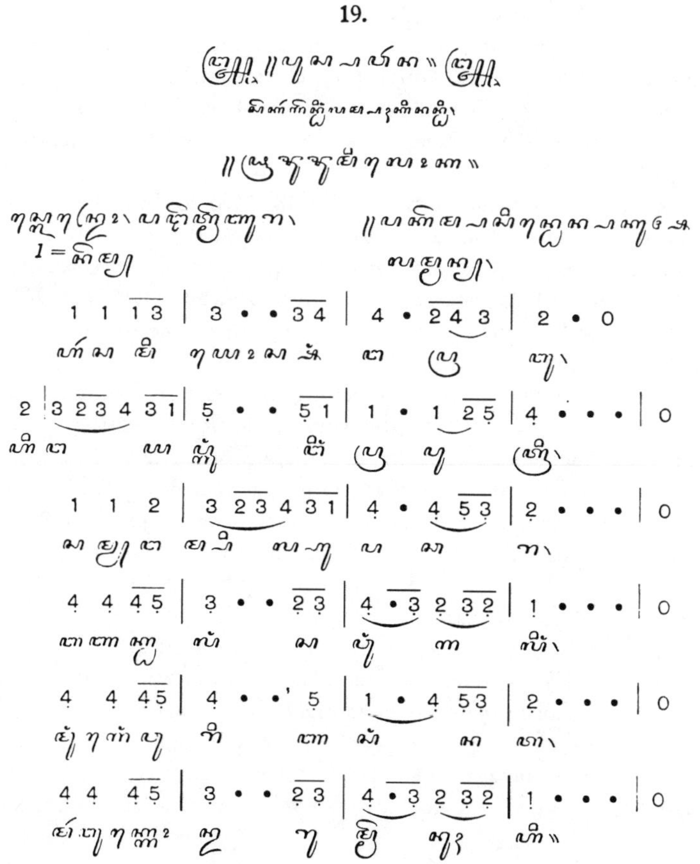

19.

1 1 1̄3̄ | 3 • • 3̄4̄ | 4 • 2̄4̄ 3 | 2 • 0

2 3̄ 2̄3̄ 4 3̄1̄ | 5̣ • • 5̄1̄ | 1 • 1 2̄5̄ | 4̇ • • • | 0

1 1 2 | 3 2̄3̄ 4 3̄1̄ | 4 • 4 5̄3̄ | 2̣ • • • | 0

4 4 4̄5̄ | 3 • • 2̣̄3̣̄ | 4 • 3̄ 2̣ 3̣̄2̣̄ | 1̣ • • • | 0

4̇ 4 4̄5̄ | 4 • •' 5 | 1 • 4 5̄3̄ | 2̣ • • • | 0

4 4 4̄5̄ | 3 • • 2̣̄3̣̄ | 4 • 3̄ 2̣ 3̣̄2̣̄ | 1̣ • • • | 0

Figure 3.7 Notation of Puspa Warna (Dewantara 1930)

Viewed from the perspective of pélog, it is clear that in sléndro there is a skipping of one key—key 4 has no comparable key in sléndro.

Moreover, if the arrangement of sléndro adopted in Sari Swara is 123451, then there is something odd about it, more odd than the omission of pitch 4. This is because lima [5] is the common name for pitch 4 in Sari Swara and nem [6] is the common name for pitch 5 in Sari Swara. About this Ki Hadjar says. . . : ". . . To combine the numerical order [in notation] with the ciphers used only as [common] names is to violate scientific rules." Based on this statement, I can say that Ki Hadjar has played around (*main komedi*) with words, as well as degraded science.[87] This is because the designation of the names lima and nem for these two pitches also has its appropriate place in the number sequence of pélog. This is a scientific observation that cannot be disputed. (1941:293)[88]

Dewantara and Poerbatjaraka used Western scientific thought in different ways. Dewantara attempted to apply Western music theory in his gamelan analysis. On the other hand, Poerbatjaraka applied Western scientific method in a historical approach, albeit speculatively.[89] Both of these Javanese intellectuals gave confused explanations in their discussions of musical practice. For example, although Dewantara was right in saying that pélog operates pentatonically, he is incorrect in saying that pitch 4 was a half step higher than pitch 3 and pitch 7 was a half-step lower than pitch 1. It would be more appropriate to think of a pélog system as consisting of more than one five-tone set. In Poerbatjaraka's elucidation of pélog ("one octave consists of 8 pitches"), the comparison with the numbering of sléndro ("Pitch 1 [bem] and pitch 7 [barang] should be made parallel, not equal, to pitch 1 and 1̇ in sléndro") is hard to understand. His claim that historically pélog is older than sléndro, and his theory that the gendèr originated in Gandhara (see note 89), are highly speculative. His attack on Dewantara and other intellectual noblemen was inspired by his increasing dissatisfaction "with the ossification of palace intellectual life" (Anderson 1984:213).[90]

Besides Sari Swara I, Dewantara also wrote a number of essays on gamelan. One of these essays was entitled *Wawaton Kawruh Gendhing Jawi* (The knowledge of Javanese gendhing). In 1936 this essay was transliterated into Latin script with the title *Kawruh Gendhing Jawa*. It had also been presented as a report (*preadvis*) on 12 December 1935 and again on 26 March 1956 at the "Parepatan Para Ahli Gendhing Jawi" (Meeting of experts on Javanese gendhing) in the hall of the Sana Budhaya museum in Yogyakarta.

With regard to gamelan theory, what is particularly pertinent in Dewantara's essay is the direct involvement of M. Ng. Najawirangka. As indicated by his name, Najawirangka was the maker of the keris sheath. But he was also known as a dhalang and a teacher of *pedhalangan* (the art of puppetry) with the name Atmatjendana. His book *Tuntunan Pedhalangan* (A guide to the art of puppetry) (1960) was widely known as a complete book of instruction on the art of dhalang. Its focus was on dramatic structure (including the narration and dialogue of one whole story), but a guide to techniques of movement and musical accompaniment was also included. As will be seen, Najawirangka had an insider's knowledge of gamelan.

In the meeting of gendhing experts mentioned above, Najawirangka was asked to respond to Dewantara's paper. He responded in "Tjentanganipun Mas Ngabehi Najawirangka" (The checkmarks of Mas Ngabehi Najawirangka) (1957). In this essay we learn the depth of Najawirangka's knowledge of gamelan. He states that his intent is first to select some of Dewantara's points and apply them to Solonese gamelan practice; second, to correct any mistakes; and third, to give explanations where necessary (p. 64).

In his essay, Dewantara proposes that irama determines how badly or well each gendhing is performed (pp. 64–65). Then he proposes two definitions of irama: irama are the formal structures of gendhing that can be grouped into three

categories: gendhing ageng (large gendhing), gendhing madya (medium gendhing), and gendhing alit (small gendhing) (p. 66). And irama also means tempo
(pp. 67–68).

Responding to these definitions, Najawirangka says that in practice irama is
lampah (course, action; p. 64). Najawirangka does not respond directly to Dewantara's first definition of irama; instead he lists several kinds of formal structure
that can be found in Solonese gamelan practice. Perhaps he does not see the
relevance of the formal structures of gendhing in defining irama. He does, however, respond at length to Dewantara's second definition of irama (or wirama):

> In wirama, what is fixed is the number of beats. For the tempi, musi-
> cians must practice expressiveness (ulat-ulatan). If there is no expressive-
> ness, a gendhing will be dead, dull, without enthusiasm or intensity of
> feeling. I will give you an example of [the playing of] gendhing Gambir
> Sawit. In Jogyakarta, the drumming is called Tjandra. Its [structure] is
> kethuk 2 kerep—three kenong [phrases] and then the fourth kenong
> is [coincides with the stroke of] gong. Each kenongan contains 16
> beats. [After the introduction] wirama should settle by the second ken-
> ong—after 32 beats. [The gendhing] should begin with fast wirama,
> then gradually slow down; it should be played steadily in three gongan.
> Then it should be gradually accelerated, a cue for [making the transi-
> tion to the] inggah. After arriving at the gong, wirama should settle
> (wirama 2 or 3 tjiblon). If suwuk (ending) is intended, the gendhing
> should speed up, then slow down [to the end]. The following is an
> illustration (1957:68–69):[91]

It is clear that Nayawirangka offers a more detailed and useful explanation of
irama than Dewantara. That is, irama refers not only to tempo but also to the
changing number of beats per gatra (the Javanese equivalent of "measure") or to
expanding the gatra to include one to four times as many beats. On the other
hand, Dewantara, who keeps his discussion general, interprets irama as the
tempo and formal structure of gendhing.

There are two points to be emphasized. First, until this time the content of
most of the texts remained at an introductory level. Thus, the theoretical con-

cepts used were rudimentary. Second, many of the authors were not active musicians. Djakoeb and Wignjaroemeksa (1913:6) state that to do research on many gendhing in preparing the book, they had to observe niyaga playing the gamelan. This seems to suggest that they were not themselves musicians. In the case of the Radyapustaka's Committee on Gamelan Instruction, perhaps Djatiswara, the music director of the European string ensemble of the court of Surakarta, was entrusted to write the committee's book on gamelan instruction. But though he was a musician in the European music ensemble, he was not a gamelan musician.

Raden Bagoes Soelardi was known as a painter. In fact, it was for his skill as an artist that Mangkunegara VII brought him to the Mangkunegaran from Wonogiri, the town where he was born and grew up (Quinn 1992:21–22). Mangkunegara VII appointed him painter, gamelan player, puppet maker, and teacher of the Javanese language. In other words, gamelan playing was only a small part of his assignment at the Mangkunegaran.

In short, most of the early theorists were court intellectuals whose musical experience was limited.[92] Their theories lack input from the musicians' perspectives of the subtlety and complexity of gamelan practice.

The Involvement of Musicians in the Formulation of Gamelan Theories

Ki Sindusawarno is an exception among the intellectuals interested in gamelan. First, he was not a high-ranking court intellectual. His interest in Javanese art and culture led him to become a member of the advisory committee for Taman Siswa and a good friend of Dewantara (Becker and Feinstein 1988:440–41). He was educated in engineering, though he did not complete his studies. At one time he was a teacher of mathematics (*ilmu pasti*) in a high school in Solo. Because of his interest in music, he discussed gamelan with both Javanese and Dutch intellectuals, and read their works. As one of the founders of the gamelan conservatory KOKAR in 1950, he was a strong supporter of gamelan research and education. He worked closely with the members of the "staff"[93] and teachers at the school, who were mostly court musicians. He also became the head of the research department at KOKAR and a teacher of Ilmu Karawitan (Theory of karawitan).[94] My point is that he had ample opportunity to communicate with gamelan players and tembang singers. Moreover, he also discussed his research with Balinese and Sundanese musicians who were in residence at the school.[95]

Sindusawarno's career was very different from that of other gamelan theorists. Writing and teaching gamelan theory became his profession. The success of his independent study of Indonesian gamelan earned him the title *Ki* before his name, an honorific given to a highly esteemed person because of his expertise in a particular field.

His most important work, which was intended as a textbook for his students at the gamelan conservatory, is *Ilmu Karawitan* (Theory of karawitan), volume 1 (1987). Although it is largely about Javanese gamelan, the book also discusses Balinese and Sundanese gamelan. Sindusawarno sheds much new light on gamelan performance practice, especially irama (tempo and density level) and lagu (melody). I believe that he gained his deep knowledge from his interaction with gamelan players of the staff division at the gamelan conservatory when he was head of its research division.

Like his contemporaries, Sindusawarno briefly discusses many aspects of gamelan practice. His treatment of melody clarifies the practice of the gamelan. He was aware of the importance of examining all aspects of melody: laras (tuning system), pathet (modal practice), *jenis-lagu* (gendhing forms), *padhang-ulihan* (question-answer melodic phrases), irama (tempo and density levels), cèngkok (melodic pattern), *luk* (vocal ornament), and wilet (ornamentation) (1984:46). Although his book is short on detailed discussion of these elements and on musical examples, he presents a wider scope toward understanding gamelan melody.

In some of his discussion, Sindusawarno reflects on the characteristics of Western gamelan scholarship at the time. He was familiar with the work of the Dutch scholars Jaap Kunst and J. S. Brandts Buys (Sindusawarno 1960:58) and the American ethnomusicologist Mantle Hood (Hood 1988:14–15).[96] Sindusawarno's discussion of laras and pathet conforms to the pattern of gamelan scholarship provided by Western scholars such as Kunst and Hood. In his unpublished *Ilmu Karawitan*, volume 2, he discusses *teori kempyung tiup* (the blown fifth theory of Hornbostel), a theory of the derivation of the sléndro and pélog tuning systems. He (n.d.:7–9) also discusses what he claims to be a Chinese *teori kempyung-kawat* (a theory of tone systems produced by a series of divisions of a monochord) and the theory of his colleague, Hardjosubroto, of the relationship between the Western diatonic and sléndro-pélog tuning systems. He provides the following chart as a comparison of the various systems (p. 8).

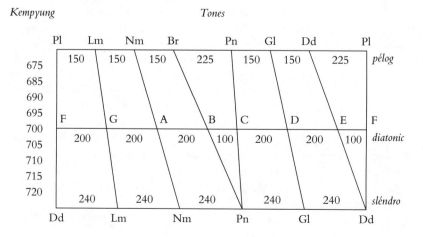

Sindusawarno, like Kunst and Hood, discusses each pathet as a type of scale. He identifies each pathet according to the level of the functions of the tones in the scale. The relationship of each functional tone between pathet is one kempyung. In this way he neatly associates kempyung as a function of laras and kempyung as a determinant of the tones in each pathet. The following is Sindusawarno's diagram of pathet in sléndro (ibid. 11).

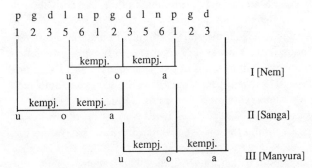

In this diagram, the vowels *o, u,* and *a* are abbreviations of *dong, dung, dang.* According to Sindusawarno, the complete series of syllables *dong, dung, dang, dèng,* and *ding* describes a descending order of weight of sounds, from the heaviest to the lightest sound. Hence, these syllables are used to label a hierarchy of the functions of the tones in each pathet system. *Dong* is the most important tone in a pathet, equivalent to the tonic in Western music. *Dung* is the second in importance, equivalent to the dominant. And *Dang* is the third in importance, equivalent to the subdominant.

In short, Sindusawarno became a specialist in the study of gamelan. His interactions with European and American scholars and his familiarity with gamelan scholarship (both indigenous and non-indigenous) gave him a broad perspective for his work on gamelan. His relationships with Balinese and Sundanese musicians in the gamelan conservatory enabled him to relate Javanese gamelan to the other two gamelan traditions, and his intimate interaction with Javanese gamelan musicians, the members of the staff division at the gamelan conservatory when he was the head of the research department, enabled him to shed more light on gamelan performance practice.

In the 1960s, R. L. Martopangrawit, a gamelan musician and composer, became directly involved in gamelan scholarship. Like Sindusawarno, Martopangrawit was not an elite intellectual. But he was a member of the family of a court musician. Because of lack of funds, his education in the Dutch school ended when he was thirteen years old (Hatch 1979:14).[98] Subsequently, Martopangrawit became a musician in the Surakarta court. When the gamelan conservatory was founded in 1950, he was appointed a member of the staff division of the school. He worked with Sindusawarno and other members of the staff division. His relationship with Sindusawarno encouraged him to write on gamelan theory and practice.[99] His first monograph, *Tetembangan: Vocaal Jang Berhubungan Dengan Karawitan* (Tetembangan: Singing which is related to gamelan), was published in 1967, two years after he was appointed lecturer at the gamelan academy (ASKI). In the following decade he wrote a number of books and monographs. His most important theoretical work is in his two-volume *Catatan-Catatan Pengetahuan Karawitan* (Notes on the knowledge of gamelan music; 1969–72).

There is no question that Martopangrawit attempted a thorough and substantive elucidation of gamelan practice. He acknowledges (1984:9) that his work is based on *praktek* (musical practice). Some of his introductory material, however, is similar to that in Sindusawarno's works. For example, both explain the function of instruments in the gamelan in terms of two basic ingredients: irama and lagu (Sindusawarno 1987:315; Martopangrawit 1984:12–13). They both recognize the difference between *laya* (tempo) and irama (density level).

What is especially useful about Martopangrawit's work is his discussion of cèngkok, and in particular his illustration of cèngkok (melodic patterns) for the gendèr (pp. 99–120). He also discusses pathet at length (pp. 45–98). He discusses not only scalar aspects of pathet, but melodic aspects, such as the role of gendèr cèngkok[100] and "modus" (scale degrees) contained in the rebab melody (1984:132–169).[101]

Martopangrawit's work exemplifies a kind of advanced gamelan theory written largely from the musician's point of view. The interdependence of music theory and musical experience is essential in musicology. This means that theorizing and music-making must go hand in hand. Martopangrawit represents this approach, and the generation of Indonesian musicologists after him follow it as well.

To summarize: Javanese contact with Western modes of thought, directly or indirectly, has consistently fostered the development of gamelan theory written by Javanese. And just as significantly, contacts with gamelan musicians determined the musical content of the theory. In order to fully understand the history of gamelan theory, one should see it in the context of interaction between the Indonesian and Western intellectuals. This interaction is continuing; a number of contemporary Indonesian gamelan theorists have graduated from European or American universities.

To what extent have Western concepts helped to elucidate indigenous concepts of gamelan, and to what extent have they been responsible for the misinterpretation of indigenous concepts? These are important questions I address in the discussion below.

In Search of the Origins and Significance of Balungan

It is clear that Dutch scholars initiated the scholarly study of gamelan. Their work is widely recognized by both Western and Indonesian theorists and has had an important influence on later theories of gamelan.

Among Dutch scholars of Indonesian music, Jaap Kunst is the most noted. His numerous works on the theory, history, and practice of Javanese music inspired many later works on gamelan.[102] As a musicologist and an official of the Dutch colonial government, he spent fifteen years in Indonesia (1920–1935). He wrote a large body of literature on the theory, practice, and history of gamelan in which he combines his own perspective with the perspectives of his Javanese informants. In classifying gamelan instruments according to their musical functions, he proposes:

> Such a great princely gamelan is apt to confound the listener who hears and sees it for the first time: the grouping of the orchestra and the manner of playing the instruments appear completely arbitrary, and only gradually does one become aware that each instrument actually performs its own fixed task within the ensemble. Little by little, one learns to distinguish:
> a. cantus firmus (nuclear theme)-instruments;
> b. interpunctuating (colotomic) instruments;[103]
> c. instruments playing a more or less independent counter-melody;[104]
> d. paraphrasing instruments,[105] and
> e. agogic instruments.[106]
> Those under *d,* the so-called *panerusan,* may, again, be subdivided into instruments that keep fairly closely to the nuclear theme, and those which, more especially, supply the variations to the theme, and are responsible for the actual filling and ornamentation (*(sa)sekaran;* L.J.: *(ka)kembangan*) of the framework of the said nuclear theme (*balunganing gending* (S.), *mlampah* (J.)). The latter of the two types of instruments are generally indicated by the name of *(h)isènan* (= "filling-in" instruments). (1973, 1:247–48)

Earlier writers had used the terms "theme" (Land 1890) and "cantus firmus" (Soerjo Poetro 1919–20:381). Kunst may have followed them in using these terms. In any event, when Kunst uses the term "cantus firmus," he has European music very much in mind. Associated with twelfth- to fourteenth-century polyphonic music, the term "cantus firmus" refers to a preexistent melody which is used as the basis for creating other melodic layers (Randel 1986:135).[107] Similarly in gamelan, according to Jaap Kunst, the cantus firmus or nuclear theme (i.e., Jaap Kunst's translation and interpretation of the Javanese term balunganing gendhing, the skeleton or melodic outline of a gamelan composition) is the basis on which other instruments construct their melodies.[108] Slenthem, demung, and saron are the instruments entrusted with the cantus firmus or nuclear theme.

Kunst acknowledges that his system of classification is not perfect. He says: "It is not, in all compositions, invariably the same instruments that come under the different categories enumerated above" (1973, 1:248). But he also emphasizes that "it is possible to associate some principal function with nearly every instrument" (ibid.).

To what extent Kunst based his findings on the opinions of the musicians is unclear.[109] It is clear, however, that he acknowledged the help of the following: First he thanked Mangkunegara VII for "his valuable collaboration and cordial hospitality; whose *niyaga's* and *gamelans* were ever standing in readiness," who had "been kind enough to go to the trouble of reading through critically the paragraphs dealing with Java Proper, and making marginal notes and corrections where necessary" (Kunst 1973, 1:xii). He had also received information from Dr. Purbacharaka (see above) and his brother Raden Kodrat, referring to them as "connoisseurs, the former of the old and new Javanese languages, the latter gamelan, wayang, and dance" (ibid.). For the Yogyanese gamelan he had received information from Raden Mas Jayadipura, whom he referred to as "a Jogya artist" (p. xiii); elsewhere he calls him "the musical expert" (p. 161).[110]

On his classification system specifically, he makes direct reference to the work of the former regent of Temanggung, R. A. A. Tjakrahadikusuma, who submitted a treatise to the 1923 competition. Using batik cloth as an analogy, he classifies gamelan instruments into two groups: *kalowongan* (outlines)—gong, kenong, kethuk, kempul, and demung; and *plataran* (background) or *isèn-isèn* (filling-in)—the instruments remaining (Kunst 1973, 1:248). He may also have had in mind Soelardi's classification (1918:16–18). (For details of Soelardi's classification, see below.) As an indication, Kunst uses the word *baku* as another term for balungan. The term baku swara was used by Soelardi to refer to the balungan. In other contexts, Kunst also often refers to Soelardi's work.

For several decades, many gamelan studies have followed Kunst's theory in examining the melodic organization of the gamelan ensemble. Recent studies of gamelan have questioned the validity of Kunst's system of classification and its wider implications for the study of gendhing (McDermott and Sumarsam 1975; Sumarsam 1975, 1976; J. Becker 1980; Hatch 1980).[111] In particular, the role of cantus firmus, nuclear theme, or balungan as providing a basis for the melodies of other instruments has been discredited. Balungan itself has been redefined.[112] My questions are now: First, when was the term and concept of balungan introduced and developed to mean the principal melody of a gendhing? Second, what might we learn about the concept of gendhing from the nineteenth-century treatises which Jaap Kunst often uses as references in the formation of his theory?

Let us return to a nineteenth-century poetic work, the *Serat Centhini*, which I discussed in the earlier chapters. Elaborate melody, the intricate network of instruments in the ensemble, performance technique, and style are described and implied in the poem. Is the term balungan or balunganing gendhing ever used in the *Serat Centhini*? It is not. Moreover, terms equivalent in meaning to balungan were not suggested by the poets.

In addition, two other nineteenth-century Javanese treatises on gamelan and other related arts, Kusumadilaga's *Serat Sastramiruda* (mid nineteenth century) and Tondhakusuma's *Serat Gulang Yarya* (1870), do not employ the term balungan either. The term also is furthermore not present in the important work of two Dutch scholars of the time, Groneman (1890) or its introduction, Land (1890).

I do not mean to say, however, that the concept of melodic abstraction of a gendhing did not exist in the nineteenth century or before. What I am arguing is that the concept of melodic abstraction was misinterpreted, and thus the term balungan, which means the melodic theme of a gendhing, was born.

Jennifer Lindsay has also searched for the origin of the notion of melodic theme in gendhing. She suggests convincingly that the introduction of the idea was the result of the gradual development of gamelan notation from the late nineteenth century onward. (For her excellent treatment of this subject, see Lindsay 1985:193–216).

As far as I know, the term balungan was first used by Djakoeb and Wignjaroemeksa (1913). They used the term as if it were of little importance. In the entire book, babalunganing gendhing is mentioned only once, in the first chapter, "Prakara nabuh gamelan" (About the playing of gamelan). After a brief explanation of the aesthetic concept of gendhing and the instrumentation of an ensemble, the authors write:

> If you want to learn to play gamelan and also to know by heart the entire babalunganing gendhing, you should first know the physical characteristics and names of gamelan instruments on which it can be learnt, such as: slenthem, demung, saron barung, and so forth (p. 6).[113]

This passage implies that the term babalunganing gendhing refers to the melody played by the slenthem, demung, and saron barung. The fact that the rest of the chapter is devoted to a discussion of the instrument slenthem, including the names of its pitches in each tuning system, the numbering of the keys, etc., indicates that the true intention of the authors is to associate the term babalunganing gendhing with this instrument. Does this insignificant mention of balungan indicate that the term was commonly understood by musicians? Or, was the term and meaning of balungan uncommon at that time? As I will show below, there is evidence for the latter conclusion.

In 1919 the authors published another book, *Serat Enut Gendhing Sléndro* (The notation of sléndro gendhing). It is a collection of the notation of 127 gendhing in sléndro, with a brief introduction. In this book the term babalunganing gendhing is never used.

With regard to notation, it is worth noting that Djakoeb and Wignjaroemeksa emphasize that it is only used to make learning gamelan easier:

> After knowing the physical appearance of the keys, their sounds [suwara] or their individual tunings [laras], then the students are allowed

to begin learning to play. However, for the beginner, in order to make learning gamelan easier, they should use notation. (1913:15)[114]

The next use of the term balungan is by Raden Bagoes Soelardi in his *Serat Pradongga* (1918). Unlike Djakoeb and Wignjaroemeksa, Soelardi explains the term balungan in greater detail. Furthermore, he is the first Javanese theorist to propose the classification of instruments according to their musical function. I will discuss Soelardi's system of classification later. But in regard to his use of the term balungan, he says:

> The rules of playing demung or slenthem: The rule for a demung or slenthem player is that he must validate balunganing gendhing in the form of ordering of the gendhing [in] notation, since that [balunganing gendhing] is the principal element of the gendhing (like the body of a gendhing). (Ibid. 17)[115]

Soelardi makes a point of emphasizing balunganing gendhing as "the principal element of the gendhing" or "the body of a gendhing," and the notation (*enut*) as a codification of these concepts. He also makes his intention clear about notating gendhing:

> For the readers, in order to know the cèngkok of a gendhing and to make it easy for them to learn [gamelan], I give directions for gendhing with numbers, which is called baku swara (the principal sound). I will shed light on only a few commonly known gendhing. In order to make it easy for anyone who is learning [to play gamelan], the baku swara of the demung [is provided]. (Soelardi 1918:18)[116]

From Soelardi's statement it is clear that balunganing gendhing is the most important part of a gendhing (baku swara). Furthermore, this part should be notated to make it easier for people to learn gamelan. Soelardi defines the term balungan more clearly than Djakoeb and Wignjaroemeksa do. As I mentioned earlier, Djakoeb and Wignjaroemeksa (1913, 1919) use the term babalunganing gendhing only once, and they never explain its significance. We should thus question whether the term is basic to the concept of gendhing. This is because we do not know if it was in common use by musicians or if it was newly invented by Djakoeb and Wignjaroemeksa or Soelardi. Doubt concerning the general use of the term balungan is somewhat strengthened by the fact that in a subsequent publication on gamelan, *Buku Piwulang Nabuh Gamelan* (Komisi Pasinaon Nabuh Gamelan . . . 1924), by the committee of gamelan instruction of the museum of Radyapustaka, the term is still missing. Since well-known musicians were on the committee—M. Ng. Lebdapradongga and M. Ng. Atmamardawa (who was later known as R. T. Warsadiningrat, a leader of the gamelan ensembles of the court of Surakarta)—the absence of the term in the work of the committee suggests it was rarely used by musicians. R. T. Wasitodipura (pers.

comm., 1989), who studied during this period with M. Ng. Atmamardawa, says that he never heard his teacher or other musicians use the term.[117]

So far we have not found a reason for the emergence of the term balungan in the practice of gendhing. By the beginning of the twentieth century, some Javanese intellectuals felt a need to elucidate the principles of their music, either as a guide to learning gamelan or simply to describe musical practice. This need had a precedent in the late nineteenth century, for example in the work of Raden Mas Harya Tondhakusuma, which I discussed earlier. But his work does not contain the kind of rudimentary discussion of gamelan that is found in the works of Djakoeb and Wignjaroemeksa and those of Soelardi. Tondhakusuma's *Serat Gulang Yarya* is also a work of belletristic literature.

There is a basic description of gamelan practice that did exist in the late nineteenth century, however; namely, J. Groneman (1890), *De Gamelan te Jogjakarta.* A Dutch physician who worked at the court of Yogyakarta, Groneman was interested in Javanese arts and ceremonies (Lindsay 1985:7–8). J. P. N. Land, who wrote the introduction, although he never visited Java, was interested in Javanese music. He was familiar with literature on Javanese music and Javanese art written by European intellectuals. On a few occasions, he had an opportunity to hear gamelan played in the Netherlands (Groneman 1890:1–2).

As I mentioned earlier, in describing the musical functions of gamelan instruments J. P. N. Land uses terms such as "theme" for the saron family, "punctuation" for the kethuk, kempul, kenong, and gong, and "figuration" for the other instruments. Explaining the realization of ladrang Girang-Girang, he says:

> The piece opened with a phrase of eight notes, which were answered with the statement of the first note repeatedly, and with a phrase of the same length. This introduction was carried out by the middle-range *bonang,* strengthened in an octave playing by *gendèr* and *gambang;* at the end-note, then falls the consolidation in the low range, the first stroke of *gong.* The theme itself is now taken up by all the strong instruments, with figuration in the high[-range] instruments and a statement in the low-range *bonang,* and is interpunctuated by *kethuk, kempul, kenong,* and *gong;* we hear the first half three times, and the second once; thus, in the whole the first division consists of 4 × 8 notes of the theme. They are repeated up to the third *gong*-stroke. The *saron* part in the second division has the same theme, but with rhythmic variations; meanwhile the figuration of the middle-range *bonang* and the low-range *bonang* are likewise accompanying accordingly. (Land 1890:17)[118]

Did Djakoeb, Wignjaroemeksa, or Soelardi know the works of Land and Groneman? Were these Javanese authors' writings inspired by the works of the Dutch intellectuals? The absence of information about Djakoeb and Wignjaroemeksa prevents us from answering these questions. But it seems likely that Soelardi was familiar with the writing of the Dutch scholars, since he was interested not only in the performing arts, but also in linguistic and cultural study in general. Nonetheless, it is difficult to determine conclusively whether the writings of Land and Groneman inspired Soelardi's works, although such a possibility cannot be ruled out. At any rate, by early in the twentieth century the terms "theme" and "cantus firmus" [119] (in writings on gamelan in Dutch) and rarely balungan (in Javanese writings) were used to refer to the parts played on the slenthem, demung, and saron barung.

Shortly after the publication of *Buku Piwulang Nabuh Gamelan* (Komisi Pasinaon Nabuh Gamelan . . . 1924) by the gamelan instruction committee of the museum of Radyapustaka, the term balungan (i.e., ambalung, mbalung, babalunging gendhing) appeared again in *Titi Asri* (1925:28–29, 30, 32). The book was written by Sapardal Hardosoekarto with the help of Mas Ngabèhi Mlayadimeja (a court musician of Surakarta with the rank of mantri) and Kyai Demang Gunasentika II (a court musician of Surakarta with the rank of panèwu). Written in macapat poetic meters, the *Titi Asri* is a compendium of knowledge about gamelan, its mythical history, its theory, and its practice. *Mbalung* is used in this passage:

> Cautious [treatment] of gendhing accomplishes
> a sturdy and firm [performance],
> one that provides support for the cèngkok.
> Attention to the saron adds to the beauty.
> It becomes a leader,
> like the demung.
>
> The meaning of demung is "the guide to order,"
> the support structure of the cèngkok,
> which when unfolded, contains the wiled,
> the guide to all, which refers to
> [any instrument] that has one mallet.
> The gendhing is *ambalung* (played in its melodic skeleton). [120]
> (*Titi Asri* 1925:28–29)

Like Soelardi's *Serat Pradongga,* the *Titi Asri* refers to the demung as a lead instrument (*kang dadya pangarsi*) that provides support (*uger-uger*) for the cèngkok of a gendhing. At the time of the *Titi Asri,* the terms mbalung, ambalung, and babalunganing gendhing were not yet common; but during the 1930s, the concept of balungan as a melodic entity that is used as the basis for the working out of gendhing became an integral part of writing about gamelan. The extent of its use among musicians is difficult to estimate. It seems clear, however, that one of the initial purposes for using it, namely as an aid in learning gamelan, remains intact. As Dewantara (see above) makes clear in a section "Titi wirama lan titi laras" (The order of time and tone) in *Wawaton Kawruh Gendhing Jawi* (1936):

> In order to present thoroughly each of the gendhing or songs, and also
> as a device to ease the learning of the notation, it is necessary to create

a notation for the melody (lagu) or gendhing whose criteria are as follows:

a. It must put in the form of gatra the skeleton (balunganing) of time and melody: that is, in the form of the ordering of tones and of time, which only illustrates the principle. (1936:47)[121]

From 1935 to 1939 Mas Ngabèhi Wirawiyaga, a court musician of Surakarta with the rank of mantri of the Kadipatèn musicians, wrote a three-volume manual on learning gamelan and vocal music, entitled *Serat Lagu Jawi* (The book of Javanese melody) (1935,1936,1937). Wignyabongsapatra (1939) wrote the fourth volume. In 1939, Wirawiyaga wrote another book with the title *Serat Mardu Swara* (The essence of sound). Wirawiyaga's and Wignyabongsapatra's works contain notations of vocal music and gendhing.

In his volumes, Wirawiyaga used the term balungan in his preface to volume 3 in a sentence *laguning gérongan dalah balunganing gendhingipun* (the melody of gérongan and the balungan of its gendhing).[122] And the titles of the musical examples of sekar macapat, he always begins with the word balunganipun: for example, "Balunganipun Sekar Maskumambang, Raras Pl. [Pélog] Pathet 6 [Nem]."

The *Serat Mardu Swara* uses and explains the already common usage of the term balunganing gendhing. In the preface Wirawiyaga remarks that

> The notation = *Noot* [Dutch for notation], which is used to give numbers to the sound of the balungan of a gendhing, is already common, and can easily be applied to the playing of all gamelan instruments and to the melody of song. Furthermore, its arrangement is flexible, without being too broad; I will explain the details of the duration of sound and the setting of meter (*maatstrip*), measuring the length and shortness of the sound. (Wirawiyaga 1939:i–ii.)[123]

We have seen a few reasons for the introduction and use of the term balungan. From the late nineteenth century to the early part of the twentieth century, a certain kind of intellectual climate provided the setting for the discussion of and writing about gamelan practice. This intellectual atmosphere was characterized by interaction between Dutch intellectuals and learned Javanese noblemen and leading artists.

In this intellectual climate, a need was felt to explain the rudiments of gamelan. Gamelan musicians and European and Javanese theorists felt compelled to write manuals for teaching and describing gamelan. The introduction of the term balungan followed soon after the introduction of notation. Consequently, a fixed idea of the medium density, the most easily represented line of the multilayer gamelan texture—the saron part—was notated and designated as the theme, cantus firmus, nuclear theme, or balungan of the gendhing.[124] This was the result of three factors: first, the initial process of theorizing about gamelan; second, the development of manuals on teaching gamelan; and last, the adoption

and use of notation. These three processes combined brought about the promi-
nence of the term and the concept of balungan or balunganing gendhing.[125]

A historical account of balungan weakens and even contradicts the centrality
of the role of balungan as it is commonly understood by many contemporary
gamelan theorists. For example, Supanggah (1988:9) in his article on balungan,
concludes that:

> The balungan gendhing is an important—if not, indeed, the most
> important—factor in the practice of karawitan, because as the frame-
> work of the gendhing it gives a composition its basic shape, and is used
> as a frame of reference and point of departure for the playing of the
> gamelan instruments [menggarap].

This same stance is also commonly adopted by Western gamelan theorists:

> Because of the balungan's special significance and because other parts
> are implied by the configuration of the balungan, it is justifiable to
> discuss Javanese compositions with reference to this one central part.
> (Sutton 1993:26)

But neither Supanggah nor Sutton really takes a strong stand on the centrality
of balungan. Sutton uses the word "implied" rather than "prescribed" in describing balungan as the basis of composition.[126] Supanggah suggests that only
gamelan students who learn from balungan notation think of a balungan as a
pre-existent melody that is the basis for working out the melody of each instrument (1986:6). He suggests that pangrawit (traditional gamelan musicians), on
the other hand, who learned gamelan aurally, conceive of gendhing in relation
to the sound of the entire ensemble.[127]

In his fifteen rules for composing gendhing, only once does Martopangrawit
use the word balungan and state what the composer should know about it:

> 12. You must be able to change the style of the *balungan*—for instance
> from *balungan mlaku* to *balungan nibani,* or to *balungan ngadhal,* and back
> again—so that the atmosphere of the gendhing can be manipulated.
> (Translated by Martin Hatch, in J. Becker and Feinstein 1984:228)[128]

Martopangrawit does not explain the relationship between balungan and other
parts of the ensemble. Instead he indicates that the variants of balungan should
be known and used by the composer to create a dynamic (i.e., changing in
mood) gendhing.

Balungan was not originally a musical term. It derives from the root word
balung, "bone." The suffix *-an* creates the meaning of "frame," which commonly refers to the skeleton of a house (*balungan omah*). But it can also mean the
outline of a story (i.e., *balunganing crita*). Both meanings are given in Gericke and
Roorda's *Javaansch-Nederlandsch Handwoordenboek* (1901:730). Other meanings

of *balungan* from this dictionary are the muscularity (of a lion) and the sketch or outline (of the main content of a work).[129] The point here is that in Gericke and Roorda's dictionary the term *balungan* is not yet associated with gamelan terminology. In fact, even in a dictionary published in 1939, the *Baoesastra Djawa* by Poerwadarminta, the term still is not related to gamelan practice.

Historically, the term and concept of balungan arose as a consequence of the need for a shorthand elucidation of gendhing. Its use in this capacity occurred shortly after the introduction of notation and gamelan theory in the late nineteenth century. Thus, the term emerged from a combination of both indigenous and non-indigenous perspectives on gamelan. Since the turn of the century, balungan has gradually been accepted as an "indigenous" aspect of gendhing. Although contemporary gamelan theorists still acknowledge the centrality of balungan, their stands on this issue have become somewhat less emphatic.

Future research should consider balungan as having the same status as other melodic parts in the ensemble (yet having a distinctive function). Balungan should be understood not so much as the central part of gendhing but rather as a useful *reference* for learning a gendhing.

Classification Systems of Gamelan Instruments

Since terms other than balungan are also used to describe the musical function of other gamelan instruments, we can extend our terminological discussion to include all these others. Particularly, I will discuss how gamelan theorists choose a coherent cluster of terms that signify the total sound of the ensemble.

As I noted earlier, Djakoeb and Wignjaroemeksa were the first theorists to use the term balungan, albeit in a minor way. Subsequently, Soelardi used it and clearly stated his position on the central role of the term. Furthermore, it is in his work that a classification of instruments according to their musical functions appeared for the first time. In the section "Bab Ugering Tatabuhanipun Gongsa" (About the rules for gamelan playing) from his *Serat Pradongga,* Soelardi divides gamelan instruments into five groups (1918:16–18):

1. Kendhang has the function of restraining the tempi (*tetalining wirama*) of all instruments. It is like the breath (*napas*) of a gendhing.
2. Demung or slenthem is entrusted to play the balungan of a gendhing (balunganing gendhing).
3. Rebab must be competent in the treatment of the melody of a gendhing, since it is the guide of the pesindhèn and gendhing. It is analogous to the feeling of a gendhing.
4. Kethuk, kenong, kempul, *kemong,* kempyang, and gong have the function of counting (*wiwicalan*) or marking (*tetenger*) in the different types of gendhing. They give clues to the character (*wateking*) of a gendhing. They must care for and make others aware of the wirama of a gendhing.

5. Gendèr, [gendèr] panerus, gambang, celempung, saron, suling, bonang, and bonang panerus, are responsible for the ornaments (*rerengganing*) of a gendhing. They are like the clothing (*sandhanganing*) of
a gendhing.[130]

What we find used as headings in this classification system is essentially a
cluster of terms that are barely related to each other (i.e., breath, skeleton, ornament or clothing, feeling, counter or marker). In other words, the terms to be
used for classifying the instruments derive from different fields: "breath" and
"feeling" are part of the human condition; "skeleton" is the framework of a
being or object; "ornament" signifies artistic decoration; "clothing" refers to
human dress; and wicalan is a mathematical expression.

Jaap Kunst's classification is similar in character. In translating the term balungan, he begins with the Western music term "cantus firmus." He then gives
"nuclear theme" as its synonym. "Nuclear" or "nucleus" is a term that is commonly used in physics or biology, referring to anything constituting a central
part, a basis, or a kernel from which other parts develop or grow or around which
they circle. Other classification terms Jaap Kunst uses, such as "paraphrase," "in-
terpunctuating," and "colotomy" are the property of discourse on language, or
simply invented. Still others, such as "agogic" and "counter-melody," are musical terms.[131]

I am not suggesting that borrowing terms from other disciplines or fields of
study is necessarily a bad thing. In fact, as Seeger reminds us, creating analogies
or metaphors is an important part of the process of inventing a theory. It is worth
noting, however, that as the study of gamelan advanced, instrument classification
systems became more focused on musical terminology. Examples of these are the
systems invented and developed by Ki Sindusawarno and R. L. Martopangrawit.
Both of these theorists used the terms lagu and irama as two primary headings in
their instrumental groupings. Lagu instruments pertain to pitch aspects, while
irama instruments are concerned with temporal features of gendhing. Each of
these categories is subdivided into two functional groups: supervisors (*pamurba*)
and supporters (*pamangku*). Thus, pamurba lagu are instruments whose function
is to supervise the pitch elements of the gendhing. In accordance with the genre
of gendhing being played, the instrument in this category is either the rebab or
the bonang barung. Pamangku lagu are instruments whose function is to support
or realize pitch aspects of the gendhing. Instruments in this category are the
gendèr (i.e., gendèr barung and panerus), gambang, bonang (i.e., bonang barung
and panerus), saron (i.e., slenthem, demung, saron barung, and saron panerus),
celempung, suling, and the vocalists (pesindhèn and gérong). Pamurba irama are
instruments whose function is to supervise the temporal elements of gendhing.
Instruments in this category are kendhang. Pamangku irama are instruments
whose function is supporting or conveying temporal elements of gendhing. This
category includes gong, kenong, kempul, and kethuk kempyang.

This classification may be interpreted in two ways. First, it seems clear that lagu simply means pitch contour melody: a single melody played by any one of the instruments or sung by any one of the singers can be called lagu. On the other hand, on a more conceptual level this classification presents the word lagu as an intangible phenomenon. This happens when pamurba or pamangku is attached to it. By stating that each instrument or group of instruments either supervises (*murba*) or supports the realization (*mangku*) of lagu, this means, as Hatch has pointed out: "No one instrument is a performer of *lagu*. indeed, all *lagu*-oriented instruments perform a role vis-a-vis *lagu*" (1980:170 n. 16).

It may be instructive to examine the terminology used in the nineteenth-century literature on gamelan. In spite of the common use of the term lagu by present-day gamelan theorists, *Serat Centhini* descriptions of playing gendhing do not use the term, even when the authors describe the melody of a single instrument (such as a rebab or gendèr). Instead, the authors consistently use the terms cèngkok and wilet (two important terms which I will return to later). As for the word lagu or lagon, the poets reserve it exclusively for describing the terbang music ensembles, referring either to the unaccompanied singing of poetry as the introduction to a composition (bawa) or the singing by a soloist or chorus of the main composition. The *Serat Centhini* also uses the term lagon as a synonym for pathetan, the song of the dhalang which is accompanied by a few instruments in the gamelan ensemble.

It is possible that the *Serat Centhini* avoids the term lagu in its description of the playing of gamelan gendhing because the melody of a gendhing is expressed in a variety of ways by different instruments. In other words, the *Serat Centhini* recognizes the melodic plurality of the gendhing by avoiding the use of the word lagu. For this reason, the poets prefer to use the term lagu or lagon to refer specifically to a clearly defined melody in vocal music.

This definition of lagu is presented unambiguously by Tondhakusuma in his *Serat Gulang Yarya*. Contrasting the terms cèngkok and lagu, Tondhakusuma says: "lagu is contained in the sung poetry (sekar), cèngkok is contained in gendhing." (1870:12).[132] (Later I will discuss the complexity of the concept of cèngkok.)

As with any other classification system, the classifications of the gamelan instruments discussed above emphasize conciseness. In order to fully understand such a classification, a supplementary explanation is necessary. Conciseness also creates problems for the category of irama instruments, because irama has different meanings depending on the context.

The *Serat Centhini* often describes the irama of a gendhing as tempo. In this poem, the words "accelerating" (*neseg*) or "slackening" (*ngandhelong*) are often used to describe irama.[133] Tondhakusuma (1870:7) describes the practice of irama as contained in the word "*kiramanggèn*" (an abbreviation of "*kira-kira amanggèn*" [approximate location]). He explains that irama means "to approximate the steadiness of the lapses or intervals." [134] It seems that he includes both temporal flow and temporal density of the music under irama (see below). Jaap Kunst's accounts of irama (1973, 1:334–35) do not contain any new information beyond what was commonly known before his time (i.e., irama as tempo), as his list of different irama indicates. [135]

Actually, the concept of irama consists of two aspects: the rate of temporal flow and temporal density. [136] Temporal density is the primary factor in irama. It is a process in which time-space in the structure of a gendhing is being contracted or expanded. A contraction of time-space means a decrease in the number of pulsations (i.e., temporal density) of certain instruments; and an expansion means an increase in the number of pulsations. As mentioned earlier, such a definition of irama was first explained by R. Ng. Najawirangka. Subsequently, using the principle proposed by Najawirangka, Ki Sindusawarno elucidates irama in more detail.

It is only by viewing irama as a process of contraction and expansion of time-space that we can make sense of the categorization of gong, kenong, kempul, and kethuk as pamangku irama instruments. That is, the process of expanding and contracting time-space is understood as the process at work in the formal structure of a gendhing (gongan unit), which is delineated by these instruments.

Essentially each of the above classification systems is a simplified way of presenting complex musical processes and diverse compositional techniques. In most cases, they do not consider the vocal parts in the gamelan in any detail. Occasionally, some writings state the importance of vocal music in gendhing, however. For example, *Serat Pakem Wirama* (1934:28) categorizes sindhènan into four types: [137]

1. Lampah gendhing: This is a gendhing accompanied by the singing of pesindhèn; for example, in gendhing Megamendhung. Thus, the basic structure is contained in the gendhing, the sindhènan accompanies it.
2. Lampah sekar gendhing: This is sung-poetry accompanied by gamelan [gendhing] with [the formal structure] ladrang, ketawang, srepegan, and the like. For example, sekar Kinanthi is accompanied by gamelan [gendhing] with formal structure ladrang, ketawang, and the like. Thus, the basic structure is sung-poetry, gamelan accompanies it, but in the manner of playing gendhing (i.e., the whole ensemble is played).
3. Lampah sekar: This is also sung-poetry accompanied by gamelan [gendhing] with the formal structure ladrang, ketawang, srepegan, and the like. For example, sekar Durma is accompanied by gamelan [gendhing] with the formal structure ladrang, ketawang, and the like. Thus, the basic melodic structure is contained in the sekar. But it differs from sekar-gendhing: the lampah sekar is accompanied

only by 1. gambang, 2. gendèr, 3. kendhang ketipung, 4. kethuk, 5. kenong, 6. gong, 7. *kemanak*.

4. *Lampah lagon lasem:* This is also sung-poetry accompanied by gamelan. The basic structure is contained in the melody [of the sung-poetry], but it differs from the lampah sekar. The lampah lagon is accompanied only by 1. rebab, 2. gambang, 3. gendèr.[138]

Although the classification is about the types of sindhènan, it is clear that categories 2, 3, and 4 point at the vocal music as the basic structure of a composition (baku gendhingipun). In this kind of classification we begin to see the diverse techniques of composition in the gamelan. Consequently, the effectiveness of general classification systems of instruments according to their functions begins to weaken. This is because such classification does not take into account vocally-based gendhing.

Kodrat Poerbapangrawit, a musician in the court of Surakarta, also reminds us of the important role of vocal music in gamelan when he offers a classification system in "Gendhing Jawa" (Javanese gamelan composition) (1984:419–21). This is particularly clear in the section "Bab Gendhing" (Concerning gendhing), which lists four genres of gendhing: *gendhing lésan, gendhing thuthuk,* gendhing gamelan lan lésan, and gendhing lésan + thuthuk. Gendhing lésan (vocal compositions) consist of unaccompanied or minimally accompanied songs, such as children's songs, selawatan, santiswaran, and laras madya (the last three categories are vocal music accompanied by mainly frame drums). Gendhing thuthuk are types of gendhing in which the melodies are played by percussion instruments, except for rebab and suling. This category includes most of the gendhing in gamelan. In this category, Poerbadiningrat classifies instruments according to their musical functions.[139] Gendhing gamelan lan lésan are any gendhing that have gérongan (a male chorus). They are also called gendhing gérongan. Gendhing lésan + thuthuk are those that accompany bedhaya and serimpi dances. The names and origins of these dance melodies are macapat poetic forms, but they are accompanied by the whole gamelan ensemble.

Poerbapangrawit's classification of gendhing not only shows us the variety of genres in gamelan composition, in which vocal music often plays an important role, but also raises a larger question about gendhing in general. With regard to gendhing thuthuk, he states: "Gendhing thuthuk (struck pieces) are so named because the gamelan, except for the rebab and suling, produces sounds by being struck." Could we translate gendhing thuthuk simply as "instrumental pieces"? It seems to me that the term "struck piece" refers to the act of producing the musical sound. The musical sound itself, however, may not be purely instrumental. In other words, the concept of gendhing thuthuk may involve more than simply instrumentally produced sounds; in most cases it also includes a vocal element. Indeed, the fact that the majority of gendhing thuthuk also employ singing suggests that further examination of this genre of gendhing is necessary.

In his detailed elucidation of gendhing, Poerbapangrawit offers further sub-categories of gendhing thuthuk. They are gendhing rebab, gendhing bonang, gendhing gendèr, gendhing gambang, and gendhing kendhang (ibid., 429). In gendhing bonang, the pesindhèn, the rebab, gendèr, the gambang, and the celempung are absent. In other words, in this particular genre, vocal parts and vocally inspired instruments do not participate in the ensemble. However, for gendhing in the other genres, vocal parts are almost always present, and vocally oriented instruments (particularly the rebab) often have an important function in the ensemble.

Poerbapangrawit himself seems to be confused when he gives examples of gendhing in these categories. Initially he proposes that gendhing thuthuk differs from gendhing gérongan. However, in the examples he gives, a number of gendhing are mentioned in both categories (1955:15–17).[140] This indicates that it is conceptually difficult to classify gendhing as either instrumental or vocal pieces.

We have focused on classification: the classification of instruments according to their functions in the ensemble, and the classification of gendhing. The existence of several different kinds of classification makes us aware of diverse types of compositions for the gamelan. In other words, the richness of the gamelan compositional process has caused many difficulties for the theorists who wish to classify gamelan instruments and gamelan gendhing with precision.

A solution that is often proposed by theorists is to classify gendhing as either vocal or instrumental. Such a division leads to broader questions about gendhing. Can we conceptually divide gendhing into vocal and instrumental music? How important is the role of vocal melodies in gendhing? We will return to these questions later.

It may be useful to recapitulate the account of the development of intellectual life in Java resulting from the relations between the Dutch, the Indos, and the Javanese intellectuals in the nineteenth century and the early twentieth century, and between Western and Javanese intellectuals from the mid twentieth century onward. Essentially, we can detect three broad categories.

First, the period from the third decade of the nineteenth century to the late nineteenth century represents the pre-modern European intellectual period. In this period, relations between Dutch scholars, Indo scholars, Javanese intellectuals (especially court pujangga, and leading court artists) were fairly close. They had ample opportunity to exchange ideas on fairly equal terms. This period produced works of literature such as *Serat Sendhon Langen Swara, Serat Sastramiruda, Javaansch Zamenspraken,* and *Serat Gulang Yarya.* From these works we can draw indigenous, pre-notational perspectives on gamelan.[141] Concomitantly, as a result of the introduction of European technology, this period also marks the beginning of experimentation with notation for gamelan. The main purpose of the early gamelan notation was for preserving gendhing from extinction. But the notation also slanted the development of gamelan theories in a certain direction, especially with regard to the formation of the melodic theme of gendhing.

Second, the early to mid twentieth century represents the peak of the Europeanization of Java. This was the time of a rapid increase in European cultural power in Java. Printing technology, European-style education, modern scientific scholarship, the phonograph, and other modern elements of European life were much more thoroughly integrated into Javanese life than they had been before. European intellectuals began to apply their up-to-date, prestigious scientific tools to study Javanese culture. The works of Jaap Kunst and his contemporaries come to mind. They superimposed the notion of "high culture" on Javanese court culture: Javanese court arts were the products of high culture; Javanese gamelan was presented in analogy with European art music. Soon afterward, the Dutch-educated Javanese elite followed in the footsteps of their European colleagues. Javanese intellectuals such as Dewantara felt compelled to study Javanese arts scientifically because Javanese arts were adi luhung. Notation for gamelan was now used by the Javanese elite to justify gamelan as a "high art," in accord with the status of European music, and the first attempts were made to develop a systematic theory of Javanese gamelan music. This theory was itself strongly influenced by the notational system, which focused on instrumentally-based melody and identified the saron part as the melodic theme of a gendhing.

During the period of national awakening, the attempt to legitimize the status of gamelan to represent Indonesian national culture created a debate among Indonesian nationalists. This debate and the discussion about national culture formed a background for the founding of gamelan schools and academies and continued to be the subject of discourse in these institutions. Concomitantly, writing on gamelan developed in these institutions.

Third, from the middle of the twentieth century there was a period of mixed European-Javanese intellectual life. Western intellectuals, mostly ethnomusicologists, have begun to look more closely at the perspectives of Javanese niyaga.[142] Many ethnomusicologists have studied not only the knowledge of gamelan, but also how to play the music. (Nowadays gamelan ensembles and gamelan clubs can be found in many Western countries.) Consequently, the interactions between Western gamelan researchers and Javanese musicians and theorists have intensified.

In this period, gamelan theory has become more comprehensive. Various methods of music analysis and cultural analysis have emerged. Gamelan theory has often been prominent in cross-cultural and interdisciplinary studies of music theory, especially in the works of Western scholars (for example, in the area of linguistic theory, J. Becker 1980, A. Becker and J. Becker 1979, Hughes 1988, and Powers 1980a; Powers 1979 on music in Muslim nations; Powers 1980b on cross-cultural study of mode).

Javanese gamelan theorists have also become familiar with the theory and methods of ethnomusicology. This familiarity has come about through the ethnomusicological literature, through personal contact with Western ethnomusicologists working in Java, and through the sending of Javanese students and scholars of gamelan to study in Europe and the United States of America.

Current intellectual discourse on gamelan is marked by the tendency of Western and Javanese gamelan theorists to work more closely together. The increased accessibility, resulting in better communication between Javanese and Western gamelan theorist-musicians (especially through programs of gamelan study in Western colleges), has strengthened this tendency. The residence of some Javanese musicians and theorists in Western countries (the author of the present study is one of them) adds to the strength of this kind of intellectual intercourse. In many ways, the current intellectual atmosphere reminds us of the intellectual life in nineteenth-century Java, when Dutch and Indo scholar-officials and Javanese intellectuals had ample opportunities to exchange ideas as equals—for example, when C. F. Winter had frequent discussions with Ronggawarsita. From the 1970s onward, eminent Javanese musicians and theorists had frequent discussions with young Western ethnomusicologists and other researchers, for example Martopangrawit of Surakarta with Marc Perlman and John Pemberton, and Sastrapustaka of Yogyakarta with Anderson Sutton and Jennifer Lindsay. This tradition continues to the present day. It is this kind of intellectual atmosphere that produces the discussion of gamelan theories in the next chapter. Beside redefining the melodic theme of a gendhing, gamelan theorists shed more light on the complexity of compositional processes in gamelan. Responding to the previous assumption of instrumentally-based melody as having the primary melodic function, in the next chapter I consider the importance of the vocal element in gendhing.

In a nutshell, the modern world provides for better cultural and intellectual communication between Javanese and Westerners. In addition, the advent of modern technologies such as audio and video reproduction has fostered the growth of our understanding of Javanese gamelan. In this kind of intellectual atmosphere, gamelan scholarship may proceed fruitfully.

FOUR

Current Theories of Gendhing

Vocal Melodies as the Melodic Precedent of the *Gendhing:* Views from the *Serat Centhini, Serat Gulang Yarya,* and *Serat Sosorah Gamelan*

It is commonly held that gamelan composition operates within the framework of formulaic organization.[1] The smallest formula of a gendhing is said to be contained in a four-note unit of balungan (melodic abstraction played by instruments of the saron family). This four-note formula is called gatra. Many gamelan studies have stressed the importance of gatra. J. Becker (1980) used gatra as the basis for studying the modal system of gamelan called pathet. Sutton (1993) employs gatra as a way of elucidating compositional techniques and variations.

Another formulaic term that relates to or is synonymous with gatra is cèngkok. It refers to the performance practice of certain "elaborative" instruments and singers. There are also other meanings of cèngkok, including "melody," "variant of melody," and "gongan" (the phrases in between two strokes of the large gong). In other words, "melodic pattern" is only one of the meanings of the word cèngkok. In light of its various meanings, closer inspection of the significance of the term is necessary.

The idea that the compositional process in gamelan involves an important role for melodic formulas can be traced in an earlier study by Hood (1954). In defense of his use of the saron part as the principal melody of a gendhing, Hood states:

> The preference for a one-octave saron as the instrument to be entrusted with the nuclear theme is directly attributable to a desire, conscious or otherwise, to preserve the melodic contour or *shape,* if you will, of the principal melody—the melodic *shape,* I repeat, of the all-important cadential formula which closes the three critical sections, which serves as the framework of the whole gending, which, in short, is one of the strongest features in the identification and, consequently, the very preservation of the patet concept itself. (1954:242)

Hood saw the importance of cadential formulas for identifying pathet. But J. Becker (1980:81) postulated even more strongly the formulaic system in gamelan:

It is not only cadences that are formulas. Gamelan *gendhing* (pieces) are formulaic from beginning to end, from the *buka* (introduction) to the final gong, and in all the musical lines whether played by saron, bonang, gendèr, rebab, suling, kendhang, or any other instrument.

Becker, like Hood, made her statement in the context of her study of pathet. But Becker's statement also alludes to a wider context of gamelan performance practice. The broader context of Becker's view of a formulaic system in gamelan can be found elsewhere in her same work. Following Albert Lord's explanation of the formulaic technique of composing epics in Yugoslavia, she suggests that "the musician in an oral tradition . . . has mastered a *technique* of composition, based upon *the manipulation of formulas,* which allows him to perform and compose at the same moment" (p. 20; emphasis added).

There is no question that Becker emphasizes the importance of formulas in gendhing.[2] It is not clear whether she is elucidating a process of composing a gendhing or a process by which the musicians rendered gendhing in a performance. But Sutton states unambiguously that such a process explains how the Javanese composer actually composes gendhing. He sees Javanese gendhing as radically different in nature from Western musical compositions such as Beethoven's *Eroica* Symphony (Sutton 1993:25–26):

> Not only is the identity of individual composers of considerably less importance in Java than in the West but the processes by which they invent and the resultant products contrast markedly. The Javanese idea of a piece (*gendhing*) is an outline which is to be filled in by musicians with similar but not identical sensibilities. If Beethoven's score is a blueprint that players must follow in detail to build their structure of sound, the Javanese gendhing is more a sketch that may serve as the basis for varied interpretation. This sketch, moreover, usually resembles others in a clearly perceivable manner—both in form and content. The traditional Javanese composer, far from being encouraged to create anything "completely original" is expected to build new pieces by the centonization method described by Hughes above. His new composition must be familiar—a variation of what already exists.

When Sutton cites the "centonization method," he refers to the process of creation of certain Gregorian chants proposed by Hughes—a process of stringing together certain standard patterns which are selected from a stock of formulas (p. 24). In gamelan this means a process of recombining a repertoire of gatra.

Having understood the crucial role of gatra patterns in the creation of gendhing, we may ask: What constitutes a repertoire of gatra? Sutton answers this question by referring to Becker's account of gatra from her analysis of pathet. Based on her analysis of some one hundred gendhing, Becker (1980:85) finds that:

Given a four-note unit with the final note fixed, there are 125 combinations possible, or 125 possible contours. Actually, fewer than thirty-eight contours occur five or more times in this collection of data. In *sléndro*, a total of either thirty-one or thirty-three contours occur regularly on any given pitch, in *pélog* even fewer, averaging only a total of twenty-six of the possible 125 contours.

Given the availability of a great number of contours, gendhing use them restrictively. For example, in sléndro gendhing, only thirty-three contours are used from the possible 125; this means that the total number of contours used is only 165 (five pitch levels times thirty-three contours). In pélog the total number of contours is around 130.

What causes the restriction of the number of gatra used in gendhing? What are the criteria for selecting and reordering gatra in creating a gendhing? These are important questions. Perhaps Becker is right to point out that one of the criteria for selecting gatra in composing a gendhing is pathet: pathet imposes certain rules on the placement of gatra patterns within the formal structures (Becker 1980:81). Whether or not the composer is actually thinking of the placement of gatra patterns when composing a gendhing is a moot question. Sutton adds to the criteria: "The sequence of gatra in the living repertory almost always entails some repetition or other type of relationship between gatra. These relationships contribute to the coherence of the gendhing" (1993:28).

Using ladrang Wilujeng as an illustration, Sutton explains the character of the balungan melody of the piece (pp. 28–29), and provides a broad explanation of what constitutes coherence in a gendhing. He concludes: "While the precise nature of these relationships will vary from one gendhing to another, the presence of perceivable relationships between passages, particularly varied or exact melodic repetition, is an essential aspect of any acceptable gendhing" (p. 29).

He then discusses and analyzes the varied or exact melodic (gatra) connections among the gendhing (pp. 30–68). Basically, his discussion confirms Becker's assertion: the manipulation or the reordering of formulas is the essential way of creating a gendhing. As Sutton puts it: "These formulas, used again and again from one piece to another, unite the tradition into a coherent whole" (p. 45).[3]

The basic assumption made by Hood, Becker, and Sutton is that gatra is an important element in creating gendhing. To what extent this concept represents the way Javanese composer-musicians do so deserves further examination. Assuming that gatra is the melodic precedent of gendhing means that instrumentally-inspired melody is primary in the process of composition in gamelan. This is because gatra is originally conceived for the melody of the saron instrument.[4]

I pointed out in chapter 3 that the introduction of notation for gamelan has caused gamelan theories to develop in a certain direction: positioning the instrumentally-based melody as the melodic theme of gendhing. In formulating their theories, gamelan theorists neglected the vocal element in gendhing. The discussion below will suggest that there are other ways in which gendhing are created; restructuring a vocal musical repertoire is one of them. Let us consider the following passages from the *Serat Centhini*.

> 7. The origin of gamelan
>   is *widayaka,*
>   which is intricately contained in a gendhing.
>   The meaning of widayaka is tembang (sung-poetry).
> 8. Song is the melody, words are the lyric,
>   *raras* is contained in gamelan.
>   The meaning of gamelan is to handle—
>   the sound of gendhing is produced by the hands.
> 9. That is the marriage between gendhèng and gendhing;
>   The love of raras
>   is originated in the sound.
>   That's only explication, brother.[5]
>   (*Serat Tjenṭini* 1912–15, 7–8:204)

The passages indicate the importance of vocal melody in the gamelan. That is, tembang or sekar is the basis for creating gendhing. The passage "the marriage between gendhèng (people singing) and gendhing" strongly supports the point above. In fact, the plural word gendhèng-gendhing is used frequently in the poems.[6]

Like the authors of the *Serat Centhini,* Tondhakusuma in his *Serat Gulang Yarya* also uses the idiom gendhèng-gendhing. He also makes his position clear with regard to the inherent link between the vocal and the instrumental embodied in a gendhing (1870:11–12).

> 7. [Kyai Gulang Rarya]: Let's cease the explanation of tembang.
>   What is gendhèng-gendhing?
>   [Setu]: Gendhing is intended for the cultivation of definable
>   sound,
>   consisting of the tying up of gendhing
>   and beautiful tembang.
>   Thus, the name gendhing
>   means the cultivation of
>   singing as it is connected with gamelan.[7]

Semantic evidence in the description of gamelan lends support to the concept of the interdependency of vocal and instrumental elements. It furthermore supports why the term and concept of balungan does not appear in the *Serat Centhini*. Balungan is conceived as a strain of pulses. Pulsation is represented clearly by the striking of an instrument such as a saron. If the basis of the concept of gendhing is not so much punctual sounds, but singing or flowing melodic motion, it is understandable that the *Serat Centhini* and other nineteenth-century treatises on gamelan did not find it necessary to bring forth a concept like bal-ungan to refer to the melodic abstraction of a gendhing.

Unfortunately, *Serat Centhini* and *Serat Gulang Yarya* do not pursue the issue of the importance of vocal music in gamelan in greater detail. Musical examples are absent. Thus, the argument for an inherent fusion of gendhèng and gendhing in the context of nineteenth-century musical practice must stop at the level of semantic evidence. In order to understand the important role of vocal music in gamelan, we have to rely more on evidence from the later period.

Elsewhere (Sumarsam 1976) I suggest that the melodic essence of gendhing is contained in an implicit form of vocally-inspired melody. I am gratified to find that there is an older reference that supports my point. In fact, I often cite the above passage from the *Serat Centhini* to support my claim. I am even more delighted to discover that, drawing the same conclusion as I, a venerable court musician, Warsadiningrat (1920s), cites the same passage.[8] Moreover, Warsadi-ningrat discusses at length the notion of vocal melodies as the basis of creating gendhing:

> Perhaps gendhing originated from the unfolding of the melody of sekar (sung poetry). The number of sekar arose gradually and so did the vari-ants of their melodies. The melodies of the unfolded sekar were then arranged in an orderly manner. They were gradually rearranged with wirama. When the rearrangement was completed, then they were called gendhing. That was the origin of gendhing—the result of [the rearranging of the melody of] sekar. (Warsapradongga 1920s:13)[9]

Clearly, Warsadiningrat believes that the melodic source of the gendhing is the melodies of sekar. He confirms a reference from the *Serat Pustakaraja,* com-posed by Ronggawarsita (mid-nineteenth century), indicating that gendhing kemanak—a type of performance consisting of a unison mixed chorus accom-panied by kemanak, kendhang, gong, and kenong—is the oldest form of gen-dhing. He calls this form of composition gendhing bawa swara. This also shows Warsadiningrat's strong belief in the importance of vocal melodies in gamelan. He then goes on to say that:

> After the creation of gendhing bawa swara, then [people] invented gamelan as a vessel of laras. Having created gamelan, the melodies of sekar were then accompanied by gamelan, and were rearranged in an orderly manner in such a way that the melodies of the sekar cannot be identified anymore. This is how gamelan gendhing came into being. (Ibid., p. 14)[10]

As an example of those gendhing based on the melody of sekar, he lists six gendhing in each of the laras. In laras pélog they are gendhing Agul-agul, Sumekar, Semang, Sarayuda, Babar Layar, and Pramugari. In laras sléndro they are gendhing Mas Kumambang, Lonthang, Gonda Kusuma, Dhandhang Gula, Lagu, and Irim-Irim. However, Warsadiningrat does not explain in what ways these pieces are related to the melody of sekar. He acknowledges that he is only assuming that this is so. Because the transformation from sekar to gendhing is "so intricate and refined, it is very hard to guess" (p. 14) which sekar was the source for a gendhing.

The names of two sléndro pieces, Mas Kumambang and Dhandhang Gula, are the same as the names of two types of macapat (sung poetry). However, the gendhing called Mas Kumambang now is in pélog. In sléndro there are now two pieces entitled Dhandhang Gula Tlutur and Dhandhang Gula Maskéntar. (The latter can be played in pélog). The melodies of these two pieces were based on macapat melodies of the same name.

Because Warsadiningrat does not explain the relationship of these gendhing to the melody of sekar, we cannot analyze his example further. But these pieces are not the only examples used by Warsadiningrat. In another section of the same work, he gives a list of pieces along with suggestions of the sekar these pieces are based on:

1. Gendhing Muncar pélog barang derives from sekar Mas Kumambang.
2. Gendhing Sinom Bedhaya pélog barang derives from sekar Sinom Logondhang.
3. Gendhing Endhol-Endhol Bedhaya pélog barang derives from sekar Nagabonda.
4. Gendhing Klèwèr pélog barang derives from sekar Nagabonda.
5. Gendhing Pucung derives from sekar Pucung.
6. Gendhing Lobong derives from sekar Kinanthi.
7. Gendhing Kinanthi derives from Pangukir. (P. 15)[11]

Warsadiningrat does not present musical analysis that confirms his statements on the connection between the melodies of gendhing and sekar listed above. But my analysis shows that to a certain extent his thesis rests on firm ground. Of the seven gendhing in his list, five are clearly related to the melodies of macapat. Figure 4.1 (p.172) shows the notation and the text of sekar macapat Mas Kumambang. Figure 4.2 (p.173) is the notation of the rebab melody and the balungan of gendhing Muncar. And figure 4.3 (p.174) shows a comparison of each line of the verse-melody with each kenongan of the gendhing.

As can be seen, the melodic structure of the first line of Mas Kumambang and of the first kenongan of Muncar are very closely related. The sustaining of pitch 5 in the first half of the verse melody parallels the *gantungan* melody of the same pitch in the second gatra of the kenongan. The third and fourth gatra of the same kenongan are taken together as one phrase. This phrase parallels the second half of the verse-melody.

The second line of Mas Kumambang (lines IIa and IIb) is paralleled by the second kenongan of Muncar. In other words, these two lines were compressed into one kenongan. In so doing, the ending-note of line IIa (tone 6) in Muncar becomes a weak tone,[12] and tone 2, the most conspicuous tone in line IIb, becomes an important tone, marking the end of the first half of the kenongan and the gatra before the gong.

The third kenongan of Muncar has no relation to the verse melody. This kenongan is a restatement of the preceding kenongan—the ending-notes of the middle and the end of the kenongan are the same.[13]

The last kenongan of Muncar parallels the last line of Mas Kumambang. However, in Muncar the kenongan approaches the gong-tone from the middle range, not from the lower range as in Mas Kumambang.

In other words, the parallel between the melodic structure of the last line of Mas Kumambang and that of the last kenongan of Muncar is not as close as that of the earlier lines. In fact, this last kenongan is very closely related to the first kenongan.

Usually, the macapat-based gendhing have the same titles as the names of the macapat from which they are derived; and they are usually in a shorter formal structure, such as ketawang or ladrang. But the above example indicates that the title of some macapat-based gendhing are different from the names of the macapat; and that some such gendhing are composed in longer formal structures, such as kethuk 2 kerep.

There is also a ketawang Mas Kumambang pélog lima, however, that is based on the sekar macapat of the same name. Figure 4.4 (p.175) is the notation of sekar macapat Mas Kumambang. Figure 4.5 (p.176) shows a comparison between the verse melody and ketawang Mas Kumambang.

Like many macapat-based gendhing, the ngelik section of the piece is the part that contains the verse-melody. In the example below, line I of the verse-melody parallels the first kenongan of the first gongan of the ngelik. The second kenongan of the same gongan is a modified version of line IIa of the verse-melody; that is, the gong-tone is 5 (the emphasized tone of line IIb), instead of the ending-tone of line IIa (tone 2̇). The first kenongan of the second gongan of the ngelik is a modified version of line IIa of the verse-melody; that is, because tone 5 is already used as a gong-tone of the previous gongan, the gérongan of this kenongan begins immediately with tone 1. Finally, the last kenongan relates to line III, and it incorporates tone 4.

Like many gedhing based on macapat melodies, ketawang Mas Kumambang begins with ompak, a type of refrain that can be used for more than one piece. The ompak has no gérongan. There is no definitive explanation for the basis of the ompak melodies. The ompak of ketawang Mas Kumambang is identical to the ompak of ketawang Langen Gita. Other typical ompak are: 6̣6̣·· 2321 3216̣ 216̣5̣ for sléndro or pélog pieces; ··26̣ 1232 6̣123 6532 for sléndro, or ··26̣ 7232 6̣723 6532 for pélog barang; ·2·3 ·2·1 ·3·2 ·1·6̣ for both sléndro and pélog.

In another example, Warsadiningrat identifies the verse-melody of Sinom Logondhang as the melodic precedent of gendhing Sinom Bedhaya pélog barang. My analysis reveals that only the second half of the piece has a connection with the verse-melody. The detailed connection of their melodic structures is not as close as in gendhing Muncar and macapat Mas Kumambang. But on the basis of the correlation of ending-tones of important phrases, we can make the connection between these two compositions. Figure 4.6 (p. 177) is the notation, with the text, of sekar macapat Sinom Logondhang. Figure 4.7 (pp. 178–79) is the notation of the rebab and balungan of gendhing Sinom Bedhaya. And figure 4.8 (pp. 180–81) shows a comparison of these two compositions.

Only the second half of gendhing Sinom Bedhaya matches the melody of macapat Sinom Logandhang. The match begins with the second half of the second kenongan ($\dot{2}\dot{2}\cdot7$ $\cdot6\cdot5$). It is in the ending-notes of the phrases that the connection between these two compositions is strongest. The connection is as follows: Lines Ib and Ic, ending on note 2, relate to the first quarter of the third kenongan ($\cdot2\cdot\dot{7}$ $\cdot3\cdot2$). Line Id, ending on 5, relates to the second quarter of the same kenongan ($\cdot327$ $\cdot\dot{6}\cdot5$). Lines IIa and IIb, ending on 2, relate to the second half of the same kenongan. Line IIIa, ending on 5, matches the first quarter of the fourth kenongan. Line IIIb, ending on 5, parallels the second quarter of the same kenongan. Finally, line IVa and IVb connect to the second half of the same kenongan.

It is true that the melodic parallel between these two pieces is not exact. But the fact that the ending-notes of the phrases are identical is enough to indicate the extent to which the melody of macapat Sinom was transformed into gendhing Sinom Bedhaya.

Warsadiningrat's second example is sekar Nagabonda as the basis for the melody of gendhing Endhol-Endhol and gendhing Klèwèr, both in pélog barang. Present-day evidence has Nagabonda as a song in pélog nem (Gunawan 1983–84, 2:14; Martopangrawit 1977:1, 7) and sléndro manyura (Martopangrawit 1977:2, 106). Although there are tantalizing similarities in arrival points between the Nagabonda songs and the two gendhing, I cannot identify the relationship of the two pieces.

For his next example, Warsadiningrat identifies sekar macapat Pucung as the melodic precedent of gendhing Pucung; this is an example of a macapat-based gendhing. There are two kinds of formal structures for gendhing Pucung, ketawang and *mérong kethuk 2 kerep*. The former is a gendhing gérongan, the latter is not. Both of them are based on the verse-melody. Except for a difference in their formal structure, basically they are the same piece. Below I will illustrate only ketawang Pucung. Figure 4.9 (p. 182) is the notation of sekar macapat Pucung. Figure 4.10 (p. 183) shows a comparison of the verse-melody and the gérongan of ketawang Pucung.

As can be seen, the melodic structure of ketawang Pucung is closely related to the verse-melody of the same name. The connection begins in the last gatra of the second gongan. It should also be noted that ketawang Pucung, like any other ketawang piece based on a macapat melody, has an ompak melody unrelated to the verse-melody.

I indicated earlier that some macapat-based gendhing do not retain the name of the verse-melody; they were given a new title. Warsadiningrat's next example illustrates another such transformation. The piece is gendhing Lobong, which was based on sekar macapat Kinanthi Sastradiwangsa.[14] Figure 4.11 (p. 182) is the notation of the verse melody of Kinanthi Sastradiwangsa. Figure 4.12 (p. 184) is the notation of the rebab and balungan of gendhing Lobong. And figure 4.13 (p. 185) shows a comparison of these two compositions.

There is a close connection between the melodic structures of these two musical compositions. We see the correlation even more clearly in the rebab line than in the balungan. This shows that the balungan has been drawn from the more fluid, vocally-inspired melody that underlies the gendhing, a melody that is more accurately reflected in the rebab than in the balungan.

Figure 4.13 shows a correlation of each line of the verse-melody and each kenongan of the gendhing. That is, lines Ia and b of Kinanthi parallel the second kenongan of Lobong; lines IIa and b correlate with the third kenongan; and lines IIIa and b parallel the last kenongan. The first kenongan of Lobong is an exact restatement of the last kenongan of the piece.

The verse melody Kinanthi Sastradiwangsa was also the basis for the ngelik part of ketawang Suba Kastawa (Darsono 1980:166–67). Figure 4.14 (p. 186) shows the correlation of each line of the verse-melody and the gérongan of the ngelik of ketawang Suba Kastawa.[15]

Warsadiningrat's next example is sekar macapat Pangukir as the basis for gendhing Kinanthi. There is no gendhing called Kinanthi by itself. But there is a composition in ketawang structure called Kinanthi Pawukir.[16] Darsono (1980: 158–59) identifies sekar macapat Kinanthi Pawukir as the melodic precedent of this piece. Figure 4.15 (p. 187) is the melody of sekar macapat Kinanthi Pawukir. Figure 4.16 (p. 188) shows a comparison of these two compositions.

The illustration shows lines Ia/b and IIa/b of the verse-melody parallel the first and second gongan of ketawang Kinanthi Pangukir. Lines IIIa/b parallel the last gongan.

In another example, Warsadiningrat identifies pathetan and sendhon as the melodic precedents for gendhing. He lists the following pieces:

1. Gendhing Kombang Mara pélog lima was taken from pathetan Pélog Lima [Wantah].
2. Tlutur dhawah Playon pélog lima was taken from pathetan Pélog Lima.
3. Ladrang Semang or Playon nem was taken from pathetan Pélog Barang.

4. Gendhing Klèwèr dhawah ladrang Playon was taken from pathetan Pélog Barang.
5. Gendhing Krawitan was taken from pathetan Sléndro Nem.
6. Gendhing Tutur dhawah (minggah) ladrang Tlutur was taken from sendhon Tlutur sléndro sanga.
7. Gendhing Merak Kasimpir was taken from pathet Sléndro Manyura. (Ibid. 6)

Of these seven pieces, I can identify the connections between only two pieces and pathetan and sendhon: I have made connections between pathetan Pélog Lima Wantah and gendhing Kombang Mara, and sendhon Tlutur sléndro sanga and gendhing Tutur (or Tlutur) of the same laras and pathet. In neither case can I correlate the entire piece with the pathetan or sendhon.

Compared to the examples discussed thus far, Kombang Mara represents the most intricate process of recomposition of a melody. Figure 4.17 (p. 189) is the notation and the texts of the pathetan. Figure 4.18 (pp. 190–93) is the notation of the rebab and balungan of gendhing Kombang Mara. Figure 4.19 (pp. 194–97) shows the correlation between these two compositions.

The connection between the melodic structures of these two compositions is not always clear. Some connections are the result of compression of certain melodic motifs; some, of expansion. Very often, the connection of melodic structures cannot be made in detail.

I cannot correlate the entire first gongan of Kombang Mara with the beginning of the pathetan. The second and third kenongan of Kombang Mara are the only sections of the piece that have a correlation with the pathetan, that is with lines Ia and b—line Ia becomes a motif in the first half of the kenongan, and line Ib, the second half. I cannot identify the source of the melodies for the first and last kenongan. In a way, the first gongan is a prefatory section of the piece similar to ompak in the macapat-based pieces in the ketawang structure discussed earlier.

The first, second, and third kenongan of the second gongan of Kombang Mara are the same as the same kenongan of the first gongan. The last kenongan of the second gongan is directly drawn from the first half of line IIa of the pathetan, concentrating on tone 3; the transformative process involves melodic expansion. In light of the connection of this last kenongan with line IIa of the pathetan, I can clearly identify the connection of these two compositions beginning with the second kenongan of the second gongan. That is, the second kenongan parallels line Ia/b of the pathetan, the third kenongan is a repetition of the second kenongan, and the last kenongan is an expansion of the first half of line IIa (Ginarebeg) of the pathetan.

The third gongan begins with the restatement of the variant melody of the last kenongan of the preceding gongan. The second half of line IIa and the first half of line IIc are compressed to become the first gatra of the second kenongan. The second gatra of this kenongan is an extension of the first. Then, the first section of the second half of line IIb (654 5421) becomes the second half of the second kenongan. The third kenongan is a melodic extension of the kenong tone (tone 1), which is carried over in the first gatra of the last kenongan. The second gatra of this kenongan relates to the last phrase of line IIb (21 6). And the second half of this kenongan parallels the first half of line IIc of the pathetan.

The fourth gongan of Kombang Mara begins with the transformation of the second half of line IIc to the first kenongan, a process of melodic expansion. Then the second and third kenongan of the first gongan are introduced again in the same kenongan of this gongan. Finally, the last kenongan is drawn from line IIIa, but the end-note or the gong-tone is 3, instead of 4 as in the pathetan.

The fifth gongan of Kombang Mara is an ompak, the transition section from mérong to inggah. The melodic source of this section cannot wholly be found in the pathetan. We can say that the first kenongan is a reiteration of tone 3 of the gong. And the whole fourth kenongan is drawn from the last phrase (line IIIa/b) of the pathetan.

We have seen in the examples of the macapat-based pieces above that, except for gendhing Muncar, the name of the gendhing is taken from the title of the macapat. Warsadiningrat's next example is in this category, but the name of the gendhing derives from the title of the sendhon: Tlutur. This gives us an indication that sendhon Tlutur relates to gendhing Tlutur. Figure 4.20 (p. 198) is the notation and the text of sendhon Tlutur. Figure 4.21 (pp. 199–201) is the notation of the rebab and balungan of gendhing Tlutur. And figure 4.22 (pp. 202–4) shows the correlation between these two compositions.

The first gongan of gendhing Tlutur is a prefatory section. However, the melodies are drawn from lines IVb and Ic of the sendhon. The connection begins on the first kenongan of the second gongan; it is drawn from line Ic of the sendhon. (Notice that the kenongan begins with gantungan 3, emphasizing the ending-tone of the phrase.) The next connection is between line Id and the second kenongan of the same gongan.

The transformation from the sendhon to the gendhing often requires composing a connecting melody that starts with a gantungan melody using the preceding tone. The connection between lines Ic, IIa, IIb and the third gongan is a case in point: the first half of the first kenongan, the second half of the same kenongan, and the second kenongan each begin with a type of gantungan melodic connector.

I. 2   3   5   5   5   5   5   6   7   5   3   2
    Pra- mi- la- né ra- ma i- bu dèn bek- tè- ni

IIa. 5   6   7   7   7   5   6
     Ki- nar- ya lan- tar- an

b. 3   2   2   2   3   5   6   2   3   2   7.   6. 5.
    A- na- né ba- né da- ni-   rè-   ki

III. 5   6   7   5   6   7   7.   6. 7. 2
     Wi- ne- ruh- ken pa-dhang ha-   wa

Figure 4.1 Sekar macapat Mas Kumambang pélog

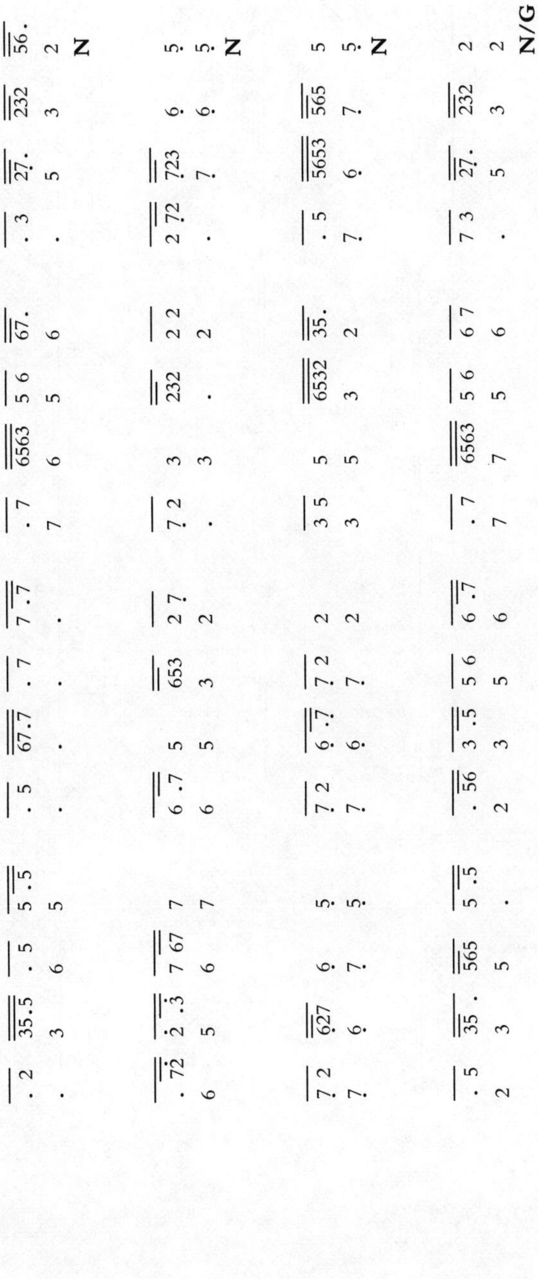

Figure 4.2 Gendhing Muncar pélog barang (rebab and balungan)

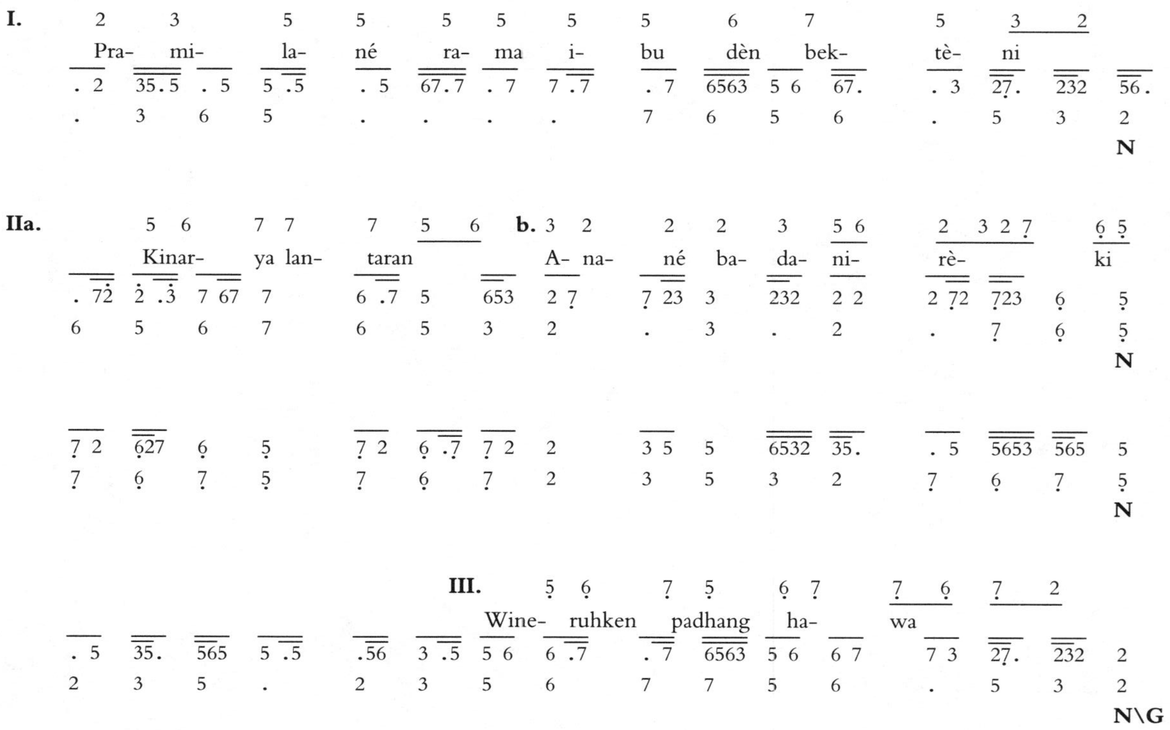

Figure 4.3 Comparison of sekar macapat Mas Kumambang pélog and gendhing Muncar pélog barang (sekar macapat, rebab, and balungan)

I.
```
5   6   i i       i   i   i    i    2̇    3̇    i   6  5
A-  ja  nggresah  yèn nu- ju   ke-  ta-  man   ka- ki
```

IIa.
```
i    2̇   3̇  3̇   i     i̲ 2̇
Wit  i-  ku  ki- nar-  ya
```

b.
```
6   5   5   5    6    i̲ 2̇      6̲ 5̲ 3    2̲ 1
Co- ba  pa- nge- sah- ing      dhi-      ri
```

III.
```
1   2   3   1   2   3        3̲ 2̲       3 5
Sa- ka  ka- pa- renging      Suks-      ma
```

Figure 4.4 Sekar macapat Mas Kumambang pélog

Ompak

2	.	1	.	2	.	3	.	2	.	6̣
								P		N/G

I/IIa.

```
 .  5   6  1 1 1 1    1 1 1 1 2  3 1 6 5    1̇     1̇        3̇ 3̇      1̇ 2̇ 2̇
 .  5   6̣·1 1̇·1       1̇·1 2̇ 2̇3̇ 1̇ 2̇1̇6̇ 5   3̇·2̇1̇  i-    .  2̇3̇ 1   1̇2̇1̇6̇  5
    Aja nggresah yèn   nu-ju keta-man ka-ki   Wit        ku ki-   nar- ya
 .      5             2̇  1   6       5          2̇    3̣    1      6        5
                                     N           P             N/G
```

IIb/III.

```
     6 5  5 5   6  1̇2̇    6  53 2 1     1 2  3 1        2  3      3 2  3 5
 .  1 1 12̇ 1   . 2  3    2 12̇    1    .1  23̇35 5   .56̣ 4   4 56  5
    Co-ba pange- sahing  dhi-   ri-      Sa-ka kapa-  renging   suk- ma
 .      5        1  1   2   1    N       2  3   5     6   4     6    5
                                           P                      N/G
```

Figure 4.5 Comparison of sekar macapat Mas Kumambang pélog and ketawang Mas Kumambang pélog lima (sekar macapat, gérongan, and balungan)

Ia. 2̇ 2̇ 2̇ 2̇ 2̇ 2̇ 3̇ 2̇ 7 6 5
Nu-la- da la- ku u- ta- ma

c. 7 6 7 5 3 2 2 2 3 5
Wong a- gung ing Ngèk-si- gan- da di

IIa. 2 2 2 2 2 3 2 7 6̣ 5̣
Ka- pa-ti a- mar- su- bra- ta

IIIa. 7 7 7̣ 3 2 7 6̣ 5̣
Pi- ne-su ta-pa bra-

IVa. 7 2̇ 3̇ 5 6 7 6 7
A- me- ma- ngun

b. 2 3 5 5 5 6 7 5 7 6 5
Tu-mrap- é wong ta-nah Ja-wi

d. 2 2 2 3 5 6 3 2 7 6̣ 5̣
Panem- bahan Sé- na- pa- ti

b. 7 7 6̣ 5̣ 6 7 5 5 5 6 5 3 2 3 2 7̣
Suda- né ha- wa lan nap- su

b. 2 2 2 3 5 6 3 5 3 2 7 6̣ 5̣
Ta-na- pi ing si-yang ra- tri

b. 2 3 5 5 5 5 5 6 5 3 2
Karyé- nak tyas-ing sa- sa- mi

Figure 4.6 Sekar macapat Sinom Logondhang pélog

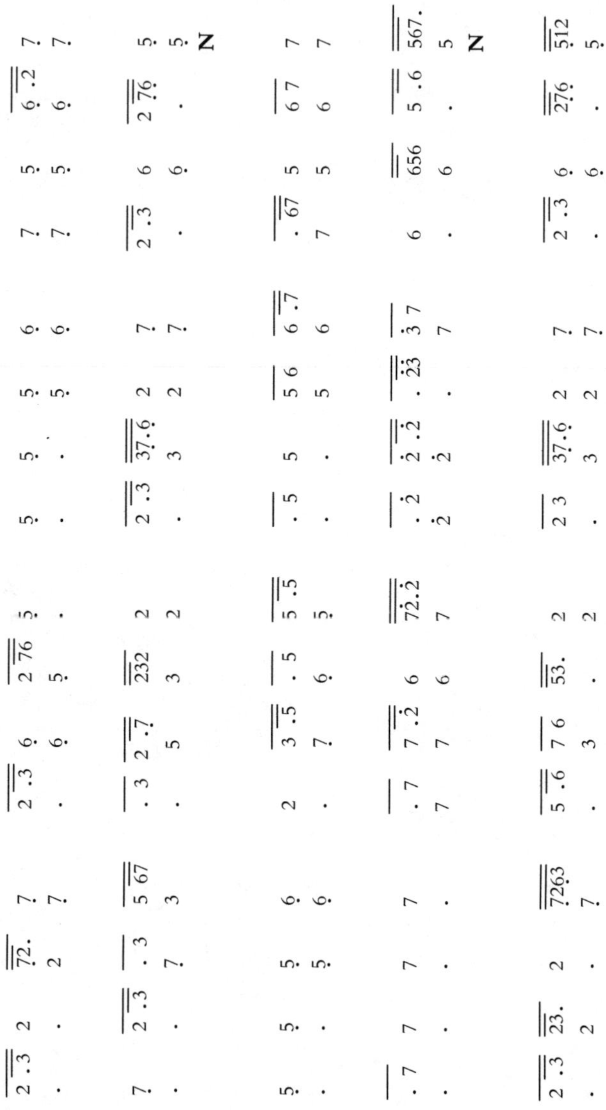

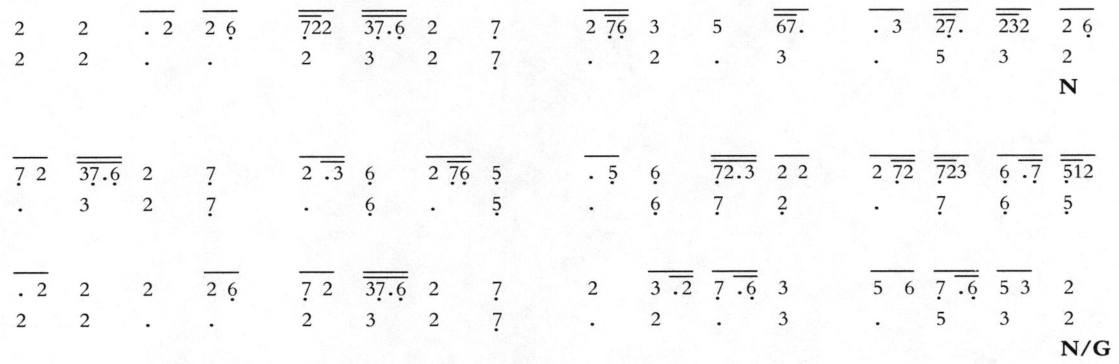

Figure 4.7 Gendhing Sinom Bedhaya pélog barang (rebab and balungan)

Ia.

... Nu- la- la- ku da u- ...

Ib.

2 3 5 5 5 6 7 ...
Tumrap- é wong tanah Ja-wi

Ic.

7 6 7 7 5 ...
Wong a- gung ing

Ngè- ksi ma gan-
da

Id.

2 2 2 2 3 5 6 3 2 7 6
Panem- bahan Séna- pa- ti

IIa.

	Ka-	pati	amar-	sudi	né	ha-	wa lan	nap-	su		
2	2 2	2 2	2 3	5	6 5	6 7	5 5	5 65	3 2	3 2	7
2	.2	2 6.	37.6		2 76.		67.	.3	27.	232	26.
2		.	7 2	3	.	5	3	.	5	3	2
2			2		2	2					**N**

IIb.

Pi-	nesu	tapa	bra-	ta		Pindha-					
7	7 7	7 7	3 2 7	6 5		7 7					
7 2	37.6	7.	2 .3	2 76.		7					
.	3	7	6.	6.		7.					
2	2		2	5.		5.					

IIIa.

IIIb.

Tana-	pi	ing	siyang	ra-	tri						
2 2	2 2	3 5 6	2 2	3 2 7	6 5						
.5	6.	72.3	72 723		6 .7	512					
.	6.	7.	2.	7.	6.	5.					

IVa.

A-	me-	ma-	ngun	Karya-	nak	tyasing	sa-	sa-	mi		
7	2 3	5 67	6 7	2 3	5 5	5 5	5	6 5	3 2		
.2	2	2 6.	37.6	7 2	3 .2	7 .6 3	56	7 .6	53	2	
2	2	.	2 3	7.	2	2.	.	5	3	2	
			2	7.		3					**N/G**

Figure 4.8 Comparison of sekar macapat Sinom Logondhang pélog and gendhing Sinom Bedhaya pélog barang (sekar macapat, rebab, and balungan)

Ia.

6	6	5 3
O-	ra	u-rus

i i 2̇
U- wos-

6 3
é tan

3 5̲ 3
é bu-

IIa.

i i 2̇
Ka- rem-

6 2̇
an- é

3 2 1
a-

1
na

b.

1 2
Mung ba-

1 3
ti- né

2 1
muring

1 6̣
mu-

6̣
ring

IIIa.

3 3
Ka- ya

3 5̲ 3
bu-

3
ta

2 2
buteng

1 6̣
be- tah

1 1
nga- ni-

1̲ 2
a-

2
ya

Figure 4.9 Sekar macapat Pucung sléndro

Ia.

3 6
Na- li-

i 2̇ 3̇
ka- ni-

i i
ra ing

i̲ 2̇
da-

6̣
lu

3 3
Wong a-

2 2
gung mang-

1 3
sah se-

3 1
mè-

2
di

1 6̇
.

IIa.

3 6
Si- rep

i 2̇ 3̇
kang ba-

i i
la wa-

i̲ 2̇
na-

6̣
ra

3 3
Sa- da-

2 2
ya wus

1 3
sa- mi

5 3
gu-

2
ling

IIIa.

3 5
Na- dyan

3 6
a- ri

5 3
Su- dar-

3 5 3
sa-

2 1
na

3 3
Wus da-

2 2
ngu dèn-

1 3
i- ra

3 1
gu-

2 1
ling

6̇
.

Figure 4.11 Sekar macapat Kinanthi Sastradiwangsa sléndro

Ompak

Ia.

Ib.

IIa/b.

Figure 4.10 Comparison of sekar macapat Pucung sléndro and ketawang Pucung sléndro manyura

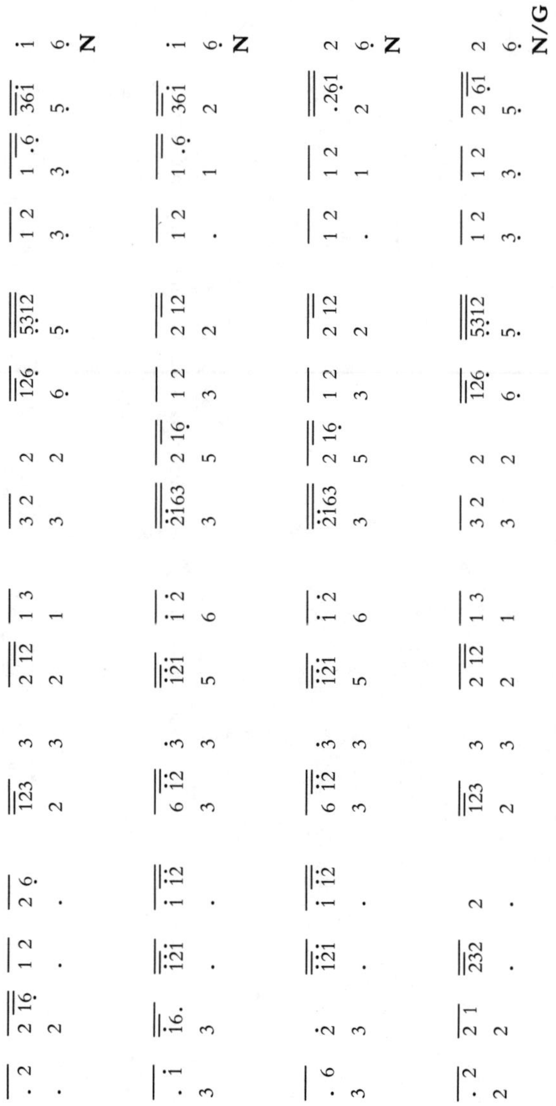

Figure 4.12 Gendhing Lobong sléndro manyura (rebab and balungan)

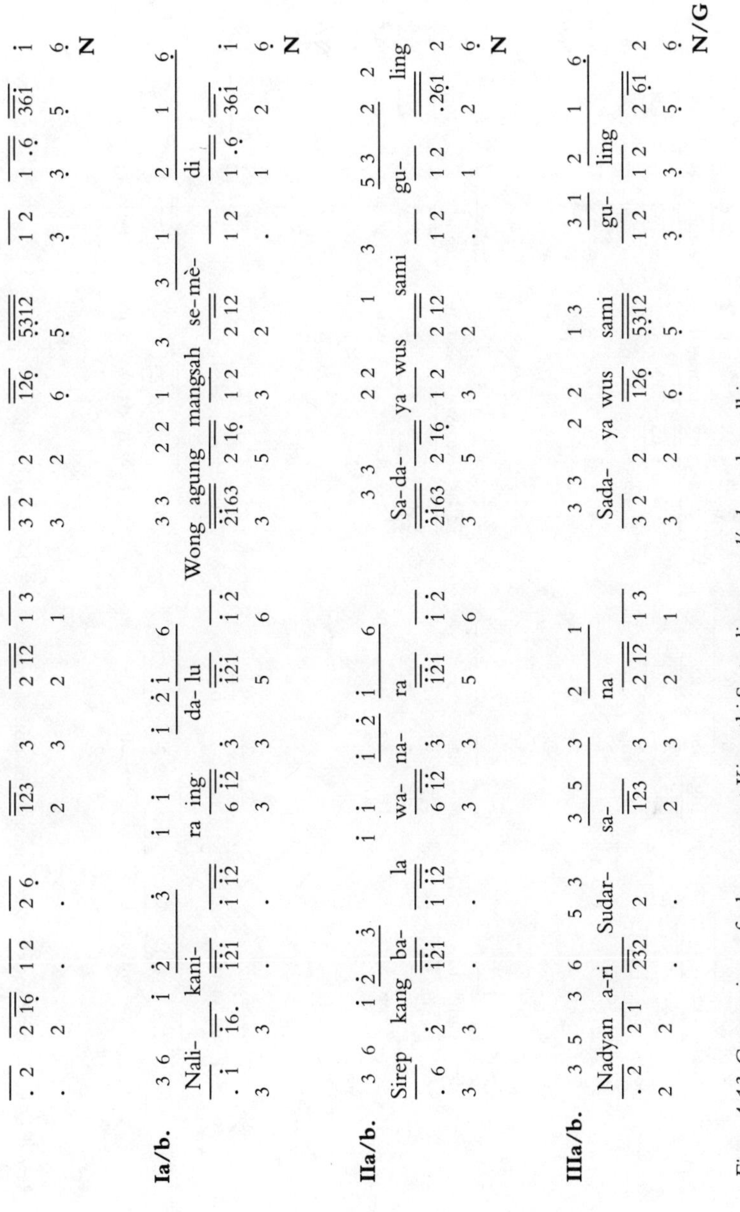

Ia/b.

Nali- kani- ra ing da- lu

Wong agung mangsah se-mê- di

IIa/b.

Sirep kang ba- la wa- na- ra

Sa-da- ya wus sami gu- ling

IIIa/b.

Nadyan a-ri Sudar- sa- na

Sada- ya wus sami gu- ling

Figure 4.13 Comparison of sekar macapat Kinanthi Sastradiwangsa *sléndro* and gendhing
Lobong sléndro manyura (sekar macapat, rebab, and balungan)

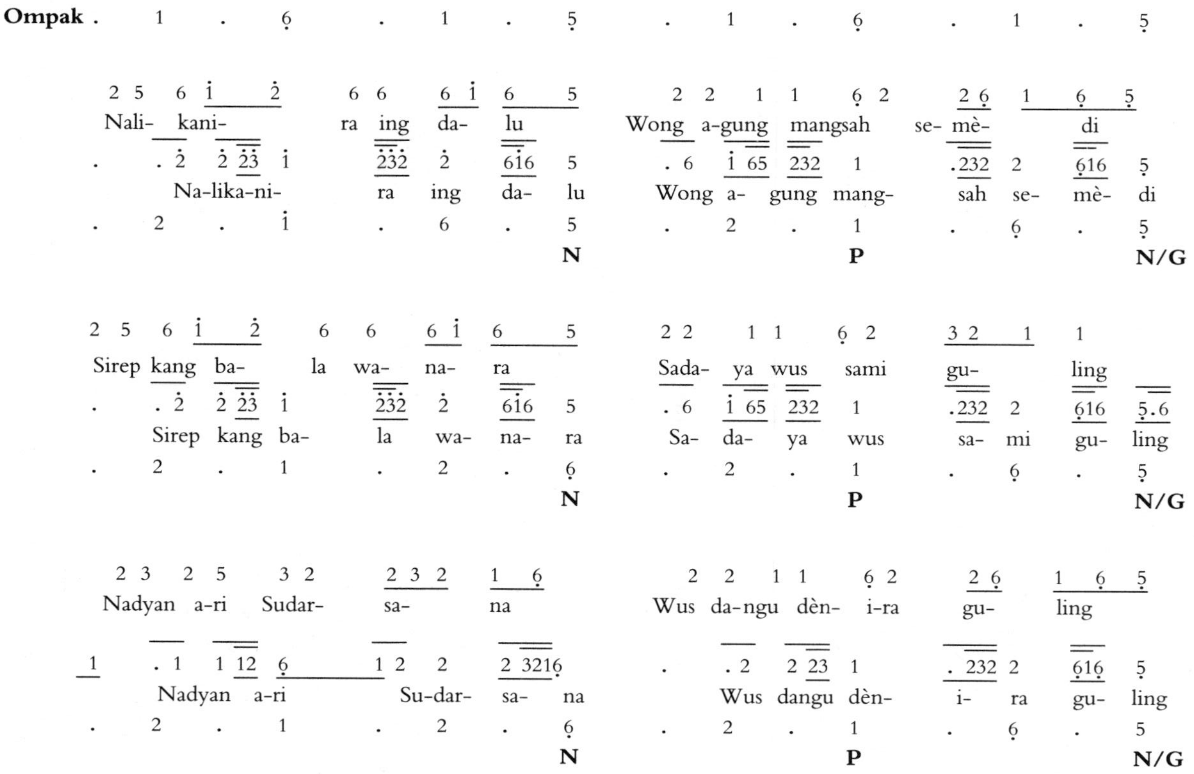

Figure 4.14 Comparison of sekar macapat Kinanthi Sastradiwangsa sléndro and keta-wang Suba Kastawa sléndro sanga (sekar macapat, gérongan, and balungan)

Ia. 3   6   i   i   i   2̣   2̇   2̇
     Na- li- ka- ni- ra ing da- lu

b.   6   3   3   3   2   2̲ 3̲   1   2
     Wong a- gung mang- sah se- mè- di

IIa. 3   6   i   i   i   2̣   2̇   2̇
     Si- rep kang ba- la wa- na- ra

b.   6   3   3   3   2   2̲ 3̲   1   2
     Sa- da- ya wus sa- mi gu- ling

IIIa. 1 2   3   3   3   3   3   3
      Na- dyan a- ri Su- dar- sa- na

b.   3   3   2   2   1   1   2̲ 1̲ 6̣̇ 6̣̇
     Wus da- ngu dèn- i- ra gu- ling

Figure 4.15 Sekar macapat Kinanthi Pawukir sléndro

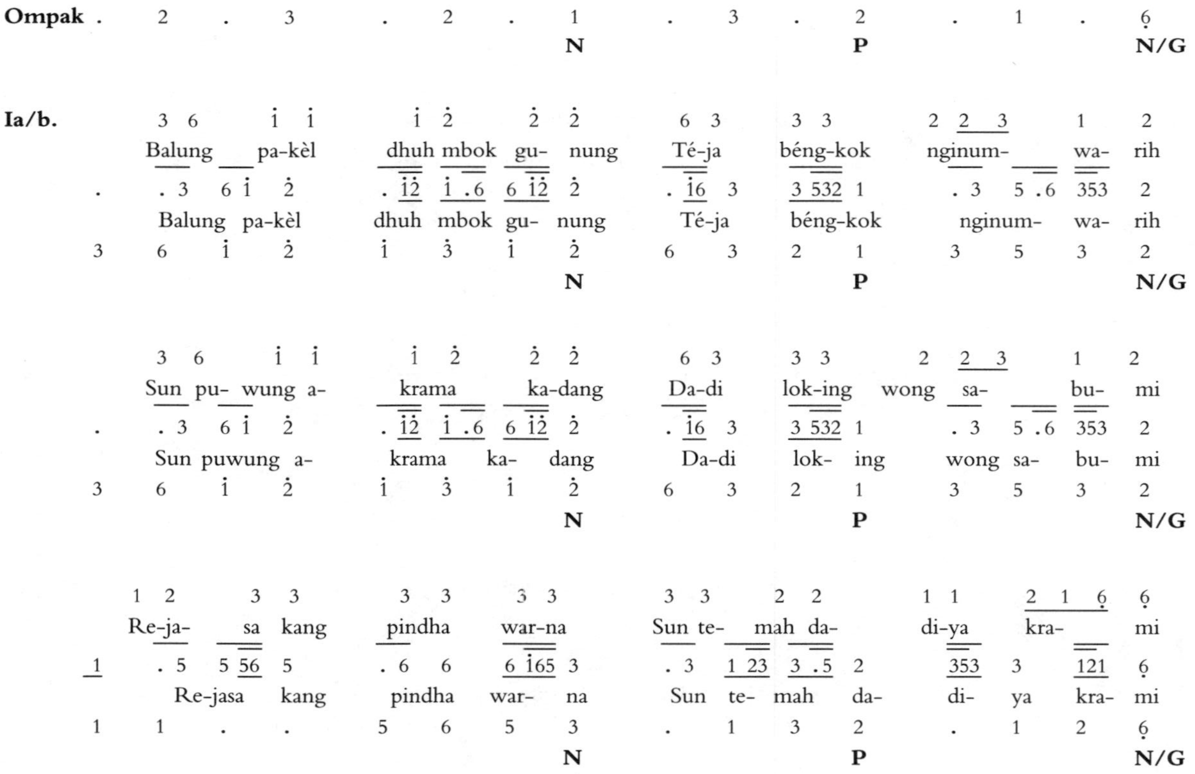

Figure 4.16 Comparison of sekar macapat Kinanthi Pawukir *sléndro* and ketawang Kinanthi Pawukir sléndro manyura (sekar macapat, gérongan, balungan)

Ia.
5̣ 6̣ 1 2   2   2 2 2   2 3 2 1   2 3 2 1
Sri- narèn-   dra miyos   sa- king   pu-ri,   ×2

b.
5̣ 6̣ 1   1 1 1   1   2 1   6̣ 5̣
Bu- sa-   na ka- pra-   bon.

IIa.
3 3 3 1   1 2 3   3 2 3 3 5   3 5   3 2 1
Gi-na-   rebeg,   ba- dha ya yu war- na- ni-   ra,

b.
1 1 1 2   4 5 5   6   5 4 5 4 2   1   2 1   6̣
sang na- ta ma-   wi-   ngit, é

c.
6̣ 6̣ 6̣ 6̣   6̣ 6̣   6̣ 1 2 2   3 2 1   6̣ 5̣
Lir hyang As-ma-   ra tu-   mu-   run,   O

IIIa.
6̣   1   2 6̣   5 4̇
    O

b.
5̣   4 2̣ 1̣
    O

Figure 4.17 Pathetan Pélog Lima Wantah

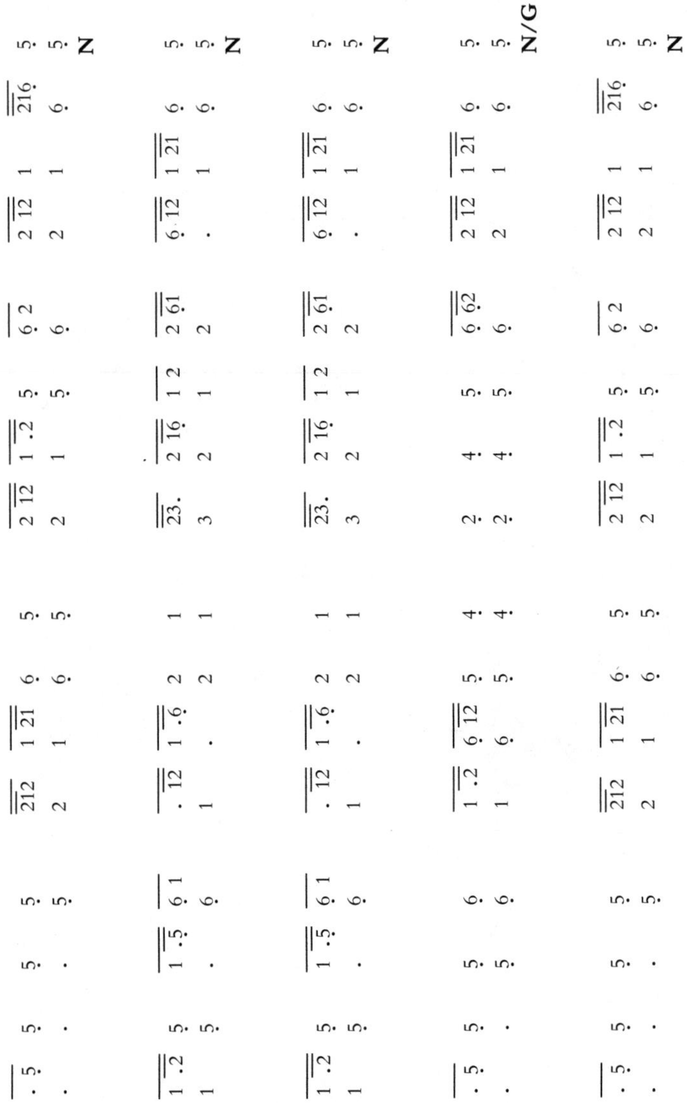

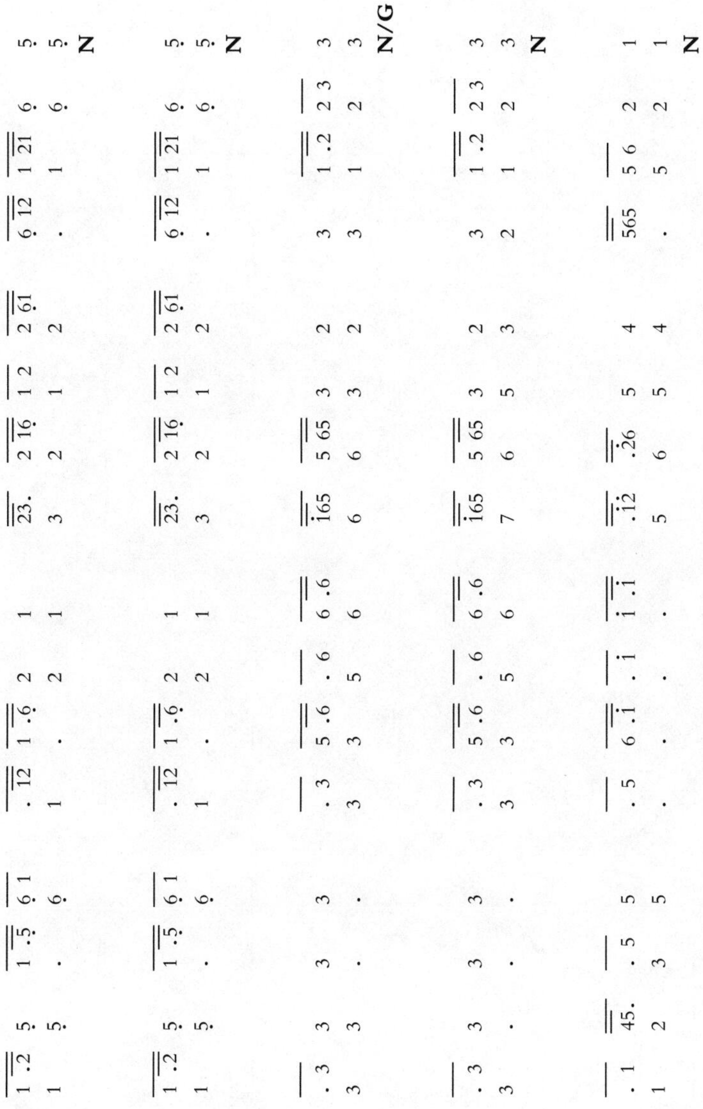

Figure 4.18 Gendhing Kombang Mara pélog lima (rebab and balungan) (continued)

Figure 4.18 (continued)

. 6	6 .6	. 6	6 .6	. 6	6 .1	5	6	1 .2	1 .2	6 1	612	5	3 .2	2 3	3	
6	6	.	.	6	6	5	6	.	1	.	6	5	3	2	3	**N/G**
. 3	3	3	3	2 3	1 .2	2 3	3	3	1	2 3	3	3	1	2 3	3	
.	.	.	3	.	1	2	3	.	1	2	3	.	1	2	3	**N**
6	1	2	2	6	1	2	1	1	1	1	2	4	5	6	5	
.	6	.	5	.	4	2	1	.	.	1	2	4	5	6	5	**N**
6	5	4	2	1	2	4	5	6	5	4	2	1	6 1	5	4	
6	5	4	2	1	2	4	5	6	5	4	2	1	6	5	4	**N**
4	4	4	4	4	4	5	6	1	6 1	5	4	2	1	2	1	
.	.	.	.	4	4	5	6	1	6	5	4	2	1	2	1	**N/G**

Iab. Sri- narèn- dra miyos sa- king pu-ri, Bu- sa- na ka- pra- bon.

Iab. Sri- narèn- dra miyos sa- king pu-ri, Bu- sa- na ka- pra- bon.

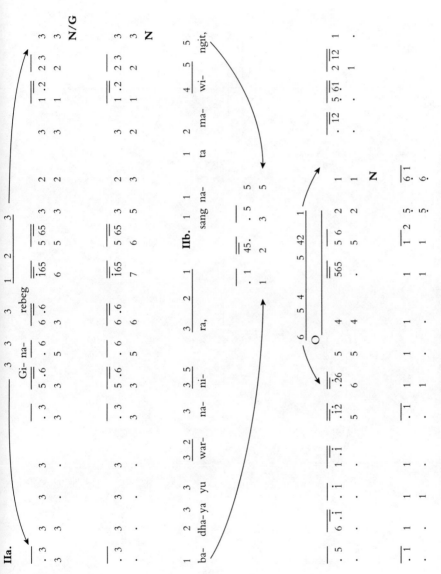

Figure 4.19 Comparison of pathetan Pélog Lima Wantah and gendhing Kombang Mara *pélog lima*, beginning in the second gongan (pathetan, rebab, balungan) (continued)

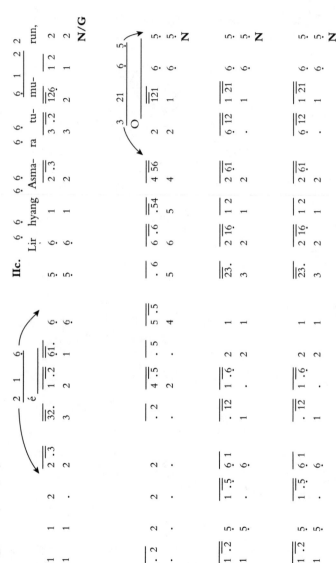

Figure 4.19 (continued)

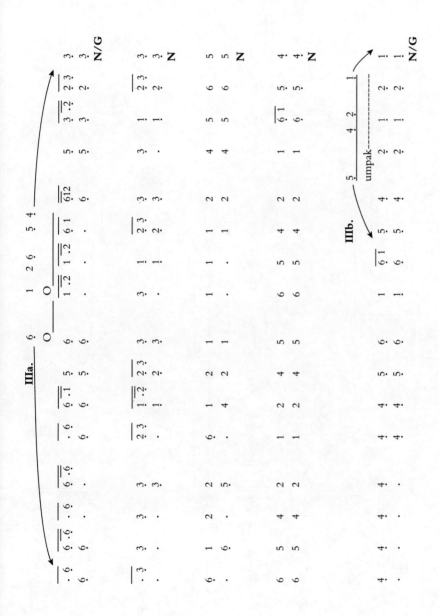

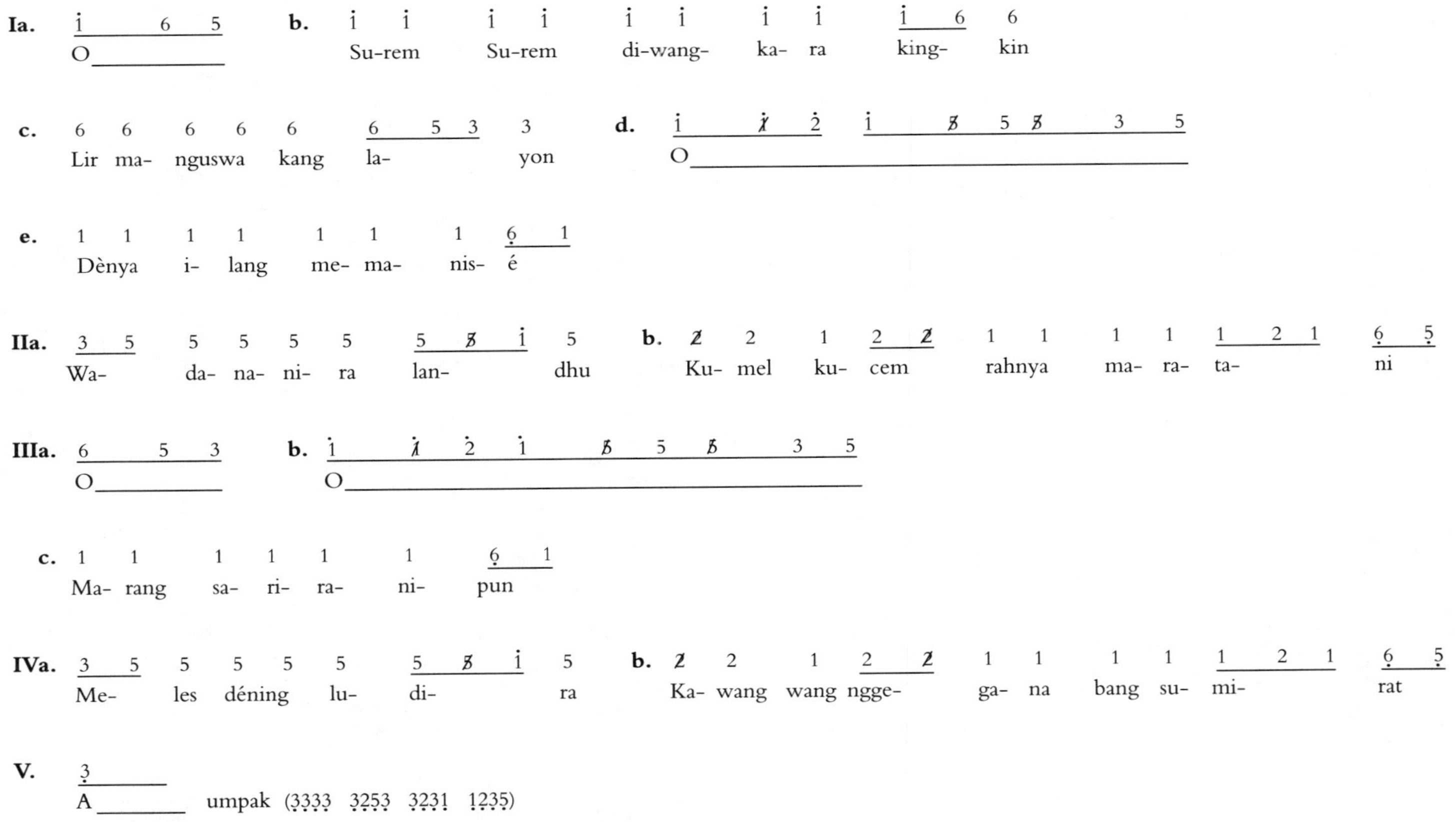

Ia. i 6 5 ◯

b. i i i i i i 6 6
Su-rem Su-rem di-wang- ka- ra king- kin

c. 6 6 6 6 6 5 3 3
Lir ma- nguswa kang la- yon

e. 1 1 1 1 1 6̣ 1
Dènya i- lang me- ma- nis- é

d. i 2̣ ʔ̣ i 5̣ 5 5̃ 3 5
◯

IIa. 3 5 5 5 5 5 5̃ i 5
Wa- da- na- ni- ra lan- dhu

b. 2̃ 2 1 2 2̃ 1 1 1
Ku- mel Ku- mel ku- cem rahnya ma- ra-

1 2 1 6̣ 5̣
ta- ni

IIIa. 6 5 3 5̃ 5 5̃ 3 5
◯

b. i 2̣ ʔ̣ i 6̣ 1
◯ ra

c. 1 1 1 1 1 1 6̣ 1
Ma- rang sa- ri- ra- ni- pun

IVa. 3 5 5 5 5 5̃ i 5
Me- les déning lu- di- ra

b. 2̃ 2 1 2 2̃ 1 1 1
Ka- wang wang ngge- ga- na bang su- mi-

1 2 1 6̣ 5̣
ra- rat

V. 3̣
A̱ ――― umpak (3̣3̣3̣3̣ 3̣2̣5̣3̣ 3̣2̣3̣1̣ 1̣2̣3̣5̣)

Figure 4.20 Sendhon Tlutur sléndro sanga

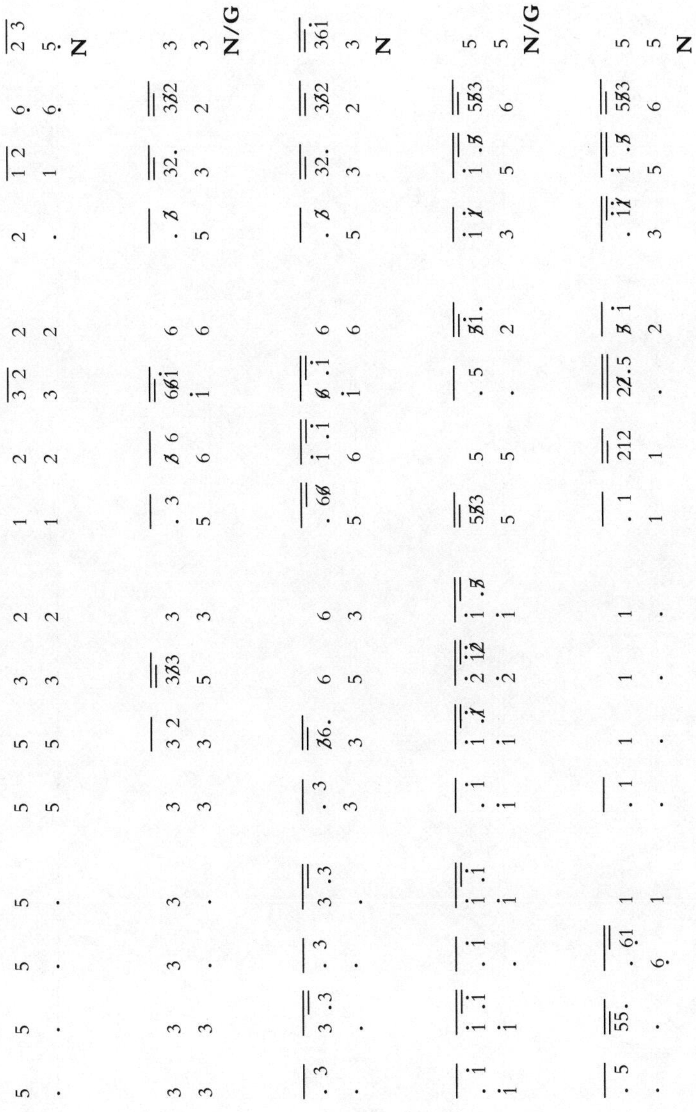

Figure 4.21 Gendhing Tlutur sléndro sanga (rebab and balungan) (continued)

Figure 4.21 (continued)

N

N/G

N

N/G

Ic.

Lir ma-   nguswa   kang   la-   yon

Id.

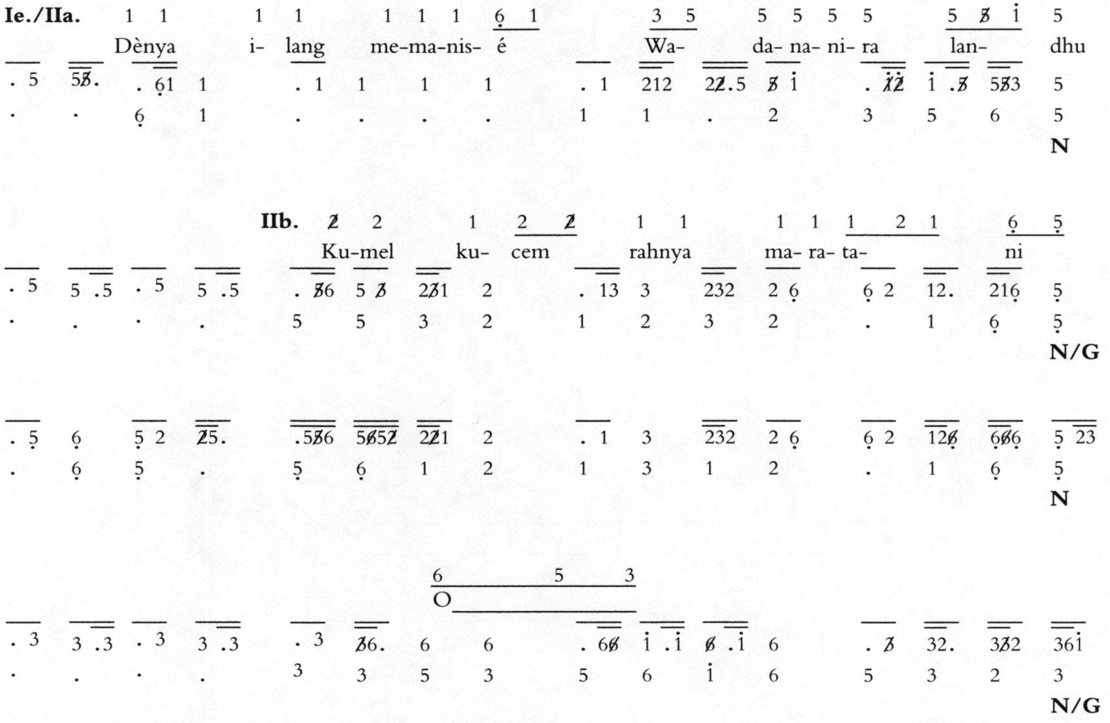

Figure 4.22 Comparison of sendhon Tlutur and gendhing Tlutur sléndro sanga (sendhon, rebab, and balungan) (continued)

Figure 4.22 (continued)

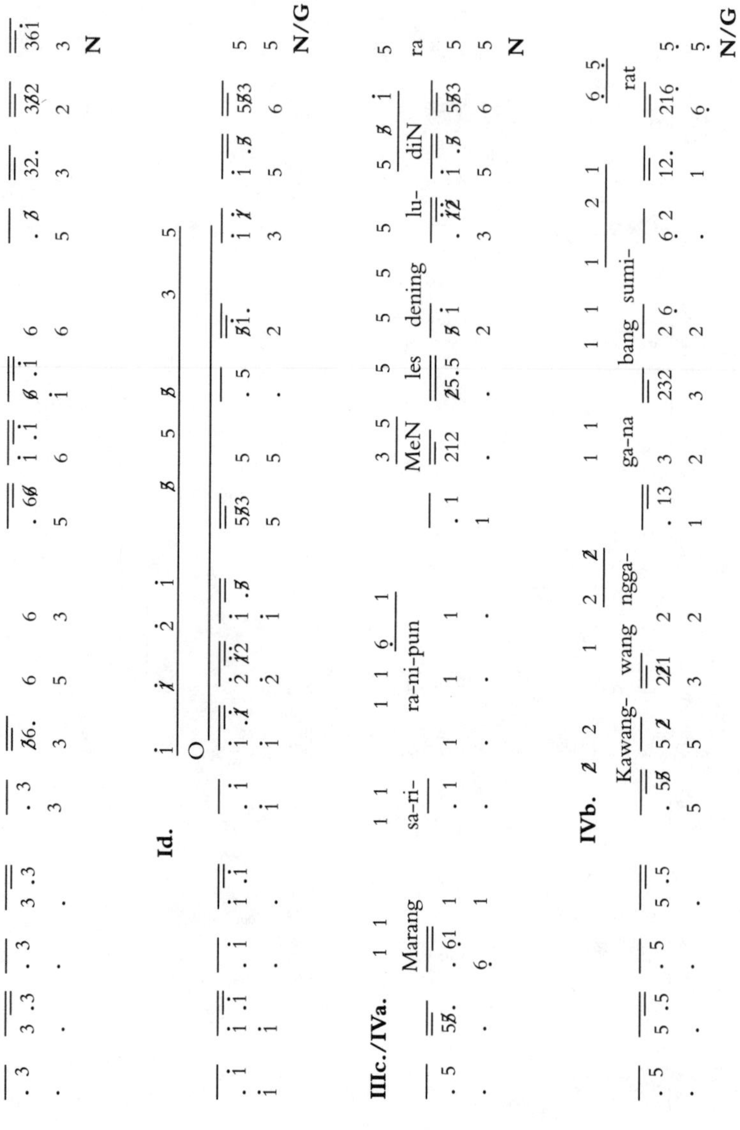

Additional Examples of the Process of Composition

From both historical and oral evidence, we can say that vocal melodies were the origin of many gendhing that were composed in shorter formal structures. These gendhing fall in the genres of gendhing gérongan, gendhing based on a macapat melody, and gendhing panembrama.[17]

Earlier, I presented examples of gendhing based on the macapat melodies, especially those gendhing in the ketawang structure. Here I wish to illustrate the transformation of ladrang Pangkur from the melody of a macapat of the same name. Unlike the process of composing the macapat-based gendhing discussed above (i.e., ketawang Mas Kumambang and ketawang Pucung), this example represents a very intricate transformative process in this genre.

There are different melodic styles of macapat Pangkur, in both pélog and sléndro. One of the Pangkur in sléndro is Pangkur Paripurna. Figure 4.23 (p. 208) is the melody of sekar macapat Pangkur Paripurna.

At first we will find it difficult to see how ladrang Pangkur originated from the above song, particularly if we think of ladrang Pangkur *irama dadi* or *tanggung*. As it is commonly practiced, ladrang Pangkur can be played in different irama: irama tanggung (I), irama dadi (II), irama wilet (III), or *irama rangkep* (IV). For irama tanggung or dadi, the balungan melody is as in figure 4.24 (p. 208).

It is difficult to find the relationship between the verse melody of Pangkur and ladrang Pangkur. A closer examination reveals, however, that the end-notes of each line of the macapat Pangkur are synonymous with the end-notes of each gatra of ladrang Pangkur, except that the third kenongan consists of two end-notes of pitch 1. Do we consider the above ladrang Pangkur an abstraction of macapat Pangkur? Yes. But it is not direct abstraction. To find out about it, let us look at ladrang Pangkur in irama wilet or rangkep (figure 4.25, p. 208).

As with ladrang Pangkur in irama dadi, the end-note of each line of the verse-melody is synonymous with the end-note of each two-gatra phrase of ladrang Pangkur irama wilet. What is significantly different is the fact that each kenongan phrase of ladrang Pangkur irama wilet is twice as long as ladrang Pangkur irama dadi. We also notice that the second and third kenongan of the former have more notes than that of the latter. Thus, a closer structural relationship between the piece in irama wilet and macapat Pangkur becomes more apparent. Figure 4.26 (p. 209) is a comparison of these two Pangkur. (Note: The first line, with the texts, is the sekar macapat melody; the second line is the rebab melody; and the third line is the balungan.)

The illustration indicates that the process of composing ladrang Pangkur involved a creative way of connecting the lines of the macapat Pangkur. That is, the composer conceived the first gatra of each kenongan of ladrang Pangkur as a melodic connection. Notice that the relationship between the fifth line of the verse-melody and the third kenongan of ladrang Pangkur differs from the others.

That is, the third kenongan of ladrang contains one line of the verse-melody, instead of two lines as in other kenongan. This is necessary in order to accommodate the longest line (12 syllables) of the verse-melody and to fulfill the requirement of the melodic structure of ladrang, i.e., four kenongan per gongan.

When the process of transformation evolved, it was necessary for the composer to modify some of the verse-melody of Pangkur. In particular, such a modification occurred in the third kenongan. But a minor modification also occurred in the first and fourth kenongan. Figure 4.27 (pp. 210–11) shows a modified version of the melody of Pangkur.

The modified melody of ladrang Pangkur can still be found in the song repertoire of langendriyan. In fact, according to Warsadiningrat, Tondhakusuma composed ladrang Pangkur for a langendriyan piece. Explaining the background of ladrang Pangkur, Warsadiningrat says, "Gendhing Pangkur [pelog barang] came from Pangkur Paripurna, slendro pathet sanga, a gendhing langen driya composed by Raden Mas Harya Tandhakusuma with no gerongan but *with a sindhenan whose text was sekar pangkur Paripurna*" (1987:155; emphasis added).[18] I believe this passage refers to the modified version of the melody of Pangkur mentioned above.

I hope I have convinced the reader that ladrang Pangkur was first conceived in irama wilet. Thus, ladrang Pangkur irama dadi is a condensed version of ladrang Pangkur irama wilet. In fact, the older generation of musicians often told me that when they were young, they played ladrang Pangkur irama dadi only once, as a transition from the buka (introduction) to irama wilet. Significantly, older musical notation of ladrang Pangkur does not have the part of irama dadi (Djakoeb and Wignjaroemeksa 1919:136). The evidence strengthens the above thesis: the composer conceived ladrang Pangkur first in irama wilet.

In present-day gamelan practice, ladrang Pangkur irama dadi commonly has gérongan with a Salisir text. It is also very common for ladrang Pangkur to be played in irama tanggung, an irama that creates an animated feeling in the piece. Perhaps dancing gave an impetus to playing ladrang Pangkur in irama tanggung.

We have seen the importance of vocal melody as the melodic precedent of gendhing. Composing gendhing involved a very creative way of modifying already existing musical material. In the cases presented above, the prior musical material was a vocal melody. In the example below, the transfer is from the vocal melody of a children's song to a stately, vocally-oriented gamelan piece: the recomposing of gendhing dolanan Witing Klapa to become the second half of ayak-ayakan Pamungkas.[19] Figure 4.28 (p. 212) shows the correlation between these two compositions.

We have seen the extent to which gamelan composition is rooted in vocal melody. In some cases the melodic source of new gendhing is not limited only to Javanese gamelan and vocal music. A panembrama piece ladrang Siyem (Siam) is a case in point. It was composed to commemorate and honor the visit of the King of Siam to the court of Surakarta in 1929 during the reign of Paku Buwana X. My own observation reveals that ladrang Siyem was a direct adaptation, with minor modification, of the Western style Siamese royal anthem, *Sarasoen Phra Barami*.[20] Figure 4.29 (p. 213) is the notation of the balungan and gérongan of ladrang Siyem. Figure 4.30 (p. 214) is a notation of the Siamese royal anthem.[21] Figure 4.31 (p. 215) shows the correlation between these two compositions.

Figure 4.23 Sekar macapat Pangkur Paripurna sléndro

notes	2 2	2 2	2 1	1	2 3 5	2	1 6.
syllable	Mingkar	mingkur-	ing	ang-		ka-	ra

notes	2 2	2 2	2 2	i i 2̇	1 2	6̣ 1
syllable	A-	ka-	ra- na	ka- re- nan	mardi-	si- wi

notes	5 6	i i	i i 2̇	6 i 6 5	6 i	i
syllable	Si-	na-	wung res-	mi- ning	ki-	dung

notes	6 i 2̇	2̇	6 i 6 5	6	2 1	6̣
syllable	Si-	nu- ba	si-	nu-	kar- ta	

notes	2̇ 2̇	2̇	i 6 2̇ 6 i	5 2	6̣ 1
syllable	Mrih ker-	tar- ta	pa- kar- ti- ning	ngèlmu	lu- hung

notes	1 2 2	5	5 3 2	2 1 6̣
syllable	Tu- mrap- é	wong	ta- nah	Ja- wa

notes	3 5 5	5	3 2 3	1 6̣ 5̣
syllable	A- ga- ma	a-	gem- ing	a- ji

Figure 4.24 Balungan ladrang Pangkur sléndro sanga (irama tanggung and dadi)

```
2 1 2 6.   2 1 6. 5
6 5 2. 1   3 2 1 6.
2 3 2 1    5 3 2 1
3 2 1 6.   2 1 6. 5
```

Figure 4.25 Balungan ladrang Pangkur sléndro sanga

```
. 2 . 1    . 2 . 6.   . 2 . 1    . 6. . 5.
6 6 . .    5 5 6 1    2. i 5 2    6. . 1 6.
. 2 . 2    . . . 1    2 1 3 2     . 1 . 6.
5 6 2. i   5 2 1 6.   . 2 . 1     . 6. . 5.
```

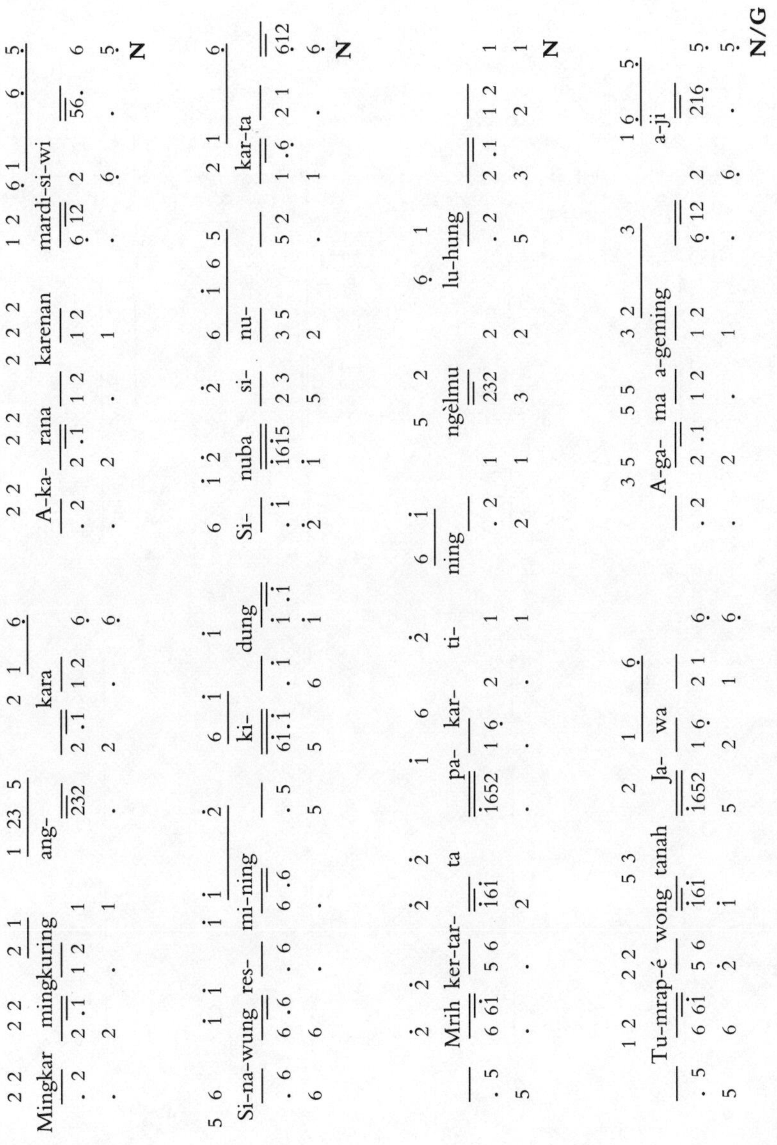

Figure 4.26 Comparison of sekar macapat Pangkur sléndro and ladrang Pangkur sléndro sanga (sekar macapat, rebab, and balungan)

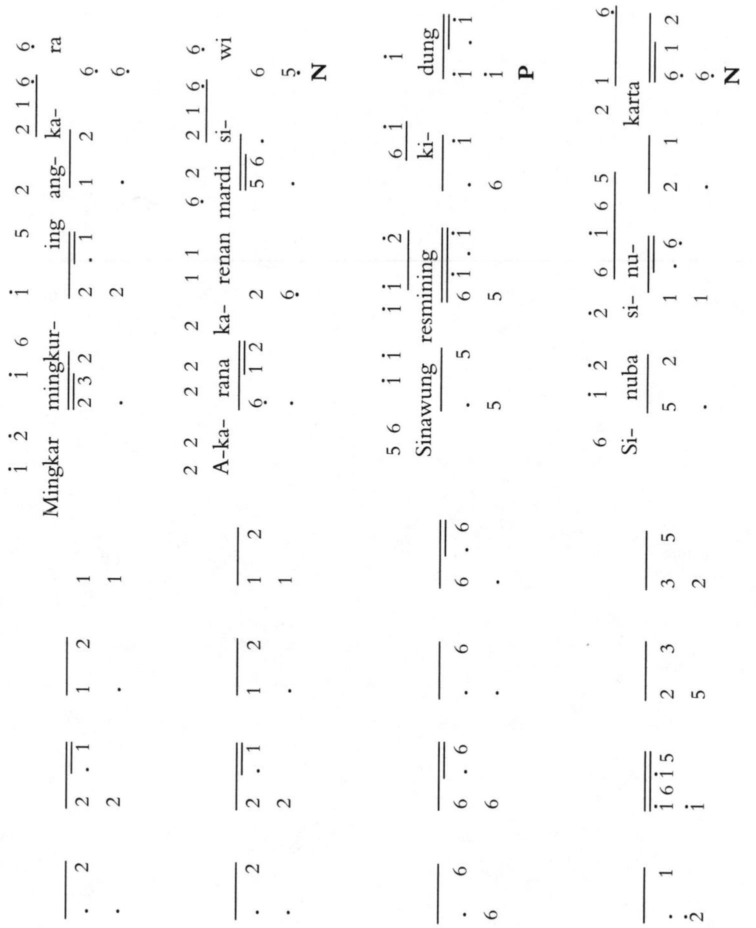
Mingkar mingkur- ing ang- ka- ra
A-ka- rana ka- renan mardi si- wi
N
Sinawung resmining ki- dung
P
Si- nuba si- nu- karta
N

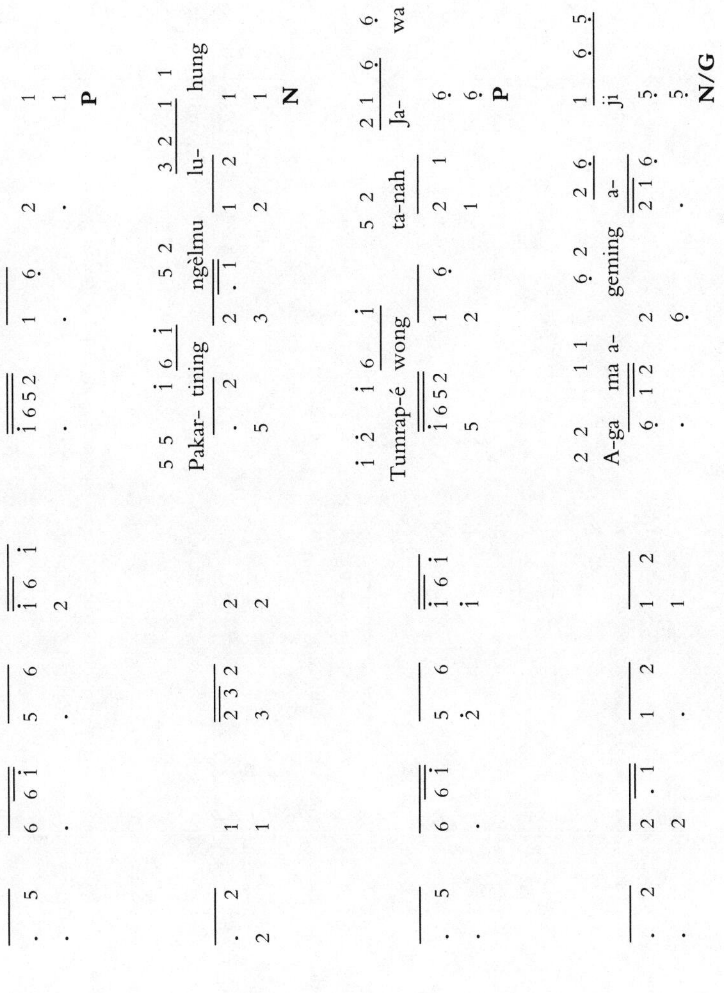

Figure 4.27 Comparison of sekar macapat Pangkur Paripurna sléndro and ladrang Pangkur sléndro sanga (sekar macapat, rebab, and balungan)

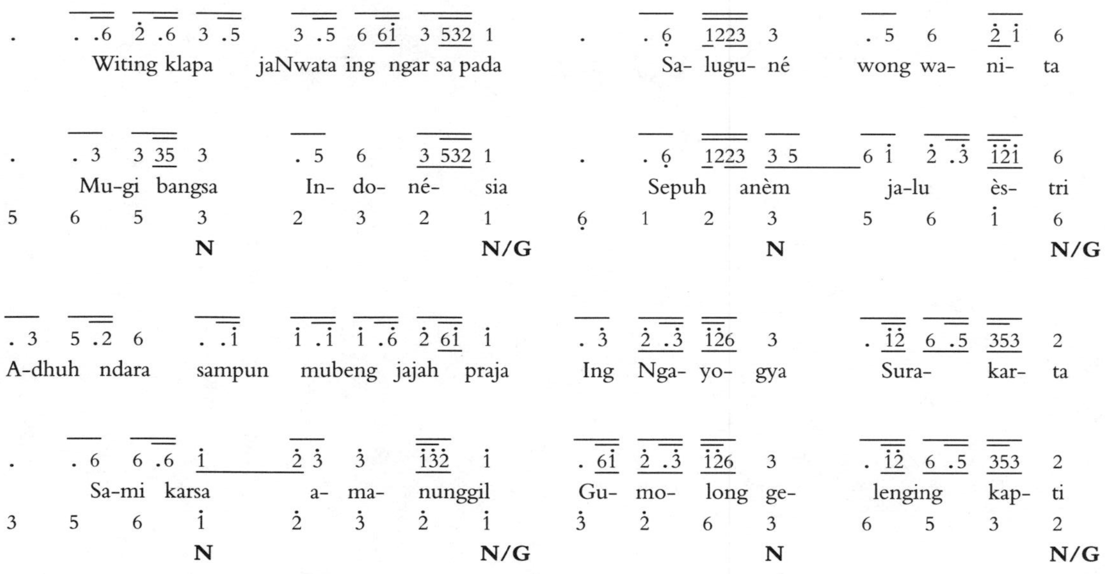

Figure 4.28 Comparison of gendhing dolanan Witing Klapa and ayak-ayakan Pamungkas sléndro manyura (gendhing dolanan, ayak-ayakan, balungan)

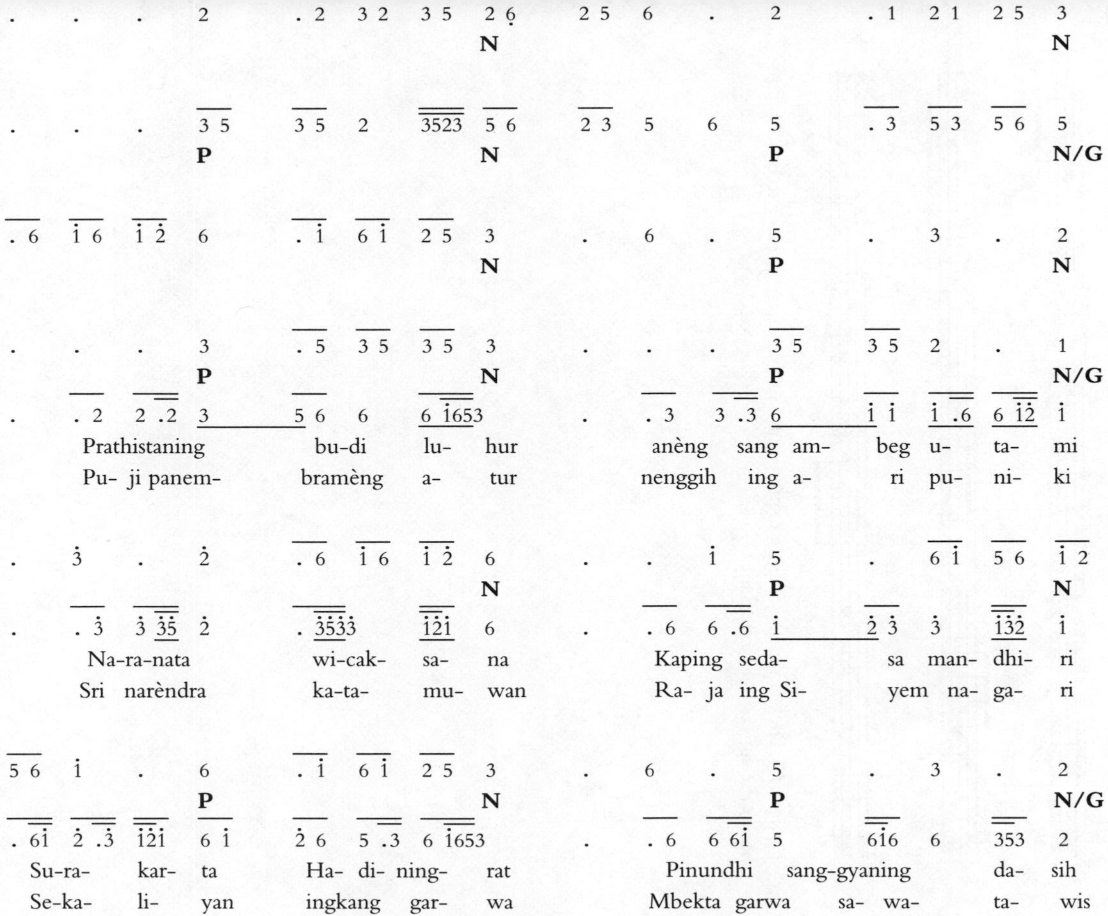

Figure 4.29 Ladrang Siyem sléndro nem (balungan and gérongan)

Figure 4.30 The Siamese royal anthem played by a military band; a piece to be played to honor the appearance of the king

Figure 4.31 Comparison of ladrang Siyem and the Siamese royal anthem. Line 1, Western staff of ladrang Siyem; line 2, cipher notation of ladrang Siyem; line 3, Western staff of the Siamese royal anthem

The Instrumental Element of Gendhing and Gendhing Bonang

Although the evidence is far from comprehensive, the foregoing discussion suggests a central role for vocal melodies in the construction of many gendhing. This does not mean, however, that the instrumental element has been excluded from the construction of gamelan pieces. There are sections of some gendhing that are based on the instrumental idiom, such as the ompak of ketawang Suba Kastawa. The balungan ·1·6 ·1·5 ·1·6 ·1·5 is a gongan which comes from the melody of an archaic instrumental ensemble called Monggang. Indeed, musicians refer to the kenong and kempul part for this section of the piece as *monggangan* technique. (In this section, kenong and kempul play the same melody as the balungan.)[22]

It is probable that a repetition of a single gatra pattern in a gendhing was inspired by the melodies for the instrumental ensembles gamelan Monggang or Kodhok Ngorèk,[23] for example, the first gongan of ladrang Dirada Meta, which contains the repetitive melody 6365 6362; the first gongan of ladrang Prabu Mataram, consisting of the repetitive melody 1216 1215; and the first gongan of gendhing Ela–Ela Pengantèn consisting of the repetitive melody ·6·5·6·3·6· 5·3·2. For some gendhing, in order to finish a gongan, it is necessary to compose a new gatra that deviates from the repetitive gatra. Figures 4.32 and 4.33 (p. 220) show two examples of gendhing in this category.

These instrumentally-inspired gendhing contain melodies in the low range. This is one of the characteristics of instrumentally-inspired melodies. It is difficult to determine when instrumentally-inspired melodies end and vocally-inspired melodies begin. Lacking evidence, I can only speculate that when a gendhing begins to employ middle- or high-range melodic motion, we should assume that the vocal element had taken over that melody.

The second gongan of ladrang Agun–Agun (figure 4.34, p. 220) employs the middle and high range. This is an indication of its vocal element. Unlike the early examples, this piece contains both regular and irregular rhythmic patterns. In the first gongan, such variety of rhythm may still be considered an extension of instrumentally-inspired melodies, especially because the melody is constrained to the low register.

Let us now turn to gendhing bonang. This is a group of compositions whose performance is without the participation of soft-sounding instruments (i.e., rebab, gendèr, gambang, celempung, and suling) or vocalists. Gendhing bonang is commonly categorized as an instrumental genre. Are gendhing bonang really instrumental pieces devoid of vocal elements? To answer this question, let us begin by examining the character and performance practice of these gendhing.[24]

Composed in large formal structures, gendhing bonang have the same compositional sections as in gendhing rebab: a gendhing bonang consists of two sections, mérong and inggah; usually it has a transitional phrase called ompak; and sometimes it has a special inggah section called sesegan and an ending section called suwukan. There are two features of performance practice of gendhing bonang. First, the range of gendhing bonang falls mostly in the low and middle registers. Second, the conclusion of gendhing bonang (i.e., the inggah or sesegan) is always played loudly in irama tanggung.[25] Some gendhing bonang employ irregular, syncopated balungan rhythms (for example, some passages in gendhing Glendheng [see figure 4.35, p. 221], gendhing Slébrak, and gendhing Klenthung). These passages make the sesegan more dynamic.

Unfortunately, there is no evidence to indicate the melodic precedents of gendhing bonang. Can we determine the melodic character of these gendhing? Do they contain only instrumentally inspired melodies, or do they incorporate vocal elements? In an attempt to answer this question, I would like to compare the way in which the bonang part is rendered in gendhing rebab and in gendhing bonang. Let me first explain the technique of bonang-playing.

Basically, there are two bonang-playing techniques: *imbal-imbalan* and *pipilan*. Imbal-imbalan (interlocking) refers to the playing technique in which bonang barung and bonang panerus play interlocking patterns.[26] Gendhing bonang do not employ imbal-imbalan technique. They employ only pipilan.

In pipilan, a bonang player plays single notes one at a time, based on each pair of the balungan notes. Because of the anticipatory nature of this pipilan pairing technique, the bonang functions as a melodic leader of the saron instruments. That is, the bonang part tells the saron player what tones will follow by anticipating a pair of balungan tones (Figures 4.36 and 4.37 on p. 221 are examples of the pipilan technique for balungan mlaku and balungan nibani). However, there are limits to the leadership of the bonang. As I have mentioned elsewhere (Sumarsam 1984:283),

> Within the pipilan technique, there are some practices that give clues to the motion of the inner melody. These techniques are gembyangan (octave playing) and *nduduk tunggal* (syncopated single notes). There are different kinds of gembyangan grouped according to their special uses in expressing the inner melody.

There are two kinds of gembyangan: (1) gembyangan that are used to express a high register of gendhing melody unattainable on the bonang (figure 4.38, p. 221), and (2) gembyangan that are used to signal a gantungan melody in the high or medium range (figure 4.39, p. 222). There is also a bonang technique called nduduk tunggal that expresses gantungan melody in the low range (figure 4.40, p. 222). These are three bonang-playing techniques whose functions are not to guide the saron player to his balungan tones, but to express the flow of vocally-inspired melody.

The question posed earlier is whether gendhing bonang are purely instrumental pieces. In comparing the bonang parts of gendhing bonang and gendhing rebab, I argue that, if the bonang part of gendhing bonang does not differ from the bonang part of gendhing rebab, the character of gendhing bonang is not fundamentally different from that of gendhing rebab.

In figure 4.41 (pp. 223–25) I have provided the balungan and bonang part for gendhing rebab Pasang. In figure 4.42 (pp. 226–28) I have given the balungan and bonang part of gendhing bonang Gondrong. These are the abbreviations used to identify bonang techniques in both gendhing:

G-1,   gembyangan gantungan
G-2,   gembyangan to accentuate the end-note of a phrase
G-3,   gembyangan to anticipate the following gantungan
DT-1, nduduk tunggal, expressing gantungan melody in a low register
DT-2, nduduk tunggal, anticipating the following gantungan
SP,   sekaran pipilan (the embellishment of pipilan playing) to heighten the effectiveness of a cadence

Pipilan playing is used in most parts of both gendhing. Both gendhing also employ the other two bonang techniques: gembyangan (G) and nduduk tunggal (DT). Another technique used in both gendhing is sekaran pipilan (SP). Thus the bonang parts in gendhing bonang do not differ from the bonang parts in gendhing rebab—that is, they share common playing techniques. This suggests that the concepts of gendhing bonang and gendhing rebab are the same. In corroboration of this argument, Soekanto, a musician and gamelan teacher whose bonang playing is the focus of McNamara's thesis, consistently explains "unusual" passages of bonang parts through analogies to the ways that rebab lines are rendered (McNamara 1980:127–33).[27]

The examples above also indicate that some passages can be found in both gendhing bonang Gondrong and gendhing rebab Pasang. In the mérong, ·253 ·2·1 in Gondrong is essentially the same as ·253 2121 in Pasang. In the inggah, 2325 2356 6676 5421 can be found in both gendhing.

There are other gendhing bonang that share the same passages. A more striking example is in gendhing bonang Jalaga and the gendhing rebab of the same name. The mérong of these two gendhing are the same, except for a few notes' difference. The difference between these gendhing lies in the inggah section.

The only important difference between gendhing bonang and gendhing rebab is in their use of melodic register. Gendhing bonang employ mostly low and middle registers; that is, the range of gendhing bonang does not go beyond the range of bonang. Another feature of gendhing bonang missing in gendhing rebab is the playing of sesegan as a conclusion to every gendhing.

Sesegan is also featured in the performance of gamelan Sekatèn. This ensemble consists of large-sized, loud-sounding instruments capable of producing very loud sounds. The Sekatèn gamelan is played for special court occasions, most notably in a week-long Sekatèn celebration to commemorate the birth and death of the Prophet Muhamad. Another important aspect of Sekatèn gamelan is its low tuning. This low-pitched gamelan produces a special effect—a weighty and dignified quality of sound.

Gendhing bonang convey a weighty and dignified quality of sound, and the low range of gendhing bonang supports this quality. The production of loud sound is another feature of gendhing bonang, especially in the playing of sesegan sections. Did Sekatèn gamelan inspire the creation of gendhing bonang? Unfortunately, lack of evidence prevents us from giving a conclusive answer to this question. But the fact that gendhing bonang were composed during a time in Javanese history when loud-sounding music was important for a variety of reasons[28] suggests a connection between gendhing bonang and gamelan Sekatèn, or gamelan that were built according to gamelan Sekatèn standards.

```
2326  2327 ⎤
2326  2327 ⎬  instrumentally-inspired phrases
2326  2327 ⎦
6765  3567 ⟶ cadence phrase
```

Figure 4.32 The first gongan of ladrang Tedhak Saking pélog barang

```
1516  2356 ⎤
1516  2356 ⎬  instrumentally-inspired phrases
1516  2356 ⎦
5563  6532 ⟶ cadence phrase

5653  6532 ⎤
5653  6532 ⎬  instrumentally-inspired phrases
5653  6532 ⎦
6616  2356 ⟶ cadence phrase
```

Figure 4.33 Ladrang Sapu Jagad sléndro manyura

```
.62.  6232 ⎤
565.  5623 ⎥  instrumentally-inspired phrases
565.  5623 ⎥
5616  5352 ⎦

..2.  2232 ⎤
6165  .32. ⎬  vocally-inspired phrases
6165  .323 ⎦
5321  6532
```

Figure 4.34 Ladrang Agun-Agun sléndro nem

```
.4  54  54  54    54  5   6   1     62  .6  1   62    .6  1   6   5
                                                                  N

.4  54  54  54    54  5   6   1     62  .6  1   62    .6  1   6   5
                                                                  N

.4  54  54  54    54  5   6   1     62  .6  1   62    .6  1   6   5
                                                                  N

 4   2   5   4     2   1   2   1     2   3   5   3     2   1   2   3
                                                                  N

 5   6   5   3     2   1   2   3     5   6   5   3     2   1   2   3
                                                                  N

 2   2   .   .     2   2   .   .     4   4   4   4     2   1   6   5
                                                                  N

.4  54  54   5     1   2   4   5    .4  54  54   5     1   2   4   5
                                                                  N

.6  54   5  .6    54   5   6   1     62  .6  1   62    .6  1   6   5
                                                                N/G
```

Figure 4.35 The inggah of gendhing bonang Glendheng pélog lima. The first kenongan, the first half of the second kenongan, and the last kenongan are phrases that have irregular, syncopated rhythms.

```
Bonang barung   2 3 2 . . 3 2 . 2 1 2 . . 1 2 .
Balungan            2       3       2       1
```

Figure 4.36 Pipilan Technique of bonang for balungan mlaku

```
Bonang barung   . 5 . 2 2 5 . . 2 5 2 . 3 5 . 3
Balungan          .     5     .     3
```

Figure 4.37 Pipilan Technique of bonang for balungan nibani

```
                            ⌒gembyangan⌐
Bonang barung   353..53.6i6..i6.  2i666..6..6..6..
Balungan        3   5   6   i    3   2   i   6
Rebab           .  6  12.  121  i  12  6  123  121  6
```

Figure 4.38 Gembyangan used to indicate the high register of the gendhing. For the bonang part, the underlined tone means octave playing (gembyangan).

⌒nduduk gembyang⌒
Bonang barung   ..3..3..3..3..3.   ..3..3..3.23.323.
Balungan   3   3   .   .   3   3   .   2
Rebab   . 3 3 .3 . 3 3 .3 . 3 2 16 1 2 2

Figure 4.39 Nduduk gembyang technique of bonang used to indicate a gantungan melody in the middle or upper octave of the gendhing

nduduk tunggal
Bonang barung   656..56.232..32. 3..3..3.363..63.
Balungan   6 5 2 3 . . 3 6

Figure 4.40 Nduduk tunggal technique of bonang used to indicate a gantungan melody in the low octave of the gendhing

G-1   **G-1**

1..1..1.121..21.   3..3..3.232..32.   323..23.535..35.   212..12.212..12.
. . 1 2   3 3 2 3   . 2 5 3   2 1 2 1

G-1   **G-1**

1..1..1.121..21.   3..3..3.232..32.   323..23.535..35.   212..12.212..12.
. . 1 2   3 3 2 3   . 2 5 3   2 1 2 1

              G-1   **G-2/3-1**

2..2..2..2..2..2   ..2..2..2..2..2.   2..2..2.232..32.   565..65.535.3..3
2 2 . .   2 2 . .   2 2 . 3   5 6 5 3

                              SP   **G-2/3-1**

..3..3..535..35.   212..12.515.61.6   121..21.262..62.   121..21.323.2..2
. . 5 3   2 1 2 6   1 2 . 6   1 2 3 2
                                                              N

                      G-1

..2..2..2..2..2.   .2..2..2121..21.   3..3..3.323..23.   212..12.616..16.
.. . . .   . 1 2   3 3 . 2   . 1 6 1

     G-1   **G-1**

2..2..2..2..2..2   ..2..2..121..21.   3..3..3.323..23.   212..12.616..16.
.. . . .   . 1 2   3 3 . 2   . 1 6 1

              G-1   **G-2/3-1**

2..2..2..2..2..2   ..2..2..2..2..2.   2..2..2.232..32.   565..65.535.3..3
2 2 . .   2 2 . .   2 2 . 3   5 6 5 3

                      SP   **SP**

..3..3..535..35.   212..12.515.61.6   353..53.525..25.   353..53.636.53.5
. . 5 3   2 1 2 6   3 5 . 2   3 5 6 5
                                                              N

     DT   **G-1**   **SP**

..5..5..5..5..5.   .5..5..5656..56.   616..16.2..2..2.   212..12.636..53.
. . . .   5 5 6 5   6 1 2 .   2 1 6 5

Figure 4.41 Bonang parts and balungan of gendhing rebab Pasang pélog lima
(continued)

Figure 4.41 (continued)

G-1	SP	DT-1	DT-2

```
     G-1                SP   DT-1                  DT-2
616..16.2..2..2.  212..12.636..53.  6..6..6.161..61.  535..35.23..3..3
  6   1   2   .      2   1   6   5    6   6   1   6     5   3   2   3
```

```
              G-1
..3..3..3..3..3.  .3..3..3..3..3..  3..3..3..3..3..3  525..25.353..53.
  .   .   .   .      3   3   .   .     3   3   .   .    5   2   3   5
```

```
       G-1              G-1          SP   G-2/3-1
..5..5..5..5..5.  .5..5..5656..56.  1..1..1.121..21.  61555..5..5..5..
  .   .   .   .      5   5   6   5    .   1   .   2    3   5   6   5
                                                              N
```

```
5..5..5..5..5..5  ..5..5..656..56.  242..42.545..45.  212..12.212..12.
  .   .   .   .      5   5   6   5    2   4   5   4    2   1   2   1
```

```
         G-1
414..14.1..1..1.  121..21.454..54.  545..45.242..42.  212..12.212..12.
  .   4   1   .      1   2   4   5    .   4   2   4    2   1   2   1
```

```
         G-1              G-1
5..5..5..5..5..5  ..5..5..5..5..5.  2..2..2..2..2..2  232..32.212..12.
  5   5   .   .      5   5   .   .    2   2   .   .    2   3   2   1
```

```
  G-1                               G-1   G-2/3
1..1..1.323..23.  21.661..616.53.5  151..51.565..65.  1..1..1.212.1..1
  .   .   3   2      .   1   6   5    1   5   .   6    1   .   2   1
                                                              N/G
```

Inggah

```
   G-1          SP         SP                          SP
3..3..3..3..3..6  .636..56.323..23.  123..23.161..61.  565..65.151.612.
  3   3   .   .      6   5   3   2    3   2   1   6     5   6   1   6
```

Figure 4.41 (continued)

```
  G-1        SP            SP                    SP
3..3..3..3..3..6 .636..56.323..23.   123..23.161..61.   565..65.151.612.
  3  3  .  .   6  5  3  2    3  2  1  6    5  6  1  6
                                                              N


  G-1        SP            SP                    SP
3..3..3..3..3..6 .636..56.323..23.   123..23.161..61.   565..65.151.612.
  3  3  .  .   6  5  3  2    3  2  1  6    5  6  1  6


             G-1                               SP
1..1..1..1..1..1  ..1..1..1..1..1.  .1..1...121..21.  353..53.636.56.5
  1  1  .  .   1  1  .  .    1  1  .  2    3  5  6  5
                                                              N


  G-1                G-1                        SP
..5..5..323..23.  1..1..1..1..1..1  ..1..1..121..21.  353..53.636.56.5
  .  5  3  2    1  1  .  .    1  1  .  2    3  5  6  5


                SP-G-2/3-1        SP
232..32.252..52.  232.3.21666..6..  6..6..67767..67.  545..45.212..12.
  2  3  2  5    2  3  5  6    6  6  7  6    5  4  2  1
                                                              N


DT-1                      DT-1
6..6..6.616..16.  323..23.161..61.  6..6..6.616..16.  323..23.161..61.
  6  6  .  1    3  2  1  6    .  .  6  1    3  2  1  6


DT-1        SP
3..3..3..3..3..6 .636.656.323..23.   123..23.161..61.   565..65.151.61.6
  3  3  .  .   6  5  3  2    3  2  1  6    5  6  1  6
                                                              N/G
```

G-1		G-1	G-1
1..12..2..2..2..	121..21.212..12.	.1..1..1121..21.	3..3..3.232..32.
. 2 . .	1 2 . 1	. . 1 2	3 3 2 3

	SP	G-1	G-1
323..23.535..35.	.2.6.2..626.12.1	..1..1.1121..21.	3..3..3.232..32.
. 2 5 3	. 2 . 1	. . 1 2	3 3 2 3

	SP	G-1	G-1
323..23.535..35.	.2.6.2..626.12.1	..1..1.1121..21.	3..3..3.232..32.
. 2 5 3	. 2 . 1	. . 1 2	3 3 2 3

	SP	G-1	SP
323..23.535..35.	.2.6.2..626.12.1	..1..1..6..6..6.	212..12.636.53.5
. 2 5 3	. 2 . 1	. . 6 .	2 1 6 5
			N

		G-1	G-2/3-1
.6.4.6...6.4.6..	565..65.454..54.	2..2..2..2..2..2	232..32.212.1..1
. 6 . 4	5 6 4 5	2 2 . .	2 3 2 1

		G-1	G-2/3-1
..1..1.3313.323.	21.1212.656..56.	2..2..2..2..2..2	232..32.212.1..1
. . 3 2	. 1 6 5	2 2 . .	2 3 2 1

		G-1	G-2/3-1
..1..1.3313.323.	21.1212.656..56.	2..2..2..2..2..2	232..32.212.1..1
. . 3 2	. 1 6 5	2 2 . .	2 3 2 1

			SP
..1..1.3313.323.	21.1212.656..56.	454..54.242..42.	565..65.454.5..5
. . 3 2	. 1 6 5	4 5 2 4	5 6 4 5

		G-1	G-2/3-1
.6.4.6...6.4.6..	565..65.454..54.	2..2..2..2..2..2	232..32.212.1..1
. 6 . 4	5 6 4 5	2 2 . .	2 3 2 1

Figure 4.42 Bonang parts and balungan of gendhing bonang Gondrong pélog lima

Figure 4.42 (continued)

		G-1	**G-2/3-1**
..1..1.3313.323.	21.1212.656..56.	2..2..2..2..2..2	232..32.212.1..1
. . 3 2	. 1 6 5	2 2 . .	2 3 2 1

		G-1	**G-2/3-1**
..1..1.3313.323.	21.1212.656..56.	2..2..2..2..2..2	232..32.212.1..1
. . 3 2	. 1 6 5	2 2 . .	2 3 2 1

		G-1	**G-2/3-1**
..1..1.3313.323.	21.1212.656..56.	2..2..2..2..2..2	232..32.212.1..1
. . 3 2	. 1 6 5	2 2 . .	2 3 2 1

			SP
..1..1.3313.323.	21.1212.656..56.	454..54.242..42.	565..65.454.5..5
. . 3 2	. 1 6 5	4 5 2 4	5 6 4 5
			N

	G-1		**SP**
..5..5..5..5..5.	.5..5..5..5..5..	242..42.545..45.	.511.1..1511.1..
. . . .	5 5 . .	2 4 5 4	2 1 2 1

DT-1			**SP**
..1. 1..141..41.	121..21.454..54.	454..54.242..42.	1511.1..1511.1..
. . 1 4	1 2 4 5	2 4 5 4	2 1 2 1

	G-1		**G-2/3-1**
5..5..5..5..5..5	..5..5..5..5..5.	.5..5..565..65.	767..67.565.6..6
5 5 . .	5 5 . .	. . 5 6	7 6 5 6

		SP	**G-2/3-**
..6..6..545..45.	242..42..42.242.	454..54.656..56.	242..42.212.1..1
. 6 5 4	2 4 . 2	4 5 6 5	2 1 2 1
			N/G

Figure 4.42 (continued)

Inggah

G-1

3..3..3..3..3...   313..13.323..23.   313..13.323..23.   161..61.454..54.
 3   3   .   .   3   1   3   2   3   1   3   2   1   6   4   5

G-1

3..3..3..3..3...   313..13.323..23.   313..13.323..23.   161..61.454..54.
 3   3   .   .   3   1   3   2   3   1   3   2   1   6   4   5
                                                                      N

G-1

3..3..3..3..3...   313..13.323..23.   313..13.323..23.   161..61.454..54.
 3   3   .   .   3   1   3   2   3   1   3   2   1   6   4   5

        SP-G-2   **G-1**

565..65.121..21.   21666..6..6..6..   6..6..6..6..6...   535..35.565.6..6
 .   6   1   2   1   6   5   6   .   6   6   6   5   3   5   6
                                                                      N

  G-1   **SP-G-2**   **G-1**

5..5..5.565..65.   767..67.535.3.61   2..2..2.232..32.   5..5..5.656..56.
 .   5   5   6   7   6   5   3   2   2   .   3   5   .   6   5

        SP-G-1

232..32.252..52.   232.3.21666..6..   6..6..67767..67.   545..45.212..12.
 2   3   2   5   2   3   5   6   6   6   7   6   5   4   2   1

  G-1   **G-1**

3..3..3.313..23.   161..61.454..54.   3..3..3.313..23.   161..61.454..54.
 3   .   3   2   1   6   4   5   3   .   3   2   1   6   4   5

  G-1

3..3..3..3..3...   313..13.323..23.   313..13.323..23.   161..61.454..54.
 3   3   .   .   3   1   3   2   3   1   3   2   1   6   4   5
                                                                      N/G

The Terms Gatra and Cèngkok

The discussion thus far directs our attention to the process of composing gendhing. In earlier writings, it has been assumed that gatra patterns are extant musical materials that are ready to be drawn on and recombined when creating a gendhing. In the above discussion I suggested that gatra patterns, except in instrumentally-inspired passages involving repetition of gatra, are not directly considered by the composer when creating a gendhing. Although gatra patterns are the means of expressing gendhing melody, in the mind of the composer they are not kernel melodic units on which a gendhing melody is based.

I should point out that in playing a gendhing the gatra patterns are useful guides for creating melody.[29] This is because these gatra patterns are important to the players in performance, as they work to realize the gendhing in their various instrumental idioms. When we consider the underlying flow of the musical sentence, however, the function of gatra as compositional material becomes less significant.

I cannot claim that vocal melodies are the basis of all gendhing. This is because I cannot show melodic precedents for all the gendhing in the current gamelan repertory. But the evidence presented above shows that the compositional process in gamelan music cannot be explained in only one particular way (e.g., the creative act of manipulating gatra). Composing gendhing is a complex process, consisting of (1) reformulation of vocal melodies, (2) creative use of existing melodic material (the result and the expansion of process [1]), and (3) consideration of instrumental elements. In other words, the bulk of the gendhing pieces have heterogeneous and even syncretic origins.[30]

I should mention that the term gatra did not appear in the literature on gamelan until relatively recently. It is not found in such texts as the nineteenth-century *Serat Centhini* and *Serat Gulang Yarya,* or the early twentieth-century *Layang Anyumurapaké Sinau Nabuh lan Panggawéné Gamelan* and *Serat Pradongga.* The term is also omitted from Kunst's *Music in Java* (1934) and Hood's *Pathet in Javanese Music* (1954).

My examination of a number of dictionaries reveals that the word *gatra* is not associated with gamelan practice. Gericke and Roorda (1901, 2:575) gave as synonyms for *gatra* the words *rupa* (appearance), *awak* (body or basic form), *pawakan* (physical character), and *gambar* (drawing). Then they define it further as: "sketch or outline; project, plan, draft, or design; something that is still in incomplete form and still must develop; an undeveloped part of the body."[31] Even a dictionary published in 1937, the *Baoesastra Jawa* by Poerwadarminta, does not yet relate the word *gatra* to gamelan practice. The *Baoesastra Jawa* defines it as: 1. *awak* (body), or *péranganing awak* (parts of the body); 2. *wewujudan* (form); 3. *péranganing ukara sing wis madeg* (part of a phrase that already stands up or has meaning).

Significantly, most early gamelan notation did not employ spaces or bar lines to separate gatra (see chapter 3): the *ranté* notation, the notation by Gondapang-rawit (late 19th c.), Paku Alaman's and Adiwinatan's systems (mentioned in Groneman 1890), Djakoeb and Wignjaroemeksa (1913, 1919), and Soelardi (1918). The *andha* notation used in the *Pakem Wirama,* a manuscript of the Yog-yakarta court, is an exception.[32] In this notation, imitating the Western staff but written vertically, a thick line was placed in every second or fourth note.[33]

In the work of the Committee of the Instruction of Gamelan of the Museum Radyapustaka, gamelan notation begins to adopt the solfège system, which uses bar lines. Bar lines continued to be used by Dewantara (1930) and Wirawiyaga (1935, 1936, 1937, 1939a/b). This was the period when Javanese increasingly describe gamelan as having a closer analogy with Western music. In particular, the Dutch term *maat* (meter) became the closest analogy to gamelan gatra. In fact, these early gamelan theorists designated the meter 4/4 for writing gendhing notation, illustrating their explanation with the hand gestures and fractional du-ration of the notes appropriate to this meter. In the widest sense, the analogy has its merit: like meter, gatra is a function of the organization of pitch and duration.

Perhaps the Dutch term *maat* validated the term gatra. It was Dewantara who first used the verb word *anggatrakaken* in his discussion of the intention of using notation as a device to teach gamelan. He says that in order to ease the use of gamelan notation, it was necessary "to draw the skeleton of meter and melody" (*anggatrakaken balungan wirama lan lagunipun*), that is, using notation and meter, which illustrate only the basic idea (Dewantara 1936:47).

Related to the term gatra is cèngkok. Cèngkok has different meanings, de-pending on the context in which the term is used. Cèngkok can mean "melodic pattern," "melody," and "melodic style." But, as Sindusawarno's definition of the term cèngkok indicates, these meanings may be hard to separate.

> As each phrase is played or sung, it is filled in, expanded, embel-lished, etc. The series of notes and intervals (*sruti*) used in this manner are called "cèngkok." In principle, one phrase contains one cèngkok. One antecedent-consequent also comprises one cèngkok. Thus one gongan may be called a cèngkok. "Cèngkok" may then be defined as an arrangement of phrases of a given lagu that are played or sung in the process of filling in and embellishing a lagu. The essential nature of a cèngkok is neither its form nor its shape, but, rather, its course of move-ment. The function of a cèngkok is to clarify and affirm the meaning of the lagu, in order to give it movement and strength. Cèngkok is that which gives soul and sense to a lagu. (Translated by Stanley Hoffman, in J. Becker and Feinstein 1984:394)

Sindusawarno's definition of cèngkok produces an ambiguous meaning. It is either melodic pattern, melodic style, melody, or the process of melodic movement. This suggests that cèngkok is a complex concept. Melodic formula is only one of the meanings of cèngkok.

Intended to mean melodic formula, cèngkok is parallel to gatra. But cèngkok is a formulaic term commonly used to refer to the melodic pattern of "elaborative" instruments,[34] particularly of the gendèr. In fact, much of our understanding of the term cèngkok as melodic formulas is based on the study of gendèr playing (See McDermott and Sumarsam 1975; Sumarsam 1975; Sutton 1978; Martopangrawit 1972–76).

The studies give us a first impression that gendèr playing is basically the result of the manipulation or recombination of cèngkok. The analysis of gendèr playing brought about the notion that the process of playing gendhing is the manipulation or recombination of melodic formulas. That is, the gamelan teacher can easily discern and classify the melodic formulas of the gendèr melodies. But classification of melodic formulas can be found to be restrictive when we analyze, say, rebab. In teaching gendèr, the teacher can write down the ordering of cèngkok (indicating which cèngkok are repeated, new or similar cèngkok but in different musical contexts, in high, medium, or low melodic range); but in teaching rebab, the teacher must write the whole rebab melody from beginning to end.

Even for the gendèr, very often a classification of cèngkok cannot be used effectively in practice. The names of cèngkok used to classify gendèr melodic patterns can reasonably represent the melodic patterns they designate. However, a particular cèngkok name will represent the intended melodic shape only in a particular musical context. Thus, the use of pattern names as the basis for classification may change the function of these names, until they are classification symbols only. In order to clarify my point, I will present a musical illustration.

In figure 4.43 (p. 236), we see that the pattern called *jarit kawung* in the rangkep playing style is comparable to the *lamba* style. However, in the playing of this pattern in ladrang Mugi Rahayu (figure 4.44, p. 236), the jarit kawung pattern is lamba style has no sense of jarit kawung melody. On the other hand, in the fifth gendèr pattern of the first kenongan of the inggah section of Wida Sari (irama wilet with the rangkep style of gendèr technique; figure 4.45, p. 237), the player conveys the true sense of the jarit kawung pattern. Usually the jarit kawung melody is sung by the pesindhèn, although she does not use the words jarit kawung; usually she uses the words *ya ramané*. Only occasionally does the penggérong sing senggakan (short vocal interjections) with the word and the melody jarit kawung (i.e., the origin of the name of this pattern).

The circled gendèr melodic patterns in Mugi Rahayu could be classified as the jarit kawung pattern. However, because of their musical contexts, none of them have the feeling of a jarit kawung melody. This is because the origin of the jarit kawung pattern corresponds to a melodic passage in which the pesindhèn and occasionally the penggérong sing the melody of this pattern and the pattern is usually associated with the rangkep playing style of the gendèr. More importantly, in Mugi Rahayu, the melodic passages in question (3612 and 6132) differ significantly from the melodic passage in Wida Sari (i.e. · 2 in the *balungan nibani* style, or 3632 in the balungan mlaku style). Thus, it is musically inappropriate for the singer to sing the jarit kawung pattern in the indicated passages in Mugi Rahayu. Even if the gendèr player plays the passages in rangkep style, the result still will not convey the melody of jarit kawung. In addition, the non-accented position of the pattern in question in the formal structure of a gendhing, also determines the sense of the jarit kawung pattern. Gendèr playing of the indicated passages in Mugi Rahayu violates both criteria: the melodic shape of the passages in question and their position in the formal structure of the composition. Thus we cannot feel the sense of jarit kawung. (Compare the fifth gendèr pattern of the inggah of Widasari, which fulfils both criteria.)

In short, in order to understand gendèr playing, we cannot depend on the gendèr cèngkok alone. We must examine cèngkok in the context of the formal and melodic structure of gendhing. The meaning of cèngkok is very broad, indeed. It may refer not only to instrumental melody, but also to vocal melody. Gericke and Roorda (1901) define *cèngkok* as "the various tunes whereby a poetic meter is sung (or a musical instrument is played)" (Hatch 1980:490). Gericke and Roorda also define *cèngkok* as "to make a variation in a song or play (and similar to *nyangkok*)." Thus, cèngkok means individual versions of a melody of a tembang (Hatch 1980:161), as well as the process by which variations in singing tembang are created. Viewed in this way, cèngkok can mean the melodic style of the whole tembang and/or the various detailed styles of singing this tembang. The former, as Hatch rightly points out, is analogous to a gongan phrase in a gendhing. In discussing Jaap Kunst's comments on cèngkok, Hatch states:

> If we regard a gong-phrase as a melodic phrase [in tembang], the unity and coherence of which is defined in part by the period of time between its beginning and its end—a period which is delineated in *gendhing* by the sounding of the *gong*—then we can refocus . . . on melodics—songs—in the minds of the performers, rather than on melodies of particular instruments in *gamelan* performances. And, if we regard "sound-combinations" as horizontal realizations—melodic contours—rather than vertical combinations of instrumental sounds, then we can refocus that point on *tembang* melodics. (1980:160)

Hatch implies that gendhing can be conceived as vocally-inspired, internally sung melodies which, in concept, can be treated as tembang. Certainly, such a view supports the notion I have touched on earlier: the sources of many gendhing are vocal melodies. Thus, the use and significance of the term cèngkok is relevant to both of these musical genres.

The foregoing discussion noted that "melodic pattern" is the restricted meaning of the term cèngkok. The concept of cèngkok is crucial to our understanding of gendhing. But its meaning should not be confined to "melodic pattern." We should discuss all the implications of the term.

The association of cèngkok with the word *cangkok* (pruning, then planting a shrub) adds to the understanding of the richness of the concept of this term. Day finds that the horticultural metaphoricity of Javanese music is intriguing. In a sense, cèngkok is a "pruning" of a melody—"a process of musical delimitation which in fact prepares and fosters the new embellishing growth of each individual melodic performance" (1981 : 20 n. 28). This implies that cèngkok refers to both musical substance (a melody one gongan long) and musical process (ongoing musical embellishment). The former delimits musical structure (definitive organization and phrasing), while the latter frees musical structure (producing melodic versions and variations).

It becomes clear that the term cèngkok has multiple meanings, comprising both musical substance and process. This developed as a result of the interrelationships between vocal and instrumental music in Java.

Another term associated with cèngkok is the term wilet. This term, which means "intertwine" or "weaving," describes musical process in the concept of cèngkok. Although at times it is used interchangeably with the term cèngkok (Hatch 1980 : 166–67), wilet (especially in Surakarta) tends to refer more to the variation or embellishment aspect of Javanese music. Tondhakusuma (1870 : 12) explains:

> 9. About the use of an expression [such as]
> "wilet intertwines,"
> this means [wilet]
> is a detailed filler[?] of
> cèngkok and lagu.
> Or, [wilet] is very intricately
> intertwining,
> encircling the plain cèngkok.
> Thus, wilet cannot defeat
> 10. the plainness of cangkok.[35]
> But it could [create] indistinctness,
> and could create different
> feeling—an unblemished feeling.
> It is truly intended so that
> the sound of gendhing Sekar Gadhung
> whose cèngkok is to succeed
> with what is searched for.
> Creating wilet means to create different feeling.
> 11. This is also comparable to
> sekar Dhangdhang Gendhis,
> anywhere,

its melody is truly the same.
The difference is a minor one.
When it is fragrantly bathed with
intricate wilet,
it becomes many kinds, Sir,
though having the same origin.[36]

The term wilet clarifies the intricacy of the concept of cèngkok. The term describes the process of ornamentation or embellishment. Actually, the term cèngkok itself already contains the practice of wilet. It is not surprising, therefore, that these two terms are often hyphenated or used interchangeably.

To summarize: Although I cannot account for all gendhing, the foregoing analysis shows the important role of vocal music in discussing gamelan gendhing. This notion is well supported by traditional Javanese views of gendhing—descriptions of gendhing presented in the *Serat Centhini, Sendhon Langen Swara, Serat Gulang Yarya,* and *Serat Sosorah Gamelan.* It seems that extensive development of gendhing for the gamelan repertoire in the mid eighteenth and the first half of the nineteenth century occurred when tembang was a flourishing art. I noted earlier that the description of tembang singing in the *Serat Centhini* and in Raffles's *History of Java* suggests that singing tembang was quite active in the eighteenth and nineteenth centuries. The interaction between the instrumental and vocal idioms provided the basis for the development of gamelan gendhing.

In the past, the terms used in talking about gendhing were associated with or originated in the terms used to describe vocal music. The terms cèngkok and wilet are cases in point. When the term cèngkok was adopted in discussions of gamelan gendhing, its meaning became very elaborate, encompassing all aspects of gendhing—melody, melodic pattern, melodic variants, melodic embellishment, formal structure, and modal practice. All these aspects are interrelated. In other words, cèngkok with its associated term wilet became an essential concept in understanding the musical processes in gamelan. It describes the crux of musical processes in Javanese gamelan. As Day (1981:19) notes: "The Javanese meanings of *cèngkok* and *wilet* point to a process of ongoing derivation and embellishment which is the very life and substance of art in Java."

The complex process in composing and playing gendhing cannot be explained with complete consistency. Composing a gendhing involves the process of restructuring pre-existing vocal melodies, consideration for integrating vocal and instrumental elements, and consideration of idioms of the different parts in the ensemble. These all point to the heterogeneous process, the multiple systems involved in creating a gendhing.

The adaptation of Western modes of thinking, particularly the introduction of notation for gamelan and the development of the idea of "melodic theme" in gendhing as contained in the saron part, was partly responsible for a certain direction in the formulation of gendhing theories, a direction that misrepresented the compositional process in gamelan. This direction led to viewing gatra as an important element of creating gendhing; it downplays the intimate relationship between vocal music and gamelan gendhing. Consequently, the heterogeneous or syncretic origins of gendhing have not been fully explored.

There is no question that the Westernization of Java is a very complex cultural transformation, resulting in a complex synthesis—a Western-Javanese intellectual outlook. It appears, however, that in the case of the development of gamelan theories, the early Western intellectualization of Java led to the formulation of a somewhat narrow view of the concept of gamelan composition. This is not to say that I regret the exposure to Western modes of thinking. To do so is to regret history. There is no question that the works of Western theorists have great value in contributing to the understanding of the history and theory of gamelan. It should be recognized, however, that only through dialogue can theory fruitfully proceed.[37] The discussion of gendhing theories in this chapter should be seen in this light.

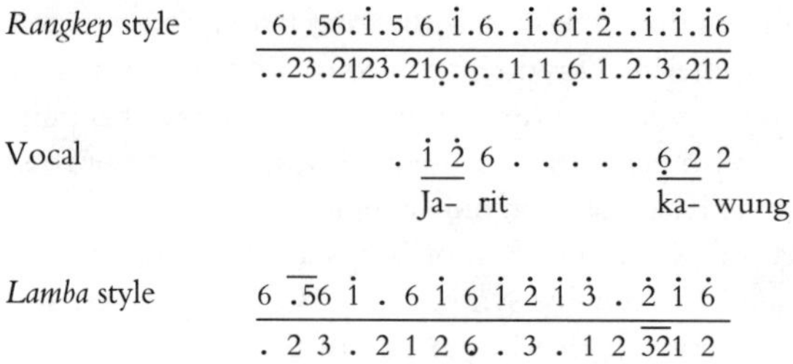

Rangkep style $\quad$ .6..56.i̇.5.6.i̇.6..i̇.6i̇.2̇..i̇.i̇.i̇6
$\quad\qquad\qquad\overline{..23.2123.216.6..1.1.6.1.2.3.212}$

Vocal $\qquad\qquad\qquad$. i̇ 2̇ 6 . . . . . 6 2 2
$\qquad\qquad\qquad\qquad$ Ja- rit $\qquad\qquad$ ka- wung

Lamba style $\qquad$ 6 .5̄6 i̇ . 6 i̇ 6 i̇ 2̇ i̇ 3̇ . 2̇ i̇ 6
$\qquad\qquad\qquad$. 2 3 . 2 1 2 6 . 3 . 1 2 3̄21 2

Figure 4.43 Cèngkok Jarit Kawung for gendèr

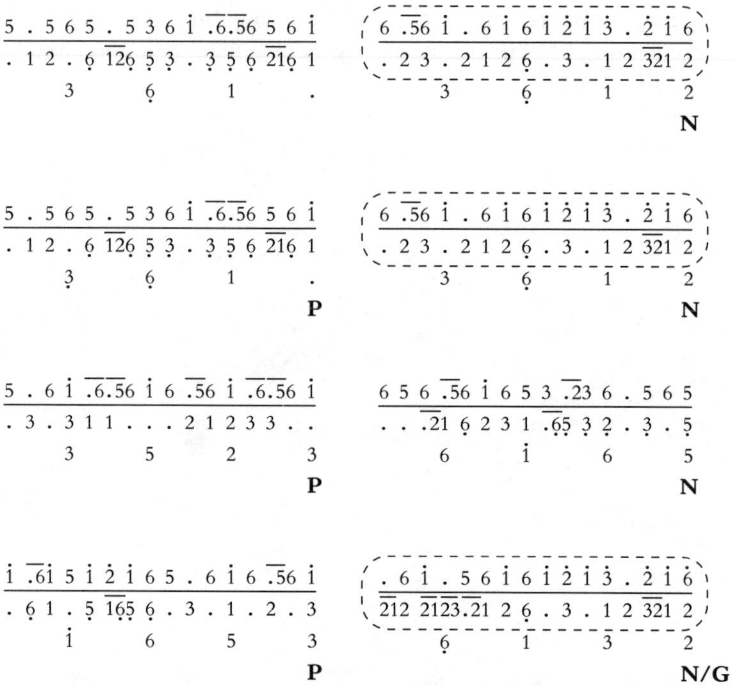

5 . 5 6 5 . 5 3 6 i̇ .6̄.5̄6 5 6 i̇ $\qquad$ 6 .5̄6 i̇ . 6 i̇ 6 i̇ 2̇ i̇ 3̇ . 2̇ i̇ 6
. 1 2 . 6 1̄2̄6 5 3 . 3 5 6 2̄1̄6 1 $\qquad$. 2 3 . 2 1 2 6 . 3 . 1 2 3̄21 2
$\quad$ 3 $\qquad$ 6 $\qquad$ 1 $\qquad$. $\qquad\qquad$ 3 $\qquad$ 6 $\qquad$ 1 $\qquad$ 2
$\qquad\qquad\qquad\qquad\qquad\qquad\qquad\qquad\qquad$ **N**

5 . 5 6 5 . 5 3 6 i̇ .6̄.5̄6 5 6 i̇ $\qquad$ 6 .5̄6 i̇ . 6 i̇ 6 i̇ 2̇ i̇ 3̇ . 2̇ i̇ 6
. 1 2 . 6 1̄2̄6 5 3 . 3 5 6 2̄1̄6 1 $\qquad$. 2 3 . 2 1 2 6 . 3 . 1 2 3̄21 2
$\quad$ 3 $\qquad$ 6 $\qquad$ 1 $\qquad$. $\qquad\qquad$ 3 $\qquad$ 6 $\qquad$ 1 $\qquad$ 2
$\qquad\qquad\qquad$ **P** $\qquad\qquad\qquad\qquad\qquad\qquad\qquad$ **N**

5 . 6 i̇ .6̄.5̄6 i̇ 6 .5̄6 i̇ .6̄.5̄6 i̇ $\qquad$ 6 5 6 .5̄6 i̇ 6 5 3 .2̄3 6 . 5 6 5
. 3 . 3 1 1 . . . 2 1 2 3 3 . . $\qquad$ . . .2̄1 6 2 3 1 .6̄5 3 2 . 3 . 5
$\quad$ 3 $\qquad$ 5 $\qquad$ 2 $\qquad$ 3 $\qquad\qquad$ 6 $\qquad$ i̇ $\qquad$ 6 $\qquad$ 5
$\qquad\qquad\qquad$ **P** $\qquad\qquad\qquad\qquad\qquad\qquad\qquad$ **N**

i̇ .6̄i̇ 5 i̇ 2̇ i̇ 6 5 . 6 i̇ 6 .5̄6 i̇ $\qquad$. 6 i̇ . 5 6 i̇ 6 i̇ 2̇ i̇ 3̇ . 2̇ i̇ 6
. 6 1 . 5 1̄6̄5 6 . 3 . 1 . 2 . 3 $\qquad$ 212 2123.21 2 6 . 3 . 1 2 3̄21 2
$\qquad$ i̇ $\qquad$ 6 $\qquad$ 5 $\qquad$ 3 $\qquad\qquad$ 6 $\qquad$ 1 $\qquad$ 3 $\qquad$ 2
$\qquad\qquad\qquad$ **P** $\qquad\qquad\qquad\qquad\qquad\qquad$ **N/G**

Figure 4.44 Gendèr melody and balungan of ladrang Mugi Rahayu sléndro manyura.
The circled passage is the "jarit kawung" melodic pattern.

```
...i...6...i...6...i...6.5.6.i.6        .i...i232.32.i..1.6..i.6.i...i.6
.123212.2123212.2123212.3.216.6.        3.356....i..6.63.5.35.5.5.532.2.
                    .          3                      .              2
            6  1  2    3  3                     6  i  2  i6  3  2 12
            Kan-cané dhé-wé                     U- jung      ja-ri


.5.6.i.6.3.5.6.i.6..56.i...6.i.6        .5.6.5.3.5.6.5.3.6.5.6.2.6.i.2.i
3.216.6..535.56.1.23.2123.212.2.        2.21612.2.21612...212.2.2.321.1.
              .          3                            .              1
                                        3 3 3 3  3 3 2 i  2   6 3  3  2 1 1
                                        Ujung jari balung rondhon-ing ka- la- pa


.6..56.i.5.6.i.6..i.6i.2..i.i.i6        .5.6.5.3.5.6.5.3.6.5.6.2.6.i.2.i
..23.2123.216.6..1.1.6.1.2.3.212        2.21612.2.21612...212.2.2.321.1.
              .          2                            .              1
        i  2  6      6 2 2               212   3 3     2  3    3 2 1  1
        ya- ra-      ma- né              ma- rama   ka- weng- ku-    a


..2.i2.i.2.2.i23.333.33321.i...i        2.232.32.i....6i.6i.6i.6.3...356
61.1....2.262163.....;....6.356.        .i...i..6.6535.35.35.35.2.612.2.
              .          3                            .              2
                                                                    N
    1  1  2   3                          2 353  2  i   2  6 3   5 3  2  2
    Gonès                                sayek- ti da-  di u- sa-    da
```

Figure 4.45 Gendèr, balungan, and pesindhèn part of the first kenongan of gendhing Wida Sari sléndro manyura (inggah section, irama wilet). The circled passage is the jarit kawung melodic pattern.

Conclusion

It is apparent that the longstanding interaction of the Javanese with foreign cultures produced complicated cultural transformations and very complex Javanese traditions. We can identify three different encounters of Java with foreign cultures: Java-Hindu, Java-Islam, and Java-Western. The encounters were both similar and distinctive in character.

The Java-Hindu and Java-Islam encounters resulted in the formation of the backbone of the traditional Javanese way of life (chapter 1). In these encounters we see the tolerance and flexibility of the Javanese toward foreign cultures. The congruence between the pre-Hindu Javanese systems of belief and the core religious systems of Hinduism and Islam gave rise to this tolerance and flexibility. The core religious system of the Javanese was the people's devotion to spiritual forces or gods. In pre-Hindu times, these spiritual forces were potent humans or potent objects which were believed to have "prowess" or "soul stuff" (Wolters 1982). In Hinduism, this is called *bhakti,* that is, a passion for access to god.[1]

In the Java-Hindu period, devotion to spiritual forces was the basis for artistic and literary activities. For example, writing poetry was a religious experience or a way to unite with god. As Zoetmulder (1974:179) says:

> For the poet this union with the god of beauty is both a means and an end. It is a means toward creating a work of beauty, his *kakawin.* The yoga, which is reflected in the opening stanzas, enables him "to bud forth sprouts of beauty" (*alung alango*), because it unites him with the god who is beauty itself. On the other hand, it is also an end, for by constant practice he will attain final liberation (*moksa*) in this union.

In their practice of this "literary yoga," the Javanese adapted Indian poetic writings. Hence, the Indian-based Javanese kakawin became a common format for writing poetry and became a popular genre sung by almost all levels of courtiers. Subsequently, kakawin became an important source for the development of Javanese vocal music and literature.

It is a mistake to assume that artistic activities served only as devotional practices. The function of performing arts in giving pleasure was also evident. Performances of music and theater were essential parts of exciting court occasions. Besides giving pleasure, these performances also had a political function—to make the ruler's subjects faithful servants. In any event, to the extent that artistic activities provided enjoyment and signs of devotion to either god or ruler, they were important parts of religious and secular activities.

Religious devotion continued to be important to the Islamization of Java. Before arriving in Java, the Islam of the Middle East had mixed with Indian Hinduism. This reduced religious conflict when Islam was introduced into Java in the fifteenth and sixteenth centuries, since the Javanese sensed the Hinduism in the new religion. The presence of Sufism in the Islam that first came to Java also made possible a syncretism between Islam and the Hindu-Javanese tradition. As in the Hindu practice of *bhakti,* Sufism had a strong tradition of devotion to spiritual leaders, the wali, or Islamic saints.

Sufism also maintained the tolerance of Javanese toward music and dance. This is because Sufism believed in the power of music. According to Sufism, music and dance could be used as conduits for communion with God. Consequently, the Javanese viewed indigenous Javanese and Islamic music as having important roles in their society. The intimate relationship between Javanese and Islamic music led to the development of new musical ideas and exchanges of musical repertoire between these two bodies of music.

To sum up, there were two important consequences of the Hinduization and Islamization of Java. First, the Javanese arts provided for religious devotion as well as enjoyment; the two cannot be separated. Second, the Javanese arts existed and developed in the atmosphere of intimate social interaction in the court. Such an intimate atmosphere made it possible for artists and noblemen to intermingle and exchange ideas.

The intrusion of Europeans and European culture into the life of the Javanese court interfered with these features. Unlike the expansion of Hinduism and Islam, which was basically the expansion of religious systems, Western religions did not have a strong impact on Javanese culture. But the influence of Western civilization was important in the intellectual and technological development of Java. The manner in which European cultures were introduced into Java—by the expansion of trade and of political domination—changed the course of sociocultural history of Java. Chapter 2 assesses this development.

It is true that during the period of contact with Europeans, Javanese aristocrats showed tolerance to European culture. This happened not for religious reasons (as in the Java-Hindu-Islamic encounter), but mainly for social and political reasons. The mestizo culture in which Indos and Europeans lived enhanced Javanese tolerance for Europeans. In fact, the interaction between Javanese aristocrats and Dutch and Indo bureaucrats, planters, and managers of companies was a benefit of cultural life in the nineteenth-century Javanese court. First, these people became social equals in many respects. More importantly, as they interacted, Javanese aristocrats became Europeanized, and Dutch and Indos became Javanized.

They formed a common society. As I mentioned above, the close relationship between Javanese aristocrats and Europeans resulted in the breakup of the close tie between court artists and their royal masters.

Europeans and Javanese aristocrats interacted in nineteenth-century Central Javanese court rituals, especially those that involved Europeans. These rituals consisted of all sorts of combinations of indigenous and European music or other sounds. There are abundant examples: the sounding together of sacred gamelan monggang and salvos of cannons or rifles at important court events; the playing of polkas and waltzes at the court meditation tower on the religiously significant Thursday evening; the playing together of the Dutch national anthem and gamelan to honor a Javanese ruler; the use of pistols in one of the most refined court female dances, the serimpi; the incorporation of European field drums and brass instruments in gendhing mares to accompany the sacred bedhaya dance; among others. The Chinese, who were fond of festive occasions, contributed to the elaboration of these lavish rituals.[2] More importantly, the gradual Javanization of the Europeans, Indos, and Chinese, as well as the Europeanization of the Javanese elite politically and culturally, was the key reason for the development of certain court rituals.

The social harmony we see between the Javanese aristocrats and the Europeans can be explained in terms of the willingness of the Javanese rulers to participate in the European colonial system. The harmony may also be thought of as the result of the political awareness of the colonial government. That is, in order to survive domination, colonial rulers had to harmonize political domination with the cultural personality of the Javanese (Nandy 1983). The alternation of the ruler and the ruled between being allies and being enemies inspired the hybrid characteristics of many court cultural productions.

These perspectives on colonialism in Java conflict with the commonly held opinion that because of the decline in their political power, Javanese aristocrats focused their activities inward; hence, the remarkable development of Javanese arts and literature in the courts. While there is a certain truth to this thesis, it suggests that the development of artistic activities in Central Javanese courts was immune to the sociopolitical context of the time. This is not the case. On the contrary, the artistic activity created in eighteenth- and nineteenth-century Java expressed a unitary political and cultural statement of colonial Java. In essence, the ruler and the ruled had the cultural consensus of which Nandy (1983:10) speaks.

> In such a culture, colonialism was not seen as an absolute evil. For the subjects, it was a product of one's own emasculation and defeat in legitimate power politics. For the rulers, colonial exploitation was an incidental and regrettable by-product of a philosophy of life that was in harmony with superior forms of political and economic organization.

Nandy, whose topic is British India, goes on to say that colonial rulers reached this kind of consensus. They were aware that

> they could not successfully rule a continent-sized polity while believing themselves to be moral cripples. They had to build bulwarks against a possible sense of guilt produced by a disjunction between their actions and what were till then, in terms of important norms of their own culture, "true" values. On the other hand, their subjects could not collaborate on a long-term basis unless they had some acceptance of the ideology of the system, either as players or as counterplayers. This is the only way they could preserve a minimum of self-esteem in a situation of unavoidable injustice. (1983:10–11)

I suggest that the diversity in the court musical expressions was a reminder of the constantly shifting position of the Javanese rulers and their cultures, from being players to being counterplayers in the colonial culture. In spite of the hybrid Javanese-European artistic expressions mentioned above, there was no significant musical syncretism between gamelan and European music. Although gamelan and European music were often played together, each kept its own identity. Perhaps musical syncretism did not happen because of the lack of compatibility of the musical elements in the two musical systems. Actually, it is a reflection of the bigger picture of Javanese culture in the context of colonialism.

At the end of the nineteenth century, as a result of their increasing exposure to Western modes of thought and technology, the Javanese elite gradually came to better understand the colonial cultural power of the West. Consequently, they learned more ways to construct their individual and cultural personalities. During this transitional period, there were two consequences: the increasing adaptation of European modes of thought, and the rise of the Indonesian national awakening.

This period of transition was during the peak of Western economic, cultural, and political domination of Java. As a result also of the continuing process of Islamic reformation, Javanese culture was in the initial period of what Anderson (1972:20 n. 9) describes as "a heterogenous, disjunctive, and internally contradictory complex of traditional and Western elements."

In this period, the Europeans and European elements became prominent. This was the pinnacle of development, such that the Dutch national anthem had to be played together with gendhing Sri Katon (the signature piece of the king Paku Buwana) whenever Paku Buwana appeared in his court chamber; in a religiously significant court event, the court musicians for European music played repertoire from a genre of European popular music. This was the period of kaélokan (mysterious, fantastic, and strange), in which Javanese traditional forces lived side by side with the secular, modern Western world.

As for the adaptation of Western modes of thought (chapter 3), the intellectual relationship between the Dutch and Indo scholar-officials and Javanese aristocrats, poets, and leading court artists was close and equal. The presence of European and Indo intellectuals in Central Java had a particular impact on the formation of the attitudes and intellectual outlook of the Javanese elite toward their arts and literature. These intellectuals gradually developed a strong relationship with Javanese traditional intellectuals, the pujangga and learned noblemen. The increasing incorporation of Western-style education and printing technology intensified the adaptation of Western ideas in Java. In gamelan, this adaptation resulted in the introduction of notation for gamelan and the proliferation of writing about gamelan, and led to the adoption of certain themes in these writings.

The Chinese had an important role in the development of intellectual life in Java. Besides being important patrons of Javanese arts and literature, some Chinese owned publishing houses.

One of the important results of the expansion of Western cultural power in Java was the rise of Indonesian nationalism, which was led by Western-educated courtiers and non-courtiers and prominent Indos. This awakening caused tensions among Indonesian intellectuals concerning the role of gamelan in their newly developed Indonesian society. The search for an Indonesian national identity or national character became important for Indonesian nationalists. (Geertz (1973:240) characterizes it as follows:

> It consists in defining, or trying to define, a collective subject to whom the actions of state can be internally connected, in creating, or trying to create, an experiential "we" from whose will the activities of government seem spontaneously to flow. And as such, it tends to revolve around the question of the content, relative weight, and proper relationship of two rather towering abstractions: "The Indigenous Way of Life" and "The Spirit of the Age."

In the search for the identity of Indonesian culture, the question was: Should Indonesians retain and cultivate their indigenous cultures ("The Indigenous Way of Life"), such as gamelan music? or, Should Indonesians create a national culture that could be appreciated by all ("The Spirit of the Age")? Some Javanese nationalists felt strongly that gamelan was the most appropriate national music for Indonesia: so much so that they talked about playing "Indonesia Raya" (the Western-style Indonesian national anthem) on gamelan. But the general diversity of Indonesian music led to opposition from other Javanese and non-Javanese nationalists. Thus, the notion of a single Indonesian culture seemed out of the question. "Multiform in the past, it would seem also to have to be multiform in the present" (ibid. 246).

Gamelan schools, which were founded in the 1950s and 1960s, inherited the same problems that nationalists had to confront. That is, the schools had to justify the relevance of their gamelan curriculum in a modern and pluralistic Indonesian society. Like some nationalists, the schools attempted to do this in two ways. First, they claimed that they would eventually produce composers who could compose music that would be appreciated by all Indonesian people. This notion was not realized, however, since the schools focused their study only on gamelan music. Music from other parts of Indonesia was never included in their curriculum. Second, the schools promoted gamelan music as classical art, comparable to Western art music. This attempt was contested because the performance contexts of gamelan were not compatible with those of Western art music. In addition, gamelan represents a homogeneous tradition. Besides the court gamelan tradition, which was viewed as classical music, there were also village gamelan traditions, whose musical concepts were basically the same as those of court gamelan.

The influence of Western-style education on the intellectual outlook of the Javanese elite was another important aspect of the Westernization of Java. The relationships between European researchers, Indo scholars, the Javanese elite, and leading Javanese court artists characterized this intellectual development. In gamelan, these intellectual relationships made possible the proliferation of gamelan writings. To what extent do Western perspectives supersede Javanese perspectives in the formulation of gamelan theories? Do Western perspectives have anything in common with Javanese perspectives? Was there any cross-fertilization between the two perspectives that benefited the formulation of gamelan theories?

It would be difficult to answer these questions, as they affect all aspects of music in Java. But the evidence shows that exposure to Western modes of thinking caused gamelan theories to develop along particular lines. Particularly as a result of the expansion of Western culture in Java at the beginning of the twentieth century, European modes of thought inspired many writings on gamelan, as did the presence of European researchers in Java at this time. The introduction of notation for gamelan and the rudimentary description of gamelan compositions for gamelan teaching was characteristic of these early gamelan writings and led to the introduction of the idea of a "melodic theme" in gamelan gendhing from which other parts are derived. This in turn led to the idea of the importance of gatra in constructing gendhing. (I discuss this and other related points in the second half of chapter three.)

In the 1950s and 1960s, these ideas were popular in ethnomusicological writing on Javanese music. Beginning in the 1970s, there was another development in the theories of gendhing. This was a period when Javanese theorists and Western scholars tended to work closely together, questioning the validity of previous theories and seeking the perspectives of Javanese niyaga in formulating theories of gendhing. (This reminds us of the intellectual atmosphere in the nineteenth century, when the Javanese intellectual elite also had close relationships with European and Indo scholars, and produced works that expressed indigenous perspectives.) Many Western researchers intensified their efforts to learn to play gamelan and to sing tembang. Audio and video production has contributed greatly to the discovery of the intricacy of gamelan performance practice. (Chapter 4 discusses the compositional process in gamelan in relation to recent studies of Javanese music by both Western and Javanese theorists, and to indigenous perspectives found in the older gamelan literature.)

Although the idea of the importance of balungan and gatra mentioned above has a certain element of truth in it, when these theories are contrasted with indigenous Javanese theories, another concept of the construction of gamelan pieces emerges: the intimate relationship between gamelan gendhing and Javanese vocal music. There is some evidence that vocal melodies are the melodic precedents of many gamelan gendhing, and that gatra exist only through the reformulation of the melodic precedents of the gendhing, after gendhing are performed or balungan are notated.

But there is insufficient evidence to show that all gendhing are based on vocal melodies. In fact, analysis of some gendhing reveals that instrumental elements are basic in the construction of some gendhing. The point is that the compositional process in gamelan is very complex. It cannot be explained in only one way, such as the manipulation of gatra patterns. The bulk of gendhing have heterogeneous, or even syncretic, origins. Thus, it is probably impossible to establish a single musical source for gamelan gendhing.

My objective has been to show the dynamics of the development and transformation of Javanese musical culture. To the extent that the Javanese had long been exposed to foreign ideas, the cultural transformation and development was a complicated process. Javanese cultural possibilities are and always have been expandable, to the extent that it is impossible to develop a mathematical characterization of the Javanese view of music. In this study I attempt to show the complex transformations that resulted in the unusually rich historical contexts and the development of theories of Javanese music in the nineteenth and twentieth centuries.

Appendix: Gamelan Instruments

Chapters 3 and 4 discuss the historical development of theories of gendhing; chapter 4 especially contains extensive musical analysis. To read these chapters, readers may need to familiarize themselves with the basic compositional process and instrumentation in gamelan music. I hope the description of gamelan instruments below will be a useful reference.

Bonang

A set of ten to fourteen small horizontal kettle gongs arranged in two rows, placed on cords strung through a wooden frame. The player sits in the center of the side with the low-octave row of kettle gongs, holding a cylinder-shaped mallet in each hand. There are three kinds of bonang, characterized by their size, octave range, and function in the ensemble.

Bonang Barung

Medium-size, middle-to-high-octave bonang. One of the leading instruments in the ensemble. Particularly in the pipilan technique, the anticipatory nature of its patterns provides a guide to the melody of the other instruments. In the gendhing bonang genre, the bonang barung introduces the piece (i.e., deciding the piece to be played) by playing buka (an introductory phrase) and leads the melodic motion and the progress of the piece. In the imbal-imbalan technique, the bonang barung does not function as melodic leader; it interlocks with the bonang panerus, forming hocketing patterns; in any important accent of the gendhing, both bonang are allowed to play sekaran (melodic ornaments), usually at the end of the phrase.

Bonang Panembung

Largest-size, low- to middle-octave bonang. It plays the low density level subdivision of the balungan, whose function is to point to important accents of the melody. The bonang panembung is more commonly found in the Yogyanese gamelan tradition. In the Solonese tradition, the bonang panembung has only a one-octave range.

Bonang Panerus

Small-size, highest-octave bonang. In the pipilan technique, it plays twice as fast as the bonang barung. Although it anticipates earlier than the bonang barung, the bonang panerus does not have the role of melodic leader. In the imbal-imbalan technique, together with the bonang barung, it plays interlocking patterns.

Celempung

A plucked zither set on four legs. The two front legs are lower—that is, shorter—than the back legs. Therefore, the instrument slopes downward toward the player. Its thirteen pairs of strings run between tuning pins (on a scroll near the top of the instrument) and hooks at the bottom. The bridge is placed on the middle across the soundboard (body of the instrument). The celempung is played with the thumbnails. In addition, damping is required, using the other fingers. The celempung delivers its melodies in the style of pulsed melodic patterns, cèngkok.

Gambang

A wooden xylophone with seventeen to twenty-one keys, encompassing a range of two octaves or more. It is played with two disc-type beaters, with long, horn handles. Most of the time the gambang plays in octaves (gembyangan) and in the style of regular pulsed melodic patterns. The gambang may also play a few ornamental styles of melody and rhythm, such as a melodic pattern that includes playing two notes separated by two keys (kempyungan), or playing two notes separated by six keys, and a melodic pattern with syncopated rhythms.

Gendèr

A metallophone with ten to fourteen keys (from two to two and one-half octaves) suspended by cords over tube resonators. It is played with two disc-type mallets (i.e., a padded disc attached to the end of a stick). According to its melodic function, melodic range, and size, there are two kinds of gendèr: gendèr barung and gendèr panerus.

Gendèr Barung

Large-size, low- to middle-range gendèr. One of the leading instruments in the ensemble. The gendèr barung delivers its melodies in the style of pulsed melodic patterns known as cèngkok. It creates the fullness or sonority of the ensemble and reinforces the modal character (pathet) of gendhing. Some gendhing have a buka (melodic introduction) which is played by the gendèr barung; these gendhing are called gendhing gendèr. In the wayang performance, the gendèr player has a demanding task to fulfill, and has to play almost non-stop, in gendhing, in sulukan, and in *grimingan* (a solo gendèr playing to support the mood of a scene in the wayang performance).

Gendèr Panerus

Small-size, high- to middle-octave gendèr. Although it is a dispensable instrument, its presence adds to the richness of the ensemble. It expresses its melodies in the style of fast-moving, pulsed melodic patterns.

Gong

An onomatopoetic word, gong specifically refers to a large- or medium-size hanging gong which produces sound when struck with a round, padded beater on its central knob. The gong marks the beginning and end of the piece and gives a feeling of balance after the longest melodic section of a gendhing. The gong is so important in marking the fundamental unit of a gendhing that this unit (i.e., the space between two gong strokes) is called a gongan. There are two kinds of gong: gong ageng, and gong suwukan or gong siyem.

Gong Ageng

A large-size hanging gong, played to mark the end of each fundamental unit (a gongan) of a piece.

Gong Suwukan

A medium-size hanging gong, played to mark the end of the piece, especially in short and concentrated pieces, such as *lancaran,* srepegan, and sampak.

Kemanak

An instrument in the shape of a hollow banana, believed to be an archaic instrument. The kemanak is played in the ensemble accompanying some bedhaya and serimpi dances and santiswaran.

Kempul

Small-size hanging gong. Like the kenong, the kempul subdivides the melodic flow of the gendhing into musical phrases. Kenong and kempul are played at points of primary and secondary importance within the period marked by the gong ageng. In relation to the gendhing melody, the kempul may play the same note as the balungan; occasionally it may anticipate the following balungan note; sometimes it plays a note which forms a kempyung interval with the balungan note to enhance the feeling of the pathet.

Kendhang

A two-headed asymmetrical drum with heads attached to leather loops interlaced in a Y pattern. The kendhang is placed horizontally on the kendhang stand and is played with bare hands (part of the palm and/or fingers). The kendhang is responsible for setting irama and leading tempi (i.e., to keep a steady tempo, control transitions to faster and slower tempi, and end the piece). Beside setting irama and leading tempi, in the dance and wayang performance the kendhang also accompanies the movement of the dancers or puppets. These functions give the kendhang an important role in the ensemble—it is one of the leading instruments in the ensemble. According to its size and its musical function, there are four kinds of kendhang: kendhang ageng, kendhang ciblon, kendhang ketipung, and kendhang wayangan.

Kendhang Ageng

The largest kendhang (*ageng* = large), played in those gendhing or sections of gendhing which have a peaceful or majestic feeling. In a technique called kendhang kalih, kendhang ageng is played in combination with the kendhang ketipung.

Kendhang Ciblon

A small-size kendhang used to accompany dance. It is also used in "concert" music, where it plays rhythmic patterns associated with the dance movements.

Kendhang Ketipung

The smallest kendhang, played in combination with the kendhang ageng in a technique called kendhang kalih.

Kendhang Wayangan

A medium-size kendhang played to accompany wayang performances.

Kenong

A set of large horizontal gong kettles placed, open side down, on a wooden rack. The kenong is the next most important instrument after the gong in delineating the structure of a gendhing. It divides the gongan into two or four kenong phrases, or kenongan. Besides its function of underlining the formal structure, the kenong also relates to the melody of gendhing. It may play the same note as the balungan; it may anticipate the following balungan note to guide the melodic flow; or it may play a note in a kempyung interval with the balungan note, to support the feeling of the pathet. In the fast style of kenong in ayak-ayakan, srepegan, and sampak, the kenong playing guides the melodic flow of the gendhing.

Kethuk-Kempyang

Two small horizontal gong-kettles placed, open side down, on a wooden rack. The kethuk-kempyang subdivides the melodic flow of gendhing into shorter musical phrases. In the fast style of kethuk, in lancaran, sampak, srepegan, and ayak-ayakan, the kethuk plays between the balungan beats, resulting in a rapid interlocking pattern.

Rebab

A two-stringed bowed lute with a heart-shaped body of wood (or a round body of coconut shell) covered with a membrane made of parchment from a cow bladder. As one of the leading instruments in the ensemble, the rebab is considered the melodic leader of the ensemble, especially in the soft style of playing gendhing. In most pieces, the rebab plays the melodic introduction to the gendhing, determining the gendhing, laras, and pathet which are to be played by the ensemble. The melodic range of the rebab is the melodic range of any composition. Therefore, the melodic motion on the rebab gives a clear direction to the flow of the melody of a gendhing. In many gendhing, the rebab also gives musical cues to the ensemble to move from one section to another.

Saron

A generic name for a metallophone with six or seven keys (one octave or one octave and one tone) placed on a wooden frame, which serves as a resonator. The saron instruments produce sound when struck with a mallet made of wood or horn. According to the size and musical function, there are three different saron: saron demung, saron barung, and saron panerus.

Saron Demung

Large-size, middle-octave saron. Demung plays the balungan of a gendhing within its limited range. In a playing technique called *pinjalan,* two demung and a slenthem form interlocking melodies. Commonly a gamelan set has one or two demung, but some gamelan have more than two demung.

Saron Barung

Medium-size, high-octave saron. Like demung, saron barung plays the balungan of a gendhing within its limited range. In a playing technique called imbal-imbalan, two saron barung form fast, interlocking melodies. A gamelan set may have one or two saron barung, but there are gamelan that have more than two saron barung. A gamelan set may have a nine-key saron wayang. As the name indicates, it is played especially for wayang accompaniment.

Saron Panerus (Peking)

The smallest saron with the highest octave. The saron panerus or *peking* anticipates and doubles or quadruples the melody of the balungan. It also often attempts to paraphrase the balungan in the context of the melody of a composition.

Slenthem

According to its construction, the slenthem belongs to the family of the gendèr; sometimes it is even called gendèr panembung. But slenthem has the same number of keys as the saron; it provides the lowest octave of the saron group. Like demung and saron barung, slenthem plays the balungan within its one-octave range.

Suling

An end-blown flute made of bamboo. The suling expresses its melodies in the style of free-metrical melodic patterns. These patterns are played intermittently, usually toward the ends of melodic phrases. Occasionally, the suling player plays short melodies in the beginning or the middle of melodic phrases.

Glossary

abdi dalem	All persons in the service of the king, regardless of their rank.
adi luhung	Glorious and beautiful. An adjective characterizing the Javanese court arts as high art.
alun-alun	Open square in front of and behind the palace (northern and southern alun-alun).
angklung	An instrument made of bamboo tubes fastened loosely on a frame, which produces sound when shaken.
arak	An alcoholic drink made from fermented rice.
ayak-ayakan	One of the formal structures of, and the name of, a gendhing.
babad	Chronicle (lit., to clear the way).
balungan	Melodic skeleton of gendhing.
banjaran sari	A Javanese dance opera invented in the Paku Alaman (the minor court of Yogyakarta) in the late nineteenth century. It is believed to be an imitation of the langendriyan dance opera of the Mang-kunegaran (the minor court of Surakarta).
barang	1. The name of a gamelan pitch; 2. The name of a pathet in the pélog tuning system (see *pathet barang*).
bedhaya (badhaya)	A genre of ceremonial dances in the Central Javanese court tradition. It is performed by seven or nine dancers. In the past, bedhaya was performed either by prepubescent boys or by female dancers. Nowadays, only female bedhaya is common.
buka	Introductory melodic phrase of a gendhing.
calapita	1. Another name for gambang gongsa; 2. Another name for kemanak.
carabalèn	A four-tone archaic gamelan ensemble.
calung	An instrument made of bamboo tubes strung on a frame, which produces sound when struck with a mallet or mallets.
cèngkok	1. Melodic style; 2. Melodic pattern; 3. A musical unit between two strokes of a gong (see *gongan*).
demang	1. The rank of a junior officer in the court's armed forces; 2. The rank of a middle-level court official.

dhikir
Islamic prayer for achieving mystical insight. It consists of the continuous repetition of a formula, usually comprising different names of God. When used together with certain rhythmic movements of the body and head, dhikir may lead the worshiper to religious ecstasy.

gadhon
A small gamelan ensemble, consisting of mainly soft-sounding, leading instruments.

gamelan angklung
A Balinese four-tone ensemble used in processions or in temple ceremonies.

gamelan caruk
A Balinese sacred ensemble, consisting of a pair of caruk (bamboo xylophone) and saron (metallophone).

gamelan gambang
A Balinese seven-tone sacred ensemble, consisting of four gambang (bamboo xylophone) and two saron (metallophone).

gamelan gambuh
A Balinese ensemble used to accompany the gambuh dance drama, consisting of four large suling (flute), rebab (two-stringed bowed instrument), kangsi (cymbal), and kendhang (drum).

gamelan luang
A Balinese seven-tone sacred ensemble, consisting of a pair of gangsa (metallophone), a set of bonang (gong-type instrument), a small bedhug (drum), and a gong.

gamelan palégongan
A Balinese five-tone ensemble, derived from an older, seven-tone Semar Pegulingan ensemble.

gamelan salunding (selonding)
A Balinese archaic and sacred ensemble, consisting of mainly metallophone-type instruments made of iron.

gamelan sekatèn
A special pélog ensemble, consisting of large, loud-sounding instruments. It is played once a year in front of the mosque to celebrate the birth and death of the Prophet Muhamad.

gantungan
From gantung, lit., hanging. It refers to sustaining a melodic passage.

garebeg
The three important Islamic religious festivals: gerebeg Mulud, garebeg Pasa, and garebeg Besar.

gembyang(an)
1. An octave; 2. An instrumental playing technique involving playing octaves.

gendhèng
To sing.

gendhing
1. A generic term for any gamelan composition; 2. A generic term for a gamelan composition with a relatively long structure, consisting of two major parts, mérong and inggah.

gendhing bonang
An "instrumental" genre of compositions in which bonang is the principal and melodic leader.

gendhing dolanan
Children's songs, or short, light-hearted pieces.

gendhing gérongan	A genre of composition whose main melodic basis is the gérongan.
gendhing mares	Gamelan marching pieces composed by the musician in the court of Yogyakarta (from the Dutch *mars*.) The playing of a gendhing mares requires the incorporation of European wind instruments and drums.
gendhing panembrama	A sub-genre of gendhing gérongan that was composed to commemorate important events in the Central Javanese court. The text of the gérongan describes the event. Usually the name of the piece starts with the word Sri.
gendhing rebab	A genre of composition with a long formal structure in which the rebab is the principal and melodic leader.
gendhing terbangan	A musical ensemble consisting of solo and chorus singing with the terbang as chief accompaniment (see *santiswaran*).
gérongan	The part of a male chorus sung with the gamelan.
gongan	The basic musical unit of gendhing between two strokes of gong.
huprup	From the Dutch title *Opperhoofd*, the Company's resident Dutch chief official.
ilmu (èlmu, ngèlmu)	Secret and sacred knowledge.
imbal–imbalan	An interlocking playing technique of bonang or saron barung.
Indo	A mixed-blood offspring, engendered usually by a European father and an Indonesian mother.
inggah	The second section of a composition of long formal structure.
irama	1. Tempo; 2. A musical concept defined by the expanding and contracting of structural units accompanied by changes of the density level of the instruments. The latter can be identified by the number of beats of the instruments in ratio with the basic beats of the gendhing. There are five irama: irama lancar, irama tanggung, irama dadi, irama wilet, and irama rangkep.
irama dadi	The irama in which the ratio between the basic beats of the gendhing and the highest density level of the instrument is 1/8.
irama lancar	The irama in which the ratio between the basic beats of the gendhing and the highest density level of the instrument is 1/2.
irama rangkep	The irama in which the ratio between the basic beats of the gendhing and the highest density level of the instrument is 1/32.
irama tanggung	The irama in which the ratio between the basic beats of the gendhing and the highest density level of the instrument is 1/4.
irama wilet	The irama in which the ratio between the basic beats of the gendhing and the highest density level of the instrument is 1/16.

jarit kawung	The name of a melodic pattern of gendèr or singing.
jathilan	A trance dance, consisting of riders on hobby horses made of plaited bamboo, a masked tiger or lion, and a masked clown.
jineman	A genre of gamelan composition in which the pesindhèn part is featured.
jumungahan	The Islamic observance of the weekly Friday prayer.
juru alok	Participants in tayuban dancing whose task is to excite the mood of the dancing party by occasionally singing stylized cries.
juru keplok	Participants in tayuban dancing whose task is to excite the mood of the dancing party by clapping.
juru senggak	See *juru alok*.
karawitan	The art of Javanese gamelan and vocal music.
Kasunanan	The major court of Surakarta.
Kasultanan	The major court of Yogyakarta.
kaul	A vow.
kaum	People who are especially devoted to Islam and live in the vicinity of the mosque, in a community called Kauman.
kemanak (kamanak)	A pair of bronze instruments which have the shape of a hollow banana.
kempyung	An interval separated by two pitches or keys.
kenongan	A musical phrase delineated by the stroke of kenong.
keris	A dagger, usually considered a magically charged item and an heirloom (pusaka).
ketawang	One of the formal structures of gendhing, consisting of 16 basic pulses per gongan.
kethoprak	Traditional Javanese drama.
kinanthi	A poetic meter of the sekar macapat often used by the penggérong.
kidung	A genre of Javanese sung poetry.
kondangan	Ritual and communal feast (a synonym of slametan).
kroncong	A genre of Indonesian popular music whose origin can be traced back to Portuguese music of sixteenth-century Java.
ladrang	A formal structure of gendhing consisting of 32 basic pulses per gongan.
lagu	Melody.
lakon	Wayang stories.

langendriyan	Javanese dance opera in which the dialogue is in the form of poetry and is sung by the dancers and accompanied by gamelan. It is known as a dance opera that is a prerogative of the minor court of Mangkunegaran in Surakarta.
laras	1. Tuning system; 2. Pitch.
larasmadya	An ensemble consisting of singing with the accompaniment of terbang, kendhang, and kemanak.
larih	The time in the tayuban when the male guest dancer is served liquor.
lawung	Court lance dance.
lurah	1. Middle rank of court officials; 2. Chieftain, such as the chief of the village.
lurah badhut	The joker of the court, whose job includes supervising the talèdhèk dancers.
luk	Aspect of musical ornamentation.
macapat	A genre of sung poetry. Each macapat song is governed by the following rules: a fixed number of lines per stanza, a fixed number of syllables per line, and a fixed vowel at the end of each line.
Mahabharata	An Indian epic that was introduced and rewritten by Javanese poets during the Hindu-Javanese period. The theme of the epic is the conflict between the Kurawa and Pandhawa brothers.
Mangkunegaran	The minor court of Surakarta.
mestizo	Derived from the Portuguese word meaning a person of mixed blood, it refers to a culture made up of different cultural influences.
monggang	A three-tone archaic gamelan ensemble played to mark important court events.
monggangan	A musical style that imitates the melody of monggang.
musikum	An oath taken by the groom in the part of the marriage ijab ceremony in which the groom declares his intention to marry the bride. The ceremony is carried out under the guidance of the religious official (pengulu).
nduduk tunggal	The bonang playing technique, consisting of syncopated rhythm of a single note.
ngabèhi	The middle-rank title of noblemen.
ngelik	Lit., rising voice. It is the second part of a composition, and usually starts in a high-register melody.
niyaga	Gamelan musicians, especially the instrumentalists.
ompak	1. Transition phrase from mérong to inggah; 2. The opening section of the gendhing gérongan, especially in the ketawang pieces, that has no gérongan part.

ordenas	From the Dutch *ordonnans,* a group of noblemen whose responsibility is to maintain and procure supplies for the palace.
padhang-ulihan	Answer-question phrases.
pagelaran	The outer hall of the court.
pakajangan	Camp-waiting. A court occasion when the king's high-ranking subjects from the outlying regions of the kingdom stay in a temporary camp at the alun-alun, waiting for an audience with the king.
pakem	Concise prose outlines of wayang stories (lakon).
Paku Alaman	The minor court of Yogyakarta.
palaran	The singing of a macapat song accompanied by a composition in srepegan structure of an ensemble consisting of gendèr, gambang, celempung, suling, kethuk, kenong, kempul, and gong suwukan.
panakawan	Companions of satriya (knight) in the wayang story.
panggih	A ceremony held around the first formal meeting between the bride and groom.
pangrawit	Gamelan musicians, especially the instrumentalists (synonym of niyaga).
paningkah	A formal marriage ceremony involving the validation of the marriage and the vows of the groom by a religious official.
panji	The indigenous Javanese stories which are associated with the period from the eleventh to the thirteenth century, the time of Kediri-Singosari kingships.
paringgitan	A ground-level area between the main hall (pendhapa) and the inner royal residence (dalem) of the court. As the name suggests, it is a space where the shadow puppet (ringgit or wayang) performance is held.
pathet	Modal classification of gendhing. There are three pathet in each of the tuning systems.
pathet barang	One of the three pathet in the pélog tuning system.
pathet lima	One of the three pathet in the pélog tuning system.
pathet manyura	One of the three pathet in the sléndro tuning system.
pathet nem	1. One of the three pathet in the pélog tuning system. 2. One of the three pathet in the sléndro tuning system.
pathet sanga	One of the three pathet in the sléndro tuning system.
pendhapa (pandhapa)	The outer hall of a house.

penggérong	Male singers in gamelan.
pengulu	An Islamic religious official.
penggérong	The male singers of gérongan.
peranakan	Mixed-blood offspring, usually engendered by a Chinese father and Indonesian mother.
pesantrèn	The Islamic religious boarding school.
pesindhèn	1. Solo female singer in gamelan; 2. Mixed chorus singers in the gamelan accompanying bedhaya/serimpi dance.
pipilan	Playing technique of bonang and gendèr in which the player plays single tones, one at a time.
prajuritan	A genre of central Javanese court processional music, consisting of a combination of Javanese and European instruments.
pujangga	Court poet. Pujangga could be a prophetic man.
pusaka	Magically charged object.
Ramayana	An Indian epic whose theme is the adventure of Rama and his wife, Sinta.
rasa	Inner feeling and experience.
rantau	Tradition among the Minangkabau in Sumatra in which a young man takes a journey, searching for life experience outside his homeland.
ratib	A kind of dhikir practiced in Aceh, North Sumatra.
reyong	1. An instrument consisting of two small gongs attached to the two ends of a pole, which is found in the Balinese gamelan angklung; 2. Balinese instrument consisting of a row of small gongs.
ringgit	1. Another term for the wayang puppets; 2. Another term for the talèdhèk dancers.
ringgit tiyang	A Javanese dance drama with characters and stories drawn from the shadow puppet performance, the wayang purwa.
ronggèng	Another term for talèdhèk.
salisir	A poetic meter often used by the male chorus (penggérong).
salomprèt (selomprèt)	A wooden oboe, the melodic instrument in the réyog ensemble.
salunding	See *selonding*.
sampak	One of the formal structures, and the name, of gendhing.
santiswaran	An ensemble consisting of singing (solo and chorus) with the accompaniment of mainly terbang (frame drum) and kemanak.
santri	People who are especially devoted to the practice of Islam.

santri meri	Santri who observe the practice of Islam but are not prohibited from the forbidden world of pleasure.
satriya	Javanese knight.
sendhon	A dhalang's song that expresses wonder or a sad mood.
serat	1. Book; 2. Letter.
sesegan	A special section in the inggah part of a gendhing that is always played in a loud style, in irama tanggung.
sekar	Sung poetry (see *tembang*).
sekar ageng	Indian-influenced Sanskrit poetry. Each stanza of sekar ageng consists of four lines. Each line has an equal number of syllables (lampah) and is divided into two or more units (pedhotan).
sekar kawi	See *sekar ageng*.
serimpi (sarimpi, srimpi)	A genre of female court dances. A serimpi dance is performed by four dancers.
sekatèn	A religious festival to celebrate the birth and death of the Prophet Muhamad.
selametan	See *kondangan*.
sindhèn(an)	The part of a female solo sung with the gamelan.
simpingan	The arrangement of wayang puppets on either side of the wayang screen. Used for decoration, the small puppets are near the center and the larger ones are on the outside edges.
srageni	Marching army.
srepegan	One of the formal structures of gendhing, but also the name of that gendhing.
sindhèn	Female solo singer in the gamelan (see *pesindhèn*).
slametan	Ritual and communal feats (a synonym of kondangan).
sloki	Small liquor glass.
sufi	An Islamic movement that emphasizes the practice of mysticism.
sulukan	A generic term for songs sung by the dhalang of the wayang performance.
Susuhunan	The title of the ruler of the Surakarta court.
suwukan	A part in the inggah section used especially for ending the piece.
talèdhèkan	A male dance party involving the males present, who dance in turn with professional dancing girls or women for this dance event (see *tayuban*).
talèdhèk	Professional dancing girls or women for the talèdhèkan dancing party.

tandhak	Another term for talèdhèk.
tanjidhur	From the Portuguese word *tangedor* (musician), a generic term for music.
tayuban	Another term for talèdhèkan; verb, nayub.
tembang	Sung-poetry (see *sekar*).
terbang	Single-headed frame drum with or without jingle.
tingalan	Birthday.
totok	Tough (pertaining to personality or character); it refers to pure-blooded, un-Javanized Dutch.
tumenggung	One of the highest ranks of officers in Javanese court.
ulama	Islamic traditional religious scholars.
wayang	In a general sense, any kind of Javanese performance whose dramatis personae are human actors or puppets. In a narrower sense, a shadow play using flat leather puppets whose stories are based largely on the *Mahabharata* and *Ramayana* epics (see *wayang purwa*).
wayang gedhog	A shadow play using flat leather puppets presenting the indigenous Javanese stories of the Panji cycle which are associated with the period from the eleventh to the thirteenth centuries, the time of the Kediri-Singosari kingships.
wayang klithik	A puppet play using flat wooden puppets presenting the indigenous Javanese stories of Damarwulan, portraying a semi-history of the fourteenth-century Majapahit era.
wayang kulit	A shadow play using flat leather puppets. Considered the oldest wayang, the wayang kulit presents stories based on the Hindu *Mahabharata* and *Ramayana* epics. It is also referred as wayang purwa.
wayang madya	A shadow play presenting the indigenous Javanese stories which are related to the period from the end of the wayang purwa dynastic genealogy to the beginning of Kediri-Singosari kingships.
wayang purwa	(Purwa means "beginning") see *wayang kulit*.
wayang topèng	Masked dance-drama presenting indigenous Javanese stories based on the Panji cycle. In the past, it also told stories based on the *Ramayana* and *Mahabharata* epics.
wayang wong	See *ringgit tiyang*.
wilet	1. Aspects of musical ornamentation; 2. The name of an irama.

Notes

Introduction

1. *Serat Sri Karongron* I. Dhandhang Gula.

> Wanci jam 7   21 menit
> prabu miyos saking prabayasa
> kinurmatan ing uniné
> gendhing Sri Katon arum
> nganyut-anyut énak pinyarsi
> irama ajeg rampak
> kendho kenceng runtut
> abareng gulet wiletan
> sayuk sampyeng ngepeng panabuhé ririh
> swara kabèh karasa
>
> Arum rarasé angraras ati
> kyai Kaduk-Manis Manis-Rengga
> déné gongsa Cara Balèn
> kiyai Sepet Madu
> Madu Pinasthika kang nami
> setrik orkès musikan
> Wihèlmis munya sru
> pra suméwa ngapurancang
> Sri Narèndra wus lenggah kursi ingukir
> lung-lungan pinarada
>
> Majeng mangétan lenggahing aji
> nèng madyaning sasana parasdya
> respati pangagemané
> cara walandi prabu
> . . . .

See Purbadipura (1913–16) for the published version of *Serat Sri Karongron*.

2. Anderson (ibid.) goes on to say: "His palace would be filled not only with the traditional array of *pusaka* (heirlooms), such as krisses, spears, sacred musical instruments, carriages, and the like, but also various types of extraordinary human beings, such as albinos, clowns, dwarves, and fortune-tellers. Being in the palace, their Power was absorbed by, and further added to, the ruler's own. Their loss, by whatever means, was seen as an actual diminution of the king's Power and often as a sign of the impending collapse of the dynasty."

3. The "old pronominal forms" of which Anderson speaks are part of the complex nature of social relations in Java. The Javanese have a complex social hierarchy of which

they are very conscious. The use of speech levels in Javanese language is the best example of the intricacy of Javanese social relations. There are two basic levels: *krama*, a polite, formal language used when addressing superiors or strangers; and *ngoko*, a colloquial language used when addressing inferiors or someone of equal status. Each basic category can be subdivided into more levels. Consequently, Javanese language has quite a few pronouns. The word "I" can be *ingsun, dalem, kawula, kula*, or *aku*, and "you," *sira, nan-dalem, paduka, panjenengan, sampéyan*, or *kowé*. Like the choice of the speech level itself, the use of a pronoun is determined by the social setting of the speakers and the rank and status of the addressor relative to the addressee. For example, *sira/ingsun* (I/you) is *ngoko* level used by high noble superiors; *dalem/nan-dalem* is *krama* level used by inferiors addressing high noble superiors (these two pronouns are used only in the court language); *kula/panjenengan* is *krama* level used by inferiors; *aku/kowé* is *ngoko* level used by commoners with equal status.

4. The severity of the breakup of the master–servant relationship can be shown in the following anecdote. It is popularly believed that Paku Buwana X was an expert in gamelan, Javanese dance, and wayang. But a story told by gamelan musicians about the king contradicts such a belief. Once, the musicians played gamelan. Suddenly the king entered in the hall and yelled: "Stop playing that piece. I command you to play Pramugari." Following the king's order, the musicians stopped playing what they had been playing and began to play Pramugari. But the piece that they had been playing before the king stopped them was Pramugari. Whether or not the story is true, the point is that some musicians were willing to portray the nobility in an unfavorable light.

Chapter One

1. Many instruments that appear in the Borobudur reliefs (e.g., harp, mouth organ, and various kinds of lutes, among others) have barely survived in the later periods of Javanese history. Some of these instruments still exist in mainland Southeast Asia. Some are clearly of Indian origin. If these instruments existed in Java at that time, why did many of them disappear from Java? Was Indian music being performed for the Javanese aristocrats, or was it only drawn on the walls of temples? These are a few of the questions that have no firm answers. What is notable about the depiction of music on Borobudur is the absence of any gamelan ensemble; even the appearance of two instruments likened to the modern *kethuk* and *saron* is highly questionable.

Insisting on the ancient origin of gamelan, Hood (1984:28) speculates that the absence of gamelan on Borobudur was caused by the political circumstances of the time. That is, because in this period Java was colonized by Indian rulers, pictorial representation of Javanese aristocracy, such as would be implied by gamelan, was suppressed for aesthetic or religious reasons. Current historical accounts, however, reject the notion of Indian colonization of Southeast Asia, a view that was favored by nationalistic Indian historians; rather, they point to a process of Indianization with persistent local adjustment (Hall 1981:15–22; Wolters 1982:52). In any event, more evidence is needed to support Hood's thesis about the antiquity of gamelan.

2. Scholars do not agree on the early meaning of the word *gendhing*. Zoetmulder (1982:514) defines it as "a musical instrument of the percussion type (a kind of gong?)"; thus he translated *gendhing strinya* as "small gongs." He also defines (p. 515) the term

gendhing stri, along with *gendhing walyan* and *gendhing parekan,* as "various *gendhing* (belonging to special groups?)." Kunst (1968:5) interprets the word *gendhing* as a generic term for orchestras, but he could not establish the identity of such ensembles.

Nowadays *gendhing* is a generic term for gamelan compositions. But the term *tukang gendhing,* which means gamelan smith, implies that the word also refers to a musical instrument.

3. The characterization of the sound of *kungkang* as booming is exaggerated, although it is true that the *kungkang* is a big frog.

4. *Kamanak* (now commonly spelled *kemanak*) is a pair of bronze or iron instruments which have the shape of an unpeeled banana. Thus, "cymbals" is an incorrect translation.

5. A Balinese kingdom ruled the eastern corner of East Java until the late eighteenth century; thus the relationship between Java and Bali did not completely end after the Islamization of Java. Some genres of music in the eastern corner of East Java, such as Gandrung Banyuwangi, are similar to Balinese genres (see Wolbers 1986).

6. With regard to the interaction between the vocal and instrumental idioms of kidung, Wallis (1980:211–12) suggests that "perhaps the poets worked with musicians in the hope of recreating in Bali certain features of Javanese musical arts. Accounts of Javanese court life in the later Hindu-Javanese period (13th–15th centuries) frequently mention an instrumental accompaniment for singing. In [contemporary] Bali, on the other hand, struck instruments and voices are strictly separated, and rarely do the two take part in the same performance simultaneously. Only in ensembles strongly influenced by Javanese musical style (e.g. *gamelan palégongan*) or recreating strictly Javanese contexts in theater (e.g. *gamelan gambuh*) do instrumentalists and vocalists perform in an integrated idiom." Concerning the separation of instrumental and vocal music in Bali, I can only speculate that this is a consequence of the primacy in Balinese music of loud-sounding large ensembles—playing outdoor musical styles—in which soft-sounding vocal music has no place.

7. In Bali, four of these instruments in combination with a pair of *saron* (a metallophone with four or five keys) constitute an ensemble called gamelan Gambang. Considered one of the sacred ensembles, gamelan Gambang is played during funeral ceremonies (*ngaben*). See Schaareman (1980) for a detailed discussion of the musical practice of this ensemble.

8. In contemporary Bali, this instrument is incorporated into the Angklung ensemble.

9. The wayang bèbèr ensemble consists of a bowed-stringed instrument (rebab), a drum (kendhang), and gongs (kempul, gong, kenong, and kethuk); the wayang klithik ensemble: a metallophone (saron), rebab, kendhang, and gongs (kenong, kethuk, kempul, and gong); the réyog ensemble: a salomprèt (shawm), gongs (kempul and two kethuk), kendhang, and sometimes angklung; an ensemble for certain bedhaya dances: kemanak and gongs (kethuk, kenong, and gong).

10. About wayang bèbèr (recitation of a story that is painted on scroll paper), Anderson (n.d.:33–81) suggests that it was originally a type of recitation of kakawin poetry performed in Hindu-Javanese courts. The decline of Majapahit, skirmishes with Islamic trading centers, and European penetration caused the loss of this recited-painting tradition. It reappeared in a contemporary rural environment in its new form—adopting, in a simplified way, the idiom of *wayang kulit purwa* performance. However, the music accom-

paniment was not adjusted to the wayang kulit purwa ensemble. Perhaps the music of wayang bèbèr is the remnant of an older Hindu-Javanese ensemble. The ensemble consists of rebab, kendhang, kenong, kempul, and gong.

It is commonly held that the rebab originated in Western Asia. But Kunst (1968:86) speculates that a bowed instrument called samepa existed in the Hindu-Javanese period. It is possible that in a later period the samepa was replaced by the rebab. A rebab with three strings exists in Thailand; it is called sǭ sām sāi. Morton (1976:96) observes that sǭ sām sāi has been used by the Thai since the early fourteenth century. Relying on Hood's hypothesis (that is, that Javanese rebab existed in Java before the advent of Islam), Morton speculates that sǭ sām sāi, along with the plucked-lute type of instrument, came to Angkor from Java during the reign of Jayavarman II (802–850). Before his ascension to the throne, Jayavarman II visited Java to pay homage to the Sailendra court (Hall 1981:112). It is possible that there was some influence of the Javanese on Cambodian culture during his reign. Notwithstanding the lack of historical evidence, this is another indication of the possible existence of rebab before the expansion of Islam.

11. For a recent study on the Indian Tantric aesthetic experience in the medieval Javanese gamelan, its adaptation in Sufism during the Islamic Javanese period, and its remnant in contemporary Java, see J. Becker (1993).

12. One of the results of this unsettled period was the flight to the island of Bali of a number of Javanese aristocrats' who wanted to maintain their Hindu religion, thereby intensifying the process of cultural transfer.

13. For a detailed background of the early Portuguese travels to Asia, see Ricklefs (1993:22–26).

14. Boxer (1969:359–60) notes the passion for music of the Portuguese kings and their subjects. The latter took with them the folk music and folk dances of Portugal to Asia, Africa, and Brazil.

15. For a summary of the background of Sultan Agung and the Mataram rulers after him, see Pigeaud and de Graaf (1976:36–74).

16. ". . . metale speelgereetschappen, ten minste van 20 tot 30 [50], soo cleijne als groote gommen . . ."

17. "Dit cleet is veelderleij, off swart met goude sterren, blaeuw met gouden ofte silveren bloemen, rood, groen, wit gemengeld enz., alle met goud of silver verciert; dat zij met waeterverw seer curieux daer op weeten te schilderen."

18. "Den Koninck nu een vrolijcken luijm hebbende, clapt sleffs in de handen, animerende dese jonge vrijsters met luijder stemme om haer wel te quijten, haer eenige gouden ringen ende verciersselen belovende. Dese nu moede zijnde, moeten d' andere groote heeren haer dansmaechden mede van huijs doen haelen, om tegens de zijne om de prijs te dansen, daermade zij alsoo den geheelen nacht dickmael doorbrengen. Om haer selffs gedurende dit spel te verheugen, drincken zij onder malcanderen seeckeren dranck, genaempt brem, van bijsondere vette risjt (plut genaempt). Dese dranck is van smaeck bijnae als onse Spaense wijn, ende is, matich gedronken, gesont voor magere ligchamen, doch te overvloedich, verhet deselve machtich, ende wiert men daer van seer haest (als van Spaense wijn) droncken."

19. ". . . veel cleijne gommekens, die met eenige fluijten ende violen een soete melodie geven."

20. For further discussion of Dutch accounts during this period, see Kunst (1973, 1: 113–18). Based on Valentijn's encyclopedic work (1723–26) he mentions, among others, a few of the ensembles, such as singing to the accompaniment of a gong, a drum, and a native zither; loud music consisting of a large number of gongs and drums; and Javanese violin and zithers to accompany dance. He also proposes a theory of the development of gamelan. According to him, in the Hindu-Javanese period two chief instrumental groupings were known: soft-sounding instruments, which were intended for indoor use (e.g., gendèr, *gambang* (xylophone), and *suling* (flute)); and loud-sounding instruments, which were to be played in the open air (e.g., drums, cymbals, and various kinds of gongs) (ibid. 113–14). He believes that at the end of the Hindu-Javanese period a marriage between these two instrumental groupings was arranged. However plausible is his theory, evidence to support it is very hard to find.

21. Haji Amad Mutamakin is the main figure of the story in the *Serat Cabolèk*. He is condemned by religious scholars (*ulama*) because of his religious doctrine and his disloyalty to the king of Kartasura. The king orders the ulama, led by Ketib Anom of Kudus, to investigate Haji Amad Mutamakin. The king also asks Demang Urawan, his trusted nephew and brother-in-law, to supervise the investigation. Ketib Anom of Kudus is an Islamic scholar who is also very knowledgeable about Javanese stories and tradition. At the end of the poem, it is Ketib Anom's elucidation of the story of Bima Suci that is given special attention by the author of *Serat Cabolèk*.

22. The terbang ensemble consists of antiphonal singing between a male soloist and a male chorus, accompanied by three or more frame drums (terbang). Sometimes a kendhang (two-headed drum) and angklung (bamboo tube instruments) are included in the ensemble. According to the *Serat Centhini,* the terbang ensemble could perform Islamic and Javanese repertoire or a combination of them. Besides being listened for its own sake, the terbang ensemble could accompany a magic show and a *tayuban*. The flexibility of the use of terbang ensembles—performing both Javanese and Islamic music, and accompanying theatrical performance or not—may account for the popularity of this music at the time of *Serat Centhini* and *Serat Cabolèk*.

23. Soebardi's translation of terbang as "tambourine" is somewhat misleading. It is true that the tambourine, like a terbang, is a single-headed frame drum. But a terbang has a deeper curved rim and is larger than a tambourine. Moreover, not all terbang have jingles around the sides, a characteristic of the tambourine.

24. Considered one of the Javanese classics, the *Serat Centhini* is the story of wanderers who travel from place to place in Java looking for celebrated teachers and searching for deeper experience and esoteric knowledge. It recounts in detail the experiences the wanderers have along the way. Its diverse subjects—music, theatrical performances, religious knowledge, topography, medicine, etc.—have earned the *Serat Centhini* its reputation as a great Javanese encyclopedic work.

25. *Serat Tjeṇṭini* 7–8:277e. Pucung.

> 10. Dé punika dhaupé marang ing èlmu
> unining gamelan
> sami lan unining lambé
> gendhingané puniku jatining niat
> 11. Paminipun nglinging dhikir pujinipun

lir cengklinging gangsa
kang dèrèng kelawan gendhing
muji dhikir lamun tan kelawan niat
12. Pujinipun sami lan unining kethuk
tinabuh dhèwèkan
uniné tan dadi gendhing
muji dhikir ngethèprès lir kecèr pecah
13. Kumarusuk blebegi kuping rinungu
lir suak-suaka
dèn kongsi sempal uangé
muji dhikir ukur cangkemé kéwala
14. Nyananipun ketrima barang jinaluk
jleg padha sedhéla
dé kongsi érak gondhangé
kari-kari inganti tan ana prapta
15. Sababipun tan nganggo gendhinging kalbu
uniné krak-okrak
yèn ta anganggoa gendhing
pesthi nyamleng kadya gendhing pathet sanga

26. It is widely held that Islam was brought to Indonesia by Islamic traders from Gujarat, on the west coast of India. There Islam had mixed with Hinduism. Since the Javanese had embraced Hinduism before Islam arrived on Java, the kind of Islam that entered Indonesia was more willingly accepted by the Javanese.

27. *Serat Babad Nitik* 2. Sinom.

130b-6. Malih ing malem Jumungah
melèk malih ingkang abdi
kahum dhikir tarebangan
pra demang panahan sami
ngabèhi nèng mandhapi
pra putra lawan tumenggung
sinegah dhedharanan [dhedhaharan]
sekul ulam nginum awis
sadayané tengah dalu papanganan

28. Ann Kumar provides a translation of passages from the *Serat Babad Nitik* of an elaborate Jumungahan observance:

He performed the Friday prayer again,
worshipping for the hundred-and-thirty-
ninth time,
on Friday-Kliwon
the seventh of Rabingulakir.

There were thirty-nine *tumpĕng* [a food prepared for this ritual],
and the purpose of the slametan
was the welfare of the Pangeran Dipati
and of all his sons and grandsons
and of all his army.
Those at the prayer numbered four hundred and fifty
one. . . .

In the evening and through the night before Friday
a vigil was kept by the army
of the senior Pangeran Dipati

who circled the courtyard.
They placed bets on their skill at archery,
while the kaum soldiers said the ḍikir in unison.
There was singing, and playing a *gamělan*
of gongs and drums, and there was a meal at midnight,
Some performed a *tayungan* [dance].
In the morning they went to the prayer once again—

it was the two hundred
and twenty-fourth [fifth] time the worship had been done,
on Friday-Kliwon
the eleventh of Běsar.
There were twenty-four tumpěng at the siḍěkah [ritual meal]
with the meat of the cow as the sacrifice
for the welfare of the Pangeran Dipati.

The number of those who performed the prayer at the mosque
was three hundred and sixty-
four, performing the prayer at the mosque (Ann Kumar 1980: 13–15).

29. Beside the "big" or annual birthday, there were *tingalan alit,* the "little" birthdays, once every thirty-five days. They occurred each time the particular days of the five-day-week and the seven-day-week on which Mangkunegara I was born coincided.

30. Santri meri practiced Islam but were not prohibited from the forbidden world of pleasure (Gericke and Roorda 1901, 2:479). Perhaps santri meri were a division of court santri that practiced a kind of Sufism in which religious activity and secular emotion were mixed. See the next section.

31. *Serat Babad Nitik* 1. Sinom.

> 13a-13. . . . .
> anulya asalin sasi
> pan Arwah ingkang sasi
> Senèn wagé dinanipun
> ing tanggal ping sakawan
> kangjeng pangéran dipati
> kang tingalan ageng anenggih kang yuswa
>
> 13a-14. Wus sèket taun semana
> mapan punjul wulung warsi
> taun Ehé sinangkalan
> liman wiyat swana jalmi
> sontennya santri ngaji
> tiyang pitung atus punjul
> pitung dasa sakawan
> gumerah santri kang ngaji
> santri meri gumeder nèng palataran
>
> 13a-15. Ing tengah dalu kondangan
> papanganan lingsir wengi
> santri meri ababakar [ambalabar?]
> samya sinebaran dhuwit

énjangé monggang muni
mariyem pating jalegur
nulya abarondongan
sunapan sadaya muni
pan gumrudug kadya rug ingkang prawata
13b-16. Sampunya sragni [srageni] priya
anulya sragni [srageni] èstri
barondongan paringgitan
kang ngabani Kangjeng Gusti
rempeg sragni [srageni] èstri
kalah kang sragni [srageni] kakung
éram sakèh tumingal
tambur èstri suling èstri
dan [dyan] kondangan . . . samya maca donga
13b-17. Sarta dinuman ardana
wong kaum santri waradin
anulya ringgit titiyang
sinelan ringgit sarimpi
lan ringgit munggèng kelir
alit wanodya kayungyun
samya njomblong tumingal
kathah gawok kang ningali
pan sinelan badhaya èstri apélag
13b-18. Tur samya nginum kang bala
mariyemé wali-wali
kang alok ambal-ambalan
saya kathah wong ningali
lurah punggawa mantri
wuru sadaya kang nginum
pan wuru-wuru dawa
kangjeng pangéran dipati
Jayèngasta sinelir wuru sadaya
13b-19. Sadina nutuk kasukan
surup akasukan ringgit
sarta bandhung talèdhèkan
sadalu sarta garimis
énjing ringgitan malih
walulang sarta adudum [adundum]
lèlèmèt [lèlèmèk] mring kang bala
daluné wayang wong malih
énjingipun akasukan talèdhèkan.

32. The atmosphere of this kind of court ritual gradually changed. By the middle of the nineteenth century, the Islamic aspect of the royal event had been minimized. See below.

33. It is a mistake to assume that a sharp distinction between rural and urban existed in this period. The court of Surakarta was no more than a big village surrounded by small villages. It is therefore safe to suggest that there was an easy flow of communication between the court and the surrounding rural areas. In other words, there was dynamic interaction between the court and the villages.

34. But the shape of the wayang puppet as we know it today can be found in the reliefs of the fourteenth-century temple of Panataran in East Java—long before the coming of the Islamic wali.

35. For further discussion of the practice of gamelan Sekatèn, see Sumarsam (1981: 54–73).

36. For additional accounts of Yasadipura's translation of stories of Islamic origin, see Soebardi 1975: 23–25.

37. Perhaps "the sound of katawang" here refers to "heavenly musical sound," since katawang is usually related to the word *tawang,* which means "sky."

38. "Mungguh awit anané talèdhèk ambarang, nalika jaman ing Demak gamelané trebang kendhang, yèn lekasing gendhing dibukani swara, mangkono mau mirit jaman kabudan, kacarita jogèding widodari, tatabuhané swara katawang, déné tekan jaman karaton ing Janggala, kacarita prabu Suryawisésa, yèn kondur ngadhaton pinethuk ing pramèswari, ana madyaning paringgitan padha angigel, saha kinurmatan ing gamelan saléndro, dadi beksa tayuban mirit nalika jumenengé prabu Suryawisésa, tekaning karaton Demak dianggit marang para santri, dulguyer birahi, yèn padha ambukani dhikir, nganggo lagon tinabuhan angklung, kendhang kalawan tarebang, sarta ana santri lanang lan santri wadon kang pinatah angémpraki, yaiku jogèd laguné angèmperi laguné gendhing pélog utawa saléndro. Sabanjuré tayub mau dadi lalangening bongsa Jawa, ing désa ing nagara, wong cilik miwah priyayi, yèn duwé gawé mantu tetakan sapapadhané, padha kasukan bujana nayub."

39. I would like to thank John Pemberton (pers.comm. 1989) for pointing out to me this passage from the *Babad Prayud.* In his dissertation, Pemberton (1989: 63–86, particularly 77–83) cites this passage in his discussion of the marriage diplomacy between the court of Yogyakarta under the Hamengku Buwana I (r. 1755–1792) and Surakarta under the Paku Buwana III (r. 1749–1788).

40. *Babad Prayud.* Dhandhang Gula.

. . . .
mangkana kang anayub
gamelannya munya ngrarangin
usé ambal-ambalan
adhahar anginum
samya wuru-wuru dawa
sadanguné Pangran Dipati Matawis
tan arsa nginum arak

Amung dhahar sekul angèrèni
wusnya dhahar talèdhèk kang medal
sekawan pethingan kabèh
pra samya ayu-ayu
sininjangan kenanga wilis
sami jingga pinrada
kadya bisa mabur
Sang nata wiwit ambeksa
kadya guntur swaraning mriyem ngurmati
barung surak gumerah

. . . .
sawusira Sri Naréndra
nulya Uprup sawusnya Uprup anuli
Pangran Mangkunagara

Wusnya Pangran Mangkunagarèki
nulya Pangran Dipati Ngayogya
Sri Naréndra timbalané
mara dhimas sirèku
anglegakna ing tyasé sami
kabèh santananira
padha kumacèlu
Pangran Dipati Ngayogya
matur nuwun kula dèrèng anglampahi
padamelan punika

Pejah gesang katur jeng kakang ji
Sri Naréndra murugi gènira
jumeneng ngarsèng kursiné
kang rayi gya tumurun
dhodhok munggèng ngarsa rakaji

. . . .
.

41. Pemberton (1989:81–82) further explains this incident as follows: "Paku Buwana III's fatherly efforts to get the prince out on the dance floor failed, and an angry and drunk Huprup Beman stepped in on the king's behalf. Forcing a brimming glass of arak on the poor prince, the Huprup reckoned:

'Your father the Sultan
who's already old and of religion devout
[is] not stubborn like you.
He'd go along for a drink or two,

because he knew what's correct,
the Company set him up as Sultan.
You are his son
but you don't follow his example.
You'll be an insolent and arrogant one,
ignorant of what's correct,
you'll toss out what's right.'

The Jogyanese courtier Urawan spoke politely on the prince's behalf, but to no avail; the irate Huprup was out of control. Smashing his glass to the floor, Beman roared:

'Hey Rawan, you animal,
did you train this Crown Prince?
Your prince is a little shit / and Rawan is a dog!'

At this point, Mangkunegara I commanded the palace gamelan to begin at once as he leapt into a dramatic solo dance diversionary relief entertainment."

42. The discussion of the visit of the crown prince of Yogyakarta to Surakarta is based on Ricklefs's *Jogjakarta under Sultan Mangkubumi* (1974:110–17).

43. Wiwahan Dalem. VIII. Pangkur.

> 6. Rampunging suba bujana
> para tuwan sagarwa sami pamit
> tan winarna lampahipun
> mangkana ing pandhapa
> gya samekta rakiting rèh ananayub
> juru alok juru senggak
> juru keplok wus miranti
> 7. Jeng gusti sasmitèng putra
> sang pangantèn kinèn beksa rumiyin
> atanggap kang sinung semu
> sigra nolih mangiwa
> ngatag marang wadyanira kinèn dhawuh
> mathet gendhing Boyong barang
> bareng gong surak swara tri
> 8. Keploké ambata rebah
> kidul wétan lor kulon golong tirip
> tarap rapet atap kempul
> nut tepi tepung papan
> surak sora sarosa gongsa jumeglug
> wor ronggèng gendhing ngumandhang
> pindha angganing prang tandhing
> 11. Patitis pacaking jongga
> solah wilet memalat mulet ati
> larih rambah kaping telu
> risang nararya putra
> bikak sampur tanggap gongsa nulya suwuk
> nulya ginantyan kang beksa
> para kadang genti-genti
> 12. Sineling lan tamu monca
> gantya-gantya kapegat pagut enjing
> . . . .

44. The passage that mentions this instrumentation is as follows: "tarebang tiga gum-rumung / barung angklung lan kendhang / calung calapita gadhing / ramya gobyog gumer geter magenturan." [Three terbang rumbled, together with angklung and kendhang, calung and ivory calapita; resounding, vibrant, festive, and thundering] (Serat Tjentini 1912–15, 1–2:4). Angklung and calung are instruments made of bamboo tubes. The identification of calapita gadhing is not clear. According to Jaap Kunst (1973, 1:217), it is an ivory clapper. Nowadays musicians refer to this instrument as either a kemanak (a pair of small bronze instruments in the shape of hollow bananas) or a *gambang gangsa* (a bronze xylophone).

Remnants of such syncretic ensembles can still be found in Java. The Laras Madya ensemble is one of them. Consisting of terbang, kendhang, and kemanak, this ensemble accompanies unison choral singing with repertoire taken from *macapat* melodies. Ensembles more closely resembling those described in the *Serat Centhini* can be found in the Yogyakarta and its vicinity, for example, the ensembles accompanying *dhadhangawuk* and *srandul* dance dramas (Soedarsono 1976:207–9). These ensembles consist of terbang, kendhang, angklung, gong, and suling (the last two instruments are found only in the srandul ensemble).

45. *Serat Tjenṭini* 1–2. 2e. Sinom.

> 20. Tur sendika mas Cebolang
> lekas bawa Gambir Sawit
> swara rum manis ngesira
> membat wilet dudut ati
> santriné naurani
> gumrembyeng bareng terbang brung
> rampak ukelé padha
> tan ana gangsul menèhi
> mas Cebolang akipat panerbangira
> 21. Nulya tandhaknya ambeksa
> bérag kabèh kang ningali
> ki dipati langkung suka
> abdiné kinèn ngleboni
> gentèn lan dèn-dhawoehi
> tombokira kabèh nyuku
> suka gantya ambeksa
> abdinira ki dipati
> sasenengé dènira jaluk gendhingan
> 22. Sawenèh ana barengan
> samya gendhing Gonjang-ganjing
> . . . .

46. In the *Serat Tjenṭini* 7–8, 1912–15, 7–8:12, 26), tayuban to the accompaniment of gamelan is also mentioned. In two places the poem mentions an ensemble consisting of rebab, gambang, kromong, gendèr, suling, kethuk, kenong, kendhang, kecèr, gong, panerus, and kademung or saron. The following pieces are mentioned as gendhing for accompanying the gambyong dance in the tayuban: Kuwung-Kuwung, Ela-Ela, Ginon-jing, Bondhèt, Pacar Cina, Génjong, Nang-Onang, Kabor, Gondrong, Jongkang, Tali Wangsa, Lara Nangis, Lung Gadhung, and Oneng-Oneng (Sedyawati 1984:132). Some of these gendhing are still used in today's tayuban. But other gendhing in the list above, especially Kabor, Gondrong, Jongkang, Tali Wangsa, Lara Nangis, are considered large and majestic gendhing, not appropriate to be used in tayuban. I assume here that in the past the performance practice (*garap*) of these gendhing was suitable for accompanying tayuban (e.g., the use of animated *kendhang ciblon*). With the decline of tayuban in the Javanese courts, more and more gendhing were then "classicalized" through more refined garap.

47. Contemporary evidence supports the relationship between terbangan and game-lan ensemble. In Warsadiningrat's *Serat Wédha Pradangga* (1987:126–28) and Martopan-grawit's *Gendhing-Gendhing Santiswaran* (1977), this relationship is made clear—a com-parison of the list of pieces in Warsadiningrat and the list and notation in Martopangrawit of terbangan repertoires indicates that the majority of these gendhing terbang are also gamelan gendhing.

48. *Serat Tjenṭini* 5–6. 117e. Kinanthi.

44. Wus luaran samya tuwuk
    nulya trap majemuk dhikir
    akupeng kepung kalangan
    amasang tutup pangèksi
    ing jarit miwah deluang
    pambukaning dhikir supi
45. dhikiranipun[?] angguyer
    kèh warnané solahnèki
    angeden nenggak asantak
    myang uninya warni-warni
    pan kongsi sedina benthang
    dènya guyeng ahli dhikir
46. ingkang wus kalenger dangu
    tangi nangis dhikir malih
    pating jakengkeng kang pana
    wenèh meksih gobag-gabig
    kèh warnané solahira
    sakèh santri jalu èstri

49. Qureshi (1986:121) lists standard manifestations of strong arousal for the practitioner of the Sufi spiritual recital in India and Pakistan as follows: sudden, uncontrolled movement, twitching, jumping; weeping; having both arms raised; shouting; standing up; dancing; walking; falling down, rolling, tossing about; dying. Notice how close these kinds of behavior are to the descriptions of Sufi dhikir found in the *Serat Centhini*.

50. *Serat Tjenṭini* 5–6. 127e. Dhandhang Gula.

50. . . . .
    byar énjang gya bubuka sami
    angguyer kepalanya
    niba ting gedebug
    lapaké anenggak napas
    anggelasah asungsun timbun matindhih
    lir babadaning pisang
51. wor winor lan jalu miwah èstri
    sadhéngahnèa kang katindhihan
    kang kawudan becik baé
    tan ana ukumipun
    wus tatané wong dul birai
    singa menang sualnya
    sala-silahipun
    santri kang kasor èlmunya
    asrah jiwa raga myang bojonèki
    katur sumanggèng kersa

51. Kusumadilaga might also have had such dhikir dances and music in mind when he speculated that tayuban originated in the Islamic Dulguyer. He also described this Islamic practice using the term santri birahi.

52. Qureshi's comments (1986:107) about the role of music in Sufism deserve full citation: "Musical sound (*ghinā*, song, music, or *achchhī āwāz*, melodious, pleasing sound, voice) has the power to stir the soul (*takrīk-e-qalb*), and to arouse emotions of love to the

point of ecstasy. Moreover, the effect of music on the receptive listener's emotion is immediate, for it transcends comprehension, as attested in Sufi verse. . . . Through the Qawwali occasion Sufism utilizes this power of music as a means for spiritual progress (*rūhānī taraqqī kā ek zariyā*), by activating and directing the listener's emotions of love toward the divine by way of its manifestations, beginning wih the sheikh, leading through saints and Prophet to cognition (*ma'rifat*) of the ultimate Truth (*haq*). According to Sufis, the primary precedent for this power of musical sound was set at the time of Creation, when the beauty of God's voice transported the human soul into a state of divine ecstasy (*wajd*). However, this premise implies that music can also stir emotions of love toward profane purposes. For this reason Sufi music is to be assigned a religious character through text choice and the invocation of *zikr,* and through rules of style and presentation avoiding profane association."

53. Snouck Hurgronje, a Dutch Islamologist who in 1889 was appointed to the colonial office of Adviser for Native Affairs. His *De Atjehers* (1893–94), which was translated into English by Wilkinson (1906), is a very important ethnological study of the late nineteenth century Acehnese. As an adviser to the colonial government, Hurgronje successfully directed Dutch Islamic policy in Indonesia.

54. The following discussion of the Acehnese ratib is based on Snouck Hurgronjes' *The Achehnese* (1906); for a brief history of ratib, see p. 216: "One *rātib,* which was introduced in Medina in the first half of the eighteenth century by a teacher of mysticism called *Sammān* whom the people revered as a saint, enjoys a high degree of popularity in the Eastern Archipelago. The same holy city was also the sphere of the teaching of another saint, *Aḥmad Qushāshī,* who flourished full half a century before (A.D. 1661), and whose Malay and Javanese disciples were the means of spreading so widely in the far East a certain form of Shaṭṭārite tariqah or form of mysticism."

55. In the course of the Islamization of East Java in the eighteenth century, a small peasant population preferred to retain Hinduism. For the past two centuries these people have lived in the Tengger highlands.

56. *Serat Tjenṭini* 1–2. 1e. Dhandhang Gula.

> 14. Wus anurut tanah ing pasisir
> malah wus bengang ping pira-pira
> saking kekathahen ronggèng
> nèng Sidayu kinepung
> andhemeni bojoning santri
> késah marang ing Daha
> mondhok wismanipun
> Ki Jamal pangulu Daha
> dhasar kathah santrinira Ki Jamali
> Ki Jamali sru bungah
>
> 15. Mring sang prapta wus sinung wismèki
> santrinira ki Jamali samya
> mring kang prapta langkung sihé
> arenes cangkem karut
> yèn kalané dipun suruhi
> ginawé pakaulan
> pangantèn tan atut
> kaul nanggap mas Cebolang

yèn lumampah kathah santri [ingkang] ngiring
santriné dhéwé papat
16. Bebektané duk késahé nguni
mung punika kang ginawé tandhak
kapat parigel beksané
tur wong wus samya surup
lamun ronggèng lanang seyekti
prandéné nèng kerengan
kwèh suduk sinuduk

. . . .

57. *Serat Tjenṭini* 1–2. 2e. Sinom.

13. Swara muluk getas renyah
angungkung arum tur manis
nges wiletnya nganyut manah
panerbangé angapipir
sabat gya naurani
tarebang tiga gumrumung
barung angklung lan kendhang
calung calapita gadhing
ramya gobyog gumer geter magenturan
14. Wor swara sru lagu lempang
oreg kang samya ningali
jejel riyel yel–uyelan
dhesekan pipit–pinipit
kèh solah bawanèki
bungah kang para calimut
cèlèr–cinèlèr ramya
kathah kang kélangan sami
opyak gègèr sakedhap nora karuan
15. Suwé–suwé tan rinasa
kélangan prelu ningali
jalwèstri carub dhesekan
wong kang dhugal mangarahi
mring wong wadon anggriming
tangan nguyel–uyel susu
nalusur gagap–gagap
gembok ginegem agemi
kèh mengkono wenèh tekem–tinekeman

58. *Serat Tjenṭini* 1–2. 4e. Dhandhang Gula

21. . . . .
wauta ki dipatya
èsmu tyasnya kanyut
mring Nurwitri ronggèng lanang
ki dipati ragi kawuron sakedhik
ing brem tapé waragang
22. Wuru kaworan alimpang brangti
mring Nurwitri kang binrangti anyar
katembèn bléré karsané

nulya binekta kondur
maring dalem gedhong kawingking
ki dipati ngandika
Nurwitri di-maju
sun saré singeben ingwang
sembari rengeng-rengenga Lompong-kèli
montro Petung-wulungan

23. Gambir-sawit lawan Gandrung-manis
matur inggih Nurwitri ngujiwat
sarwi pinathet lathiné
ki dipati agupuh
ngrangkul gulunira Nurwitri
gregeten cinuwolan
lathi pipinipun
dèn-ingsep ingaras-aras
matur mangké dhuh mangké kangjeng kiai
turéné kinèn nembang

24. Angandika lah ia dèn-becik
nulya rengeng-rengeng swara raras
lompong-kèli kaluluté
jalirit merit arum
kaleleran ambelèr ati
pan lagya rong egongan
ki dipati muwus
wis menenga sun tarima
dèn mrénéa aja sira wedi-wedi

. . . .

59. Transvestism also existed in court tradition. Sources from the late eighteenth and the nineteenth century frequently mention male dancers performing the most refined and sacred of court dances, the bedhaya, which is now usually performed by female dancers. For a discussion of transvestism (viewed as "the ability to concentrate opposites") as an important sign of power, see Anderson (1972:28–29). For a provocative discussion and analysis of homosexuality and the magic spectacle described in the *Serat Centhini*, see Anderson (1990b:271–89). For an account of transvestite elements in contemporary ré-yog performances, see Kartomi (1976:105–9). She points out that "the transvestite element of reyog may be seen not only as a way of coping with life but also as a way of representing a frame of mind. In the context of Javanese religion and ritual, it becomes respectable and acceptable" (p. 108). Other transvestite practices can be found in other regions of Indonesia: in the Balinese *gandrung* performance, the old *seblang* performance in Banyuwangi, and among the *basir* and *bissu* priests in Kalimantan and Sulawesi.

60. *Singir* here means singing a eulogy.

61. The words in these three lines are onomatopoeic sounds of the terbang.

62. *Serat Tjenṭini* 1–2. 37e. Dhandhang Gula

256. Sigra gegabusan Jamal Jamil
penthung-pinenthung ing linggis samya
Jamal pinenthung rainé
sru banéné kumepruk

bathuk pecah tiba ing siti
getih adeladagan
kelosodan mujur
pinindho nganteban séla
sirah remuk balung renyek badanèki
ngalumpruk gobrah-gobrah
257. Kang ningali cep getun tan sipi
gumun samya manahé sumelang
sedaya pucat ulaté
Jèngwèsthi manthuk-manthuk
gèdhèg-gèdhèg ki Jayèngragi
Suarja Wira-dhustha
myang Kula-wiryèku
samya angungun sedaya
prié kuwé mengko akalé ki Jamil
agawé gegawokan
258. Ki Jamil salin anuwun gendhing
Sekar Gadhung kang landhung lon-lonan
pan mengkana saurané
ulung asamber ulung
ya maolé si ulung mati
ngelayung ya maola
roké pida yakun
Jayèngraga gupuh mojar
mring gus Surat Senu lah ngadega singir
nuta Jamil kéwala
259. Matur sendika kang sinungan ling
nulya ngadeg mring Jamil winulang
wus linuruban wangkéné
Jamil nèng wurinipun
sarwi bekta angklung kekalih
kang jisim ingubengan
sindhèn ulung-ulung
samber ulung ya maola
si ulung mati ngelayung molé rokin
pida yakun mengkana
260. Sareng ngelik methit anjelirit
alantik lir pulung kang pipitan
kadya nangisi isthané
mring bangké kang amujung
kang ningali samya kèh nangis
trebang lirih satunggal
lan angklung tetelu
lawan kendhangé satunggal
ukur jawil imbal angepinjal bincil
kempyang nyampyeng pincatan
261. Ting salentik pang ping pek pak pik pik
thung plek thung plek tong ting bung pang peng byang
nguk nguk dhung dhung thong thung thur thèr
kutugipun kumelun

mayid obah nulya anglilir
lurubé ingungkaban
ki Jamal wus lungguh
ambekané arenggosan
ingadhepan ronggèng ro lawan ki Jamil
Jamil lir welas mulat

63. The vestiges of such performances can still be found in Java and Sumatra. J. Vredenbregt (1973) reported that he saw similar magical performances in West Java with a similar name, *dabus*, in 1970. He acknowledges that such performances were then dying out (p. 303). Not unlike those described in *Serat Centhini*, the dabus of West Java is also related to the Islamic tradition, in particular the Sufi brotherhoods Rifaiya and Kadiriya (p. 304). Moreover, other characteristics of the dabus of West Java—the important role of *sèh*, the leader of the performance, the use of a syncretic musical ensemble (Islamic and Javanese musical instruments), and the mixing of the spectacle with dancing and singing— are also shared by the magic spectacle described in the *Serat Centhini*.

64. Certainly this is the case in the dabus of West Java, in which the sèh, the leader of the performance, was also the leader of the Sufi *tarékat*. For further discussion of the knowledge of invulnerability and the concept of *jago* (charismatic rural leaders), see Onghokham (1975 : 63–71).

65. As reported by Claire Holt (1972 : 85–88), the same magic spectacle, called *dabuih*, was also known in Minangkabau. Holt saw such a performance in 1938.

Chapter Two

1. This discussion of court intrigues in Central Java in the eighteenth century is based on Ricklefs (1974 : 39–141). The following background for the Chinese rebellion is also drawn from Ricklefs (p. 38). The Chinese rebellion began with a conflict between Dutch and Chinese residents of Batavia which resulted in a massacre of the Chinese there. Groups of Chinese that escaped from the massacre fled eastward along the north coast of Java and attacked many Dutch outposts along the way. They besieged the main Dutch position in Semarang. At this point Paku Buwana II decided to join the Chinese rebels. Soon the Chinese began to lose the war. Realizing that it was not possible to win the war, Paku Buwana II asked the Dutch leaders for forgiveness. But with the support of many Javanese and local Chinese populations, the rebellion continued, and the court of Kartasura became one of the targets of the rebels.

2. More recently, such interchange has occurred through the accessibility to musicians of recordings and broadcasts of these styles of gamelan and through the teaching of these styles in gamelan and dance schools.

3. The following discussion is drawn from Lindsay (1980 : 69–88).

4. One means of distinguishing themselves from the major courts was to deliberately build close relationships with the Dutch and to integrate European customs in the best way possible.

5. Unlike *langendriyan,* this dance opera did not become popular, and no trace can be found today. It is said that the stories of banjaran sari were based on the Panji cycle, the stories which were originally performed in *wayang gedhog* puppet theater.

According to Warsadiningrat (1987 : 166), a dance opera similar in form to langendriyan was created by the son of Paku Buwana X in the Kasunanan in the early part of the twentieth century. It was called *pranasmara*. The stories were based on the Panji of the wayang gedhog stories. But this dance opera was short-lived.

6. There is a dispute about the origin of langendriyan that reflects the rivalry between Yogyakarta and Surakarta. Lindsay (1980:83 n. 70) summarizes the debate: "The Mangkunĕgaran claim that it originated there during the reign of Mangkunĕgara IV (1853–1881), and was later taken to Yogyakarta by Tandakusuma. A Yogyakarta version of the story says that Langĕn Driya was actually the creation of R. T. Purwadiningrat, a son of Hamĕngku Buwana III, who developed the genre in 1876. After the death of Mangkubumi IV it was no longer performed in Yogyakarta, but continued in the Mangkunĕgaran, where the form was modified, using an all-female cast whereas previously the female roles had been danced by young boys. . . . It is ironical that there are doubts about the origin of the Mangkunĕgaran's most distinctive art forms, but significant that the Mangkunĕgaran claims the form as its own. Yogyakarta later developed a similar art form to the Langĕn Driya using stories from the Ramayana [it is called Langen Mandra Wanara]. Tandakusuma from the Mangkunegaran is credited with helping to establish this form in Yogyakarta, after he left the Mangkunĕgaran court, and performances were held at his residence in Yogyakarta (Tandakusuman)."

7. See the recent study by Theresia Suharti (1990:68–110) of the development of dance in the Mangkunegaran under the auspices of Mangkunegara VII (r. 1916–1944). I am indebted to F. X. Widaryanto for making available to me a copy of Suharti's thesis.

8. Anderson (1984:205 n. 28) is right to comment that the destruction of Java had been going on for two centuries before the middle of the eighteenth century, since the fall of Majapahit in the 1500s. He describes this period as "a kind of deepening Javanese Dark Ages, scarred by incessant wars, deportations, rapine, massacres, and famine. How catastrophic the period of destruction was can be judged by the extent to which present-day knowledge of Old Javanese civilization depends on manuscripts found not on Java but on Bali and Lombok. By the time that Javanese literary culture began to revive, in the later eighteenth century, a large part of Old Java's Sanskritic literature was either lost or had become nearly incomprehensible; it did not become accessible until the late nineteenth-century florescence of Dutch academic philology. In the meantime, a whole tradition of poetry making among gentlemen courtiers had essentially disappeared" (pp. 203–4).

9. She began to serve as court dhalang of the Kasunanan of Surakarta in the 1920s (L. Sears, pers. comm., 1991).

10. The author of *Serat Pustaka Raja Madya* was Ronggawarsita. At this time Ronggawarsita was occupied with writing a mythical history of Java. He composed *Serat Pustaka Raja Madya* as a sequel to his previous work, the *Serat Pustaka Raja Purwa*. Wayang madya ("intermediary wayang") was created for the purpose of linking the stories of two other wayang that existed before it: wayang purwa and wayang gedhog. Following Ronggawarsita's modes of thinking, Javanese relate these wayang story cycles to the genealogy of Javanese dynasties. Wayang purwa is considered the oldest wayang, presenting stories based on the *Mahabharata* and *Ramayana* Hindu epics. Its main heroic characters are believed to represent the oldest ancestors of Javanese dynasties. Wayang madya presents the indigenous Javanese stories which are related to the period from the end of the wayang

purwa dynastic genealogies to the beginning of Kediri-Singosari. Wayang gedhog presents stories based on the Panji cycle, which are associated with the period from the eleventh to the thirteenth centuries, the time of the Kediri-Singosari kingships.

11. Examining the development of the Yogyakarta wayang wong, especially on the basis of her reading of the *Babad Ngayogyakarta* (1847), Lindsay (1985:87–88, notes that it was only in the latter half of the nineteenth century that wayang wong's stories began to follow the format of wayang purwa. In its early development, from the late eighteenth century to the latter half of the nineteenth century, the performances of wayang wong were less structured, more informal, and more spontaneous. Moreover, stories performed in the wayang wong at this time might include the indigenous Javanese stories of the Damar Wulan and Panji cycles. Lindsay also suggests that the early wayang wong of the Mangkunegaran had closer connections to wayang topèng than to wayang purwa. This is indicated by the participation of women dancing as female actors (the performers of Yogyakarta wayang wong were all men), which was the common practice of wayang topèng.

It is difficult to find the reason for the movement to adopt the dramatic structure of wayang purwa in wayang wong. One may assume that the popularity of wayang purwa, both in literature and in performance, had something to do with this development.

12. Originally these stories were performed in *wayang krucil* or wayang klithik (a type of drama that used flat wooden puppets).

13. Lindsay states that in both the Yogyakarta and Mangkunegaran courts, "Wayang wong was developed specifically as a theatrical dance form to entertain guests, especially Dutch dignitaries, and became an important part of the ceremonial interchange between Dutch colonial officials and the Javanese nobility" (1985:91). Perhaps this was true in the nineteenth century, the period Lindsay discusses. However, the *Serat Babad Nitik* (late eighteenth century) describes wayang wong performed both with and without the presence of Dutch dignitaries. For example, there is no mention of Dutch presence at the regular wayang wong performances for the birthdays of Mangkunegara.

In the late nineteenth century, the wayang wong of the Mangkunegaran declined. Under the patronage of Chinese and Indos, the Solonese wayang wong survived in a commercial form, which was played on a stage with backdrop scenery (see below).

14. From the early seventeenth century, Java was administered by the Dutch East India Company, the V.O.C. (Vereenigde Oost-Indische Compagnie). Because of corruption and mismanagement, in 1800 the VOC was formally dissolved, and the French-dominated Dutch regime seized the Company's property and took control of Java (Ricklefs 1993:110).

15.

Tuwan Anu: Tiyang Jawi punika sumerepipun dhateng Kawi kados pundi, déné ing ngriki boten wonten pemulangan?

Radèn Ngabèhi Gunawan: Aliya saking pujongga, ing negari Surakarta ngriki kénging kawestanan boten wonten ingkang sumerep ing Kawi, wondéning ingkang sumerep ing Kawi punika, sami turunipun dhateng anak putunipun piyambak. Tiyang Jawi, ingkang dédé turunipun ing pujongga, awis-awis ingkang purun angguguru Kawi, awit boten kanggé kedamel pawicantenan, kanggénipun namung wonten in serat waosan, kalih déning prasat boten wonten fa'édahipun, dados amrelokaken anggènipun ngupajiwa, sanès kados bongsa sampéyan welandi, sami amerdi pencaring kagunan kawruh serta kesagedan, amergi dados kauntungan komuk serta kajènipun.

TA: Menawi tiyang Jawi kathah ingkang boten sumerep ing Kawi, sabab déning punapa kathah ingkang remen maos serat, punapa pemurihipun?

RG: Menawi priyantun, pemurihipun namung sumerepa ing ceriyos boten mawi anggalih werdining tembung, menawi titiyang alit, kathah-kathahipun namung kadamel cagak elèk, sampun ngantos kedhatengan ing pandung, wondéning ingkang sami maos wau kelimrahanipun namung sumerep uruting ceriyos kémawon, dhateng tembungipun kathah ingkang boten sumerep, sampun ingkang nama serat Kawi yèn sumerepa, serat jarwa kémawon awis ingkang saged merdèni, dados anggènipun golak-galok sadalu punika, lugunipun kemit, suwenèh sadé swara dhateng tongga-tangganipun, supados kahalema saged maos, serta saé swaranipun.

TA: Kula saweg mireng saking pengandika sampéyan punika, yèn tiyang Jawi kathah ingkang boten sumerep dhateng tembungipun piyambak.

RG: Saèstu yen mekaten, kula piyambak sampun naté ngayoni pitakèn dhateng titiyang ingkang sami remen maos, samukawis ingkang kula pitakènaken, boten saged nerangaken, menawi wonten ingkang purun negesi, inggih boten petitis, malah kathah kang kelintu.

16. As far as I know, this is the earliest source giving rather detailed information about the outlines of wayang stories and gendhing performed for each episode of these wayang performances.

17. These conventions are the number of lines per stanza, the number of syllables per line, and the ending vowel of each line.

18. Each stanza of sekar ageng consists of four lines. Each line has an equal number of syllables (*lampah*) and is divided into two or more units (*pedhotan*).

19. For an excellent discussion of the updating of Old Javanese poetry to a modern, nineteenth-century poetic form, see Day 1981, especially pp. 24–77.

20. *Serat Tjenṭini* 3–4. 48e, Kinanthi.

228. . . . .
suawi paman Lawatan
dika nembang Sulanjari
ki Lawatan tur sendika
ngalesed ngéwahi linggih
229. Dhèhèm watuk segu-segu
mapanaken swaranèki
mèsem mathet atrap sila
tangané siduwèng wentis
dumancunging dhestar thinap
nulya nembang Sulanjari
230. Uloné landhung amuluh
remek (rempek?) geng membat rum manis
gedheg lénggok gulunira
moyog-moyog lambungnèki
dariji genah wilangan
angkat wolu nem ping kalih

21. Raffles explains that there were five ways to sing Asmaradana: *salobog, jakalola, sarup-sasi-bawaraga, sendon-pradapa,* and *palaran* (1982:403). Sinom, which was also called Sri Nata or Perdapa, could be sung in the style of *bengak, garundel, gadung-malati, jayeng-asmara, babar layar, merak nguwuh, kagok-surabaya,* and palaran (p. 405). There were two styles of singing Pangkur: palaran and *kadaton* (ibid.). Durma could be sung in the style of *serang, rangsang, bedaya, madura,* and palaran (ibid., 406). For the last two sekar gangsal, Mijil and Kinanthi, Raffles did not mention different ways of singing the songs.

Hatch (1980:474–75) relates Raffles' points to the different manner (*cèngkok*) in which each sekar is chanted in recent times. See his explanation of the cèngkok of Pangkur, Sinom, Pucung, and Gambuh in his appendix 2 (pp. 413–72).

22. Babad Prayud. Dhandhang Gula.

> Makajangan sagung pra dipati
> bekta gongsa anèng makajangan
> umyung gumuruh swarané
> tuwin jroning kadhatun
> pitung dina munya sekati
> pélog saléndronira
> munggèng sitiluhur
> miwah Kamangkunagaran
> pitung dina anguyu-uyu sakati
> sawétaning pandhapa
>
> Pélog saléndro pasowan jawi
> jawi pisan pipi galedhegan
> wong beksani cara balèn
> . . . .

23. Kunst (1973, 1:266) reported that besides accompanying the sekatèn week, the gamelan Sekatèn was also played to celebrate other important court events, such as the jubilee of the king, the birthday of the king according to the Javanese *wuku* calendrical reckoning, and the circumcision and wedding of the crown prince. Along with the decline of the power of the king, especially because of the abolition of the appanage system orchestrated by the Dutch government, the court celebrations decreased. The splendor of pakajangan diminished. The use of gamelan Sekatèn was curbed, to the degree that after Indonesian independence it was played only to celebrate a religious event, the sekatèn week.

24. Female groups of various sorts seem to have been the specialty of Mangkunegara I. There were female gamelan musicians. There were also female armies and female army marching bands. In fact the author of the *Serat Babad Nitik* was a woman scribe and soldier (*prajurit carik èstri*). For further discussion of this woman scribe's accounts of women soldiers in the Mangkunegaran and elsewhere in Indonesia, see Kumar 1980a:3–9.

25. In his survey of the number of gamelan in the 1930s, Jaap Kunst (1973, 2:560) found there were more sléndro than pélog sets in the principalities. The total number of sléndro gamelan was 1982 sets; the pélog total was only 674 sets.

26. The instruments in present-day the Kanyut Mèsem gamelan are as follow: Sléndro set: rebab (two), gendèr barung, gendèr panerus, gambang, gambang gangsa, slenthem, slentho, demung (two), saron barung (four), saron panerus (two), bonang barung, bonang

panerus, engkuk-kemong, kethuk-kempyang, kenong (a set of three tones), kempul (a set of three tones), gong suwukan (two), gong ageng, kendhang (ageng, ciblon, ketipung), bedhug, kecèr.

Pélog set: rebab, gendèr barung bem, gendèr barung barang, gendèr panerus bem, gendèr panerus barang, gambang bem, gambang barang, gambang gangsa, slenthem, slentho, demung (two), saron barung (four), saron panerus, bonang barung, bonang panerus, kethuk-kempyang, kenong (a set of three tones), kempul (a set of three tones). The pélog set uses the same kendhang and bedhug as the sléndro.

I thank Jennifer Thom and Molly McNamara for confirming my inventory of this gamelan.

27. Actually it is one of the keys of a pélog saron that has a *sengkalan* (chronogram) *Pangéran Dipati Sang Lelana Gala 00,* indicating the Javanese year 1700.

28. I am indebted to Marc Perlman for this reference, which he found in a recent thesis by T. Slamet Suparno (1990). *Babad Mangkunegara I* also testifies that Mas Said owned a sléndro gamelan named Udan Riris. He brought it into the war camp, and his musicians played it for his own pleasure.

29. Warsadiningrat (1987:165–66) attributes the creation of a complete set of kenong to the grand vizier of the Surakarta court, K. R. A. Sosrodiningrat IV (1889–1916). But Warsadiningrat also mentions that someone told him that the practice of using a complete kenong set was established by the son of Paku Buwana V (r. 1820–1823) (ibid.).

30. Kunst (1973, 1:161) suggests that the increase in the number of kenong tones happened first in Solo. Then, in 1907, a new gamelan with a complete kenong set was made for the Yogyanese crown prince.

31. For a brief discussion of Raffles's gamelan, see Fagg (1970). Another zoomorphic gamelan resembling Raffles's gamelan was brought to Chicago and was used in performance there at the World's Columbian Exposition in 1893. This gamelan was from the regency of Sukabumi, West Java. For a discussion of this gamelan, see DeVale (1977).

32. The wooden stand of a Central Javanese gamelan instrument that commonly has a dragon (*naga*) design is the gong stand. Sometimes the two ends of the bonang frame also have a naga design, but this is intricately combined with floral designs.

33. According to Raffles (ibid.), gamelan Miring was used to accompany wayang klithik (a wooden-puppet play that presents the Damarwulan story cycle). Gamelan Srunèn was used in processions and in war (ibid.).

34. The following is a list of gamelan instruments drawn from Raffles's accounts and illustrations of gamelan: rebab, suling, celempung, gendèr barung, wooden gambang, gambang gangsa, slenthem, demung, saron barung, bonang barung, kethuk, kenong, kempul, gong, kendhang, ketipung, kecèr.

Raffles's gamelan had some peculiarities. Compared to the present-day gamelan, the gendèr is exceptionally tall; it is similar to the Balinese gendèr. In both Raffles's gamelan and the gamelan illustration in his book, only one kenong and one kempul are found and there is no kempyang. There are only two drums: ketipung and kendhang (ciblon). Raffles's gamelan has four demung (saron) barung, and two demung; there are no saron panerus, gendèr panerus, and bonang panerus. Raffles's illustration indicates that the celempung has no legs, the tuning pegs are on the side of the body of the instrument, and there is a pair of plectrums.

35. When Mataram was divided into two court centers in 1755, a pair of gamelan Sekatèn was also divided. The court of Surakarta inherited a Sekatèn set named Kyai Guntur Sari, and the other set (named Kyai Guntur Madu) was given to the Yogyakarta court.

36. For a discussion of gendhing bonang, see chapter 4.

37. The instruments in the Kyai Udan Arum and Udan Asih gamelan are: Sléndro set: gendèr barung, gendèr panerus, gambang, gambang gangsa, slenthem, slentho (two), demung (four), saron barung (eight), saron panerus (two), bonang barung, bonang panerus, kethuk-kempyang, kenong (a set of two), kempul (a set of two), gong ageng, kendhang (ageng, ciblon, and ketipung), bedhug, suling. Pélog set: gendèr barung bem, gendèr barung barang, gendèr panerus bem, gendèr panerus barang, gambang bem, gambang barang, gambang gangsa, slenthem, slentho (two), demung (four), saron barung (eight), saron panerus (two), bonang barung, bonang panerus, kethuk, kenong (a set of two), kempul (a set of two), gong ageng, suling. The pélog and sléndro sets use the same kendhang and bedhug.

38. It is true that *pasar malam* (night fair) also presents a ramé occasion, which is very popular with the common people. But the pasar malam was invented much later. It is possible that pasar malam was modeled on court celebrations, but under the sponsorship of Europeans and Indos.

39. The Malay language may have been the means of communication. But interpreters, mainly Indos, were essential in the social and formal interactions between the Dutch and Javanese aristocrats.

40. As part of a scheme to promote trade colonization, both the Portuguese and the Dutch authorities encouraged white men to marry Eurasian or Asian women and settle down in the East (Boxer 1965:220–21). As Van der Veur (1955:191–207) shows, in later periods, these Eurasians presented to the European colonial government special political and cultural problems.

41. *Serat Babad Nitik* 1. 1. Mijil.

> 1a-2. Saking kamar sakawan wus mijil
> pinarak sang katong
> mungging kursi tata lenggah kabèh
> samya larih sadaya waradin
> gamelan ngrarangin
> kagengan [kagungan] sang prabu
> 1a-3. Munya salomprèt piyola sami
> lawan tambur awor
> nulya dhahar myang santana kabèh
> mepro lan nyonyah para upesir
> myang para pinutri
> padha dahar bangku
> 1a-4. Para wadana miwah pasisir
> samya mangan ngisor
> sarta ganti-ganti badhayané
> badhayane wadana myang patih
> tan pegat alarih
> dènya dhahar dangu

1a-5. Urmat mariyem awali-wali
lan gamelan awor
sampun dangu wusnya dhahar kabèh
tata lenggah tan pegat alarih
pra wadana sami
myang pasisir wuru

42. *Serat Babad Niik* 1. 1. Mijil.

1a-6. Nulya ameng-ameng sri bupati
lan delèr tan adoh
kuliling ngulon ngétan parané
mopro [mepro] ratu pra nyonyah tut wuri
myang para upesir
sang nata dyan wangsul
1a-7. Pinarak wonten ing loji malih
sadaya wus lunggoh
munggwèng kursi tan pegat larihé
nulya kang anèm pangran dipati
badhayané mijil
nulya sanga prabu [sang aprabu]
1a-8. Badhaya Kuwung-Kuwung tulya sri
mung senggak gumuroh
nulya surup wisan badhayané
dhuk semana main [-main] api
sadaya ningali
nata lenggah panggung

43. *Serat Babad Nitik* 1. 4. Dhandhang Gula.

9b-4. Nata dhahar munggèng kampung loji
pra upesir myang para santana
ambal-ambalan mriyemé
dangu dhahar anginum
lan badhaya sasra[h] apatih
ganti para wadana
ing badhayanipun
sasampunira adhahar
kangjeng ratu lan nyonyah kartu
walandi
dangu dènya kasukan
9b-5. Kongsi dalu karetu walandi
nulya kang badhaya putra nata
pangran adipati anèm
ping kalih wedalipun
nulya ingkang badhaya aji
ping kalih wedalira
pan wus tengah dalu
nulya kundur sri naréndra

. . . .

44. The full title of the manuscript is *Babad Krama Dalem Ingkang Sinuhun Kangjeng Susuhunan Paku Buwana kaping sanga ing Nagari Surakarta-Adiningrat* [The chronicle of the marriage of his highness Susuhunan Paku Buwana IX of Surakarta].

45. *Babad Krama Dalem*. Mijil.

> Para tamu sukèng tyas anuli
> sagung para mipro
> samya dhangsah lan para tuwané
> ramé gendhingnya salin sumalin
> yèn capèg gya brenti
> linariyan nginum
>
> Sukèng driya kang samya ningali
> solahing pra mipro
> apepanthan lir lèyèk laguné
> uga lir ranté kanthèn astèki
> wudharira salin
> jejodhon rinangkul
>
> Lambungira miproné ngreketi
> agulet pupunton
> isthanira lir ngliling sutané
> obah jongga gung amanjer liring
> miproné ngèsemi
> keketing pangrangkul

46. Boxer also notes the high musical talent and skill of the Malay slaves in the Cape of Good Hope, who played entirely by ear. He gives the following account from Lichtenstein (1803): "I know of many great houses in which there is not one of the slaves that cannot play upon some instrument, and where an orchestra is immediately collected together, if the young people of the house, when they are visited in the afternoon by their acquaintances, like to amuse themselves with dancing for an hour or two. At the nod, the cook exchanges his saucepan for a flute, the groom quits his curry-comb and takes his violin, and the gardener, throwing aside his spade, sits down to the violincello."

Boxer also noted that "William Hickey [?], who prided himself on being a connoisseur of music as well as of wine and of women, averred that the slave flute-players who accompanied his party in their ascent of Table Mountain provided 'the sweetest harmony I ever heard.'"

47. I thank Lois Anderson for this reference. It is a drawing from Cortemünde's *Dagbog fra en Ostindiefart 1672–75*. The drawing is of the delegation with the Sultan and his entourage inside the left hall, two dancers[?] in the middle of the hall, a marching guard of honor led by the drummer on the left side in front of the hall, the playing of a native music ensemble on the right side in front of the hall (consisting of a pair of conical, side-up drums, two horns, a set of gongs and metallophone[?]), and the sounding of two cannons, one on each side of the front of the hall.

48. *Serat Babad Giyanti*. Dhandhang Gula.

> Tedhakira kangjeng kang siniwi
> pra prajurit kumpeni lan jawa
> urmat drèl atri swarané

sinauran mriyem gung
magenturan anggegeteri
slomprèt tambur musikkan
suling bendhé barung
munggang kodhok ngorèk ngangkang
cara balèn pradongga munya ngerangin
horeg wong sanagara
(Yasadipura, quoted in Poedjosoemarto 1967:101).

49. Marching bands consisting of different combinations of European and Javanese instruments can still be found in Yogyakarta courts. They are all of a type that can be called *prajuritan* (military) music. For brief descriptions and pictures of this type of music in the late nineteenth-century Yogyakarta court, see Groneman (1895:80–87).

50. The poem mentions the sounding of the string ensemble to honor the appearance of Paku Buwana, and also the performance of this music every Thursday evening in the court tower. The poem does not specify the instrumentation of this string ensemble; it may consist of a combination of string and wind instruments.

51. *Wiwahan Dalem*. V. Pucung.

> 11. Wusing rampung rapal rèhirèng musikum
> pangulu gya donga
> sadaya sami ngamini
> satelasé pangulu dènira donga
> 12. Klilan mundur ngulama dumulur pungkur
> tuwan risdhèn sigra
> nanting glas arsa kundhisi
> para tamu sami jumeneng sadaya
> 13. Tembungipun asarèh sora swara rum
> hèh sagung pra tuwan
> tuwin tamu ingkang prapti
> neksènana dhumateng ing kajat kula
> 14. Sung rahayu mring kangjeng pangéran prabu
> tuwin ingkang garwa
> pamuji kula kang mugi
> lestantuna anggènipun palakrama
> 15. Wusnya rampung para tamu surak barung
> musik tuwin monggang
> kapyarsa sora swara tri
> wira kuswa urmat drèl rambah ping sanga
> 16. Sinung bantu mriyem ping sanga lumintu
> titining kurmatan
> jeng gusti pangran dipati
> gya jumeneng kundhisi wilujengira
> 17. Para tamu kang sami pinarak ngriku
> rampung nulya surak
> musik myang monggang ngurmati
> para wadya ngrakit glaring lumaksana

52. *Wiwahan Dalem*. VII. Mijil.

> 19. Kalihira sawusing ngabekti
> jeng gusti gya miyos

ngirid tuwan risdhèn lan garwané
tatabéyan samya sung basuki
kang tumuntur wuri
pra nyonyah kumrubut
20. Myang pra tuwan sami sung basuki
majeng gentos-gentos
yèn ginagas kadi ta anggané
pra jawata lawan pra apsari
tumurun sasanti
mring kang sampun dhaup

53. The series of events, *babalangan* (the bride and the groom throw flowers to each other) and *wijikan* (the bride washes the groom's feet), was held in the paringgitan (a section of the front hall). Other important events of panggih were held in the inner hall: *ujungan* (the bride pays respects to the groom by making a *sembah* gesture at his feet), *pangkon* (the newlyweds sit on the lap of the Mangkunegara), and *ngabektèn* (they pay respects to their parents and their elders).

54. *Wiwahan Dalem*. VII. Mijil.

21. Ri sampuning tatabéyan sami
residhèn gya miyos
lawan para tamu sakathahé
pukul astha antaraning wanci
wit bujana munggwing
pandhapi geng kemput
22. Gongsa tratag tan kalilan muni
sinimpen mring gedhong
amung musik tansah sadanguné
kapiyarsa wèh énggaring galih
kanan tuwin kéring
ganti ungelipun
25. Sawusira bujana pra sami
andrawina katog
dyan luwaran pra tamu sakèhé
tuwan-tuwan tuwin nyonyah sami
kakanthèn lumaris
mubeng runtung-runtung
26. Dhangsah wales mubeng jro pandhapi
ing rèh gentos-gentos
galup kadril manéka gelaré
mung pra tuwan ingkang sepuh sami
lenggahan main wis
papanthan gènipun
27. Myang jro dalem wus luwaran bukti
pangantèn sakloron
gya kasukan nèng tengah enggoné
para putri apepanthan sami
lalangen mawarni
ing sasenengipun

55. The term tanjidhur originated from the Portuguese word *tangedor* (musician). In the passage above, it refers to a musical ensemble. Probably the court tanjidhur ensemble

consisted of brass instruments (trumpets and drums) with the addition of violin. The *Serat Babad Nitik* says these three instruments played in the loji. An English visitor to the Sura-karta court in 1828 also mentions an ensemble that played to honor the arrival of the Dutch Resident: "A band of Javanese musicians, with European brass instruments (in front of which a fiddle was conspicuous) attempted to play Willem of Nassau, the national air of the Netherlands, when the Resident passed" ("Journal of an Excursion" 1853, 7:9).

56. *Babad Krama Dalem.* Sinom.

> . . . .
> sawusnya antara nulya
> tuwan risidhèn kundhisi
> sadaya gelas isi
> nembungken wilujengipun
> panggih dalem sang nata
> wusnya sareng usé sasami
> langkung ramé gumuruh ambal-ambalan
>
> Asareng mangunjukira
> gya urmat tanjidhur muni
> nenging tanjidhur ginantyan
> gongsa kalenèngan ririh
> . . . .

57. Ibid. Sinom.

> . . . .
> wilujengé tanah Jawi
> usé samya gya jumeneng bibar dhahar
>
> Gongsa tanjidhur tinembang
> pélog saléndro senggani
> arungan datan parungyan
> calapita amelingi
> sang nata tedhak maring
> pandhapi lèr lan pra tamu
> . . . .

58. Kartomi (1981:235) suggests that "the belief of traditionally-minded Javanese in their own cultural superiority has protected their musical tradition from stylistic European influence, both in court and village." Perhaps Kartomi's assertion applies well to post-colonial Javanese perspectives. I am not sure if it is applicable to the Javanese colonial experience when Java was overwhelmed by many aspects of modern European life.

Some European musical ideas have had an impact on gamelan. This impact includes the use of notation and the European attitude toward music (See chapter 3).

59. There is one minor exception, however (Sindusawarno 1984:402). In 1914, Wreksadiningrat of Surakarta made a gamelan set that could play both Javanese gendhing and European songs. Called gamelan Gentha (or Genthana), this ensemble was played in a cultural congress in Magelang in 1948 and again in Bandung in 1952. There is no mention of this gamelan other than its appearance in these congresses. Sindusawarno at-tributes its limited use to the shortcomings in the quality of the instruments. Warsadining-rat (1987:166) notes that it was invented by a court servant, Raden Lurah Sastrawidata, during the reign of Paku Buwana X (1893–1939). The ensemble had the name Pramuni.

60. The Kasultanan musicians of Yogyakarta were very self-conscious about these Javanized mares pieces. They refer to the drumming pattern specially composed for these pieces as *kendhangan sabrangan* ("foreign drumming").

61. The descriptions in *Babad Giyanti* of the moving of the Mataram palace from Kartasura to Surakarta alluded to such an ensemble. This indicates that prajuritan music already existed during the Kartasura period (1680–1788).

62. *Babad Krama Dalem.* Mijil.

> Abdi bedhaya mijil ring puri
> sang ayu kinaot
> lir pangantèn kembar paraboté
> nulya gongsa sasendhon umuni
> wus praptèng pandhapi
> tatasilanipun
>
> Wiwit beksa nèng ngarsaniraji
> araras sri tinon
> para tamu éram panduluné
> madyèng beksa mundhi péstul muni
> arempek kapyarsi
> wus antara suwuk
>
> Nulya ginantyan langen sarimpi
> catur ayu kaot
> nedheng samya kembar paraboté
> beksa munggwèng ngarsanirèng aji
> aluwes tarampil
> sareng mundhi péstul
>
> Sru jumebrèt arempek kapyarsi
> kagyat ingkang nonton
> mung sababak nulya suwuk rèrèn
> kèndeling sarimpi ngunjuk sami
> sasenengirèki
> tan cuwa ing kayun

63. My thanks to Anthony Day for pointing out this reference. The following discussion on the meanings of the Mangkunegaran court ritual is based on Day's responses to my paper on the same topic (Day's letter of October 1, 1984).

64. *Serat Sri Karongron* 2. Asmaradana.

> . . . .
> Déné malem Jumungah
> kanca musikan malebu
> nèng panggung Songga Buwana
>
> Munya lagon solan-salin
> Katriya Sekoltis Polkah
> Mares Pasre Dubledansé
> Galop Pantasi Krispolkah

pan dhe Katermasokah
Opisir Pradhemares sru
Wales kapyarsèng mandrawa

lamun wus jam rolas muni
musikan kèndel bibaran
. . . .

65. ibid. Asmaradana

Makaten salami-lami
saben ri malem Jumungah
sri nata sawusnya dandos
tedhak mring kamar pusaka
misungsung asung sekar
pepundhèn dalem sang prabu
jeng kyai ageng pusaka

Ingkang sinekar rumiyin
pusaka dalem sang nata
jeng kyai gondhil namané
gya jeng kyai prajuritan
sangupati ingaran
sasampunira punika
ingkang dèn caosi sekar

Agem dalem jeng sang aji
jeng kyai ageng wangkingan
tansah kumelun kutugé
nuli kangjeng kyai nama
camethi sapu jagad
gya pusaka caping luhung
kangjeng kyai basunanda

66. Walter Spies eventually settled in Bali, becoming a well-known painter, whose interaction with Balinese artists contributed to the development of the modern style of Balinese painting. But he was also a practitioner of other arts, among them music.

67. De Vereeniging of Yogyakarta was opened in 1822 (Taylor 1983:130).

68. According to an oral account, Tuwan Godlib (also spelled Godlip or Godliep) was the owner of a batik-making company. Even today a suburb where he used to live is named after him: Godliban. Among the stories of the rise of langendriyan, Partohudoyo's account is the most informative. He says that when Tondhakusuma was ready to stage his new creation (i.e., langendriyan), he asked R. G. Kiliaan (Tuwan Godlib), a patron of the Javanese performing arts, to finance its production. Mangkunegara IV saw langendriyan for the first time when it was performed in the residence of K. P. H. Gondha Siswara. Enraptured by this new work, the prince asked that the dance drama should become the prerogative of the Mangkunegaran.

69. Kroncong is a type of Indonesian music that was developed by the Christianized slaves of the Portuguese. Komedie Stambul told popular stories based on the Arabian Nights such as "Ali Baba" and "Aladdin," and fairy-tales from the West such as "Snow

White" and "Sleeping Beauty" (Van der Veur 1968:52). The komedie actors also sang popular kroncong songs of the time, and dance music was also part of the musical repertory (ibid.). The musical accompaniment was an ensemble consisting of guitar, violin, and flute (ibid.).

70. *Serat Sri Karongron* 3. Mijil.

. . . .
sri naréndra nyanjata karendhi
myang ana in warih
asarana jungkung

wus dumugi wangsul lenggah malih
leladèn lumados
dhedhaharan sapanginumané
kangjeng ratu miwah para putri
sampun dèn ladosi
mundhut kang kinayun

sumawana putra santanabdi
kang dhèrèk nèng kono
kawaratan kabèh mangan ngombé
tanana kang kaliwatan siji
sesambèn miyarsi
pangrasaning piyul

gitar suling tarebang mandholin
panabuhé alon
pra metengan lan kalawijané
wiwit gendhing kembang kacang muni
nganggo dèn bawani
ing tembang megatruh

suwuk nuli gendhing pinggir kali
banjur muni kroncong
gendhing bintang surabaya lèrèn
sawatara nuli munya malih
setambul awiwit
siji loro telu

ingkang nabuh ngiras anyindhèni
dadi maju loro
tangan cangkem milu nyambut gawé
suprandéné katon seneng ati
. . . .

71. Day's observation on kaélokan are based on his study of Ronggawarsita's poem *Serat Cemporèt*. This is a study of the text itself and its relationship to other texts of the same period and before: *Tantu Pagelaran, Serat Jayabaya, Pustaka Raja,* and others, including a number of European texts (see Day 1981:246–302).

72. Not until the late nineteenth century were Chinese women allowed to come to Java. Before that, many Chinese men married Javanese women.

73. Although Liem Thian Joe wrote *Riwayat Semarang* in the 1930s, he based his book

largely on the older written sources he found in the archives of the Chinese Council (Kongkoan) of Semarang. He discusses a Chinese wedding in Semarang in the context of other important events, such as the beginning of the use of paper money, the beginning of the postal system, and the expansion of the railroad system, that occurred from the mid nineteenth to the beginning of the twentieth century.

74. I cannot find the original text or the original date of this report. From internal evidence, I assume that the description of this Chinese tayuban was written in the late nineteenth or early twentieth century.

75. Kapitein (captain) is a title for a tax collector and regulator of trade and trade communities. They were usually Chinese.

76. Originally, the word paséban meant a place in the court where the king's subjects are summoned by, or pay respects to, the king.

77. "Djika di waktoe terang boelan toean Tan Tiang Tjhing bersama ia poenja sanak familie sering tjari hiboeran diatas paseban sembari dengerken sinden atawa klonengan, kerna itoe Kapitein ada poenjaken wijogo sendiri, compleet berikoet gamelan pelok dan slendro jang indah! Atawa kadang-kadang bersama ia poenja sobat-sobat ia orang tjari kasenengan dengen mainken tetaboean Tionghoa, sembari minoem arak dan bikin sairan Tionghoa (Sie).

Ia ada tertjatet sebagi orang Tionghoa jang taro perhatian atas kunst Priboemi atawa gamelan, kerna pada itoe tempo gamelan belon populair diantara orang Tionghoa. Sedari toean Tan Tiang Tjhing kemarihin, baroelah gamelan banjak ambil bagian dalem berbagi-bagi perajahan jang dilakoekan oleh orang Tionghoa."

78. "Ini soerat kabar diterbitkan tiga kali seminggoe dan ditambah dengen hoeroef-hoeroef Djawa jang moeat berbagi-bagi tembang, kerna diantara orang Tionghoa itoe koetika poen banjak jang fahamken hoeroef dan bahasa Djawa, berhoeboeng dengen ang-gepan bahoea hoeroef Tionghoa ada lebih soesah dipladjarin. Maka tatkala ini soe-rat kabar terbitken feuilleton Sam Kok dalem hoeroef Djawa pake tembang, telah tarik abonne Tionghoa boekan sedikit. Pengarang dari ini tjerita adalah toean R. Goenawan di Maospati, Madioen, jang telah dapetken banjak poedjian dari bagoesnja itoe karangan, siapa ternjata sampe pande soeroepken pangkat-pangkat Tionghoa pada pangkat-pangkat di dalem lelakon wajang.

Djoega di lain-lain bilangan di Djawa Tengah kemadjoean orang Tionghoa boeat pladjarin hoeroef dan literatuur Djawa semingkin besar djoemblahnja, maka pada itoe djaman telah banjak kloear boekoe-boekoe salinan dari hoeroef Tionghoa ka dalem hoeroef dan bahasa Djawa (pake tembang), antaranja ada tjerita Siek Djien Koei, Yo Tjong Poo, Tek Thjing, njonjah Koewi dan lain-lain lagi."

79. Both the Sunan of Surakarta and the Sultan of Yogyakarta, along with their fami-lies, were regular money borrowers from the Chinese. Unable to pay the money back, periodically the courts asked the Dutch colonial government to pay their debts (Carey 1984).

80. Carey gives an example of how the Chinese tax collectors increased their income by sponsoring occasions in which music and dance were an integral part. At tollgates, Chinese tax collectors inspected and collected payments for farmers' goods and gave the right of passage. The farmers were made to wait for a long time; some even had to stay overnight. During their wait, the farmers would face the "beguilements of country danc-

ing girls/prostitutes (*ronggeng*) and gambling parties, which would further tax the farmers' meager savings" (1984 : 38). Certainly this was a form of exploitation. The Chinese knew how to use Javanese customs for their own financial gain.

81. *Wiwahan Dalem.* I. Asmaradana.

> 13. . . . .
> yèka minongka unggyané
> titingalan ringgit cina
> kang saking Singapura
> lekasé dènira talu
> tinamtu dinten punika
> 14. Dumugi sadasa hari
> ing ngangkah panggelarira
> lamun rahina kawité
> tabah tri kongsi tumeka
> surupé sanghyang surya
> déné ta kalamun dalu
> tabah astha lekasira
> 15. Tekèng wanci madya ratri
> . . . .

82. Ibid. VIII. Maskumambang.

> 15. . . . .
> nihanta samana
> kori wétan wonten kèksi
> obor abyor marakata
> 16. Tatabuhan gubar bèri mungging ngarsi
> thong-thong grit kalawan
> salomprèt puksur saruni
> oreg kang sami umiyat
> 17. Gumer gumrah gumuruh ramé dènya mrih
> prayogining prenah
> mimilih ywa kongsi tebih
> tebaning dènira mulat
> 18. Marang jenggi yèka ingkang lagi prapti
> tantara lumampah
> ingkang minongka pangarsi
> dan-édanan néka warna
> 19. Rupa sarpa sungkara mundhing karendhing
> kukila pragosa
> kidang rangutan raseksi
> giyak-giyak sarwi surak
> 20. Lampahira urut iringing pandhapi
> terus paringgitan
> mangilèn alon lumaris
> satelasé dan-édanan
> 21. Nulya wau lampahing jenggi pangarsi
> pinindha kagendra
> tinumpakan dyah respati
> senen pamuluné jenar

83. Ibid. VIII. Maskumambang.

> 26. Dupi prapta ngarsaning pangantèn nuli
> kèndel awiraga
> nolih mandeng aningali
> mring sakaloron lenggahan
> 27. Dangu datan sinapa lumampah malih
> remben kang rembatan
> semunira kadya purik
> umarak tan antuk karya
> 28. Dupi praptèng jawi kilèning pandhapi
> mangidul kang lampah
> isthanira dèn tingali
> lir mérang angungkur rena

84. "Abdi dalem wayang wong banyak yang diberhentikan. Untuk pertunjukan hiburan diadakan sekedarnya, tidak seperti pada tahun 1896. Kemudian bekas para abdi dalem mendirikan perkumpulan wayang wong di kampung-kampung. Tidak lama kemudian, tampil beberapa Orang Cina, Belanda dan Indonesia yang mengumpulkan mereka, mengadakan pertunjukkan Wayang Wong keliling kemana-mana. Itulah permulaan Wayang Wong tersebar luas di Indonesia."

85. This is probably the Rieneeker mentioned in Sayid.

86. According to Sayid (1981:59), the Sri Wedari wayang wong was founded by Babah Lie Wat Gien, on the order of the prime minister of the Surakarta court, Sasradiningrat IV (the founder of the Sri Wedari park in 1899).

87. There is no evidence of direct influence of the Chinese theatre on Javanese dance drama. But the face makeup of Chinese and Javanese dancers is similar. It is also possible that the development of commercial wayang wong was influenced by the komedie stamboel; often the performers in these plays were Indos and Chinese.

88. *Serat Tjentini* 7–8. 276e. Kinanthi.

> 40. Ya talah temen nak bagus
> nyata prenjana ing gendhing
> wasis lungiding yakmaka
> ngenorken wong juru gendhing
> tan mambu putrèng ulama
> wignya langening pakerti
> 41. Nanging dhi ragil puniku
> mungguh wong kang ulah rawit
> dadya cegahing agama
> ing temah amelarati
> melarat dunya akérat
> tanpa iman ing agami
> 42. Sabab wong gendhing puniku
> atiné mangéran gendhing
> tan ana liyan kacipta
> namung rasaning ing gendhing
> sinungku sajroning nala
> nalika lakuning gendhing

89. For a translation of other stanzas of this section of the *Serat Centhini,* see Kunst I, 1973:267–268.

90. *Serat Tjenṭini* 7–8. 277e. Pucung.

1. Kang punika dhi ragil Kulawiryèku
mungguh gagendhingan
mrih sampurnaning awaril
kedah dunungaken [ing] ilmu rasanya
2. ungelipun gamelan srancak puniku
pan unining gangsa
tan dadya werdining ilmi
mung gendhingé dhi ragil kang dadya rasa

91. Ibid. 278e. Asmarandana.

3. Yèn wus wruh rasaning gendhing
lan sasurasaning niat
gendhing dadya pangateré
marang sejatining niat
tumekaning kasidan

. . . .

92. Hatch (1980:188) has described this debate as follows: "Connections between music and matter—concrete functions of the body and nature in general—become ritualized aspects of Javanese religion (*agama Jawa*)—the more so perhaps in response to Islam. In this ritualized form they are actually represented as a threat to Islamic religion (*agama Islam*). But, when one of the protagonists in the debate attempts to resolve the conflict through a spiritualization of music—making it into a non-material, non-functional entity (except perhaps to the extent that it was an exercise of devotion), a discipline—he made it not a threat, or perhaps only a threat to the extent that it took time away from other activities."

93. "Jeng Gusti nulya dhawuh mring kang rayi Jeng Pangran Suryadiningrat, tumanggap ngimbalaken pangandika dhateng mas Pengulu, kang kinon handongani ajad dalem wiyosan dinten Akat Legi. Mas pangulu sandika, saksana andonga. Sora swaranya rum kapiyarsa pratela tur patitis kiratilapal rambah kaping tiga, gentosan kaliyan ketip kekalih, dènira handongani."

94. Also see Pigeaud (1938:295) about the support given by Sasradiningrat and his brother Wreksadiningrat to the revival of *santi swara*. Pigeaud also says that these two patrons of the arts were the founders of the popular *kethoprak* play.

95. "Vormde het ten gehore brengen dezer liederen niet lang geleden nog een onderdelen van het programma van uitvoeringen, welke in de kraton van Soerakarta met meerdere of mindere regelmaat zijn aangewezen om gegeven te worden bij verschillende gelegenheden en op de verschillende hoogtijden van het jaar."

96. "elke Donderdagavond (Malem Djoemoengahan) de Abdi Dalem Ngoelama hun opwatching kwamen maken in de Panepen (een der gebouwen in het middelste gedeelte van de kraton) en de Koer'an reciteerden (of zongen, in koor, anderes Koer'an) tot middernacht (bedoeg). Toen ter tijd bestonden de santiswara-lieren nog niet, athans niet in de huidige vorm."

97. In the nineteenth century, Europeans became interested in archaeology and antiquities, in digging up old objects and reconstructing old monuments. This interest was followed by the Javanese elite, as is seen in Sasradiningrat's attempt to revive the terbang ensemble. See also the discussion of early gamelan notations in chapter 3.

98. Sasradiningrat IV is known to have been receptive to Western ideas. Shiraishi (1990:38) notes that Sasradiningrat "established one of the earliest modern-style religious schools, Madrasah Mamba'oel Oeloem, attached to the Great Mosque, and took the initiative to modernize the Kasunanan religious bureaucracy." It is possible that his interest in reviving terbangan music was related to his activity in modern religious affairs.

99. *Mung mung jir* are the onomatopoetic words for the gamelan music.

100. These words are imitations of the sound of terbang.

101. *Babad Mangkunegara VII.* 43. Pangkur.

> Sangka bungah-bungahira
> kawulalit kumedah-medahnèki
> katona mèlu misungsung
> déné ratuné krama
> antuk garwa putri putrané sang Ratu
> marma kumpul padha ngédan
> anékad praya sumiwi
>
> mlebu bleng marang plataran
> cikrak-cikrak dèn gameli mung mung jir
> ana ingkang mung lumaku
> dhampyak jèjèr nyakawan
> bengak bengok tinabuhan terbang brang brung
> géla-gélo lailolah
> muhamad rasullulahi
>
> ngenceng ngalor mlebu bangsal
> metu ngétan mangalor mlebu maring
> paringgitan maksih brang brung
> latdholit pak pak dhung blang
> tekan kulon mangidul nulya ametu
> ngubengi sakèhing dalan
> kèh bocah cilik kekinthil

102. One impetus for the flourishing of Javanese arts in the court was the presence of the Dutch in the court and their relationships with the courtiers.

103. See Yampolsky 1985; see also Hatch (1976:59–64).

104. The word gérong already appeared in Hindu-Javanese literature (Kunst 1968). But scholars propose meanings ranging from singing, to composition, to a musical instrument.

105. *Serat Tjenṭini* 1–2. 2e. Sinom.

> 12. . . . .
> anulya nyandhak tarebang
> sasolahira respati
> dhasar radi kinardi
> apacak terbang pinangku

ing dhengkul dhangak ladak
beranyak Anggunung-sari
adan lekas sajak Jawi Sekar Lémpang
13. Swara muluk getas renyah
angungkung arum tur manis
nges wiletnya nganyut manah
panerbangé angapipir
sabat gya naurani
tarebang tiga gumrumung
barung angklung lan kendhang
calung calapita gadhing
ramya gobyog gumer geter magenturan
17. Kang sauran rebut sora
swarané samya sru angrik
rahab ungkul-ingungkulan
santri barung naurani
yèn nuju sèlèhnèki
sauran dènya gumrumung
yèn kabèh tibèng gongan
mas Cebolang kang nampèni
ngelik melung ngungkung membat angemandhang

106. Yampolsky (1985:6) suggests that this is the case. He points out that before the 1870s, gamelan had taken over many terbangan pieces. Indeed, the *Serat Centhini* suggests that the lively interaction between gamelan and terbangan happened much earlier in the nineteenth century, perhaps even in the late eighteenth century.

107. According to Tondhakusuma (1870:22), Mangkunegara IV also composed *ladrang* Maésa Liwung, *ayak-ayakan* Kaloran, and many pieces for *jineman*, such as Lara Kèwes, Petung Liris, Candhi Retna, Céré Méndé, and Glathik Glindhing. Of these four jineman, Glathik Glindhing is the only one that is still well known today.

It is possible that Céré Méndé was the name for today's jineman Uler Kambang; occasionally the term *céré méndé* is used for senggakan (short melodies to enliven the mood of the piece) of this jineman.

Ayak-ayakan Kaloran is now played as the closing piece for gamelan performances in the Mangkunegaran court.

108. "Punika Sendhon Langen Swara, anggitan dalem Kanjeng Gusti Pangeran Adipati Harya Mangkunagara: ingkang kaping IV, kagem bilih bojana kaliyan para putra, santana saha wadya, mawi kabawanan ura-ura, katampèn ing gongsa, gendhingipun manut laguning sekar."

109. Today these pieces are performed without bawa. According to the *Sendhon Langen Swara,* each of the pieces had its own bawa. The bawa, listed in the order of the pieces above, are: sekar ageng Citra Mengeng, Kumudasmara, Pamularsih, Kusumastuti, Minta Jiwa, sekar tengahan Palugon, Pranasmara, Pangajab Sih, and sekar macapat Kinanthi.

Sometime early in this century, one of the pieces, ketawang Puspa Warna, became a signature piece of the Mangkunegaran: it was played to honor the appearance of Mangkunegara at the outer hall of the palace.

110. I have not found evidence regarding the way panembrama were performed at the time of Paku Buwana X. But panembrama were still performed at many of the year-

end celebrations of grammar or high schools in Surakarta in the 1960s. Accompanied by the gamelan, the songs were sung on the stage by a dozen or more boys and girls, usually wearing uniforms.

111. For a complete list of gendhing panembrama, see Soewandi 1926 (Serat Panembrama). He includes panembrama which are not necessarily associated with the acceptance of gifts or the visits of foreign dignitaries, such as ones for weddings and those associated with certain organizations. See also *Noot Gendhing lan Tembang* (1926). It contains the lyrics and notation of thirty gendhing panembrama.

Chapter Three

1. I should mention here early scientific studies of the Javanese that preceded the works of Dutch scholar-officials in the mid nineteenth century: the early nineteenth-century works of the British Lieutenant-Governor of Java, Thomas Stamford Raffles, and the British Resident of Yogyakarta, John Crawfurd. Raffles and Crawfurd interacted with Javanese informants and noblemen. Raffles's two-volume *History of Java* (1817) is the first work in a European language on the history, ethnography, performing arts, and literature of the island and people of Java. Crawfurd wrote the three-volume *History of the Indian Archipelago* (1820). Both Raffles and Crawfurd provide glimpses of musical life and practice in Java in the early nineteenth century. But it was in the mid nineteenth century that the European-style scientific study of Javanese culture was institutionalized.

2. Ronggawarsita's *Serat Kalatidha* (Song poem of a time of darkness) expresses clearly the King's loss of cultural legitimacy in this colonial period: it was "the period of the general crisis of the 19th century Javanese spirit, as Dutch colonial rule steadily consolidated itself" (Anderson 1979:220).

3. For a discussion of the characteristics of the chirographic tradition, see Becker (1984:xi–xiii).

4. *Serat Sastramiruda,* which was written earlier than *Serat Gulang Yarya,* also explains gamelan, although only sporadically. However, the book is mostly about wayang.

5. *Serat Gulang Yarya.* I. Dhandhang Gula.

> 9. Setu matur saléndro kiyai
> wijinipun wilahan mung gangsal
> satunggal enam namané
> tegesipun pangumpul
> myang panata kajengirèki
> panatanirèng laras
> kumpul embatipun
> kaliyé nama geng Asal
> tegesipun geng ageng = Asal wiwinih
> dados pikajengira
> 10. Lamun arsa adamel wiwinih
> sorog ageng saking wilah gengsal
> punika wau yaktiné
> déné katiganipun
> wilah tengah labet nengahi
> sakawan wilah jongga
> dumunung nèng gulu

wilahan barung gangsalnya
tegesipun barung bareng angrangkepi
nimbangi wilah gengsal.

6. See also Becker 1979:237–38, for the use of jarwa dhosok by dhalang in wayang kulit.

7. Interpreting the meaning of the names of gamelan keys has continued to fascinate theorists. See, e.g., Sindusawarna 1960; Sastrapustaka 1984.

Here are some other etymological interpretations from the *Gulang Yarya: Mirong,* alteration of the word *rimong* (to cover), is a section that should be uncovered. Ayak-ayakan derives from *ayak,* which means *kira* (to approximate); thus, ayak-ayakan is analogous to the word *kira-kiranen,* which means to be approximated by the musician. This refers to the playing techniques for the piece. *Salebegan (Srepegan)* derives from *angglabeg seseg wradin* (tough, fast and even).

8. *Serat Gulang Yarya.* 8. Mas Kumambang.

      6. Ingkang nama tembang tuwin sekar kawin
         ageng lan tengahan
         macepet tuwin talisir
         cacah wiji wijangira
      7. Sampun kawrat wonten pèngetan piningit
         ing nalikanira
         jeng Gupremèn ambawani
         sakolahanirèng Jawa
      8. Tuwan Karel Prédrik Winter jrubasaning
         kang kinèn ngumpulna
         ing cacah utawi nami
         wewiji wijanging tembang

9. I have not yet found the dates of the birth and death of Yasadipura II. In 1826 Yasadipura II became the minister of the *kadipatèn* (the household of the crown prince) and assumed the name of Raden Tumenggung Sastranegara. In 1825 Winter was appointed the Javanese interpreter in the court. Thus, Yasadipura II was a contemporary of Winter.

10. According to Tondhakusuma, the singing style of Macapat Paringgitan was developed by Paku Buwana III. Kusumadilaga composed the tembang songs Sinom Pangrawit, Mijil Larasati, Mijil Tombaneng, Dhandhang Gula Bawang Sumilir, Dhandhang Gula Dhalang Krahinan, Dhandhang Gula Marwata, Kinanthi Petung Langking, Kinanthi Genjong, and the sekar tengahan song Jru Demung. Nowadays, only a few of these songs, such as Sinom Pangrawit, Mijil Larasati, and Juru Demung, are known.

11. As Perlman (1991:46) points out, the first use of Western staff notation for gamelan was by Raffles (1817) and Crawfurd (1820). This notation was intended for the English reader. The Javanese probably did not know this notation. For a discussion of Raffles's and Crawfurd's notations of gendhing in comparison with contemporary notations of the same gendhing, see Brinner (1993).

12. "Ananging para guru Jawa mau: sanyatané duru[ng] ana kang bisa nut / sabab mauné ora kawulang, dadi pamulangé guru Jawa mau marang muridé: ora nurut papathokané swara iku, mulané wus masthi ora isa bener, awit pamulangé mung saka mèl / lan

saapilé laguné dhéwé-dhéwé baé. Yèn pamulangé lastari mangkono: anané nut sekar kawi tanpa guna, sarta laguné sekar kawi i[ng] kana kéné gèsèh kabèh, ora sumurup endi kang bener."

13. Perlman (1991:48–53) finds two stages of development in the invention of nut ranté, involving the precision and refinement of the notation.

14. Evidently, there are two notation systems that predate andha notation. The first notation consists of five, six, or seven horizontal lines with letters below the lines, representing the pitches; the letters are connected with lines. This notation is similar to the ranté notation. According to Kunst (1973, 1:349), this is the oldest notation, coming from Paku Alam V (r. 1878–1900). Groneman (1890:54) attributes it to Paku Alam IV (r. 1864–1878). The second notation consists of the names of each note written in full vertically, the kethuk, kenong, kempul, and gong written alongside them. Groneman (p. 55) identifies this notation as belonging to G. P. A. Adiwinata, the brother of Hamengku Buwana VII and the supervisor of the music and dance activity in the court. The notation was dated 1886 A.D., three years before the invention of ladder notation (Lindsay 1985:205). Lindsay (p. 206) suggests that the andha notation in the *Serat Pakem Wirama* was developed on the basis of Adiwinata's system.

15. Perlman (1991:58) reports that the oldest ranté notation is dated 1879/1880. He also suggests the year 1859–60 as the date of the writing of the first stage of this notation.

16. I must admit that the information given by Warsadiningrat is the only evidence I can find to suggest a link between Western staff notation and nut ranté. Warsadiningrat was born in 1886, after the invention of nut ranté. But he received his information from his father, Demang Warsapradangga, a gendèr specialist at the court of Surakarta, as well as from the prime minister Sasradiningrat IV (1889–1916).

Another piece of evidence that corroborates the notion of the involvement of a European musician comes from a typed comment pasted on the cover of the nut ranté manuscript kept in the Department of Literature at the Universitas Indonesia (Perlman 1991: 59). It says: "Noet Gending Ranté. Jasanipun M. Demang Goenapangrawit abdidalem pangageng Nijaga kala djaman Sinoehoen P. B. IV, kabiyantoe Entjik Béngkok, abdidalem Moesikan. . . ." (Chain notation of gendhing. The invention of M. Demang Goenapangrawit, the director of court musicians in the reign of Paku Buwana IV [sic], assisted by Encik Béngkok, a court musician of European music [of the Surakarta court]. . . .)

17. Besides Karini, Perlman (1991:45–46) suggests that perhaps Nagabanda is another member of the European staff of the Mangkunegaran court who was responsible for the creation of nut ranté. During the reign of Mangkunegara IV (1853–1881), Nagabanda was sent to Batavia to study music (Dhèsibèl 1915d, quoted in Perlman 1991:63).

18. An example of Dutch interest in archaeology was the restoration of the ninth-century Buddhist monument Borobudur. The considerable deterioration of the monument in the late nineteenth century brought about the founding in 1900 of a special committee. The restoration itself started in 1907.

19. Lindsay's full statement deserves quotation here. "While the stimulus to notate [gendhing] may indeed come from the Dutch, the impulse to save or preserve at this point of time, was, I believe, particularly Javanese. It was part of a larger cultural reaction to the encroaching control of the Dutch colonial government, and to the more visible presence

of the Dutch in daily life. In the principalities (Yogyakarta and Surakarta) there was an expansion of European plantations in the last quarter of the nineteenth century. At this time there was also a rapid increase in population in the principalities (as the rest of Java) and a decline in the well-being of the Javanese people. This general decline continued when the Liberal Policy was introduced in the 1870s, and climaxed in a severe economic depression in the 1870s. A sense of alarm was not something taught to the Yogyanese kraton, but rather the stronger colonial presence led to a sense of loss of both political and cultural identity."

Lindsay was responding to Judith Becker (1980:12–13), who suggests that the introduction of notation for gamelan is not an indigenous concept. "It was introduced by foreigners who mistakenly believed that a gamelan piece is a fixed entity which, if captured in notation, would be preserved from extinction" (ibid.).

20. See Lindsay (1985:201–16) for a discussion of the origins of the *Serat Pakem Wirama*.

21. The topics include the myth of the origin of gamelan, the names of parts of the instruments, the rules of playing gendhing for particular functions (for weddings, circumcisions, *nguyu-uyu* or enjoyment, *pakurmatan* or honorific functions), a guide for sindhenan, gendhing for wayang, inventory of gamelan in the kraton with each of their functions, a list of lagon songs for wayang, and a list of gendhing, each with its kendhangan, pathet, and the number of its wirama line.

22. This is a version of solfège originated by Jean-Jacques Rousseau in 1742. Subsequently the system was promoted by Emile and Nanine Chevé in the early nineteenth century and was widely used in France. The system is known as the Chevé Method. In the latter part of the nineteenth century, use of the system spread to the Netherlands. In the early part of the twentieth century, Dutch music teachers introduced the system into Indonesia.

23. See Brandts Buys (1940) for a discussion of the use of cipher notation by early gamelan theorists.

24. Based on Shiraishi (1981), especially pp. 96–99.

25. Scherer (1975) notes that Tjipto was a son of lesser priyayi and was a Malay language teacher in a Dutch native primary school. He was also a medical doctor and had graduated as the best student from STOVIA (School tot opleiding van inlandsche artsen [School for training native doctors]). In 1916, Tjipto was married for the third time, to an Indo woman, Mrs. Vogel, who was chairwoman of the local chapter of a nationalist organization, Insulinde. For further discussion of Tjipto's background and role in the Indonesian national movement, see Scherer (1975:102–81).

26. The following discussion of the marginalization of the Vorstenlanden in the Indonesian National movement is based on the chapter "Solo in the Pergerakan" (Shiraishi 1990:175–215).

27. See Lindsay 1985:1–80.

28. For discussion of Soetomo's views of gamelan, see Scherer (1975:218–39). Soetomo felt that the musical concept of gamelan could be used as a model for the ideal harmonious society, in which each member "knows his place and his role and accepts his social status as ascribed to him by his community" (p. 221). Soetomo also "stressed that the merit of people working together harmoniously, as in playing the gamelan, is that not only must people concerned know how to play and be expert in doing so, but also they

must *manut* or follow the rules and obey the discipline. In this manner, Soetomo said that, 'they can work together, not jealous or concerned with displaying personal contribution'" (p. 231).

29. The first two individuals are the grandsons of Paku Alam V, the third the son of the regional vizier of the Yogyanese prime ministry. Noto Soeroto, who initially studied law, became known as a poet, politician, journalist, and historian (Djajadiningrat-Nieuwenhuis 1993:45; for a full account of the life of Noto Soeroto, see pp. 41–72). Soeryo Poetro began studying engineering (Dewantara 1967:344), but later he became known as a music theorist. His work includes a series of short essays on gamelan that appear in the *Nederlandsche Indie, Oud and Nieuw*. Jodjana began studying business, but he ended up becoming a Javanese dancer, performing traditional Javanese dances and his own dance creations; once he performed before the king of Belgium (Dewantara 1967: 325–27).

30. For further discussion of Dewantara, see Scherer 1975:57–100; Lindsay 1980: 74–75, 104–22.

31. "*Pasinaon gendhing* punika boten namung prelu kanggé *ngudi kawruh saha kasagedan gendhing* kémawon, nanging wigatos ugi kanggé *tuwuhing gesang kabatosan,* awit tansah nenuntun dhateng *raos kawiraman* (rhythmisch gevoel) . . . anggegesang *raos kasulistyan* (aesthetisch gevoel) . . . ngeningaken *raos kasusilan* (ethisch gevoel) . . . (Kasebut ing wewarah *Sultan Agungan,* tuwin piwulanging para *sarjana kilènan.*)."

32. "2. Ing tanah Jawi kacariyos para *pandhita lan wali* sami anggatosaken dhateng kagunan gendhing, malah kathah ingkang sami tumut ambangun wewangunan gendhing tuwin kidung, (Sunan Kali Jaga, Sunan Giri, Sri Sultan Agung lsp.). Makaten ugi ing tanah kilènan para *manggalaning agama tuwin gréja* (para paus lan pandhita) sami ngecakaken daya prabawaning gendhing, minangka *pambikaking raos kabatosan* (religieus gevoel), punapa déné minangka *pangasahing budi* (karakter vorming) ingkang adhedhasar landheping cipta, alusing rasa tuwin kiyating karsa."

33. McVey discusses Dewantara as the creator of the Taman Siswa education system. "We can trace the Taman Siswa idea, if we wish, from Suwardi Surjaningrat's Netherlands exile of 1913–17, when he obtained a teaching certificate, attended the First Colonial Education Congress in The Hague, and participated in discussion regarding a 'national' modification of the Indies school system, a subject of some debate among Dutch educators at the time. We can find its origins equally well in a culturally traditional group, the Pagujuban Selasa-Kliwon, which met under the well-known Yogyakarta mystic Pangeran Surjamataram to discuss questions of Javanese mysticism (kebatinan)" (McVey 1967:130).

34. "Ing djaman samangké para ahli kabudajan prelu sanget anggatosaken, *pasinaon gending kangge para muda,* . . . margi . . . *djedjering gending Djawi* punika jektos pantjen *èdi* miwah luhur, pantes dados busananing bangsa ingkang kinaot. Kadjawi ingkang makaten, raos anggadahi kagunan adi luhung makaten saged damel *mantep tuwin murnining raos kabangsan* (superioriteits gevoel)."

For another adi luhung image of gamelan from a contemporary of Dewantara, see Sumanagara (1935:1–2). Dhandhang Gula.

> Kang ing ngaran krawitan winarni
> tatabuhan gongsa lawan tembang
> katriné winastan jogèd
> kumpuling telu iku

karawitan dipun wastani
tegesé kaalusan
alus trusing kalbu
dadi tetengering bongsa
ing sadhéngah bongsa masthi andarbèni
lalangen karawitan.

Marma parlu kudu pinarsudi
amamardi sambada lebdaa
dadi ana pratandhané
lamun ana wong ngaku
bongsa Jawa nanging tan ngerti
maring rèh karawitan
yekti nistha saru
béda lan bongsa Eropah
wiwit bocah padha disinau bangkit
ngertiya karawitan.

Lah kacèka apa bongsa Jawi
iya darbé langen karawitan
malah ngluwihi alusé
gathuk kalawan kawruh
nawung rasa tekèng rahswa di
éman tan mangertiya

· ·

What is referred to as *karawitan*
is gamelan playing and singing;
the third is dancing.
These three [arts] together
are called karawitan.
It means refinement,
refining deep into the mind.
[Karawitan] becomes the identity of the nation;
any nation always has
the art of karawitan.

Therefore, [karawitan] must be ascertained,
in search of worthy experience.
Thus, this indicates that if one claims
to be Javanese, but does not understand
about karawitan,
that is truly shameful and indecent.
This is different from the European nations.
There, from childhood people are taught to rise to the point of
understanding karawitan (music).

What is the difference [between other people and] Javanese?
We also have karawitan,
even more refined [than European music].
[Javanese karawitan] is matched with the sacred knowledge,
integrated in feeling, reaching the sublime.
It is a pity if we do not understand karawitan.

· ·

35. I mentioned earlier that when European "cultural power" expanded rapidly in the beginning of the twentieth century, European intellectuals, followed by the Javanese elite, felt compelled to study gamelan in European scientific ways. Then followed the concept of "high culture." European and Javanese intellectuals referred to Javanese court arts as the products of "high culture."

36. See above regarding the use of notation to legitimize the status of gamelan as a "high art."

37. For more on the cult of adi luhung as a modern image of traditional Javanese literature, see Florida (1987), especially pp. 1–4.

38. "Kebudajaan nasional Indonesia ialah segala puntjak-puntjak dan sari-sari kebu-dajaan jang bernilai diseluruh kepulauan, baik jang lama maupun jang ciptaan baru, jang berdjiwa nasional."

Although Dewantara's definition appeared in print only after Indonesian independence in 1945, he often expressed it before then in the weekly meeting of teachers of Taman Siswa (Koentjaraningrat 1985:109).

39. I am indebted to Umar Kayam for this point (pers. comm., 1990).

40. "Kebudayaan bangsa ialah kebudayaan yang timbul sebagai buah usaha budi-daya Rakyat Indonesia seluruhnya. Kebudayaan lama dan asli yang terdapat sebagai puncak-puncak kebudayaan di daerah-daerah diseluruh Indonesia, terhitung sebagai kebudayaan bangsa."

41. Dewantara's notion that the superiority of Javanese arts could create sturdy and pure national feelings was so strong in the 1930s that some individuals proposed that "Indonesia Raya," the Western-style Indonesian national anthem, should be played on gamelan (Dungga and Manik 1952:32, 87).

42. Other non-Javanese nationalists who opposed the elevation of Javanese court culture to the status of national culture included Sutan Takdir Alisjahbana (see Alisjahbana 1954), Sutan Sjahir (see Lindsay 1985:27–28), and Aidit (see McVey 1986:30–31).

43. I am indebted to Philip Yampolsky for this reference material.

44. For a brief mention of kroncong, see chapter 1.

45. This is an exaggerated description of kroncong. There are no Chinese, Arab, or Rumanian elements in this music.

46. "Hal itoe memboektikan kerontjong mengandoeng tenaga jang segar. Kerontjong memperloeas diri kesegala joeroesan, keloear dan kedalam."

47. Here Resink included gamelan traditions from other regions as part of his consideration: those of Sunda, Bali, Madura, West Lombok, Banjarmasin, and South Sumatra.

48. In 1932, Mangkunegara presented at the Cultuur-Wijsgeerigen Studiekring a lecture entitled "Over de wajang koelit (purwa) in het algemeen en over de daarin voorkomende symbolische en mystieke elementen" (On the wayang kulit (purwa) and its symbolic and mystical elements). The lecture was about the true and deep meanings of wayang. In developing the point that Javanese art was the product of high culture, Mangkunegara discussed the wayang with the Western-educated Javanese elite and European Javanologists. The lecture appeared in Djawa (1933) and was translated into English by Claire Holt (1957).

49. For instance, program notes were provided for a langendriyan performed as part of the celebration of the marriage of the daughter of the Patih of the Mangkunegaran court to the son of the Regent of Banjarnagara in October 1934. Written in Dutch, the

program notes contain a brief summary of the story, the list of characters in the story, and details of the action in each scene of the play.

50. The discussion of lurah badhut as having an important role in the patronage of talèdhèk dancers is based on *Djèdjèrèngan,* compiled and transliterated by Soewandi (1938: 122–55), except as otherwise indicated.

51. Stutterheim received his information about canthang balung from two princes: Pangeran Aria Kusumayuda and Pangeran Aria Hadiwijaya. Regarding the last duty of canthang balung, the princes describe it as follows: "For the so-called *gajah ngombé* dance ('the drinking elephant') the dance postures *jèngkèng* and *kalang kinantang* are used, with the right and left hand stretched out and with their bodies slightly bent forward and hopping like birds the dancers hold a small glass of gin in their right hands. In their left hands they hold between their fingers four *chantang balung,* called collectively a *kĕpyak* and made of four long, flat leaf-shaped bones, strung on a string and kept apart by knots; they are held between the fingers and make a rhythmical, rattling noise. The dancers make twittering sounds while at every gong-beat they drink the gin, which is replenished from a jug on the floor, for the dance is performed in a crouching position. At the same time the dancers shake their head in a ridiculous manner. The gamĕlan play the tune *undur-undur kajongan* and the dancers are called *badut* or also *kridastama.* The *chantang balung* are white, one finger long and two fingers wide, made of buffalo bone and strung on white thread wound into cords" (1956:95).

52. Perhaps the promotion of prostitution by a court through its canthang balung activity mirrored a ruler's attempt to enhance his power—since virility was an important sign of a ruler's power (Anderson 1972:18). It was common for a ruler to have many *selir* (concubines), among whom were talèdhèk. For example, Hamengku Buwana II (r. 1792– 1810) had a talèdhèk concubine named Mas Ajeng Ratamsari (Suharto 1980:44).

53. This identification card was stamped with pictures of the male and female genital organs (*kuwadonan lan padjaleran*) (Soewandi 1938:122). The canthang balung's Seal of Office "was oval in shape, with an ornamental rim and in the centre the representation of a phallus which was inside a *heart*-shaped vulva; the two were enclosed by the functionary's name, the date and the words '*abdi dalem lurah badhut.*'" (Stutterheim 1956:96).

54. There were two other canthang balung, Sukaastama and Gunaastama, whose ranks were lower than Gunaléwa and Sukaléwa. Stutterheim (ibid.) says that originally there were only two canthang balung. The low-ranking canthang balung were a new addition (Soewandi does not mention them).

55. One particular affair cited in the report as the cause for abolishing the practice of lurah badhut was the kidnapping of teenage girls by lurah badhut entourages. The parents had to pay ransom to the lurah badhut in order to free their daughters from the brothel.

56. The secondary schools of Javanese performing arts are Konservatori Karawitan Indonesia (KOKAR; now Sekolah Menengah Karawitan Indonesia, SMKI), founded in Surakarta in 1950; and Konservatori Tari Indonesia (KONRI), founded in Yogyakarta in 1961. The tertiary schools of Javanese performing arts are Akademi Seni Karawitan Indonesia (ASKI; now Sekolah Tinggi Seni Indonesia, STSI), founded in Surakarta in 1964; and Akademi Seni Tari Indonesia (ASTI; now a department of the Institute Seni Indonesia, ISI), founded in Yogyakarta. There are also secondary and tertiary schools of gamelan and dance in West Java, Bali, Sumatra, and Sulawesi.

57. "Mereka dengan saksama melakukan penjelidikan2 berbagai ragam kesenian di-daerahnja. Setjara tidak langsung kesenian asli kedaerahan itu, jakin akan dapat didjadikan bahan2 perkembangan seni suara Indonesia jang sifatnja umum."

58. Becker (1980:37–77) also discusses at length the attempts of modern gamelan composers to compose new gamelan pieces. She suggests that such works were attempts by the modern composers for gamelan "to reach an all-Java if not a Pan-Indonesian audience" (p. 103).

59. It is true that the word pangrawit had already been used as part of the names of court musicians (e.g. Martopangrawit and Prawirapangrawit). But the term pangrawit as a generic term for gamelan player was a new development.

60. As a graduate of KOKAR and ASKI, I remember well other attempts to elevate the status of gamelan. For instance, the faculty and students always felt it necessary for gamelan instruments to be placed on a stage, instead of on the floor; thus the instruments and the musicians would be on the same level as the guests who sat down on chairs. Dewantara (1967:213) suggests that gamelan should be built taller, and the musicians should sit on chairs. For another example, a gamelan group consisting of faculty and students of KOKAR, who often played gamelan as an after-school activity, required its musicians to wear suits and ties instead of Javanese costume when they played gamelan. The group felt that the audience would pay more respect to the musicians and their music if the musicians wore suits and ties.

61. For further discussion of pesindhèn, talèdhèk, and tayuban see Sutton 1984b: 119–33; Hughes-Freeland 1990:36–44.

62. To him, the word karawitan referred to gamelan, singing, and dance. Today the term refers to gamelan and singing only. Earlier I mentioned Sumanagara's work in connection with the process of classicizing gamelan. Like Dewantara, he was a proponent of gamelan as adi luhung.

63. For a study of regional gamelan musics in Java, including their interactions with the Central Javanese court gamelan traditions, see Sutton (1991).

64. Recent musicologists play down the relevance of this characterization, for it is basically evaluative (Randel 1986:172). However, it is important to know the history of the term and its application to Javanese arts. The word "classic" (from Latin word *classicus*, which means "Roman citizen of the highest class") was chosen to categorize European literature and arts on the basis of social class. And it was on the same basis that the term was applied to Javanese court arts.

65. For an excellent discussion of the Indonesianization of the Western European classical-folk paradigm, see Lindsay (1980:35–80).

66. "Ini prinsip dasar karawitan tradisi tulen yang tidak pernah berusaha meniru suara-suara wantah yang didengar sehari-hari, seperti hujan, petir, orang menangis, mengeluh, kuda berlari, dsb. Karawitan tradisi tulen menciptakan nada-nada karawitan khas dalam hubungan sruti tertentu dan menyusunnya dengan tempo dan ritmo yang langsung mencapai kita.

> 'Tan karungu gamelan nang nong gungipun
> Tate tetenira
> Sadaya datan kapyarsi
> Mung rarasing gending kang nganyut ing dria.'"

The macapat verse quoted by Humardani is from the *Serat Centhini*.

67. "Kiblat kini sekalipun kelanjutan kemarin, juga kreasi kita sendiri sekarang. Nilai-nilainya bukan identik dengan nilai kemarin—nilai tradisi—melainkan nilai-nilai yang kita hayati dan yakini—entah dari tradisi kita entah bukan."

68. "Wujud dan arah perkembangan ini dapat berbagai macam [,] mulai dari tradisi secara berkembang atau kreatip dengan perbendaharaan tradisi yang dihayati oleh pribadi sampai bentuk-bentuk yang hanya bernafas tradisi."

69. The Arts Council of Jakarta has been prominent in this activity. Since 1979 the Council has sponsored an annual festival called *Pekan Komponis Muda* (The Festival of Young Composers). Young composers from music institutions in Bali, Central Java (Sura-karta and Yogyakarta), West Java, and Jakarta have participated in the festivals each year. Occasionally, there have also been young composers from Sumatra and East Java. For detailed reports of the festival, see Hardjana (1986).

70. The sound of the gong ageng produced by hitting not the knob of the gong, but around the knob.

71. "Komposisi kami tersebut adalah merupakan garapan baru yang bertolak dari bahan-bahan karawitan tradisi. Landasan ide adalah kenyataan bahwa didalam karawitan, tradisi mempunyai potensi musikal kuat. Kenyataan telah menunjukkan bahwa ada unsur-unsur yang lemah, antara lain kurangnya penggarapan volume, kwalitas suara, tempo, di-namik dsb, disamping adanya unsur yang sangat positif yaitu pada kebebasan interpretasi pada kerangka gending oleh masing-masing pengrawit, di samping kwalitas suara dari masing-masing instrumen gamelan itu sendiri. Garapan kami bertitik tolak dari hal-hal tersebut."

72. This is in contrast with traditional gamelan pieces in which dynamic changes are not so prevalent.

73. This passage from the *Serat Tjentini* (1912–15, 7–8:204–5) is relevant to this discussion: 277e. Pucung

    1. . . . .
       mungguh gagendhingan
       mrih sampurnaning awaril
       kedah dunungaken ing ilmu rasanya
    2. Ungelipun gamelan srancak puniku
       pan unining gangsa
       tan dadya wredining ilmi
       mung gendhingé dhi ragil kang dadya rasa

   10. Dé puniku dhaupé marang ing èlmu
       unining gamelan
       sami lan unining lambé
       gendhingané puniku jatining niat
   11. Paminipun nglinging dhikir pujinipun
       lir cengklinging gangsa
       kang dèrèng kelawan gendhing
       muji dhikir lamun tan kelawan niat
   12. Pujinipun sami lan unining kethuk
       tinabuh dhèwèkan
       uniné tan dadi gendhing

    . . . .

28. Campuhipun lawan niat kang nulya nung
    anunggé ing kanang
    kinengan kunenging ati
    ati ingati-ati kalawan niat

[1. . . . .
    concerning the playing of gendhing,
    in order to truly understand its meaning,
    the sacred knowledge of its rasa must be explained.
 2. The sound of the set of gamelan
    is merely the sound of metallic instruments.
    It alone will not reveal the true meaning of the sacred knowledge.
    Only the gendhing, my brother, can become rasa.
10. Concerning the compatibility of the gamelan with the sacred knowledge,
    the sound of gamelan
    is the same as the sound of the lips.
    The gendhing is the true niat (striving after the sublime).
11. The sound of the dhikir prayer is analogous to
    the clanging of the gamelan instruments,
    but without the gendhing.
    If praying dhikir is without niat
12. The prayer is like the sound of kethuk,
    played alone.
    Its sound cannot become gendhing.
    . . . .
28. The union [of the gendhing] with sublime and defined niat
    gives the clear way to the suitable goal,
    the way to inner peace and tranquility,
    [resulting in] our heart uniting with niat.

See also my translation of some passages from the same poem in chapter 1.
74. *Serat Titi Asri*. Asmaradana.

> Surasa ngèlmining gendhing
> lan ngèlmining pepathetan
> lamun nora winiraos
> sayektiné kaélangan
> surasaning gamelan
> mongka iku wulang wujud
> sanyata karosèng driya
>
> Ingkang akarsa dumeling
> midhanget laras gamelan
> pesthi kacaryan ing tyasé
> tumulya mosiking driya
> midhanget ajenggirat
> iba mangretia putus
> sasat wruh ngèlmuning Alah

75. Dhandhang Gula.

> Marsudiya kawruh jroning gendhing
> taberiya ngrasakké irama

pangolahé lan garapé
ngrasakna wosing lagu
witing pathet saka ing ngendi
ing kono golèkana
surasaning lagu
rarasen nganti kajiwa
karya padhang narawang nora mblerengi
tatas nembus bawana

76. The first klenèngan mentioned in the poem is the one held during the preparation for the wedding of Amongraga (the central figure in the poem) (*Serat Centhini* 1912–15, 1–2:245). It begins with Jayèngraga playing gambang. Then Kulawirya joins in, singing the drum part. Subsequently, Jayèngraga gets the idea of regrouping into a small *gadhon* ensemble. Thus, the gadhon performance takes place while people are preparing for the wedding celebration.

77. Here again an Indo played an important role in the development of gamelan theory. Hinloopen Labberton was a prominent Indo-Javanologist and theosophist.

78. Unfortunately I have no information about either Djakoeb or Wignjaroemeksa. Djoko Waluyo (pers. comm., 1988), a gamelan instructor at the Institute Seni Indonesia in Jogyakarta, told me that according to his uncle, the late Sri Handoyokusuma (who was an expert on tembang), Djakoeb was of Arab descent and lived in Surakarta. According to R. T. Wasitodipuro (pers. comm., 1989), he was an employee of the museum of Radyapustaka in Surakarta.

79. The exponent of the Daminatila notation system of West Java was R. M. A. Kusumadinata, an expert on Sundanese music. I cannot find an explanation for Soelardi's use of this Daminatila-like system.

80. The other two drumming techniques are *kendhang kalih* and kendhang ciblon. Kendhang kalih (two drum [technique]) is played by combining the sounds of the kendhang ageng (the largest drum) and *kendhang ketipung* (the smallest drum). Kendhang ciblon is played on a medium-size drum. Its patterns are associated with the movements of Javanese dance. In the Solonese gamelan tradition, there is also a drumming technique called *kendhang wayangan* (drumming for accompanying wayang performance). It is played on a drum somewhat larger than the kendhang ciblon. For further discussion of these drumming techniques, see Susilo 1967, Martopangrawit 1972, and Sumarsam 1987.

Djakoeb and Wignjaroemeksa (1913:49–53) list and discuss all drumming patterns of kendhang satunggal: These are kendhangan for *ketawang* (a gendhing structure), ladrangan, [ketawang] gendhing kethuk 2 kerep minggah ladrangan, gendhing kethuk 2 kerep minggah kethuk 4, gendhing kethuk 2 arang minggah kethuk 4, gendhing kethuk 4 kerep minggah kethuk 4, gendhing kethuk 4 arang minggah kethuk 8, and gendhing kethuk 8 kerep minggah kethuk 16. Soelardi's list (1918:61) is less extensive than Djakoeb and Wignjaroemeksa's.

81. Djakoeb and Wignjaroemeksa (1913:53–60) and Soelardi (1918:63–65) give the same examples of drumming notation: the notation of kendhangan for ketawang, ladrangan sléndro and pélog, [ketawang] gendhing kethuk 2 kerep, gendhing kethuk 2 kerep minggah kethuk 4 sléndro and pélog. Except for minor differences, the notation of drumming from these two books is basically the same.

82. Information about this competition is drawn from Brandts Buys's article (1923: 1–17).

83. Note the collaboration between a Dutch author and a Javanese author here.

84. Unfortunately, I have not found examples of Wreksadiningrat's original notation. But it is commonly held that he is the inventor of today's Kepatihan notation system (Sindusawarno 1960:61–63; Warsadiningrat 1979:97–98). I do not know if he originally used spaces or bar lines to separate the basic metrical units (gatra) of gendhing.

85. There is no clear evidence of who actually used this book. Perhaps it was used by gamelan students in gamelan training at the museum Radyapustaka.

For another European approach to notating gamelan pieces, see Wirawiyaga's *Serat Lagu Jawi* (1935).

86. According to Dewantara, because of a lack of funds, the publication of volume 2 of Sari Swara, which would have contained the pélog system, was canceled.

87. This passage typifies the tone of Poerbatjaraka's criticism—throughout his essay he uses strong language, condemning Dewantara for having little knowledge of gamelan. Dewantara was very hurt by Poerbatjaraka's remarks. In a letter to the editor of *Poedjangga Baroe* he says Poerbatjaraka's essay "is not proper criticism at all, but merely an attack, using ridicule and insult that is uncalled for from the pen of a scholar, and also is inappropriate to appear in a journal of the level of 'P. B.'" (Dewantara 1941–48:2).

88. "Kesalahan besar, kata Dewantara, bahwa no. 4 didalam slendro dilompati oleh Kepatihan-schrijft, 'sedangkan sebenarnja tidak ada soeara jang dilompati.' Djikalau kita hanja mempoenjai slendro sadja, barangkali bisa betoel perkataan ini, akan tetapi kita djoega mempoenjai pelog; dan toea pelog dari pada slendro. Oleh karena itu pembitjaraan akan gamelan Djawa haroes didasarkan kepada pelog. Didalam pelog satoe octaaf ada 8 wilahan. No. 1 (bem) dan no. 7 (barang) disamakan (boekan sama) dengan no. 1 dan 1̇ slendro. Djadi bandingannja seperti dibawah ini.

pélog	1	2	3	4	5	6	7
slendro	1	2	3		5	6	1

Kalau dilihat dari djoeroesan pelog, njata sekali bahwa slendro itoe meliwati satoe wilah, wilah no 4, jang didalam slendro ta' ada bandingannja.

Dan lagi kalau nomoran slendro itoe ditoeroetkan Sari-swara 123451, lantas ada hal jang gandjil, lebih gandjil dari pengliwatan angka 4. Sebab no. 4 dan no. 5 didalam Sari-swara itoe namanja oemoem lima dan nem. Tentang hal ini Dewantara mengatakan di penghabisan fatsal 13: 'karena mentjampoerkan angka nomoran (rangnummer) dengan angka jang terpakai sebagai nama; ini melanggar sjarat wetenschap.' Dengan perkataan jang begitoe kami berani menjeboet, bahwa Dewantara disini main komedi dengan perkataan, sambil merendahkan wetenschap. Sebab nama lima dan nem itoe diberikannja kepada wilahan kedoea tadi djoega beralasan tempatnya (rangordenja) didalam deretan soeara pelog. Inilah wetenschappelijk tidak boleh dibantah lagi."

89. It is true that in his response to Dewantara, he speaks only in passing of his historical approach to gamelan. But in 1957 (in Becker and Feinstein 1987:261–84) he wrote a long article on the modal systems (pathet) in gamelan and the origin of pélog and sléndro. Agreeing with Kunst, he pointed out that pélog is older than sléndro; it was

brought to the kingdom of Sriwijaya by Mahayana Buddhists from Gandhara of India, via Nalanda and Sriwijaya and from there to Java and Bali. In Sriwijaya, sléndro was formed as an alteration of seven-tone pélog; and the word sléndro is related to *shailendra,* the name of a dynasty in the Sriwijaya kingdom. Furthermore, based on the change of pronunciation of the Javanese language, he offered a theory that the words gendèr, gendar, and gandhara are related. Thus, the word gendèr is derived from gandhara; and the instrument gendèr or the tuning of gendèr originated in Gandhara.

90. See Anderson (1990:213–14).

91. "Wirama punika ingkang adjeg tjatjahipun, manawi rikat rindikipun mawi ulat-ulatan, manawi tanpa ulat-ulatan, ladjeng pedjah, kemba, boten gadah grengseng utawi greget, kula ngaturaken tulada, upami gending Gambirsawit, manawi ing Ngajogja, kendangan: Tjandra. Punika ketuk kalih kerep, kenong 3 (4 gong). Ing dalem sakenongan 16 tutukan. Punika selehing wirama manawi sampun kenong kalih = 32 tutukan. Wiwitipun wirama seseg, sangsaja tamban adjeg 3 gongan. Ladjeng anggremet seseg ater-ater bade minggah, dawahing gong wirama sampun dados (wirama 2 punapa 3 tjiblon), bade suwuk inggih mawi sesegan, ladjeng tamban. Tulada idjeman sakedik makaten:"

92. Knowing Poerbatjaraka and his brothers (Kodrat and Wiradat) personally, Anderson says that Poerbatjaraka knew how to play gamelan, but was not an expert in gamelan performance. On the other hand, his brothers could play gamelan quite well. At any rate, none of their writings on gamelan reflect the intricacy of gamelan practice. This is because Poerbatjaraka tended to focus his treatment of gamelan on the historical aspects of the music, while Kodrat wrote introductory descriptions of gamelan (see below).

93. The "staff" was a division of the school whose members were mostly musicians who served in the Surakarta Kasunanan. Besides serving as resources for research, the staff presented performances for both the public and the students of KOKAR. Some staff members were also teachers. The staff still existed when I was a student at KOKAR in the early 1960s. Perhaps because of a lack of funds, the staff section was discontinued sometime in the late 1960s.

94. I would like to thank Pak Minarno, a gamelan teacher at the Indonesian Embassy in Washington DC. in 1972–1976 and 1985–1990, for sharing information about Sindusawarno's career in the gamelan conservatory. Pak Minarno has been a faculty member of the gamelan conservatory since 1957 and is familiar with Sindusawarno's work at the school.

95. Although the emphasis is on the teaching of the theory and practice of Central Javanese music (especially Solonese style), Sundanese and Balinese music are also parts of the curriculum.

96. In fact, Sindusawarno knew Mantle Hood very well. Hood researched gamelan in Java in 1957–58. He states that Sindusawarno was the prominent theorist of the time, and that he was trained in Western music theory and was fluent in English (1988:14).

97. This kind of diagram can also be found in Kunst's discussion of pathet (Kunst 1973, 1:83–84).

98. See also the biography of Martopangrawit by Sri Hastanto in J. Becker 1988: 431–33.

99. My thanks to Pak Minarno for confirming this point (pers. comm., 1988).

100. When Martopangrawit began to write about theory at ASKI, I was appointed

his assistant. Our discussions resulted in the writing of his theory of pathet as it is viewed from the perspective of gendèr playing. He originally presented his notion of the importance of gembyang and kempyung in gendèr playing as a way of identifying pathet in a paper he gave at the first ASKI graduation in 1967.

101. Inspired by Martopangrawit's theory of pathet in sléndro, particularly with regard to the shifting of intervallic patterns according to the changing of pathet, Martin Hatch offers an elaborate theory of the same subject (see Hatch 1980:130–58).

102. Kunst also studied music from other Indonesian islands: Bali, Nias, Flores, Kei, and Western New Guinea (Irian Jaya). Kunst was not only an expert on Indonesian music but also one of the founders of the field of ethnomusicology. In fact, Kunst is commonly held to have coined the term ethnomusicology, which replaced the earlier term comparative musicology.

103. Gong, kenong, kempul, and kethuk-kempyang.

104. The two-string bowed lute (rebab), a flute (suling), and a female solo singer (pesindhèn).

105. Bonang, whose melodies, according to Kunst, follow "fairly closely to the nuclear theme." The other instruments in this category, which are "responsible for the actual filling in and ornamentation" of the balungan, are gendèr, gambang, and celempung.

106. The set of drums (kendhang).

107. The application of European musical terms to Javanese gamelan was initiated by Dutch intellectuals in the late nineteenth century. Dr. J. P. N. Land uses the terms "theme," "paraphrase," "punctuate," and "figuration," among others (1890:17).

108. The comparability of the working processes of Javanese music and Gregorian chant is confirmed by Jaap Kunst's student, Mantle Hood (1958:18), later the major exponent of gamelan study in the United States: "In the 12th and 13th century [in Europe] three voices were used, and rhythm is no longer free in following the words but has a definite meter. This style has been called 'stratification', i.e., the melodies were combined in layers. The lowest voice sings a melody in which the tones are far apart, like the melody played by the gender panembung. The next higher voice has a melody with more notes, similar to the left-hand part of the gender barung. The highest voice is the most active and might be compared to the right-hand part of the gender. *Organum* of the late 12th century was this type."

109. Heins, a student of Kunst, says (1976:100) that Kunst was not able to communicate with musicians because "the mutual social barriers . . . were insurmountable, no Dutchman or other foreigner would or could dream of entering the tightly-closed unit of a gamelan-group in those days."

110. Jayadipura was a second-prize winner of the competition for monographs on gamelan sponsored by the Java Instituut (see above). Kunst (p. 161) also mentions that in 1907 Jayadipura was responsible for making a court gamelan with a complete set of kenong—a kenong for each tone in sléndro and pélog. This gamelan was made for the crown prince of the Yogyanese Kasultanan.

111. Defending her use of saron melodies for pathet analysis, Judith Becker (1980:240) objects to the term "nuclear theme" for the saron part: "Sometimes the saron is prominent and dominating, other times it is in the background. Some instruments sometimes focus their melodic patterns to coincide with the saron part, others never do. The

division of the gamelan into three parts, 'nuclear theme,' 'colotomic,' and 'elaborating' parts is a theory invented by Kunst (never used by Javanese), which helped him and many since to organize mentally and listen to gamelan music. In the sense that it is a limiting way of listening to gamelan, placing undue emphasis on the saron part, which may or may not be prominent in a given gendhing, and especially since the tri-part division of the gamelan instruments is foreign to the native sensibilities of the Javanese, the "nuclear theme," "colotomic," and "elaborating part" theory should be viewed as a tool, not as a dogma, to be discarded when the listener can comprehend the melodic importance of all three parts of the gamelan."

In her recent study, Lindsay (1985:196) voices a similar objection to the above tri-partite division of the gamelan instruments: "I myself have used this simplified concept to explain the composition of gamelan music to non-Javanese non-gamelan-musicians hearing gamelan for the first time. Lindsay 1980. This type of simplification remains useful as an initial concept, but is obviously further questioned, qualified and even discarded in the endless process of learning Javanese gamelan music."

112. In my "Inner Melody in Javanese Gamelan" (1976, 1984), I suggest that there is an implicit melody which each musician shares and which he uses as the basis for working out his part. I also draw a contrast between the one-octave melody of the saron and the balungan. Balungan is an abstraction of a gendhing melody whose range can be as wide as two and one-half octaves. Thus, since no instrument entrusted to play balungan has this wide a range, balungan is only in the mind of the musicians. On the other hand, the saron does play the balungan, but only within its one-octave range.

113. "Manawa arep sinau nabuh sarta apal kabèh marang babalunganing gendhing, kudu anyumurupi dhisik marang wujud sarta parincèning gamelan kang kena ginawé sinau, kayata: slenthem, demung, saron barung sapanunggalané."

114. "Yèn wis bisa anitèni marang wujuding wilahan lan suwara utawa siji-sijining larasé, kena wiwit sinau nabuh. Nanging sarèhning nembé murih gampangé kudu nganggo enut."

115. "Ugering andemung utawi anylenthem. Ugeripun tiyang andemung utawi anylenthem kedah apsah dhateng balunganing gendhing, awawaton paugering gendhing (enut), awit punika dados bakuning gendhing, (saéngga awak-awakaning gendhing)."

116. "Para maos supados saged nyumerepi cèngkoking gendhing, saha murih gampil anggènipun sinau, kula damel ancer-ancering gendhing sarana angka, inggih punika ingkang kawastanan baku swara, amung anerangaken gendhing sawatawis ingkang acakan kémawon. Supados gampil tumrap dhateng ingkang saweg sinau, inggih punika baku swara tabuhan demung."

117. Currently retired from teaching at the California Institute of the Arts in Valencia, California, R. T. Wasitodipura was a gamelan director in the court of Paku Alam of Yogyakarta. In the 1930s and 1940s, he studied the Solonese gamelan style under the guidance of M. Ng. Atmamardawa.

118. "Het stuk opent met een phrase van acht noten, die met weglating der eerste noot herhald, en met een phrase van dezelfde lengte beantwoord wordt. Deze inleiding wordt voorgedragen door den middelsten bonang, door gender en gambang in octave versterkt; op de slotnoot valt, naast een versterking in den bas, de eerste gong-slag. Hetzelfde thema wordt nu door al de instrumenten streng rhythmisch, met figuratie in de

hoogere instrumenten en uitlatingen in den bas-bonang, overgenomen, en door ketoek, kempoel, kenong, en gong geinterpungeerd; driemaal verneemt men de eerste helf, en eens de tweede; in het geheel bestaat dus de eerste afdeeling uit 4 × 8 themanoten. Zij wordt herhaald, en zoo komen wij tot den derden gong-slag. De tweede afdeeling heeft in de saron-party hetzelfde thema, doch met rhythmische afwijking, terwijl de middelste bonang het figureert en de bas-bonang insgelijks zijne begeleiding wijzigt."

119. Jennifer Lindsay (1985:194–95) clearly describes the use of the terms "theme" and "cantus firmus" in this period: "In 1919 a Javanese gamelan musician from the Paku Alaman, Soorja Poetra [1919–20:381], who was living and writing in Holland, used the term 'cantus firmus' to refer to that which Groneman called the 'theme,' namely that part of a gamelan composition which he thought remained firm and was the basis for the parts played on the other instruments. This is the part now known as the balungan (literally 'skeleton'). The word 'balungan' is now used, as Groneman and Land used the word 'theme' and Soorja Poetra and other writers used the term 'cantus firmus,' to refer to the part played on the saron (and frequently also on the slenthem and demung), the part that still forms the notation of gendhing." However, she fails to mention that by the early part of this century the word balungan was also already used by a few Javanese writers. She also suggests that "the saron line was not chosen to be notated because it was [not] inherently or exclusively the balungan of a gendhing, but rather the word 'balungan' came to be applied to the saron part to refer to its role as the notated gendhing outline" (p. 195).

As I mentioned earlier, Soorja Poetra is a grandson of Paku Alam V. Although he may know how to play gamelan, it is not clear to me whether he is a gamelan musician. There is also no evidence to show whether he received formal training in musicology in Holland. Initially, he came to Holland to study engineering.

120. *Serat Titi Asri.* Mijil

> Prayitnaning ing gendhing netesi
> apan kukuh bakoh
> dadya uger-uger cecèngkoké
> titi saron amuwuhi sari
> kang dadya pangarsi
> miturut ing demung

> Tegesé demung pituduh titi
> ger-ugeré cèngkok
> kang binabar mengku wiwileté
> tuturuté sadaya pan nami
> ingkang tabuh siji
> gendhingé ambalung

121. "Kanggé mudjudaken satunggal-tunggaling lagu gendhing utawi sekar ingkang sarwa pepak, sarta kangge pirantos anggampilaken pasinaonipun titilagu wau, prelu dipun wontenaken titilagu utawi titigendhing, wewatonipun:

a. Kedah anggatrakaken balunganning wirama lan lagunipun: dados awujud titilaras tuwin titiwirama, ingkang namung anggambar pokokipun."

On 26 March 1936, Dewantara presented this speech during a *Musyawaratan ing pare-patanipun para ahli-gendhing djawi* [Discussion at a conference of gendhing experts] which was held in the hall of the Sasanabudhaya in Yogyakarta. Mas Ngabèhi Najawirangka, a representative of the museum Radyapustaka, was the respondent to Dewantara's lecture. His comments and his corrections of many of Dewantara's points (1957:64–89) indicate his musical insight, since he was a dhalang and also a musician. He also uses the term balung in referring to the melodies played by slenthem, demung, and [saron] barung (p. 76).

122. I am indebted to Marc Perlman for pointing this out to me.

123. "Titilaras = Noot, ingkang kangge ngangkani raras balunganing gendhing wau sampun umum, sarta gampil katindakaken tumrap sadaya thuthukan gongsa, tuwin lagoning sekar (tembang), tur panatanipun luwes boten karowan, tambah katerangaken princèn panjang celaking swara mawi tata wirama (maatstrip) ukuran panjang celaking swara."

124. See J. Becker (1980:14) for her perceptive statements about this. However, she does not provide an account of the history of the term balungan. She seems to imply that the term balungan is only a recent phenomenon, a term familiar "only to those who have had contact directly or indirectly with the music conservatory in Surakarta, [and] the Akademi Seni Karawitan Indonesia." It is true that the term balungan is commonly used only in Surakarta. Formerly, Yogyanese musicians referred to the bonang panembung part as balungan.

For a consideration of the introduction of notation for gamelan as a consequence of Western influence, see Becker (1980:10–23). There she points out that notation was introduced as a result of Dutch intellectuals' concern to save gendhing from extinction. Lindsay (1985:210–11), on the other hand, suggests that "while the stimulus to notate may indeed have come from the Dutch, the impulse to save or preserve at this time" was particularly Javanese. In either case, it was partly the result of the intellectual climate of the time and the beginnings of the development of a new technology, namely, printing.

125. With regard to notation, Seebass (1987) says that a sort of skeletal notation was already known in Java, perhaps during the Majapahit era (14th–15th c.). The extent of such notation can be found and traced in its development in Bali. The notation was very much associated with vocal repertoire—a guide for the priest in reciting kidung poetry. Some scholars suggest that the notation was also used as a guide for the instrumentalists of the gambang ensemble when they accompanied kidung (Wallis 1980:208–9; McPhee 1966:280). It is also thought that subsequently the gambang pieces stopped being used as the accompaniment for kidung. Because of the loss of this practice in contemporary Balinese gamelan and the lack of evidence, scholars have not come to a definite conclusion about notation in Bali. The fact that the term balungan or its equivalent disappeared in Java (to appear again in a different form in the early years of this century), but still existed in Bali, is a subject that needs to be studied.

126. However, in another section of the same work, relying on contemporary evidence, he indicates that in composing a gendhing, the composer conceived balungan first (Sutton 1993:25).

127. "Sedangkan untuk para pengrawit dan para penyusun gending (komponis) menganggap bahwa gending telah ada lebih dahulu pada dirinya. Pada waktu mereka menyajikan ricikannya ataupun didalam menyusun sebuah karya, sebenarnya didalam sanubarinya telah terjadi semacam "klenengan" yaitu suatu penyajian karawitan karawitan lengkap dengan segala suara garapan ricikan (dan vokal) yang terlibat didalam garapan komposisi tersebut."

As an example of a similar attitude, Sri Hastanto states (1985:39): "When a Javanese musician imagines a gendhing, he has the music of the entire gamelan in his mind. However, when he is asked to write it down he does not write all the details he knows but only an outline of the melody on which it is based. This melodic outline is generally known as the balungan (lit., 'skeleton,' 'frame') or balungan gendhing."

128. Balungan mlaku, balungan nibani, and balungan ngadhal are the rhythmic variants of balungan melody. Balungan mlaku generally consists of a melody which has one note per pulse. Balungan nibani consists of alternation between rests and notes (e.g., · 2 · 1 · 6̣ · 5̣). Balungan ngadhal (usually appearing as part of a gendhing in balungan mlaku) is a type of balungan melody in which each pulse contains two or more notes. There are still other kinds of balungan variations (see Martopangrawit 1984, vol. 1).

129. "II–Balungan of babalungan . . . , het voornaamste houtwork *bij het bouwen;* gespierdheid *van een leeuw;* . . . *ook* schets, hoofdtrekken, hoofdinhoud *van een work;* in hoofd-*of* grondstrekken. Pakem."

130. "1. Ugering kendhangan. Tiyang ngendhang punika kedah sumerep dhateng wirama, awit wirama kendhang punika dados tatalining wiramanipun sadaya tatabuhaning gongsa (saéngga napasing gendhing), panyigeg utawi panyuwukipun gendhing kedah ingkang leres. . . .
2. Ugering andemung utawi anylenthem. Ugeripun tiyang andemung utawi anylenthem kedah apsah dhateng balunganing gendhing, awawaton paugering gendhing (enut), awit punika dados bakuning gendhing, (saéngga awak-awakaning gendhing). Wiramanipun kedah anut kendhang.
3. Ugeripun angrebab. Tiyang ngrebab punika kedah pratitis dhateng saulah laguning gendhing, awit punika dados tuturutaning sesindhèn tuwin gendhing, (saéngga raosing gendhing), . . .
4. Ugeripun angethuk ngenong, ngempul ngemong, ngempyang, tuwin ngegong, . . . sadaya wau sami dados wiwicalan sarta tetenger béda-bédaning gendhing, (saéngga wateking gendhing), pramila kedah awas dhateng wiramaning kendhang.
5. Ugeripun anggendèr, menerus, anggambang, nylempung, nyaron, nyuling, ambonang, tuwin ambonang penerus. Sarèhning warna wolu wau dédé bakuning gendhing dados amung rerengganing gendhing, (saéngga sandhanganing gendhing, ukeling tabuhan utawi lagunipun kénging sasenengipun uger boten éwah saking punapa dhongipun demung utawi slenthem. Amung semu lirih ing panabuh kedah racak kaliyan panunggilanipun."

131. For a classification of instruments by another Javanese theorist, see Najawirangka (1957:74–78). He employs terms that are related more to musical practice. He categorizes kendhang and keprak as the creators of rhythm (*yasa wirama*); rebab is the connector of the sounds (*panggandhènging swara*). Bonang guides (*damel margi*) the balungan. Bonang panerus doubles the bonang. Gendèr and gambang fill in with ornamentation (*ngisèni kembangan*). Gendèr panerus doubles the gendèr, similar to celempung. Suling answers the ornamentation (*nyauri kembangan*). Slenthem and demung play the bones (balung), and [saron] barung doubles the bones. Saron panerus is the chopper (*panacah*) of balung. Kethuk, kempyang, engkuk kemong, and ketipung stabilize or create wirama. Kenong marks a phrase (*salampah*). Kempul plays in between (*nyelani*) the kenong. Gong is the marker of a section (*pada, sacèngkok*).

132. "Lagu punika kiyai, dumunung wonten ing sekar, cèngkok dumunung in gendhing."

133. For example, "wus antara dangunira / gya nesek iramanèki / Kinandhelongaken suwuk" (After a while, the irama accelerates; then it slows down for the ending).

134. His original words are: "déné ngirama punika / purba saking kiramanggèn / pikajengipun angira / ajegé lelongkangan / utawi antaranipun" (the irama derives from kiramanggèn [the settling of approximation]).

135. He lists the following wirama (p. 335): Wirama kencheng, seseg, tanggung or dadi, antal or kendo or rangkep, toyamili, sedeng, tembang, telu and chekapan. He also says that at that time the identification of irama with numbers (1, 1 1/2, 2, 3, and 4) was gradually gaining ground. Although most of the terms signify the passage of time, labeling irama numerically may have another purpose.

136. For a perceptive cross-cultural treatment of "rhythm," see Powers' entry on "Rhythm" in 1986:700–5.

137. Jaap Kunst (1973, 1:127–28) includes this sindhènan category in his book, but no credit is given to *Serat Pakem Wirama*. He also adjusts the explanation for each category according to his theory of gendhing.

138. "1. Lampah gendhing: Punika gendhing lajeng dipun sindhèni, kadosta: gendhing Mégamendhung, lajeng dipun sindhèni, dados poenika ingkang gadhah baku gendhingipun, sisindhènipun ingkang nunut.
   2. Lampah sekar gendhing; Poenika sekar lajeng dipun gangsani, (dipun sarengi gongsa), ladrangan, ketawangan, sarta srepegan sapiturutipun kadosta: sekar Kinanthi lajeng dipun sarengi gongsa ladrangan ketawangan sasaminipun, dados punika ingkang gadhah baku sekaripun, gangsanipun ingkang nunut, nanging thuthukanipun gongsa dipun cara gendhing, gongsa mungel sadaya.
   3. Lampah sekar: Punika sekar ugi dipun sarengi gongsa, ladrang, ketawang, srepegan sapiturutipun, kadosta: sekar Durma lajeng dipun sarengi gongsa ladrang ketawang sasaminipun, dados punika ingkang gadhah baku sekaripun, namung béda katimbang sekar-gendhing; inggih punika yèn lampah sekar punika gangsanipun namung 1 Gambang, 2 Gendèr, 3 Kendhangketipung, 4 Kethuk, 5 Kenong, 6 Gong, 7 Kemanak.
   4. Lampah lagon-lasem; Punika ugi sekar dipun sarengi gangsa, punika ingkang gadhah baku inggih lagunipun, nanging ugi wonten bédanipun katimbang lampah sekar; inggih punika yèn lampah lagon punika gangsanipun namung 1 Rebab, 2 Gambang, 3 Gendèr."

139. He divides instruments into six groups: balungan (skeleton), rerenggan (ornamentation), wiletan, *singgetan* (sectional marker), *kembang* (flower or ornament), and *jejeging wirama* (stabilizer of wirama). Instruments that are the carriers of balunganing gendhing are slenthem, demung, and saron. Rerengganing gendhing is the responsibility of gendèr, gambang, bonang, and clempung. Singgetaning gendhing are played by kempyang, kethuk, kempul and kenong. Kembanging gendhing is the role of suling and sindhèn. The instrument that stabilizes wirama is kendhang. It is evident from this explanation that Poerbapangrawit misses one category, namely, wiletan. Perhaps rebab is meant to be in this category, since it is not mentioned in the other categories.

140. In his section "Banjuré bab gendhing" (More about gendhing) he provides fur-

ther explanation and examples of repertoire in each genre of gendhing. He subdivides each of the headings—gendhing lésan, gendhing thuthuk, and gendhing gamelan lan lésan—into three sub-genres: *gendhing cilik* (small), *gendhing sedhengan* (medium), and *gendhing gedhé* (large). The examples of gendhing in gendhing thuthuk and gendhing gamelan lan lésan are the same gendhing for both categories: Puspa Warna, Sri Katon, Gambir Sawit, and Bondhèt.

141. We should include *Serat Centhini,* although it was written in the early part of the nineteenth century.

142. The perspectives of Javanese musicians were long neglected. Many past studies, including several that are discussed in this book, present the elite aspects of gamelan discourse. However, several recent studies correct this one-sided view. Engaging in discussions with Javanese musicians is essential to the study of gamelan performance practice.

Chapter Four

1. At the 1990 annual meeting of the Society for Ethnomusicology in Oakland, California, I presented a paper based on the notions discussed here. I would like to thank Anderson Sutton and Harry Powers, among others, for their invaluable comments on the paper, which I considered in writing the present section.

2. Subsequently, based on her conviction of the importance of gatra, Judith Becker in collaboration with Alton Becker (1979) wrote an elaborate study of a genre of gendhing called srepegan. Becker persisted in her claim: "As basic in gamelan music in defining paradigms of notes as is tonality in the West is the concept of shape or contour, *above, below, same.* Four-note melodic contours and their paradigmatic and syntagmatic relationships are prime definers of the coherence system of Javanese gamelan music" (Becker and Becker 1979:7–8); but later the authors reconsidered their srepegan article (Becker and Becker 1983). Recently, Hughes (1988) launched a similar study. For comments on Becker and Becker's study, see Perlman (1983). See also Susilo (1989).

3. Sutton extends his discussion to the process of variation of the balungan, which he attributes to different performance contexts (1993:69–75). He also discusses the variational differences in the balungan between the Solonese and Yogyanese versions of the same gendhing (pp. 75–87). On the premise that melodic parts in the gamelan are variations of one another, he then discusses at length the nature of such variations in the loud and soft ensembles, in the practice of irama, and in individual performance (pp. 88–195).

4. But see Hoffman (1975) for a discussion of the complexity of gamelan practice; he explains it in terms of multiple epistemologies. Vocal melodies are a part of this epistemological complex. He talks about the creation of gendhing in terms of the coincidence between cyclical (instrumentally-derived) and linear (vocally-based) musical movements. His work has much value for gamelan theory, although his musical illustrations are few. However, gamelan theorists after him rarely refer to his work. Consequently, the emphasis on gatra in the generation of gamelan gendhing persists. For another initial discussion of vocal melody as the basis for composing gendhing, see Wallis (1973).

5. *Serat Tjentini* 7–8. 277e. Pucung.

> 7. Purwanipun wonten gamelan puniku
> sakèng widayaka
> anawung rawiting gendhing
> tegesipun widayaka wong anembang

8. Tembang lagu tembung peparikanipun
rarasing gamelan
tegesing gamel nyekeli
gendhing muni tinabuh kelawan tangan
9. Dadya dhaup gendhèng lawan gendhingipun
asmaraning raras
sakèng swara kang murwani
niku saweg dhi ragil kératanira

6. *Serat Centhini* gives another perspective on the meaning of the word gamelan. As noted in the second stanza above, gamelan does not mean "percussive ensemble," as we commonly understand this word, instead, the word *gamel* means "to handle"—that is, to handle, render, or present gendhing through the hand of the musician. The poets perceive the word gamelan not as an object, but as the process of an event.

7. *Serat Gulang Yarya*. V. Sinom.

7. Sigegen wijanging tembang
kang sinebut gendhèng gendhing
gendhing punika angkahnya
pangolahing swara titis
ingkang ginandhèng gendhing
tuwin tembang sekaring rum
gantya gendhing winahya
angkahira pangolah mrih
gita swara kang ginandhèng ing gamelan

8. His name at the time was Mas Ngabèhi Warsopradongga. His *Serat Sosorah Gamelan* (1920) was a lecture he presented at the meeting of a vocal music organization called Mardiguna. I would like to thank Walidi, a good friend of mine, a teacher at the Sekolah Menengah Karawitan Indonesia (SMKI) in Surakarta, who made available to me Warsadiningrat's writing on this subject. When I studied with Warsadiningrat at KOKAR and ASKI, he was already very old. Conducting classes in gamelan groups and private lessons, he rarely talked. Actually, he was a perceptive thinker. His *Wédha Pradongga* is a semi-historical book on gamelan.

In the 1920s, Warsadiningrat was appointed to the Komisi Pasinaon Nabuh Gamelan of the Museum Radyapustaka (see chapter 3). This committee published a book for gamelan instruction. But, in writing down the balungan, the committee used the Western solfège notation system. Perhaps Djatiswara, a member of the Komisi and the European music director of the court of Surakarta, dominated the work of the committee. Perhaps Warsadiningrat was never a forthcoming person. In fact, he very reluctantly gave permission for his *Wédha Pradongga* to be published.

9. "Wiwitipun wonten gendhing punika, kinten-kinten inggih saking pambabaripun lagunning sekar. Sekar wau lami-lami saya mindhak-mindhak cacahing sekar, saha mindhak warni-warni lagunipun. Lagunning sekar-sekar ingkang sampun kababar wau, lajeng dipun tata kalayan saé. Dangu-dangu dipun tata mawi wirama. Sareng sampun dados lalaluning sekar ingkang sampun katata runtut lajeng winastan gendhing. Inggih punika mula bukanipun wonten gendhing jalaran saking lelaguning sekar."

10. "Sareng sampun wonten gendhing bawaswara wau, dangu-dangu lajeng tuwuh

pamanggihipun angawontenaken gamelan, minongka dados wawadhahing raras. Sareng sampun wonten gamelan, laguning sekar-sekar wau lajeng tinut ing gamelan sarta kabe-sut tinata runtut ngantos boten katawis tabeting sekar, temahan lajeng dados gendhing gamelan, . . ."

11. Warsadiningrat also explains that some of the melodies of sekar were used as the source for the melodies of pathet, sendhon, and *ada-ada*. (For a description of these types of compositions, see Brinner 1990:1–34.) He also says that the melodies of pathet were recomposed, given wirama, and accompanied by gamelan, thus becoming ayak-ayakan. When ayak-ayakan is played faster, it becomes srepegan. When srepegan is played faster, it becomes sampak. I suggest the same in my early work (Sumarsam 1984:279), using as an example Srepegan sléndro manyura. But Susilo (1989) suggests a different interpreta-tion. He shows Sampak and Srepegan as two pieces that are derived from ada-ada, songs used by dhalang to create a tense mood (*sereng*).

12. In fact, the phrasing of the Mas Kumambang also indicates that line IIa alone is an incomplete phrase that should be completed by line IIb. In other words, lines IIa and IIb are a single phrase.

13. Marc Benamou (1989) points out that melodic restatement, which he identifies with the Javanese term gantungan or "hanging," is commonly found in gendhing. He identifies two types of "hanging": "*endogenous* hanging (that is, hanging which is gener-ated within a rhythmic group)" and "exogenous hanging (which grows out of a note that belongs to a different rhythmic group)" (p. 36). The melodic restatement mentioned above falls in the first kind of hanging. It moves the melody immediately away from an important tone and returns to it later on.

14. I thank Mas Darsono (pers. comm., 1990), a vocal teacher of Sekolah Tinggi Seni Indonesia (STSI, the Indonesian Institute of Art) of Surakarta, who pointed out to me the derivation of gendhing Lobong from sekar macapat Kinanthi Sastradiwangsa.

15. For more examples of macapat-based gendhing, see Darsono (1980).

16. Nowadays the word Pawukir is more common than Pangukir. According to Pak Martopangrawit (M. Hatch, pers. comm.; see also Hatch 1976:63), the word Pawukir is a corruption of Pangukir. This happened when Pangukir was sung in association with the "woman of the mountains" in a love dance called Gathutkaca Gandrung (Gathutkaca is in love). Pangukir means "woodcarver." The name of the piece reflects its association with a singer whose profession was woodcarving, who was perhaps the first to sing this melody of Kinanthi.

17. Other lighter genres of gendhing can be added to this list, such as *gendhing dolanan*, palaran, and jineman.

18. In contemporary practice, ladrang "Pangkur" is commonly played in pélog barang with gérongan using the "Kinanthi" text. According to Warsadiningrat (1987:155), Paku Buwana X ordered the transfer of ladrang Pangkur from sléndro sanga to pélog barang and the addition of the gérongan. Paku Buwana also ordered the creation of the ngelik part of ladrang Pangkur. Adopted from the ngelik of ladrang Kasmaran, this new part was then played in irama rangkep (ibid.).

19. I would like to thank Pak Martopangrawit (pers. comm., 1968), who told me about the connection of these two gendhing. He recounted an incident he witnessed at a concert of the RRI (Radio Republik Indonesia) gamelan. Sometime after Indonesian

independence, ayak-ayakan Pamungkas became a standard closing piece of the RRI klenèngan. Once, when the RRI gamelan group played the piece, the composer of Pamungkas was among the musicians. Coming to the second half of the piece, the gambang player (who apparently detected the melodic basis for the second half of ayak-ayakan Pamungkas) played the melody of gendhing dolanan Witing Klapa, while the other musicians played Pamungkas. The composer was offended.

20. A weekly newspaper of Surakarta, *Darmo Kondha* (1929, quoted in Perlman 1991: 43), reports that when the Siamese king entered the Srimanganti hall of the court, the court string ensemble played the Siamese national anthem. Perhaps this national anthem was the Western-style Siamese royal anthem mentioned above.

21. I heard this piece played by a Siamese army marching band on a Playasound recording (PS 33512). The transcription is based on this recording. I thank Maria Mendonça and Neil Sorell for their help in transcribing this piece.

22. Earlier I mentioned that the melodic precedent of the ngelik section of Suba Kastawa is sekar macapat Sastradiwangsa, the same sekar macapat that was used as the basis for creating gendhing Lobong.

23. I must admit that the following discussion of instrumentally-based gendhing melodies is based on my personal observation. I have not yet had time to check with other gamelan musicians.

24. For detailed discussion of gendhing bonang, see McNamara (1980). The following discussion, unless indicated otherwise, is drawn from McNamara (1980:63–157).

25. There are a few gendhing rebab that are played in this way. For example, gendhing Rebeng and Bondhan Kinanthi (both are in pélog nem).

26. For further discussion of this bonang-playing technique, see Sumarsam (1984: 285–87).

27. For example, in · 1 · 2   3 5 6 5 of gendhing bonang Pari Gentang, pélog barang, Soekanto considers 3 5 as sustaining note 5 of the rebab melody; thus on the bonang he renders this passage as "hanging" in the octave-playing of 5, instead of using the pipilan pairing.

Balungan				·	·	1	2		3	5	6	5
Imagined rebab		·	1	1	2	3̄5̄ ·		·	5	5̄6̄5̄3̄5̄6̄ ·		5
Bonang	1̲ · · 1̲ · · 1̲ · 1 2 1 · · 2 1 ·			3 5 · · 5 · · · 5 6 3 · 5 6 · 5								

(based on McNamara 1980:131).

28. See chapter 2. I pointed out that, for sociopolitical reasons, it was necessary for the courtiers to produce loud, empowering musical sound. To fulfill this need, a copy of gamelan Sekatèn was built, but the instruments were larger and heavier. In addition, the court of Surakarta and Mangkunegaran also made sets of ordinary gamelan, but, like gamelan Sekatèn the instruments were larger and heavier. There were twice as many saron as in the usual gamelan. Also as in gamelan Sekatèn, the tunings of these extra-large gamelans are low.

29. Below I discuss the usefulness and limitation of gatra as a pedagogical tool in gamelan, especially as they are rendered in the cèngkok patterns of the gendèr.

30. I am indebted to Harold Powers for pointing this out to me.

31. "Schiets, ontwerp, iets dat nog maar in een onvolkomene gedaante is en zich nog eerst ontwikkelen moet, onontwikkeld lichaamsdeel."

32. See chapter 3, figure 3.2.

33. My thanks to Philip Yampolsky for pointing out this to me.

34. I put the qualifier "elaborative" in quotation marks in order to prevent misunderstanding. It has long been assumed that "elaborative instruments" means instruments that elaborate balungan. I believe such a premise misinterprets gamelan practice. My use of "elaborative" here simply means any instrument that plays elaborate melody in its own right.

35. The word *cangkok* is not a misprint for *cèngkok*. In fact, Tondhakusuma used these two words interchangeably. This means that, as Gericke and Roorda indicate, these two words are interrelated.

36. *Serat Gulang Yarya.* V. Sinom.

> 9. Déné kang kanggé babasan
> wilet wilelet nguleti
> punika pikajengira
> linangkung sumela saking
> ing cèngkok lan laguning
> utawi linangkung langkung
> anglelet let–uletan
> ngubedi cèngkok luguning
> dados wilet wau tan saged ngalahna
> 10. Dhateng cangkok lugunira
> ananging saged nyamari
> myang saged damel prabéda
> ing pangrasa rasaning writ
> yektiné kados ta mrih
> mungel gendhing Sekar Gadhung
> kang lulus cèngkokira
> aliyan ingkang pinardi
> miletaken punika pangraos béda
> 11. Makaten ugi timbangnya
> lamun sekar Dhandhang Gula
> inggih ing pundi–pundiya
> laguné saèstu sami
> sanèsa mung sakedhik
> wangsul sareng kasiram rum
> ing wilet let–uletan
> dados sanès–sanès kyai
> ingkang awit ing dalem sacepurinya

37. For a stimulating discussion of gendhing theories, I would like to refer readers to a recent dissertation by Marc Perlman (1993). He focuses on the development of a contemporary concept of implicit melody in Javanese gamelan. But he also provides his readers with an expansive study of the development of gendhing theories from the past century to the present.

Conclusion

1. For further discussion of "men of prowess," "soul stuff," and *bhakti* in Southeast Asia, see Wolters 1982:6–15, 101–4.

2. The Chinese, especially Chinese peranakan, had intimate relationships with Javanese aristocrats, especially as financial backers. And the love of the Chinese for the Javanese arts led them to become important patrons of gamelan, wayang, and Javanese dance.

References

The Surakarta Manuscript Project (SMP), sponsored by Cornell University, preserves on microfilm copies of manuscripts located at the courts of Surakarta. References to these documents are by location, reel, and item number. KS = Kasunanan; MN = Mangkunegaran. Both are courts in Surakarta.

al-Faruqi, Lois Ibsen. 1985. "Music, Musicians and Muslim Law." *Asian Music* 17:3–36.

Alisjahbana, Takdir. 1954. "Menudju Masjarakat dan Kebudajaan Baru" [Toward new society and culture]. In *Polemik Kebudajaan,* ed. Achdiat K. Mihardja. Djakarta: Perpustakaan Perguruan Kementerian P. P. dan K.

Anderson, Benedict. 1972. "The Idea of Power in Javanese Culture." In Anderson 1990a:17–77.

———. n.d. "The Last Picture Show: Wayang Beber." In *Conference Proceeding of the Conference on Modern Indonesian Literature, Madison, Wisconsin, 28–29 June 1974,* pp. 33–81. Madison: Center for Southeast Asian Studies.

———. 1979. "A Time of Darkness and a Time of Light: Transposition in Early Indonesian Nationalist Thought." In *Perceptions of the Past in Southeast Asia,* ed. Anthony Reid and David Marr, pp. 219–48. Singapore: Heinemann.

———. 1984. "Sembah Sumpah (Courtesy and Curses): The Politics of Language and Javanese Culture." In Anderson 1990a:194–240.

———. 1990a. *Language and Power: Exploring Political Culture in Indonesia.* Ithaca: Cornell University Press.

———. 1990b. "Professional Dream: Reflections on Two Javanese Classics." In Anderson 1990a:271–98.

Appadurai, Arjun. 1991. "Global Ethnoscapes: Notes and Queries for a Transnational Anthropology." In *Recapturing Anthropology: Working in the Present,* ed. Richard G. Fox, pp. 191–210. Santa Fe, N.M.: School of American Research Press.

Atmadikara, R. 1865–66. *Babad Krama Dalem Ingkang Sinuhun Kangjeng Susuhunan Paku Buwana Kaping Sanga ing Nagari Surakarta Adiningrat* [The chronicle of the marriage of his highness Susuhunan Paku Buwana IX of Surakarta] (ms. SMP KS 104/4, inscribed Surakarta, mid–late nineteenth century).

Becker, Alton. 1979. "Text-Building, Epistemology, and Aesthetics in Javanese Shadow Theater." In *The Imagination of Reality: Essays in Southeast Asian Coherence System,* ed. A. L. Becker and A. A. Yengoyan, pp. 211–43. Norwood, N.J.: Ablex.

Becker, Alton, and Judith Becker. 1979. "A Grammar of the Musical Genre Srepegan." *Journal of Music Theory* 23:1–43. Reprinted in *Asian Music* 14 (1983):30–72.

———. 1983. "Reflection on 'Srepegan': A Reconsideration in the Form of a Dialogue." *Asian Music* 14:9–16.

Becker, Judith. 1980. *Traditional Music in Modern Java*. Honolulu: University Press of Hawaii.

———. 1993. *Gamelan Stories: Tantrism, Islam, and Aesthetics in Central Java*. Arizona State University: Program for Southeast Asian Studies.

Becker, Judith, and Alan Feinstein, eds. 1984, 1987, 1988. *Source Readings in Javanese Gamelan and Vocal Music,* 3 vols. Ann Arbor: The University of Michigan Center for South and Southeast Asian Studies.

Benamou, Marc. 1989. "Approaching and Hanging: Metrical and Melodic Organization in Javanese and Western Music." M.A. thesis, University of Michigan, Ann Arbor.

Boediardjo, Ali. 1941. "Volkskoncert P.P.R.K. Jang Pertama" [The first P.P.R.K. folk music concert]. *Poedjangga Baroe* 8/10:252–55.

Borel, Henri. 1916–17. "De Indische Kunstavond in Den Haagschen Schouwburg." *Nederlandsch Indie Oud en Nieuw* 1:119–25.

Boxer, C. R. 1965. *The Dutch Seaborne Empire 1600–1800*. New York: Knopf.

———. 1969. *The Portuguese Seaborne Empire 1415–1825*. London: Hutchinson.

Brandts Buys, J. S. 1924. "Uitslag van de Prijsvraag inzake een Javaansch muziekschrift." *Djawa* 4:1–17.

———. 1940. "Het Gewone Javaansche Tooncijferschrift (Het Salasch-Kepatihan-Schrift)." *Djawa* 20:87–106.

Brandts Buys-van Zijp, Anna. 1941. "De Eenheidmuziek." *Poedjangga Baroe* 9/5: 137–39.

Brown, Robert, and Nancy Pemberton. 1977. *Javanese Court Gamelan,* vol. 3 (liner notes). Nonesuch H72074.

Brinner, Benjamin. 1990. "At the Border of Sound and Silence: The Use and Function of Pathetan in Javanese Gamelan." *Asian Music* 21:1–34.

——— 1993. "A Musical Time Capsule from Java." *Journal of the American Musicological Society* 46:221–60.

Carey, Peter. 1984. "Changing Javanese Perceptions of the Chinese Communities in Central Java, 1755–1825." *Indonesia* 37:1–48.

Citrasantana, R. Ng. 1920s. *Serat Babad Dalem Kangjeng Gusti Pangran Adipati Arya Prabu Prangwadana kaping VII* [The chronicle of Pangran Adipati Arya Prabu Prangwadana VII] (ms. SMP MN 230; composed and inscribed Surakarta, 1920s.)

Crawfurd, John. 1820. *History of the Indian Archipelago,* vol. 1. Reprinted Delhi: B. R. Publishing Corp., 1985.

Cohn, Bernard S. 1983. "Cultural Contradictions in the Construction of A Ritual Idiom." In *The Invention of Tradition,* ed. Eric Hobsbawm and Terence Ranger, pp. 165–209. Cambridge: Cambridge University Press.

Dajoh, M. R. 1948. "Lagu Nasional: Krontjong atau Gamelan" [National music: kroncong or gamelan]. *Poedjangga Baroe* 10/1–2:26–29.

Dam-Mikkelsen, Bente, and Torben Lundbæk, eds. 1980. *Ethnographic Objects in the Royal Danish Kunstkammer 1650–1800*. Copenhagen: Nationalmuseet.

Darsono. 1980. "Gending-Gending Sekar" [Gendhing based on verse melodies]. B.A. thesis, Akademi Seni Karawitan Indonesia, Surakarta.

Day, Anthony. 1981. "Meanings of Change in the Poetry of Nineteenth-Century Java." Ph.D. dissertation, Cornell University.

———. 1983. "Islam and Literature in Southeast Asia: Some Pre-modern, Mainly Javanese Perspectives." In *Islam in South-East Asia,* ed. M. B. Hooker, pp. 130–59. Leiden: Brill.

———. 1986. "How Modern Was Modernity, How Traditional Tradition, in Nineteenth-Century Java?" *Review of Indonesian and Malaysian Affairs* 20:1–37.

DeVale, Sue Carole. 1977. "A Sundanese Gamelan: A Gestalt Approach to Organology." Ph.D. dissertation, Northwestern University.

Dewantara, Ki Hadjar. 1930. *Sari Swara* [The essence of sound]. Groningen-Den Haag-Weltevreden: J. B. Wolter.

———. 1931. *Beoefening van Letteren en Kunst in Let Pakoe-Alamsche Geslacht.* Djokja: Buning. English trans., Lindsay 1980:104–22.

———. 1936. *Wawaton Kawruh Gendhing Jawi* [Fundamental knowledge about Javanese gendhing]. Yogyakarta: Wasita. Transliterated as *Kawruh Gending Djawa* [Knowledge about Javanese gendhing]. Solo: Sadu Budi, 1957:41–63.

———. 1941. "Metode 'Sari-Swara' dan Bedanya dengan Kepatihanschrift" ['Sari-Swara' system and its difference from the Kepatihan notation]. *Poesara* 11/4 (April 1941). Reprinted, with a foreword " 'Sari-Swara' dan 'Kepatihan Schrift'," in *Poedjangga Baroe* (1941/48):2–8.

———. 1967. *Karja,* vol. 2a: *Kebudajaan.* Jogjakarta: Madjelis-Luhur Persatuan Taman Siswa.

Djajadiningrat-Nieuwenhuis, Madelon. 1993. "Noto Soeroto: His Ideas and the Late Colonial Intellectual Climate." *Indonesia* 55:41–72.

Djakoeb and Wignjaroemeksa. 1913. *Layang Anyumurupaké Pratikelé Bab Sinau Nabuh Sarta Panggawéné Gamelan* [Book about learning and making the gamelan]. Batavia: Drukkerij Eertijd H. M. van Dorp.

———. 1919. *Serat Enut Gendhing Sléndro* [The notation of sléndro gendhing]. Batavia: Drukkerij Eertijd H. M. van Dorp.

Dungga, J. A., and L. Manik. 1952. *Musik di Indonesia* [Music in Indonesia], vol. 1. Djakarta: Balai Pustaka, 1952.

Fagg, William. 1970. *The Raffles Gamelan: A Historical Note.* London: British Museum.

Florida, Nancy K. 1981. "Javanese Language Manuscripts of Surakarta, Central Java: A Descriptive Catalogue," 3 vols. Ithaca: John M. Echols Collection, Olin Library, Cornell University.

———. 1987. "Reading the Unread in Traditional Javanese Literature." *Indonesia* 44:1–16.

Furnivall, J. S. 1939. *Netherlands India: A Study of Plural Economy.* London: Cambridge University Press.

Geertz, Clifford. 1968. *Islam Observed: Religious Development in Morocco and Indonesia.* Chicago: University of Chicago Press.

———. 1973. *The Interpretation of Cultures.* New York: Basic Books.

Gericke, J. F. C., and T. Roorda. 1901. *Javaansch–Nederlandsch Handwoordenboek,* 2 vols., ed. A. C. Vreede. Amsterdam: Muller; Leiden: Brill.

Goens, Rijklof van. 1856. "Reijsbeschrijving van den weg uijt Samarang nae De Konincklijke Hoofdplaets Mataram Mitsgaders de Zeeden, Gewoonten ende Regeringe van den Sousouhounan Groot Machtichste Koningk van 't Eijlant Java." *Bijdragen tot de Taal-, Land-en Volkenkunde van Nederlandsch-Indie* 4:307–67. Original work, 1656.

Gondapangrawit, Ki. *Buk Gendhing Sléndro, Buk Gendhing Pélog* [The book of sléndro gendhing, the book of pélog gendhing] (ms. SMP MN 85/3; composed and inscribed Surakarta, late 19th century).

Groneman, J. 1890. *De Gamelan te Jogjakarta.* Amsterdam: Johannes Muller.

Gunawan Sri Hastjarjo. 1983–84. *Sekar Ageng,* 2 vols. Surakarta: ASKI.

Hadiwidjojo, K. G. P. H. 1981. *Bedhaya Ketawang* [The Bedhaya Ketawang dance]. Jakarta: PN Balai Pustaka. Original work, 1971.

Hall, D. G. E. 1981. *A History of South-East Asia,* 4th ed. New York: St. Martin's.

Hardjana, Suka, ed. 1986. *Enam Tahun Pekan Komponis Muda 1979–1985* [Six years of the festival of young composers 1979–1985]. Jakarta: Dewan Kesenian Djakarta.

Hastanto, Sri. 1985. "The Concept of Pathet in Central Javanese Gamelan Music." Ph.D. dissertation, University of Durham, England.

Hatch, Martin. 1976. "The Song is Ended: Changes in the Use of Macapat in Central Java." *Asian Music* 7:59–71.

———. 1979. "Theory and Notation in an Oral Tradition: Some Notes on ASKI, Surakarta." In *What Is Modern Indonesian Culture?* ed. Gloria Davis. Athens: Ohio University Center for International Studies, Southeast Asia Program.

———. 1980. "Lagu, Laras, Layang: Rethinking Melody in Javanese Music." Ph.D. dissertation, Cornell University.

Hefner, Robert W. 1987. "The Politics of Popular Art: Tayuban Dance and Culture Change in East Java." *Indonesia* 43:75–94.

Heins, Ernst. 1975. "Kroncong and Tanjidor: Two Cases of Urban Folk Music." *Asian Music* 7:20–32.

———. 1976. "Letter to the Editor" (a response to Becker's review of Kunst 1973). *Ethnomusicology* 20:97–101.

Hoffman, Stanley B. 1975. "Epistemology and Music in Java." M.A. thesis, University of Michigan, Ann Arbor.

Holt, Claire. 1972. "Dances of Minangkabau: Notes by Claire Holt." *Indonesia* 14:73–88.

Hood, Mantle. 1954. *The Nuclear Theme as a Determinant of Pathet in Javanese Music.* Reprinted New York: Da Capo, 1977.

———. 1958. *Javanese Gamelan in the World of Music.* Jogjakarta: n.p.

———. 1984. *The Evolution of Javanese Gamelan,* book 2: *The Legacy of the Roaring Sea.* Wilhelmshaven: Noetzel.

———. 1988. *The Evolution of Javanese Gamelan,* book 3: *Paragon of the Roaring Sea.* Wilhelmshaven: Noetzel.

Hughes, David W. 1988. "Deep Structure and Surface Structure in Javanese Music: A Grammar of Gendhing Lampah." *Ethnomusicology* 32:23–74.

Hughes-Freeland, Felicia. 1990. "Tayuban: Culture on the Edge." *Indonesia Circle* 52:36–44.

Humardani, S. D. 1972. "Masalah-Masalah Dasar Pengembangan Seni Tradisi" [Basic issues of the development of traditional arts], ms. Surakarta: Pusat Kesenian Jawa-Tengah.

Hurgronje, Snouck C. 1893–94. *De Atjehers*. Trans. as *The Achehnese* by A. W. S. O'Sullivan. Leiden: Brill, 1906.

"Journal of an Excursion to the Native Provinces on Java in the Year 1828, During the War with Dipo Negoro." 1853–54. *Journal of the Indian Archipelago and Eastern Asia*, 7 (1853): 1–19, 138–57, 225–46, 358–78; 8 (1854): 80–174.

Kartodirdjo, Sartono. 1966. *The Peasants' Revolt of Banten 1888, Its Conditions, Course and Sequel: A Case of Social Movements in Indonesia* (Verhandelingen van het Koninklijk Instituut voor Tall-, Land- en Volkenkunde, 50). Leiden.

————. 1972. "Agrarian Radicalism in Java: Its Setting and Development." In *Culture and Politics in Indonesia*, ed. Claire Holt, pp. 71–125. Ithaca: Cornell University Press.

Kartomi, Margaret J. 1976. "Performance, Music and Meaning of Reyog Ponorogo." *Indonesia* 22:85–130.

————. 1981. "The Processes and Results of Musical Culture Contact: A Discussion of Terminology and Concepts." *Ethnomusicology* 25:227–49.

Koentjaraningrat. 1985. "Persepsi Tentang Kebudayan Nasional" [The perceptions of national culture]. In *Persepsi Masyarakat Tentang Kebudayaan*, ed. Alfian, pp. 99–141. Jakarta: Gramedia.

Komisi Pasinaon Nabuh Gamelan ing Paheman Radyapustaka Surakarta. 1924. *Buku Piwulang Nabuh Gamelan* [The book of instruction in gamelan playing]. Surakarta: Swastika.

Kornhauser, Bronia. 1978. "In Defence of Kroncong." In *Studies in Indonesian Music*, ed. Margaret J. Kartomi, pp. 104–83. Melbourne: Centre of Southeast Asian Studies, Monash University.

Kraemer, H. 1932. "Het Instituut voor Javaansche Taal to Soerakarta." *Djawa* 12/6: 261–75.

Kumar, Ann. 1980a. "Javanese Court Society and Politics in the Late Eighteenth Century: The Record of a Lady Soldier. Part 1: The Religious, Social, and Economic Life of the Court." *Indonesia* 29:1–46.

————. 1980b. "Javanese Court Society and Politics in the Late Eighteenth Century: The Record of a Lady Soldier. Part II: Political Developments: The Courts and the Company. *Indonesia* 30:67–111.

Kunst, Jaap. 1924. "De Muziek in den Mangkoe Negaran." *Djawa* 4, extra number: 24–31.

————. 1973. *Music in Java*, 2 vols. 3d. enlarged edition, ed. E. L. Heins. The Hague: Nijhoff. (Revised English ed. of *De Toonkunst van Java*, 2 vols. The Hague: Nijhoff, 1949.)

————. 1968. *Hindu-Javanese Musical Instruments*. The Hague: Nijhoff (Revised English ed. of *Hindoe-Javaansche Muziekinstrumenten, Speciaal die van Oost-Java*, in collaboration with R. Goris. Batavia, 1927.)

Kusumadilaga, Kangjeng Pangeran Harya. 1930. *Serat Sastramiruda* [The book of Sastramiruda]. Solo: De Bliksem. Original work, 1879.

Kusumadiningrat, Kangjeng Pangeran Arya, and D. van Hinloopen Labberton. 1913. *Serat Rarya Saraya* [Child's companion book]. Bogor: Widya Pustaka.

Land, J. P. N. "Over Onze Kennis der Javaansche Muziek." In Groneman 1980:1–24.

Langendriya. 1934. Program notes accompanying langendriya dance drama performed in Surakarta, Kepatihan Mangkunagaran.

Layang Wuwulang Nut: Papathokané Unggah-udhun lan Dawa-cendhèké Swara. Teteladan Saka Tanah Eropah [The book of instruction on notation: Rules of the register and rhythm of melodies. Examples from Europe]. 1874. Batawi: Kantor Pangecapan Gupremen.

Liem Thian Joe. 1931–33. *Riwajat Semarang* [The history of Semarang]. Semarang-Batavia: Boekhandel Ko Him Yoe.

Lindsay, Jennifer Mary. 1980. "The Paku Alaman: The Foundation and Functions of a Javanese Minor Court in the Nineteenth Century." M.A. thesis, Cornell University.

———. 1985. "Klasik Kitsch or Contemporary: A Study of the Javanese Performing Arts." Ph.D. dissertation, University of Sidney, Australia.

Mangkunegoro IV, Kangjeng Gusti Pangeran Arya. 1853–81. *Sendhon Langen Swara* [The art of singing] (ms. SMP RP 80/4; composed Surakarta 1853–81; inscribed Surakarta mid–late 19th c.).

Mangkunegara VII, Kangjeng Gusti Pangeran Arya. 1933. "Over de wayang koelit (poerwa) in het algemeen en over de daarin voorkomende symbolische en mystieke elementen." *Djawa* 13:79–98. Trans. Claire Holt, "On the Wajang kulit (purwa) and its Symbolic and Mystical Elements." Ithaca: Cornell University, 1957.

Marcus, George E., and Michael M. J. Fischer. 1986. *Anthropology as Cultural Critique.* Chicago: University of Chicago Press.

Marle, A. van. 1951–52. "De Groep der Europeanen in Nederlandsch-Indie, iets over onstaan en groei." *Indonesie* 5:98–121, 314–41, 481–85.

Martopangrawit, R. L. 1967. *Tetembangan: Vocaal jang berhubungan dengan karawitan* [Tetembangan: Singing which is related to gamelan]. Surakarta: Dewan Mahasiswa ASKI.

———. 1969–72. *Pengetahuan Karawitan* [Knowledge of gamelan music], 2 vols. Surakarta: Dewan Mahasiswa Akademi Seni Karawitan Indonesia. Trans. Martin Hatch, in Becker and Feinstein 1984:1–244.

———. 1972–76. *Titiraras Cengkok-Cengkok Genderan dengan Wiletannya* [The notation of gender melodic patterns and their variations], 2 vols. Surakarta: Akademi Seni Karawitan.

———. 1977. *Gending-Gending Santiswara,* 2 vols. Surakarta: Akademi Seni Karawitan Indonesia.

McDermott, Vincent, and Sumarsam. 1975. "Central Javanese Music: The Patęt of Laras Sléndro and the Gendèr Barung." *Ethnomusicology* 19:233–44.

McNamara, Molly. 1980. "Solonese Gendịng Bonang: The Repertoire and Playing Style." M.A. thesis, Wesleyan University.

McPhee, Colin. 1966. *Music in Bali.* New Haven: Yale University Press.

McVey, Ruth. 1967. "Taman Siswa and the Indonesian Awakening." *Indonesia* 4: 128–68.

———. 1986. "The Wayang Controversy in Indonesia." in *Content, Meaning and Power in Southeast Asia,* ed. Mark Hobart and Robert H. Taylor, pp. 21–52. Ithaca: Cornell University Southeast Asian Program.

Mellema, R. L., ed. 1933. *Serat Gancaran Warni-warni ing Jaman Sapunika* [The book of various prose writings at the present time]. Groningen: Wolters.

Merriam, Alan. 1964. *The Anthropology of Music.* Evanston, Ill.: Northwestern University Press.

Moertono, Soemarsaid. 1968. *State and Statecraft in Old Java.* Ithaca: Cornell Modern Indonesia Project.

Morton, David. 1976. *The Traditional Music of Thailand.* Berkeley and Los Angeles: University of California Press.

Mrázek, Rudolf. 1972. "Tan Malaka: A Political Personality's Structure of Experience." *Indonesia* 14:1–48.

Najawirangka, Raden Mas Ngabehi. 1957. "Tjentanganipun Raden Mas Ngabehi Najawirangka" [The checkmarks of Radèn Mas Ngabèhi Najawirangka]. In *Kawruh Gending Djawa.* Solo: Toko Sadu Budi. Original work, 1936.

———. 1960. *Serat Tuntunan Pedhalangan* [Guide to the art of puppetry], 4 vols. in 2. Jogjakarta: Djawatan Kebudajaan, Departemen P. P. dan K.

Nandy, Ashis. 1983. *The Intimate Enemy: Loss and Recovery of Self Under Colonialism.* Delhi: Oxford University Press.

Noot Gendhing lan Tembang [Gendhing and tembang notation]. 1926. Published under the auspices of Paku Buwana X. Solo: Toko Buku Sadubudi.

Onghokham. 1975. "The Residency of Madiun: Pryayi and Peasant in the Nineteenth Century." Ph.D. dissertation, Yale University.

Pane, Armijn. 1941. "Kerontjong Disamping Gamelan" [Kroncong rather than gamelan]. *Poedjangga Baroe* 8/10:256–60.

Parkin, David. 1978. *The Cultural Definition of Political Response.* London: Academic Press.

Partohudoyo, Raden Ngabehi. 1924–44. "Bab Langendriyan" [Concerning Langendriyan] (ms. SMP MN 193/14; inscribed Surakarta 1924–44).

Pemberton, John. 1987. "Musical Politics in Central Java (or, How Not to Listen to a Javanese Gamelan." *Indonesia* 44:17–30.

———. 1989. "The Appearance of Order: A Politics of Culture in Colonial and Postcolonial Java." Ph.D. dissertation, Cornell University.

Perlman, Marc. 1983. "Reflection on 'Srepegan': Notes on 'A Grammar of Musical Genre Srepegan.'" *Asian Music* 14:17–29.

———. 1991. "Asal Usul Notasi Gendhing Jawa di Surakarta, Suatu Rumusan Sejarah Nut Rante" [The origins of notation for Javanese gendhing in Surakarta, the historical formulation of the chain notation]. *Jurnal Masyarakat Musikologi Indonesia* 2/2:36–68.

———. 1993. "Unplayed Melodies: Music Theories in Post Colonial Java." Ph.D. dissertation, Wesleyan University.

Pigeaud, Theodore G. 1938. *Javaanse Volksvertoningen.* Batavia: Volkslectuur.

———. 1960. *Java in the Fourteenth Century,* 5 vols. The Hague: Nijhoff.

———. 1967. *Literature of Java,* 3 vols. The Hague: Nijhoff.

Pigeaud, Theodore G., and H. J. De Graaf. 1976. *Islamic States in Java 1500–1700.* The Hague: Nijhoff.

Poedjosoemarto, Soepomo. 1967. "The Establishment of Surakarta, a Translation from the Babad Gianti." *Indonesia* 24:88–109.

Poerbapangrawit, Raden Mas Kodrat. 1955. *Gendhing Jawa* [Javanese gendhing]. Jakarta: Harapan Masa. Trans. J. Becker, in Becker and Feinstein 1984:408–38.

Poerbatjaraka, Raden Mas Ngabehi. 1941. "Metode 'Sari-Swara' dan Bedanja dengan Kepatihanschrift" [The 'Sari-Swara' system and its difference from the Kepatihan notation]. *Poedjangga Baroe,* 8/11:287–96.

Poerwadarminta, W. J. S. 1939. *Baoesastra Djawa* [Javanese dictionary]. Batavia: Wolters.

Powers, Harold. 1979. "Classical Music, Cultural Roots, and Colonial Rule: An Indic Musicologist Looks at the Muslim World." *Asian Music* 12:5–39.

———. 1980a. "Language Models and Musical Analysis." *Ethnomusicology* 24:1–60.

———. 1980b. "Mode." In *The New Grove Dictionary of Music and Musicians,* ed. Stanley Sadie, 12:376–450. London: Macmillan.

Purbadipura, R. Ng. 1913. *Serat Sri Karongron* [The book of Sri Karongron], 3 vols. (ms. SMP KS 113/5. composed and inscribed Surakarta 1913).

———. 1913–16. *Serat Sri Karongron,* 4 vols. Surakarta: Budi Utama.

Quinn, George. 1978. "The Case of the Invisible Literature: Power, Scholarship and Contemporary Javanese Writing." *Indonesia* 35:1–36.

———. 1992. *The Novel in Javanese.* (Verhandelingen van het Koninklijk Instituut voor Tall-, Land- en Volkenkunde, 140). Leiden.

Qureshi, Regula Burckhardt. 1986. *Sufi Music of India and Pakistan: Sound Context and Meaning in Qawwali.* Cambridge: Cambridge University Press.

Raffles, Thomas Stamford. 1817. *The History of Java,* 2 vols. Reprinted Kuala Lumpur: Oxford University Press, 1982.

Randel, Don, ed. 1986. *The New Harvard Dictionary of Music.* Cambridge: Harvard University Press.

Ranger, Terence O. 1975. *Dance and Society in East Africa, 1890–1970: The Beni ngoma.* Berkeley and Los Angeles: University of California Press.

Resink, G. J. 1941. "Indonesische toekomstmuziek." *Kritiek en Opbouw* 4/5:74–77.

Rhodius, Hans, and John Darling. 1980. *Walter Spies and Balinese Art,* ed. John Stowell. Amsterdam: The Tropical Museum, 1980.

Ricklefs, M. C. 1974. *Jogjakarta under Sultan Mangkubumi 1749–1792.* London: Oxford University Press.

———. 1993. *A History of Modern Indonesia c.1300,* 2d ed. Stanford: Stanford University Press.

Robson, S. O. *Wangbang Wideya.* 1971. The Hague: Nijhoff.

Rush, James R. 1990. *Opium to Java: Revenue Farming and Chinese Enterprise in Colonial Indonesia 1860–1910.* Ithaca: Cornell University Press.

Sajarah Kanthi Babad Lalampahanipun Kangjeng Gusti Pangéran Adipati Arya Mangkunagara ingkang kaping IV ing Surakarta [The Accompanying history of the chronicle of Kangjeng Pangéran Adipati Arya Mangkunagara IV in Surakarta]. 1853–63. (Ms. SMP MN 16-17/1; composed and inscribed Surakarta, 1853–63).

Sastrapustaka, B. Y. H. 1953–78. "Wedha Pradangga Kawedhar" [Sacred knowledge of gamelan revealed]. Trans. J. Becker, in Becker and Feinstein 1984:305–34.

Sayid, Raden Mas. 1981. *Ringkasan Sejarah Wayang* [Summary of wayang history]. Jakarta: Pradnya Paramita.

Schaareman, Danker H. 1980. "The Gamelan Gambang of Tatulingga, Bali." *Ethnomusicology* 24:465–82.

Scherer, Sawitri. 1975. "Harmony and Dissonance: Early Nationalist Thought in Java." M.A. thesis, Cornell University.

Sears, Laurie. 1987. *Authority, Text, and Performance in Javanese Shadow Theater.* Unpublished ms.

Sedyawati, Edi. 1984. "Gambyong Menurut Serat Cabolang dan Serat Centini" [Gambyong dance according to Serat Cebolang and Serat Centhini]. In *Tari,* ed. Edi Sedyawati, pp. 129–61. Jakarta: Pustaka Jaya.

Seebass, Tilman. 1986. "Between Oral and Written Tradition: The Origin and Function of Notation in Indonesia." In *The Oral and the Literate in Music,* ed. Tokumaru Yoshihiko and Yamaguti Ozamu, pp. 414–27. Tokyo: Academia Music.

———. 1987. "Theory (English) and Lehre (German) Versus Teori (Indonesia)." Paper presented at XIVth International Congress of the International Musicological Society, Bologna.

Seeger, Charles. 1977. "On the Moods of a Music Logic." In *Studies in Musicology 1935–1975,* pp. 64–101. Berkeley and Los Angeles: University of California Press.

Seltmann, F. 1976. "Wajang Titi: Chinesisches Schattenspiel in Jogjakarta." *Review of Indonesian and Malayan Affairs* 10:51–75.

Serat Babad Nitik Mangkunegaran wiwit taun Alip 1707 ngantos dumugi Je 1718 [The chronicle of Mangkunegaran from A. J. Alip 1707 to A. J. Je 1718]. 1929. (Ms. SMP MN 16-41/5 [typed transliteration of Koninklijk Instituut ms. KITLV Or. 231]; composed Surakarta 1791, inscribed Surakarta).

Serat Babad Panambangan [The Chronicle of Panambangan], 2. 1900. (Ms. SMP MN 56/4; composed Surakarta early 19th century; inscribed Surakarta).

Serat Centhini Latin [Romanized Serat Centhini]. 1985–91. 12 vols. Transliteration by Kamajaya. Yogyakarta: Yayasan Centhini Yogyakarta. Original work, 1814.

Serat Kikidunganing Gendhing Ingkang Sampun Kalebet Langen Swara [The book of the singing of gendhing which have been included in Langen Swara]. (Ms. SMP MN 193/6; composed and inscribed Surakarta, late 19th century).

Serat Pakem Ringgit Purwa [The book of plot synopses of the wayang purwa stories]. 1770. (Ms. SMP KS 145/6; composed and inscribed Surakarta).

Serat Pakem Wirama Wileting Gendhing Pradongga Laras Suréndro utawi Pélog [The book of guide to the melodies of gamelan gendhing in sléndro or pélog]. 1934. (Ms. Sasana Budaya PB.18, PB.19 [typed transliteration]; composed Yogyakarta 1920s, inscribed Yogyakarta).

Serat Pasindhèn Badhaya [The book of bedhaya singing]. 1832–33. (Ms. SMP KS 156/10; composed Surakarta 18th–19th centuries).

Serat Pasindhèn Badhaya [The book of bedhaya singing]. 1893–1939. (Ms. SMP KS 156/14; composed and inscribed Surakarta).

Serat Tjentini: Babon asli Saking Kita LEIDEN ing negara Nederland [Serat Tjentini: The original is from Leiden in the Netherlands]. 1912–15. 8 vols. in 4, transcribed and edited by R. Wirawangsa with the assistance of M. Ardjawidjaja. Batavia: Ruygrok. Original work, 1814.

Shiraishi, Takashi. 1981. "The Disputes between Tjipto Mangoenkoesoemo and Soetatmo Soeriokoesoemo: Satria vs. Pandita." *Indonesia* 32:93–108.

———. 1990. *An Age in Motion: Popular Radicalism in Java 1912–1926.* Ithaca: Cornell University Press.

Sindusawarno, Ki. 1960. "Radyapustaka dan Noot-Angka" [Radyapustaka and the cipher notation]. In *Nawawindu Radyapustaka,* pp. 57–60. Surakarta: Paheman Radyapustaka.

———. 1984. "Faktor Penting Dalam Gamelan" [The important factor in gamelan]. Trans. Stanley Hoffman, in Becker and Feinstein 1984: 311–87. Original work, 1956.

———. 1987. "Ilmu Karawitan" [Theory of karawitan]. Trans. Martin Hatch, in Becker and Feinstein 1987: 311–87. Original work, 1955.

———. n.d. "Ilmu Karawitan" [Theory of karawitan], vol. 2 (ms. Surakarta: Konservatori Karawitan Indonesia).

Soebardi, S. 1969. "Raden Ngabehi Jasadipura I, Court Poet of Surakarta: His Life and Works." *Indonesia* 8: 81–102.

———. 1971. "Santri Religious Elements as Reflected in the Book of Tjentini." *Bijdragen tot de Taal-, Land-en Volkenkunde* 127: 331–49.

———. 1975. *The Book of Cabolèk.* The Hague: Nijhoff.

Soedarsono, ed. *Mengenal Tari-Tarian Rakyat di Daerah Istimewa Yogyakarta.* Yogyakarta: Akademi Seni Tari Indonesia, 1976.

Soekanto. 1953. "Konservatori Karawitan dan Kebudajaan Nasional" [The karawitan conservatory and national culture]. *Sana-Budaja* 2: 21–25.

Soelardi, Raden Bagoes. 1918. *Serat Pradongga* [The book of gamelan]. Weltevreden: Widya-Poestaka nr. 2.

Soerjaatmadja, R. M. 1957. "Konservatori Karawitan Indonesia." *Sana-Budaja* 1/5: 207–15.

Soetrisno. n.d. *Mengungkap Kembali Wayang Madya* [Uncovering wayang madya]. ms.

Soewandi, Raden Mas. 1926. *Serat Panembrama* [The book of panembrama]. Kediri: Tan Khun Swi.

———. 1938. *Djèdjèrèngan bab: Beksa Tajoeb, Bondan Toewin Wireng* [The descriptions of tayuban, bondhan, and wirèng dance] Yogyakarta, ms.

Soorjo Poetro. 1919–20. "Muziekschrift voor Java's Toonkunst II." *Nederlandsch Indie Oud and Nieuw* 4: 380–84.

Steinberg, David Joel, ed. 1987. *In Search of Southeast Asia,* rev. ed. Honolulu: University of Hawaii Press.

Stutterheim, W. F. 1956. "A Thousand Years Old Profession in the Princely Courts on Java." In *Studies in Indonesian Archeology* (Koninklijk Instituut voor Taal-, Land- en Volkenkunde, translation series), pp. 93–103. The Hague: Nijhoff.

Suharti, Theresia. 1990. "Tari di Mangkunagaran, Suatu Pengaruh Bentuk dan Gaya Dalam Dimensi Kultural 1916–1988" [Dances in the Mangkunagaran, an influence on the form and style in its cultural dimension, 1916–1988]. Sarjana S-2 thesis, University of Gadjah Mada.

Suharto, Ben. 1980. *Tayub, Pengamatan dari Segi Tari Pergaulan serta Kaitannya dengan Unsur Upacara Kesuburan* [Tayub: its observation as social dance and its relation with aspects of fertility ritual]. Yogyakarta: Proyek Pengembangan Institut Kesenian Indonesia.

Sumanagara, K. R. M. T. 1835. *Serat Karawitan* [The book of karawitan]. Sragen: n.p.

Sumarsam. 1975. "Gendèr Barung, Its Technique and Function in the Context of Javanese Gamelan." *Indonesia* 20: 161–72.

————. 1976. "Inner Melody in Javanese Gamelan." M.A. thesis, Wesleyan University.

————. 1981. "The Musical Practice of the Gamelan Sekaten." *Asian Music* 12:54–73.

————. 1984. "Inner Melody in Javanese Gamelan." In Becker and Feinstein 1984: 245–304.

————. 1987. "Introduction to Ciblon Drumming in Javanese Gamelan." In Becker and Feinstein 1987:171–204.

Supanggah, Rahayu. 1979. "Gambuh." In Hardjana 1986:37–41.

————. 1988. "Balungan." Paper presented at the International Gamelan Festival-Symposium, Vancouver, Canada. English translation by Marc Perlman, *Balungan* 3/2:2–10.

Suparno, Slamet T. 1990. "Pemunculan dan Pengembangan Karawitan Mangkunegaran: Kronologi Peristiwa Karawitan di Mangkunegaran 1757–1881" [The emergence and development of karawitan Mangkunegaran: Chronological accounts of karawitan in the Mangkunegaran 1757–1881]. Sarjana S-2 thesis, Fakultas Pasca Sarjana Universitas Gadjah Mada.

Supriyanto, Mathihas. 1980. "Langendriyan Mangkunagaran." Thesis Akademi Seni Karawitan Surakarta.

Susilo, Hardja. 1967. "Drumming in the Context of Javanese Gamelan." M.A. thesis, University of California, Los Angeles.

————. 1989. "The Logogenesis of Gendhing Lampah." *Progress Reports in Ethnomusicology,* 2/4:1–17.

Sutherland, Heather. 1979. *The Making of a Bureaucratic Elite: The Colonial Transformation of the Javanese Priyayi.* Singapore: Heinemann.

Sutton, Anderson, R. 1978. "Notes Toward a Grammar of Variation in Javanese Gender Playing." *Ethnomusicology* 22:275–96.

————. 1978. "Notes Toward a Grammar of Variation in Javanese Gender Playing." *Ethnomusicology* 22:275–96.

————. 1984a. "Change and Ambiguity: Gamelan Style and Regional Identity in Yogyakarta." In *Aesthetic Tradition and Cultural Transition in Java and Bali* (Monograph Series, No. 2), ed. Stephanie Morgan and Laurie Jo Sears, pp. 221–45. Madison: University of Wisconsin, Center for Southeast Asian Studies.

————. 1984b. "Who is the Pesindhèn? Notes on the Female Singing Tradition in Java." *Indonesia* 37:119–34.

————. 1991. *Traditions of Gamelan Music in Java.* Cambridge: Cambridge University Press.

————. 1993. *Variation in Javanese Gamelan Music: Dynamics of a Steady State* (Monograph Series on Southeast Asia, Special Report No. 28). DeKalb: Center for Southeast Asian Studies, Northern Illinois University.

Taylor, Jean Gelman. 1983. *The Social World of Batavia: European and Eurasian in Dutch Asia.* Madison: University of Wisconsin Press.

Titi Asri. 1925. Ed. Sapardal Hardasukarta and M. Ng. Mlayadimeja, based on the instruction of Kyai Demang Gunasentika. Surakarta: N. V. Budi Utama.

Tondhakusuma, Raden Mas Harya. 1870. *Serat Gulang Yarya* [Joy of Learning] (ms. SMP MN 80/3; composed and inscribed Surakarta).

Trimingham, J. Spencer. 1971. *The Sufi Orders in Islam.* London: Oxford University Press.

Tsuchiya, Kenji. 1990. "Javanology and the Age of Ronggawarsita: An Introduction to Nineteenth-Century Javanese Culture." In *Reading Southeast Asia,* 1:75–108. Ithaca: Southeast Asia Program, Cornell University.

Uhlenbeck, E. 1964. *A Critical Survey of Studies on the Languages of Java and Madura.* The Hague: Nijhoff.

Undang-Undang Dasar [The constitution]. 1945. n.p.: Team Pembinaan Penatar dan Bahan-Bahan Penataran Pegawai Republik Indonesia.

Valentijn, François. 1723–26. *Oud & Nieuw Oost-Indien,* 3 vols., ed. S. Keyzer. Amsterdam: Dordrecht.

Van der Veur, P. W. 1955. "Introduction to a Socio-Political Study of the Eurasians of Indonesia." Ph.D. dissertation, Cornell University.

———. 1968. "Cultural Aspects of the Eurasians in Indonesian Colonial Society." *Indonesia* 6:38–53.

———. 1969. *Education and Social Change in Colonial Indonesia (1).* Athens: Ohio Center for International Studies Southeast Asia Program.

Vetter, Roger R. 1986. "Music for 'the Lap of the World': Gamelan Performance, Performers, and Repertoire in the Kraton Yogyakarta." Ph.D. dissertation, University of Wisconsin, Madison.

Vickers, Adrian. 1987. "Hinduism and Islam in Indonesia: Bali and the Pasisir World." *Indonesia* 44:31–58.

Vlekke, B. H. M. 1959. *Nusantara: A History of Indonesia.* The Hague and Bandung: van Hoeve.

Vredenbregt, J. 1973. "Dabus in West Java." *Bijdragen tot de Taal-, Land-en Volkenkunde* 129, 2/3:302–20.

Wallis, Richard Herman. 1973. "Poetry as Music in Java and Bali." M.A. thesis, University of Michigan, Ann Arbor.

———. 1980. "The Voice as a Mode of Cultural Expression in Bali." Ph.D. dissertation, University of Michigan, Ann Arbor.

Warsadiningrat, R. T. [Mas Ngabehi Warsapradongga]. 1920s. *Serat Sosorah Gamelan* [A speech on gamelan] (ms. Solo).

———. 1987. *Serat Wédha Pradangga* [The book of sacred knowledge about gamelan music]. Trans. Susan Walton, in Becker and Feinstein 1987:1–170. Original work, 1944.

Winter, C. F. 1874. *Tembang Jawa Nganggo Musik Kanggo ing Pamulangan Jawa* [Javanese song written in music to be used in Javanese educational institutions], 2 vols. Betawi: Kantor Pangecapan Gupremen.

———. 1848. *Javaansche Zamenspraken,* vol. 2. Amsterdam: Muller.

Winyabongsapatra, Ms. Bèhi. 1939. *Serat Lagu Jawi* [The book of Javanese melody], vol. 4. Surakarta: Boekhandel "S. T. M."

Wirawiyaga, Mas Ngabèhi. 1935–39. *Serat Lagu Jawi* [The book of Javanese melody], 4 vols. Surakarta: N. V Sie Dhian Ho.

Wirawiyaga, Mas Ngabèhi, and Th. S. Martasudirja. 1939. *Serat Mardu Swara* [The book of the essence of sound] Surakarta: n.p.

"Wiwahan Dalem Kangjeng Pangeran Adipati Ariya Prabu Prangwadana" [The celebration of the honorable crown prince Ariya Prangwadana]. 1927. In *Serat Serat Anggi-*

tan Dalem K. G. P. A. A. Mangkunagara IV. Ed. Th. Piegeaud, 1:139–280. Soerakarta: Java-Instituut (de Bliksem). Original work, mid 19th c.

Wolbers, Paul; Arthur. 1986. "Gandrung and Angklung from Banyuwangi: Remnants of
a Past Shared with Bali." *Asian Music* 18:71–90.

Wolters, O. W. 1982. *History, Culture, and Region in Southeast Asian Perspective.* Singapore: Institute of Southeast Asia.

Yampolsky, Philip. 1985. "Development in Central Javanese Gamelan Music, 1850–
1930." Paper presented at the Society for Ethnomusicology, Vancouver, Canada.

Yasadipura, R. Ng. 1854. *Babad Prayud* [The chronicle of Prayud] (ms. SMP KS 212;
composed Surakarta, late 18th century; inscribed Surakarta).

Zoetmulder, P. J. 1974. *Kalangwan: A Survey of Old Javanese Literature.* The Hague:
Nijhoff.

———. 1982. *Old Javanese–English Dictionary,* 2 vols. The Hague: Nijhoff.

Zurbuchen, Mary Sabina. 1987. *The Language of Balinese Shadow Theater.* Princeton:
Princeton University Press.

Index